Second Edition

READING PROBLEMS
Assessment and Teaching Strategies

MARGARET ANN RICHEK
Northeastern Illinois University

LYNNE K. LIST
Professor Emeritus—University of the Virgin Islands

JANET W. LERNER
Northeastern Illinois University

PRENTICE HALL, ENGLEWOOD CLIFFS, NEW JERSEY 07632

LIBRARY OF CONGRESS
Library of Congress Cataloging-in-Publication Data

Richek, Margaret Ann,
 Reading problems: assessment and teaching strategies / Margaret
Ann Richek, Lynn K. List, Janet W. Lerner. — 2nd ed.
  p. cm.
 First edition has subtitle: Diagnosis and remediation.
 Bibliography:
 Includes indexes.
 ISBN 0-13-761107-2
 1. Reading disability. 2. Reading—Remedial teaching. I. List.
Lynne K., (date). II. Lerner, Janet W. III. Title.
LB1050.5.R53 1989
428.4′2—dc19   88-22472
              CIP

Editorial/production supervision and
 interior design: Barbara DeVries
Cover design: Lundgren Graphics, Ltd.
Manufacturing buyer: Peter Havens

 ©1989, 1983 by Prentice-Hall, Inc.
A Division of Simon & Schuster
Englewood Cliffs, New Jersey 07632

Previously published under
the title *Reading Problems: Diagnosis and Remediation.*

Printed in the United States of America
10 9 8 7 6 5 4 3 2 1

ISBN 0-13-761107-2

Prentice-Hall International (UK) Limited, *London*
Prentice-Hall of Australia Pty. Limited, *Sydney*
Prentice-Hall Canada Inc., *Toronto*
Prentice-Hall Hispanoamericana, S.A., *Mexico*
Prentice-Hall of India Private Limited, *New Delhi*
Prentice-Hall of Japan, Inc., *Tokyo*
Simon & Schuster Asia Pte. Ltd., *Singapore*
Editora Prentice-Hall do Brasil, Ltda., *Rio de Janeiro*

To our parents, our first and most loving teachers . . .

CONTENTS

Part IV Special Concerns

13 TEACHING THE SEVERELY DISABLED READER 286

14 USING MICROCOMPUTERS IN READING INSTRUCTION 314

15 ORGANIZING AND DELIVERING REMEDIAL READING SERVICES 326

APPENDIX A REMEDIAL INSTRUCTIONAL MATERIALS 341

LIST OF TABLES

LIST OF TEST INVENTORIES

Preface

This book is concerned with helping the many children, adolescents, and adults who encounter difficulty with reading. Designed as a text for undergraduate and graduate students, it guides prospective and present teachers in assessing and teaching remedial readers.

Reading Problems: Assessment and Teaching Strategies is a comprehensive survey of research, theory, assessment techniques, and teaching strategies for remedial reading. The reader will find both information from the field of reading and relevant information from other fields, such as special education, bilingual education, and policy studies. Together, this forms a coherent framework for treating students with reading problems.

The book combines time-tested methods with newer, more innovative ideas. It is important for today's teachers to be familiar with traditional methods of diagnosis and instruction. In addition, the recent research in reading gives us a clearer picture of the reading process. New insights provide a rich source of innovative diagnostic methods and teaching strategies. This text integrates traditional methods with newer perspectives to provide an effective remedial reading program. It brings the old and the new together in a workable and practical framework.

The text is a valuable resource for teachers. There are extensive lists of available assessment instruments and instructional materials. Forms, checklists, and informal tests throughout the book are designed for teacher use. However, the text also gives readable, understandable summaries of the research and theory that comprise the basis of the methods and materials suggested.

The book is divided into four parts. Part I (chapter 1) deals with the consequences of reading problems, a definition of reading, and an overview of remedial reading.

Part II deals with assessment. Chapter 2 gives principles of assessment. Chapters 3 and 4 present correlates of reading problems and how they may be assessed. Chapter 5 is an extensive survey of informal reading assessment techniques. Chapter 6 deals with formal tests.

Part III deals with teaching strategies. Chapter 7 presents principles of remediation. Chapter 8 gives strategies for teaching beginning word recognition; chapter 9 continues with the teaching of advanced word recognition and word meanings. Chapter 10 describes strategies for teaching comprehension of narrative text and for improving oral language. Chapter 11 concentrates on comprehension of expository text and on studying. Chapter 12 details the reading/writing connection and gives ideas for developing writing and other language arts abilities. Throughout these chapters, sections are given for using strategies diagnostically. In addition, "strategy snapshots" show actual examples of teaching situations.

Part IV deals with special concerns. Chapter 13 presents the characteristics of severely disabled readers and gives instructional options for them. Chapter 14 discusses the use of computers in the remedial reading program. Chapter 15 deals with organizing for remedial instruction and provides background in the laws and practices that affect all teachers.

Appendix A presents an extensive resource list of materials useful for teaching remedial students. Appendix B lists publisher addresses. Appendix C provides a partially completed sample diagnostic report. Appendix D presents a model informal reading inventory.

This second edition retains the comprehensiveness and clarity of the first edition. In addition, however, the second edition adds both new insights into reading and new developments. These include an emphasis on reading as an interactive process, further development of informal assessment techniques, inclusion of many new strategies for teaching reading, and an emphasis on cognitive strategies/self-monitoring. Updated sections on developments in service delivery, the field of special education, and the use of computers also reflect new trends.

Many people have contributed to this book. We wish to thank the reading professionals who deepened and extended our understanding of techniques by taking the time to answer personal inquiries. The indispensible reference librarians of Northeastern Illinois University worked tirelessly in ensuring accuracy for references and publishers. The Learning Services Department of Northeastern Illinois University provided the excellent photographs and line drawings used in the text. Steve Kushner and Jerry Stecker conducted a field study to validate the reading inventory in Appendix D. Ignacio Nguyen gave technical help in preparing the manuscript. Finally, our editor, Barbara DeVries, has helped us immeasurably with her fine editing skills, her eye for detail, and her care and interest in the development of the manuscript.

Margaret Ann Richek
Lynne K. List
Janet W. Lerner

1

READING DISABILITIES
A Personal and National Dilemma

The consequences of poor literacy are poignantly revealed in a newspaper report of an attempted bank robbery. The would-be thief handed this threatening note to a bank teller (Miami Herald, 1980):

> I GOT A BUM.
> I ALSO GOT A CONTOUR.
> IM GOING TO BLOW YOU SKY HEIGHT.
> IN NO KILLEN.
> THIS IS A HELD UP.

Unable to decipher the note, the teller asked the robber for help in reading it. During the time the two of them were working out the words, the police arrived and arrested the bank robber. Unfortunately for the thief, the police were also able to trace him to other bank holdups in which the same written errors were made. This news report of a thwarted bank holdup illustrates the point that literacy is required in most occupations today—even to be a successful bank robber.

INTRODUCTION

Educators, parents, physicians, and psychologists, as well as society in general, share a common concern about individuals who do not learn to read. All teachers have the responsibility of understanding and helping their failing and frustrated students. Elementary classroom teachers, reading teachers, special education teachers, and secondary teachers all need knowledge about the assessment and treatment of reading difficulties. The field of remedial reading is concerned with diagnosing and providing programs for individuals who, for a variety of reasons, are not learning to read in a normal fashion.

This text conveys important concepts, methods, research, and practices from the field of remedial reading. This first chapter provides an introduction by discussing (1) the impact of poor reading upon the individual, society, and the school; (2) the reading process and its definition; (3) programs for serving poor readers in our schools; and (4) a survey of the field of remedial reading. This chapter also provides an overview of the book.

THE IMPACT OF READING PROBLEMS

Reading disability is a debilitating problem for many children, adolescents, and adults in North America and throughout the world. Without help, these individuals are destined to suffer throughout their lives. As a primary cause of school failure, poor reading ability leads to lowered self-esteem and serious emotional overlays. Moreover, reading problems prevent individuals from reaching desired career goals and rob them of the opportunity to read for pleasure and enjoyment.

Studies of the literacy level in our nation are alarming. The New York Telephone Company (NYNEX) recently reported that it gave a simple 50-minute exam on basic reading and reasoning skills to 21,000 applicants for entry-level jobs. Only 15 percent passed (Simpson, 1987). The U.S. Department of Education estimates that almost one-third of the school population has significant learning problems (Will, 1986), and most of these problems are reading related. Studies show that almost 80 percent of children with learning disabilities have their primary educational problem in the area of reading (Lyon, 1985). The reading problems of all these students have a substantial impact on their ability to master other subjects in school.

Consequences to Society

Because illiteracy is associated with many social problems, society as a whole suffers the consequences of poor reading among its citizenry. Many of the ills of our society have been related to illiteracy. The unemployed, school dropouts, juvenile delinquents, and criminals in our prisons tend to have very poor reading skills. The problems of our schools, the persistence of poverty, and the concerns of troubled parents all show some association with poor reading.

How serious is the problem of illiteracy in the United States? About 23 million adults are functionally illiterate, having basic skills at fourth grade level or below. Another 35 million are semi-literate, with skills below the eighth grade level. Illiterate and semi-literate adults account for 75 percent of the unemployed, one-third of mothers receiving Aid to Families with Dependent Children, 85 percent of the juveniles who appear in court, 60 percent of prison inmates, and nearly 40 percent of minority youth. Of people in the work force, 15 percent are functionally illiterate. This includes 11 percent of professional and managerial workers and 30 percent of semi-skilled and unskilled workers (Orton Dyslexia Society, 1986).

A recent study of the literacy skills of young adults warned that unless improvements are made in education, the labor force in the United States will become progressively less capable of doing highly skilled work (Venezky, Kaestle and Sum, 1987). The study found that literacy skill levels are not adequate for maintaining world leadership in a changing, technological society. Furthermore, the lack of reading skills among large numbers of young adults threatens to divide society deeply between the literate and a low-income, low-achieving underclass unequipped for educational and professional advancement. We need citizens who can adapt to change, whose literacy skills allow them to master new jobs and new economic and political structures (U.S. Department of Education, 1986).

Consequences for the Individual

The consequences of reading problems upon an individual can be devastating. Emotionally, the strain of being unable to read in school may cause the individual to feel lost and frightened and to experience rejection and defeat. In the case of failing students, there is no escape. They are forced to face their inadequacies day after day in school and to be subjected to degradation or grudging tolerance by others (Roswell and Natchez, 1977). Frequently, students with reading handicaps display overt disruptive behaviors, or they may simply "give up," convinced that they are not capable of doing any better. Thus, they develop a response of "learned helplessness."

The poor reader finds that doors for personal growth and career opportunities are closed. Reading is a key tool for acquiring and maintaining employable skills. With the rapidity of change in today's world, old jobs become obsolete, and there is need for continual retraining. Automation has caused the elimination of many jobs that once were filled by unskilled or semiskilled workers, and the number of jobs for uneducated workers is diminishing. When workers are functionally illiterate, they are likely to become chronically unemployable (Venezky, Kaestle, and Sum, 1987).

How do individuals try to deal with severe reading limitations? Many find ingenious ways to *cope, compensate,* and *conceal* their inability to read. *Coping* involves dealing successfully with the situation. *Compensating* requires that the individual "make up for" the deficiency. *Concealing* involves hiding the handicap.

One man *coped* by accepting his menial work status and low income as inevitable. He rationalized that his father and grandfather before him had held the same station in life and that he should be content with his lot. A school-aged youngster convinced herself that she was stupid and that she just could not do any better. Interviews with psychologists revealed that she sincerely believed she was "dumb." Her failure was, therefore, easy to accept, since she did not have to blame herself. Both these individuals had learned to cope with their reading handicap.

A young boy with a severe reading problem learned to *compensate* by reading with one eye shut. In this way he could more clearly discern the letters. Since he did

"Read me my report card, Dad."
From *The Wall Street Journal,* August 29, 1977. Reprinted with the permission of Cartoon Features Syndicate.

not realize that he was suffering from a visual problem, he compensated in the best manner he knew how. A woman compensated by devoting her energies to the development of her artistic abilities. The recognition and acceptance that she achieved through her talent overshadowed her lack of ability to read even the newspaper.

The act of *concealing* has stimulated some ingenious behavior. Some people have mastered the art so well that their close associates never suspect the truth. For example, an elderly widowed gentleman, who was caught up in the social dating whirl, would enter a restaurant with his lady friend, put down the menu, and exclaim, "Please order for us both, dear. Whatever you select will please me." When this same gentleman explained that he hired professionals to handle all his personal matters, including his checkbook, his friends attributed his actions to wealth; they never suspected a lack of reading ability. A nonreading adolescent spent hours listening to the news on television and radio so that he could converse with his friends. He pretended to have read the information in newspapers and magazines, successfully concealing his reading handicap.

A poignant letter came to our reading clinic from the wife of a nonreader. It revealed her husband's tragic plight.

> Dear Clinic Director:
> I am writing to you about my husband's desperate need for help. He is a very kind and considerate husband and a good father to our daughter. Shortly after our marriage, I began to notice that he never read a newspaper or a book. He asked me to read labels and directions to him. He said his eyes weren't strong enough to see small print. Yesterday, our seven-year-old daughter was reading a book aloud and she asked her father to help her with a word. He grew red in the face and ran out of the room.
> Later, he admitted the truth to me. He can't read. Please help this fine man and our family. Teach him to read.

Consequences for the Schools

Schools are affected by the poor reading levels of their students. A critical report, *A Nation at Risk* (National Commission on Excellence in Education, 1983), alerted educators to the fact that the mastery of basic skills is dangerously deteriorating and that children will not be able to compete in a highly skilled, technological world. In response to the report's dramatic call for change in our educational system, many states undertook steps toward educational reform.

Educational reform has led to state testing programs to measure reading achievement. Many states have established standards for high-school graduation and for promotion at other grade levels. Some states have developed state-wide tests of reading. In effect, the educational-reform movement is leading to more emphasis on reading assessment.

At the same time, many teachers are receiving training in the "effective schools" strategies (Hunter, 1978; Robbins and Wolfe, 1987). These strategies focus on planning good lessons and teaching them effectively to children. Specifically, effective schools strategies stress motivating students, making instructional objectives clear, maximizing student learning time, and providing feedback to students on their progress. The concepts, research, and practices of the effective schools movement are included throughout this text.

THE READING PROCESS

What is reading? How do skilled readers read? What do unskilled readers lack? To answer these questions, we must first understand the nature of the reading process.

Dimensions of the Reading Process

Reading research of the past twenty years has led to significant advances in theory and practice. A comprehensive summary of this research explains that the skilled reading process includes several dimensions (Anderson, Hiebert, Scott, and Wilkinson, 1985).

1. *Skilled reading is constructive.* No reading passage is completely self-explanatory. To bring meaning to the printed text, readers draw upon their existing store of knowledge and prior experiences. Thus, readers "construct" the meaning of the written passage by filling in the gaps in a text with pieces of information they possess. Unfortunately, sometimes a reader cannot supply this information correctly. For example, when reading about computer software, a reader came across the word, "utilities." Using his prior knowledge, he constructed the meaning of this text to be about "electric power companies." Of course, "utilities" in this context refers to programs that help computer users.

2. *Skilled reading is fluent.* Fluency refers to the ability to identify words easily. If readers must concentrate on figuring out words, they are unable to focus on meaning. In skilled reading, the word identification process must be automatic, not a conscious, deliberate effort. Research shows that children who earn the best scores on reading comprehension tests in the early grades are those who made the most progress in fast and accurate word identification (Stanovich, 1986a).

3. *Skilled reading is strategic.* Skilled readers are flexible and use strategies that are appropriate to each reading situation. They change and direct their reading style depending upon their purpose for reading, the complexity of the text, and their familiarity with the topic. Unlike poor readers, skilled readers monitor their reading comprehension. If something in the text is puzzling, they will go back and use fix-up strategies, such as re-reading, rephrasing the text to improve comprehension, or looking ahead.

4. *Reading requires motivation.* Learning to read requires sustained attention over a long period of time. Since it takes several years to learn to read well, teachers must plan to engage the interest of beginning and poor readers during the learning

period. Pupils must not lose hope that they will eventually become successful. Many studies show that poor readers have lost motivation (Licht and Kistner, 1986; Anderson et al., 1985). Remedial readers tend to be listless and inattentive. They give up easily and do not complete their work. It is important that teachers make reading enjoyable, conveying the belief that students will be successful.

5. *Reading is a lifelong pursuit.* Reading is a continuously developing activity, one that constantly improves through practice. It is not mastered once and for all. At all stages of reading, from the beginning on, it is important that the learner has sufficient opportunities to practice and engage in the process of reading. Teachers must search for ways to encourage their students to read.

The Search for a Definition

For many years, reading specialists have attempted to define reading. There is general agreement that reading involves the ability to construct meaning from printed symbols. Research of the past twenty years has enabled us to refine our definition further. A comprehensive definition of the reading process based on this research was developed by the state of Michigan (Wixon, Peters, Weber, and Roeber, 1987, p. 750).

> Reading is the process of constructing meaning through the dynamic interaction among the reader, the text, and the context of the reading situation.

Let us look at this definition point by point.

A. *Three components* (the reader, the written language, and the reading situation) are present in every reading act. They *interact* to affect what the reader gets from reading, that is, how the reader constructs meaning.
   1. The *reader's existing knowledge and interest* affect what he or she is willing and able to read. For example, a remedial reader may be able to read sports material on a sixth grade level, but be limited to a third grade level in history text.
   2. The *text*, or written language, is the information presented to the reader. The clarity and organization of the text will affect the reader's ability to make sense of it.
   3. The *context of the reading situation* also affects the reading process. Some children find tests so frightening that they have difficulty reading them. However, these children would be able to read the same material in a less threatening situation. The *purpose* or *task* of reading is also part of the reading situation. People read one way when trying to understand detailed directions and another when reading a novel for enjoyment.
B. The *interaction of these three components is dynamic* and may change as the reader reads through the text. For example, when readers find information in the text that conflicts with their existing knowledge, the reading act becomes less comfortable. On the other hand, when the information in the text agrees with readers' knowledge, they become more comfortable with the material.

This definition implies that a person does not have one single reading level. Rather, background knowledge, interest, and the nature of the reading situation affect the level of the material he or she can read. Reading is not one task, but a variety of complex tasks. Thus, to understand why an individual student is having difficulty in school, we need to find out how that student learns and performs in different situations and with different types of text (Wixon and Lipson, 1986).

SERVING POOR READERS IN THE SCHOOLS

Students with reading problems are found throughout our schools. Some students are served by school-sponsored remedial reading programs. Other students are served through Chapter I Programs. (Chapter I, federally-sponsored program funded by the U.S. Department of Education, offers compensatory basic-skills education for students in low-income areas.) Still other students are served through special education programs. However, most poor readers receive no supplementary help from specialists, and are instructed only by the regular classroom teacher (see Figure 1.1).

At the present time, most children who receive supplementary instruction are taken out of their regular classrooms and instructed in "resource rooms." Some educators believe that supplementary instruction should be provided in the regular classroom, rather than in a resource (or "pull-out") program. Thus, reading and special education teachers would co-teach in the child's classroom. This delivery system (sometimes called "push-in") is thought to be preferable because it would foster closer coordination between the regular classroom teacher and the reading or special education teacher (Reynolds, Wang, and Walberg, 1987). However, "push-in" systems are not problem free and may be hampered by limited space and excess noise (Lerner, 1987).

Wherever supplementary instruction is provided, coordination between the reading teacher and the regular classroom teacher is essential. Supplementary reading instruction should be aligned with the core curriculum of the classroom in which the child spends most of the day (Allington and Shake, 1986).

Figure 1.1 School Programs for Serving Students with Reading Difficulties

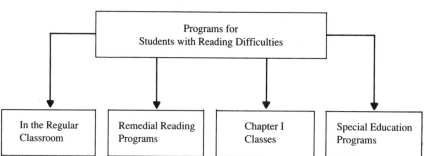

THE FIELD OF REMEDIAL READING

Remedial reading is a special category within the broader field of reading. Remedial reading teachers are dedicated to helping individuals with reading problems. The roots of remedial reading can be traced back to the period of the 1920s when standardized tests first began to be used widely (N.B. Smith, 1965). The results of these tests revealed that thousands of children were failing to make normal progress. By the 1930s, remedial reading had become established as a professional endeavor; the number of research studies increased, and reading clinics were organized in schools and universities. In the 1940s, a major effect of World War II was the shocking discovery that thousands of young men in the military services could not read well enough to follow simple printed instructions for camp life. Ways of teaching reading to young men in army camps was a product of the war years and another impetus to the development of remedial reading (Kirk, Kliebhan, & Lerner, 1978). Interest in remedial reading has continued to grow over the years and the field has now become a vital subspecialty of its own.

Remedial and Developmental Reading

Remedial reading is often differentiated from *developmental reading*. Developmental reading is concerned with the normal growth of the reading process, as well as with materials and methods to enhance this growth. In contrast, remedial reading concentrates on those students who have difficulty in learning to read. Despite this difference in focus, many reading authorities see basic similarities between remedial and developmental reading. For example, Harris and Sipay (1985, p. 327) state that

> In many ways remedial teaching resembles good classroom teaching. Both have the same desired outcomes and both involve application of the same basic principles of learning and motivation. Many of the factors that contribute to teacher effectiveness also contribute to effective remediation.

Thus, principles, methods, and techniques that hold true for developmental instruction are also appropriate for remedial reading. The major differences are that (1) there is more individualization in remedial reading; (2) highly specialized nondevelopmental techniques, which are not used in the regular classroom, are used for students with very severe and particular types of problems; and (3) reading instruction is based on a careful diagnosis of the problem.

Remedial Reading in Special Education Programs

Since many students in special programs are poor readers, classroom teachers and reading teachers must participate in the evaluation and treatment of exceptional students. It is important, therefore, for teachers who deal with reading problems to understand the structure of special education. The field of special education consists of several categories of atypical individuals, that is, individuals who deviate from the norm in some way—physically, developmentally, emotionally, or in the ability to learn. Special education can be defined as instruction that is designed specifically to meet the unique needs of exceptional students. This means that special materials, special teaching techniques, special equipment, or special facilities may be required.

The Scope of Special Education.   Approximately 4 million handicapped children in the United States, ages three to twenty-one, are receiving special education and related services. This is about eleven percent of the students enrolled in schools (U.S. Department of Education, 1988). Twenty years ago, many of these students would not have been recognized or identified as handicapped. They might have been ignored in the classroom or excluded from school altogether. The responsibility of educating the handicapped was relegated completely to parents or institutions. In today's world, the education of the handicapped is considered among the responsibilities of the public schools under Public Law 94-142.

Special education students are classified under several handicapping conditions (see Chapter 15). About 63 percent of all handicapped students need remediation in reading, or in oral or written language (U.S. Department of Education, 1980).

Reading problems become a concern for children who fall into three categories of *mild handicap:* (1) learning disabilities, (2) emotional disturbances, and (3) mental retardation. Most mildly handicapped students are in need of special instruction in reading.

Relation of Remedial Reading to Learning Disabilities.   The special education category that is allied most frequently with the perspectives and procedures used in remedial reading is that of learning disabilities. Almost 5 percent of the school population has been identified as learning disabled (U.S. Department of Education, 1988). While only a small minority of students with reading problems is classified as having learning disabilities (Harris and Sipay, 1985), about 80 percent of learning-disabled students have reading problems (Kirk and Elkins, 1975; Lyon, 1985). In fact, it is sometimes difficult to determine whether a student with a reading problem should be served by the school's remedial reading or learning disabilities program. Whatever the placement, the primary objective should be to improve the student's reading ability. Reading teachers and classroom teachers play increasingly important roles in the identification, evaluation, and treatment of learning-disabled students with reading problems.

OVERVIEW OF THIS BOOK

This book presents theoretical and practical information about remedial reading. Both assessment and remedial procedures are surveyed from beginning levels through advanced levels. Part I is an introduction, and Chapter 1 examines the field of remedial reading and the many consequences of reading disabilities.

Part II deals with assessing reading problems. It includes a discussion of the factors associated with reading disability and methods of evaluation and diagnosis. Chapter 2 deals with some general principles of assessment. Chapter 3 examines environmental factors (such as the home and school) and emotional and physical correlates associated with reading difficulties. In Chapter 4, intellectual and language factors that affect reading are analyzed.

Chapters 5 and 6 present methods of assessing both reading achievement and the components of reading ability. Chapter 5 explores informal assessment tools, including informal reading inventories, miscue analysis, observation, and diagnostic teaching. Formal assessment methods, including commercial tests, are presented in Chapter 6.

In Part III, methods for treating reading problems are examined, and many practical suggestions and activities are given. Chapter 7 discusses general principles of remediation. Chapters 8, 9, 10, 11, and 12 deal with ways to improve reading ability. Chapter 8 examines methods for teaching students to recognize words. Chapter 9 discusses ways of teaching advanced word recognition and meaning vocabulary. Chapter 10 explores the challenging topics of teaching reading and listening comprehension. Chapter 11 deals with teaching the comprehension of textbooks and the use of study strategies. Chapter 12 examines ways of fostering the relationship between reading and writing.

Part IV presents some special concerns of the remedial reading program. Chapter 13 deals with assessing and treating the severely disabled reader. Chapter 14 looks at ways to use computers in remedial reading instruction. Chapter 15 discusses the problem of organizing remedial reading programs and delivering instructional services.

Appendix A describes remedial instructional materials. Appendix B provides addresses of publishers. Appendix C is a Sample Diagnostic Reading Report. Appendix D gives readers a model Informal Reading Inventory.

SUMMARY

A reading disability can be devastating to society, to the individual, and to the schools. Illiteracy leads to problems of unemployment and crime for society. For the individual, it can cause emotional upheaval, prevent the completing of education, and block career opportunities. In schools, low reading achievement has lead to educational reform.

Research during the past twenty years has contributed to our understanding of the reading process. Based on this research, the current definition of reading takes into account the process of constructing meaning and the interaction of the reader, the text, and the context of the reading situation.

In the schools, poor readers can receive supplementary instruction in several types of programs, including a remedial reading program, a Chapter I program, or a special education program.

Remedial reading designates instruction for individuals who are not learning to read in a normal fashion. Developmental reading refers to the regular reading program of the school. Many children with learning disabilities have reading problems.

This book provides practical and theoretical information needed to treat remedial readers. The major sections of the book are (I) introduction, (II) assessing reading problems, (III) strategies for teaching reading, and (IV) special concerns.

2

AN OVERVIEW
OF ASSESSMENT

Part II of this book deals with the assessment of reading problems. In this chapter we provide general information about assessment. In Chapters 3 and 4, some correlates (or factors) related to reading problems are presented. Chapter 3 reviews environmental correlates of the home, school, social situation, and culture, and also analyzes emotional and physical factors. Chapter 4 discusses the correlates of intelligence and language. The topic of Chapters 5 and 6 is assessing reading achievement. Chapter 5 concentrates on informal tests of reading assessment. Chapter 6 focuses on formal measures of reading assessment.

INTRODUCTION

Reading assessment is concerned with collecting data for making educational decisions about reading. The focus is on the measurement and evaluation of some aspect of reading or factors related to reading. In this chapter, we also refer to a *reading diagnosis*. In formulating a reading diagnosis, the teacher analyzes and synthesizes the assessment information, determines the nature of the reading disability, and then finally evolves a plan for teaching.

In this chapter we consider (1) the purposes of reading assessment, (2) ways of gathering assessment information, (3) the phases involved in formulating assessment data into a reading diagnosis, (4) general principles of the reading diagnosis, and (5) the role of related correlates (or factors) in reading problems.

THE PURPOSES OF READING ASSESSMENT

There are many different purposes for assessing reading. Measures of reading are useful for screening, determining placement, instructional planning, measuring student progress, and evaluating the instructional program (Salvia and Ysseldyke, 1988). Assessment also gives teachers the information needed for formulating a reading diagnosis.

Screening

The screening process identifies those individuals who may be in need of special attention. In some cases, screening procedures are designed to prevent possible future problems. For example, a screening procedure can be used for early identification of high-risk preschoolers so that an intervention program can be implemented to prevent the predicted failure from occurring. In addition, remedial readers are sometimes screened to see if there is a need for referral to other professionals, such as medical specialists. For example, a student's vision can be screened to see if an examination from an eye care specialist is needed.

Determining Placement

Assessment information can lead to a student's classification or assignment to a class or a program. Placement decisions depend upon many factors, including the nature and severity of the problem, facilities and personnel available in the school, the input of the parent, needs of the student, and legal requirements for placement (especially in the case of special education students). Assessment data helps educators to decide if the poor reader can best be taught through general classroom instruction, needs supplementary instruction, or requires full-time specialized placement.

Instructional Planning

Assessment information also provides the basis for developing a plan of instruction. Based on assessment findings, the teacher selects instructional strategies, methods, and materials for teaching reading.

Measuring Student Progress

The progress of a student or a group of students can be monitored by using educational assessment information. The end-of-the-year achievement tests often given in classrooms are common ways to measure progress. Information is gathered which can provide a baseline to measure later progress. Improvement in reading can be gauged by comparing the later measures with the level at which the student began.

Evaluating the Program

Assessment information can be used to evaluate an entire curriculum or educational program. For example, judgments about the success of an organizational plan (such as a nongraded school), or specific teaching materials (such as a particular mathematics series), or a teaching method (such as finger math) can be based on this type of assessment information. This purpose is achieved as teachers monitor the ongoing reaction of a number of students to teaching methods and materials.

Developing a Reading Diagnosis

Finally, assessment information can be used to develop a reading diagnosis. A careful and objective reading diagnosis can be a turning point in a student's academic career. To formulate a reading diagnosis, assessment information must be carefully synthesized and analyzed. A productive diagnosis enables the teacher to learn enough about the failing reader to develop a viable teaching plan. *The instructional plan is the heart of the reading diagnosis.*

The depth of the reading diagnosis depends upon the nature of the problem and on the available time, facilities, and resources. Therefore, reading diagnoses vary in form, comprehensiveness, and level of intensity. Although the diagnosis is generally conducted prior to instruction, diagnostic decision making continues throughout the teaching process as well.

WAYS OF GATHERING ASSESSMENT INFORMATION

Tests are one source of assessment information, but there are other excellent ways to obtain data. Each method offers a different view of the student. The use of multiple assessment sources creates an opportunity to corroborate findings. For example, the parents of 13-year-old Jesse stated that he loved to read and that he was an avid reader at home. However, observations of Jesse in the classroom and library, and informal conversations with him, indicated that he did not enjoy reading, he did not read frequently, and he generally avoided reading activities. In this case, the different sources provided contradictory information; consequently, further investigation was needed. Several methods for collecting assessment data are noted briefly in this section. However, each is also discussed more fully in Chapters 5 and 6.

Formal Tests

There are two types of formal tests. (1) *Standardized tests* compare the student's performance with that of other students of comparable age and grade levels. (2) *Criterion-referenced tests* determine directly if the student has mastered specific reading skills.

Informal Tests

Informal tests include teacher-made tests and other nonstandardized measures. Informal tests permit the teacher to gather information in an unconstrained and relaxed manner. Although these tests have not been normed on a large population, they often provide information which is not available from formal tests.

Interviews

An interview involves discussions with parents, teachers, or the student. The purpose of the interview is to gain a more comprehensive picture of the student's attitudes, behaviors, and reading habits.

Reports from Related Professionals

Often, other professionals have useful information to contribute. Such information may come from sources such as medical reports, psychological reports, or speech and language reports. Reports done by school-based teams, such as Individualized Educational Programs (IEPs), developed for special education students, also provide useful information.

Cumulative Records

Cumulative records are kept by the school and present an overview of a student's school history. These records contain attendance reports, changes of schools, report card grades over the years, grade repetitions, age of beginning school, and so on. Cumulative records might show, for example, that 10-year-old Sara was absent for two months of the fall term in first grade due to an automobile accident. During this time, Sara missed some vital reading instruction, a factor which contributed to her later reading disability.

Observations

Observing the student's behavior in a variety of settings provides important assessment information. By observing students in a classroom situation, the teacher can note their ability to attend to a task, their level of frustration, and the frequency of disruptive behaviors. Observations in the lunchroom or at recess show how students interact with peers in social situations.

Sample Teaching Lessons

This method refers to the use of work samples (or diagnostic teaching) in which students are given an instructional task for the purpose of gathering diagnostic information. By actually trying out an instructional technique during the diagnostic period, the teacher gains valuable information about the student's likelihood of success using that particular strategy. For example, Barbara was taught six words using a sight word approach to see if she learned well using this method.

Each of these methods contributes valuable information to the diagnosis. Familiarity with these assessment sources enables teachers to select those most appropriate for a specific student.

THE READING DIAGNOSIS: PHASES OF THE PROCESS

There are several phases in the process of conducting a reading diagnosis. Because the diagnosis varies according to the needs of different students, the exact sequence of the diagnostic process may also vary. At times, several phases are accomplished simultaneously. Occasionally, the teacher must go back to an earlier phase. Nevertheless, there is general agreement that a reading diagnosis proceeds from more general to more specific concerns. The sequential phases of the diagnosis, as shown in Figure 2.1, serve as a guide. All of these phases would be used in a very thorough, comprehensive diagnosis. However, for some cases, this intensity is not needed.

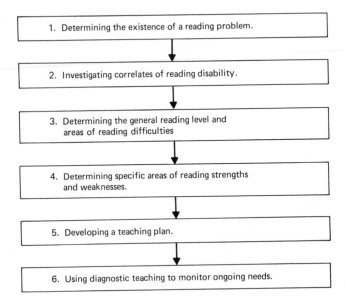

Figure 2.1 Phases of the Reading Diagnosis

1. Determining the Existence of a Reading Problem

A first consideration is to decide if the student has a reading problem. Objective evidence is needed to substantiate the existence of a reading disability. In some instances, students are referred for remedial reading instruction, but further investigation reveals that they are reading as well as can be expected or that their primary problems are not in the area of reading. Since time for diagnosis is limited and resources for remediation are in short supply, it is important, as an initial step, to decide which students are most likely to benefit from remedial help.

Several procedures can be used to determine the existence of a reading disability. In one procedure, the teacher compares the student's performance on a test of potential ability or intelligence with performance on a reading achievement test. In another procedure, the student's ability to function in the current classroom situation is examined carefully. Techniques for judging whether the student has a reading disability are presented in Chapter 4.

2. Investigating Correlates of Reading Disability

Reading disabilities are often accompanied by related problems known as *correlates*. Correlates of reading disability are nonreading factors that may impinge upon learning to read. These include environmental, emotional, physical, intellectual, and language factors. An investigation and analysis of these correlates can deepen the teacher's understanding of a student's reading problem. However, the relationship of a correlate to an individual's reading problem is quite complex. In any individual case, it is difficult to determine the precise relationship between a factor and the reading problem. Therefore, teachers should be cautious about interpreting a correlate as the *cause* of a reading problem. Cautions for interpreting the effect of correlates are discussed later in this chapter.

3. General Reading Diagnosis: Determining the Reading Level and the General Areas of Reading Difficulties

An important phase of the general reading diagnosis is assessing the student's present level of reading performance. How well can the student read and understand what is read? When gathering this information, it is important to remember that the student's reading level may vary depending upon factors such as interest and background for the text being read and the context in which the reading takes place. For example, students often find recreational reading easier than textbook reading. Thus, we often need to think of reading ability as being a range of levels, rather than one set level for any individual (Wixon and Lipson, 1986).

During the general diagnosis we also determine the major areas of reading in which the student is experiencing difficulty. Remedial students have trouble with one or more of the major areas of reading, which are (1) word recognition, (2) comprehension, (3) meaning vocabulary, (4) study strategies, and (5) reading rate. In addition, pupils may also lack the readiness skills needed to begin formal reading instruction.

Depending upon the abilities of the students, different areas of reading assume importance in the diagnosis. For remedial readers at beginning levels, the diagnosis must often concentrate on word recognition, the ability to identify words. At higher levels, the diagnosis of meaning vocabulary and comprehension assumes greater importance. Remedial readers at advanced levels need an assessment of study strategies and reading rate.

4. Specific Reading Diagnosis: Determining Specific Reading Strengths and Weaknesses

Once the general areas of reading difficulty are noted, the teacher tries to pinpoint specific areas of reading strengths and weaknesses. It is very important to assess abilities (or strengths) as well as disabilities (or weaknesses). What the student *can* do is as essential to the diagnosis as what the student *cannot* do. Even students with the most severe reading problems will have some areas of strength.

This phase involves the detailed analysis of the student's reading abilities. For example, the teacher might already know that a student is poor in the general area of word recognition. It is now appropriate for the teacher to gather more specific information about the student's word recognition abilities. To gather this information the teacher (1) assesses the precise abilities and needs in word recognition and (2) analyzes the strategies the student is using to recognize words.

As we gather this information, we need to remember that our aim is to help the student succeed in the regular classroom situation. Therefore, an emphasis should be placed on tasks which are similar to those done in the classroom. For example, when evaluating comprehension, students might be asked to read and comprehend a chapter from their social studies book or a selection from their basal reader. These tasks allow teachers to evaluate how students function in classroom situations and to plan instructions which will enable them to cope more effectively with class demands.

Assessment tools for determining specific reading strengths and weaknesses include tests, observations, informal probing, and diagnostic teaching.

5. Developing a Teaching Plan

After all the information gathered in the diagnostic process is analyzed and synthesized, a plan for teaching is developed. The teaching plan includes the areas of reading to be taught; the appropriate level of reading for instruction; the materials to be used in the teaching; the instructional methods; and time, frequency, and duration of the teaching.

6. Using Diagnostic Teaching to Monitor Ongoing Needs

Even after the formal diagnosis is concluded, the teacher should remain sensitive to changing needs. Ideally, remedial teaching continues to be diagnostic in nature. For example, if the student's response to teaching indicates that an instructional strategy is not effective, the teacher should change the instructional plans. In short, good remedial teaching continues the diagnostic process through continual questioning and decision making.

During all phases of the diagnosis, the teacher also looks at affective behaviors such as the student's motivation for reading, anxiety about reading, reading choices, and purposes for reading. These are important because the ultimate success of instruction is strongly affected by the reader's attitudes. For example, students who view reading as a meaningful activity will be more highly motivated that those who view reading merely as a school requirement.

THE READING DIAGNOSIS: SOME GENERAL PRINCIPLES

Conducting a diagnosis is an exciting intellectual challenge. In a way, the process is rather like solving a mystery. The teacher is confronted with the mystery of a student who has a reading problem. Like the famous detective Sherlock Holmes going about his work, the mystery is solved by using clues gathered from many sources. Sources in the reading diagnosis include: the student, parents, classroom teachers, cumulative school records, observations, sample teaching lessons, and tests. The alert diagnostic teacher pulls together the entire picture to solve the mystery. The following general principles serve as guidelines for conducting the reading diagnosis.

The Diagnosis Is a Decision-making Process

It is important to remember that a diagnosis is not merely testing; rather, it is a decision-making process. Although the diagnosis involves the administration of tests, they are only one vehicle for making judgments about the student's reading problem. The decisions should not be limited by information generated from test scores but should include other types of information as well.

Decision making involves searching for patterns in the student's behavior. For example, Ignacio, a nine-year-old boy, was observed to yawn while reading orally. Upon questioning, his mother reported that he generally yawned when under stress. When the teacher observed Ignacio, he seemed uncomfortable in the classroom when doing schoolwork but not on the playground. When he was given an intelligence test, he scored particularly poorly on subtests that were timed and required working under pressure. Combining all these clues, the teacher hypothesized that the pressure of schoolwork was making Ignacio nervous.

Sometimes one test or observation can be used in several ways. For example, an oral reading inventory is usually used to determine the level of a student's reading. But careful observation during the oral reading can also reveal the strategies that the student uses to recognize words.

The Diagnosis Evaluates the Student Objectively

For many students, the reading diagnosis is the only attempt ever made to counsel their educational and personal problems. For this reason, it is important that the teacher remain as objective as possible. For example, the teacher should realize that information from classroom teachers or parents can be subjective. Students with reading problems often acquire negative "reputations" in their schools and homes and even with themselves. The diagnostician owes the student a fresh, unbiased look.

The Diagnosis Considers the Whole Individual

Reading is but one part of the student's life. The teacher must consider the student's past experiences, future plans, likes and dislikes, fears, and interests. Every attempt should be made to perceive the student as an entire person—not just as some-one who is failing in reading.

Diagnosis and Remediation Are a Continuous Process

As noted earlier, diagnosis and remediation are not independent processes, but are highly interrelated. Since the plan of action changes as teachers and students work together, diagnosis continues through the instructional process. In a very real sense, the diagnostic process never ends. The teacher must continuously adjust instruction to the student's changing needs by continuing to monitor the pupil's responses to instruction.

CORRELATES OF READING DISABILITY

In the following discussion, correlates, or factors, contributing to reading disability are reviewed briefly; each is discussed in further detail in Chapters 3 and 4. These correlates include the areas of environment, emotional status, physical well-being, intelligence, and language.

Cautions in Interpreting Correlates

It is important to understand that correlates relate to reading in multiple and complex ways. For this reason, we use the term correlates, rather than causes. Several cautions should be observed in interpreting the impact of these correlates:

1. Precise causes of reading difficulty may be extremely difficult to determine. A reading disability and a correlate may occur together. This does not mean, however, that one causes the other. For example, the appearance of storks near a Caribbean Island correlated highly with an increase in the birth rate. This does not mean that the storks caused the increase in the birth rate!
2. People are affected differently by their handicaps. Thus, not every student with poor vision will have reading difficulties. Some learn to work around their visual problems, whereas others may find a similar visual problem insurmountable.
3. Reading failure is often the product of several interacting factors. In a classic study of the causes of reading disability, Robinson (1946) concluded that poor reading was generally the result of several causes, all interacting with each other.
4. Even when a specific cause can be identified, it is sometimes impossible for the reading teacher to alleviate the situation. For example, specific family difficulties may be identified as the causal factor of a reading problem. However, the school cannot control the home situation. The situation must be accepted while the teacher concentrates on dealing with the reading problem.

Despite these limitations, it is important to investigate correlates. Often they provide a key element in the understanding and successful remediation of the reading problem.

Correlates Affecting Reading

Environmental Factors. Each human being functions in many complex environmental systems. A student may be uncomfortable in the school environment and therefore unable to learn effectively. Problems at home or in social settings may also affect learning. The cultural group can influence the importance of reading for the student (see Chapter 3).

Emotional Factors.   Many students with reading problems have accompanying emotional problems. In some cases, the emotional problem is the root of the learning difficulty. In other cases, reading problems trigger the emotional distress. In either case, the teacher must try to understand the student's emotional condition and provide a warm, supportive environment (see Chapter 3).

Physical Factors.   A variety of physical factors can contribute to reading disabilities. These include visual and auditory impairment and general health problems. In addition, physical factors can include subtle neurological problems and perceptual deficits (see Chapter 3).

Intelligence.   Intellectual abilities are related to reading ability. In fact, remedial readers are sometimes defined as students who are reading below the level predicted by intelligence tests. However, true intelligence is difficult to measure, and the nature of the relationship between reading ability and intelligence is imperfect (see Chapter 4).

Language.   Reading is one form of language. If language abilities are not well developed, poor reading may result. For example, students who lack a language base of rich vocabulary and sentence structures will find it difficult to acquire higher-level reading skills. The role of language in the reading process is discussed throughout this book, but receives concentrated treatment in Chapter 4.

SUMMARY

Reading assessment is concerned with measuring and collecting data on reading. The purposes of reading assessment include: (1) screening, (2) determining placement, (3) planning instruction, (4) monitoring progress, (5) evaluating the program, and (6) developing a reading diagnosis.

Ways of obtaining assessment information include formal tests (standardized and criterion-referenced tests), informal measures, interviews, reports from related professionals, cumulative records, observations, and sample teaching lessons. Although each of these methods can provide valuable information, the teacher should select those methods that are the most appropriate for the particular situation.

The reading diagnosis uses assessment information to develop an analysis of the student's reading problem.

There are a number of elements in a reading diagnosis. They include (1) determining the existence of a reading problem, (2) investigating related factors, (3) determining the reading level and general areas of reading difficulties, (4) determining specific areas of reading strengths and weaknesses, (5) developing a teaching plan, and (6) using diagnostic teaching to monitor ongoing needs.

Several general principles are useful for the teacher to keep in mind during the reading diagnosis: the diagnosis is a decision making process, the diagnosis should consider the student objectively, the diagnosis should consider the whole individual, and diagnosis and remediation are a continuous process.

Factors contributing to a reading disability are called correlates. A correlate cannot be assumed to be the cause of a reading problem. Correlates of a reading disability include environmental, emotional, physical, intelligence, and language factors.

3

CORRELATES OF READING DISABILITY I
Environmental, Emotional, and Physical Factors

This chapter and the next consider factors (or correlates) that may be related to a student's success or failure in learning to read.

INTRODUCTION

In this chapter, we discuss three correlates of reading: (1) *environmental* factors (the home, school, social, and cultural environments in which the student operates), (2) *emotional* factors (the psychodynamic factors that affect learning), and (3) *physical* factors (vision, hearing, neurological, and other health factors).

We refer to these factors as correlates of reading disability (rather than causes) because the exact nature of the cause-and-effect interaction cannot be known with certainty. Yet, in formulating a diagnosis, it is valuable to consider these correlates and their relevance to the student's reading problem.

ENVIRONMENTAL FACTORS

The different environments in which students live and grow have a strong impact on their desire and ability to learn. The total environmental (or ecological) system within which the student operates includes the home, the school, the social group, and the cultural milieu. Each of these environments has an effect on the student, but the various environments also interrelate with each other, and the student's actions and behaviors can affect the entire system.

Complex interactions form between the individual and each of the environmental settings. For example, a student's behavior and reactions may be quite different in a clinical or formal testing situation than they are in a classroom. In fact, a description of a student in a clinical setting is often so different from that of the student in the classroom that one wonders if the same individual is being described. Since formal testing usually occurs in a rather unnatural situation—one that is divorced from the child's usual environment, it is important that the evaluation include situations that occur in the student's natural setting.

What can we learn about the student and the reading problem through these four environments—home, school, social, and cultural?

The Home Environment

The home environment is the child's first environmental system. Early formative years in the home are the foundation for tremendous growth and development. Environmental experiences during these critical first five or six years are a powerful influence upon a child's cognitive growth and intelligence. Language development is greatly influenced by the child's home experiences with a parent (Bloom 1976; White, 1975).

Parents provide emotional well-being as well as intellectual stimulation. A crucial interaction known as "bonding" takes place during the early months of infancy and becomes the basis for later emotional health. Bonding depends upon a successful interactive relationship between the mother (or primary parent figure) and the infant (Bowlby, 1969). The early development of the ego and self-concept are also dependent upon the support and encouragement of parents. Studies that compare good and poor readers show that the good readers are more likely to have a favorable home environment (Abrams and Kaslow, 1977).

The parent also provides a role model for the child. Through activities such as doing recreational reading, going to the library, and reading stories aloud, parents teach children to value reading. Experiences with a parent are a very important factor in stimulating good reading and a love for reading. The parent's role continues to be crucial after the child enters school. Students who experience difficulty learning to read are in special need of satisfying family relationships.

Children are profoundly affected by what happens to parents. In today's society, children are often dramatically touched by moves to new locations, divorce or separation of parents, death of relatives, or leave-taking of older siblings. Parents and teachers can often work together to help the student cope with these changes. However, teachers should not automatically assume that the home situation is the sole cause of the reading problem.

Coping with Parental Separation. In recent years, an unprecedented number of children are affected by the divorce or separation of their parents. It is estimated that 60 percent of all Americans born in 1984 will spend some time living in a single-parent household before reaching age eighteen (Norton and Glick, 1986). Understandably, these children may be under stress, particularly if the family change is recent. Teachers can help such students through these trying times by:

1. Talking to students and allowing them to express their feelings. Try to be nonjudgmental about the family situation.
2. Temporarily lessening academic and behavioral demands in the classroom or clinic.
3. Being sensitive to the student's living and legal custody arrangements. Make sure the appropriate parent receives communications. With permission from the custodial parent, both parents can be informed of the student's progress.

Parents' Role in Reading. Parent cooperation is a valuable asset for the remedial teacher. Parents are able to relate important and significant information about their child. By simply talking to the parents, the teacher can learn much about the reading problem. Parents are also able to alleviate some of the psychological and emotional consequences of reading failure by what they do in the home environment. They can provide love, acceptance, and other opportunities for success.

Sometimes very concerned parents think it is their responsibility to provide direct reading instruction by themselves, even though the student is already receiving remedial help. Usually parents are not effective teachers of their own children because they are so deeply involved in their child's welfare that they cannot be objective.

In an emotionally charged atmosphere, the parent displays disappointment when failure occurs, and the child is overly sensitive to parental reactions. In general, parents should not be expected to teach their own children to read. Of course, each individual-parent-child relationship is different, and some parents may be effective in providing limited kinds of instruction. For example, in our reading clinic, with careful teacher guidance, mothers successfully learned how to read with their children on a regular basis.

What can parents do to help their children improve in reading without actually teaching reading? Some suggestions that teachers can give the parent are:

1. *Share in the child's success.* Children enjoy the experience of reading material that they have mastered to the parent. The parent should be an enthusiastic listener.
2. *Provide a reading model in the home.* Parents can surround their children with books in the home and demonstrate the value of reading. They can also take trips to the library and bring home materials that the child selects.
3. *Read to the child.* It is important to read stories aloud from the time the child is a toddler. This activity promotes language learning, stresses the value of the printed word, and encourages a close relationship between parent and child.
4. *Accept the child as he or she is.* It is often difficult to admit that one's own child has a problem. When parents deny that the problem exists or hold unrealistic expectations, children are sensitive to their parents' disappointment. This situation may trigger a difficult parent-child relationship.
5. *Help the child to feel secure and confident.* Look for ways in which the child can succeed and encourage those activities. Help the child to be happy and healthy in the home environment.
6. *Share in the excitement of reading success.* Every bit of reading acquisition is an important step for the disabled reader. Parents, as well as teachers, should emphasize and enhance successful learning experiences.

The School Environment

Children and adolescents spend a substantial portion of their waking hours in school. Their experiences and relationships in the school environment profoundly affect their entire lives. For the remedial reader, however, school experiences are too often unhappy ones; the school does not offer a setting of joyful learning.

Interactions within the School.   For the poor reader, interactions with adults in the school environment are not satisfying. Studies show that poor achievers tend to be perceived negatively by teachers, teacher aides, and principals. In fact, adults form negative impressions of students with learning problems based on very short observations. Research shows that adults make relatively harsh judgments of low-achieving students after viewing them on videotape for only a few minutes (Pearl, Donahue, and Bryan, 1986).

Studies also show that classroom teachers disapprove of students with learning problems. Keogh, Tchir, and Windeguth-Behn (1974) found that teachers associate characteristics such as aggressiveness and lack of self-discipline with failing students. Other investigators have found that low-achieving students receive both less praise and acknowledgment from teachers and are more likely to be criticized (Good, 1983).

In her book, *Teachers Pets, Troublemakers, and Nobodies,* Gouldner (1978) summarizes an extensive anthropological study of kindergarten and primary classrooms. Gouldner concludes that teachers concentrate their energies and the bulk of their interactions on only a few children, generally high-achieving girls. This pattern is established early in the first grade and is maintained in subsequent years. Other students become "nobodies." They tend to be ignored by teachers and do not develop normal patterns of classroom social interactions. By the fifth or sixth grade, these "nobodies" may be ignored almost totally.

These findings have serious implications for students with reading problems. School does not provide a satisfying environment for them.

Instructional Factors in Reading Disability.   In many cases, the reading problem is related to poor or inappropriate instruction; sometimes immature children are given formal reading instruction before they can profit from it. As a result, the child is initially frustrated, achieves poorly, and eventually develops a substantial lag behind classmates. In other cases instruction is not geared to the needs of a student. For example, a teacher may routinely use reading material which does not meet the needs of a specific child. This practice may result in failure and a negative attitude about reading. It is important to remember that teachers may unintentionally provide inappropriate instruction because of the difficulty they encounter in meeting the needs of 25 to 35 students in a class.

Looking into past instructional practices may provide clues about the reading problem. The school history often reveals such information. Questions that may be investigated include:

1. Was the student given initial reading instruction before he or she was ready?
2. Was a method of instruction inappropriate to the student's needs used?
3. Were the student's initial school experiences positive and successful?
4. When did the reading problem begin?
5. Were there frequent moves or transfers which resulted in changes in instructional methods and materials?

The Social Environment

The student's social environment is another important environmental system. Social relationships and interactions with friends and peers provide an environment in which students grow and develop socially, emotionally, and cognitively. Successful interaction with friends should provide many satisfactions and opportunities to gain confidence. For some disabled readers, however, the social sphere is another area of dismal failure. A sizable body of evidence shows that social unpopularity tends to accompany school failure. Poor achievers are often rejected by their classmates. They are uninvolved in school activities and ignored by other children. Such students present social interaction problems and exhibit poor social perception skills (Bryan, 1986 a,b; Vaughn, 1985).

When children develop normally, they learn social skills in a casual and informal manner. Through incidental experiences, they learn appropriate ways of acting with people: what to say, how to behave, and how to give and take in a human situation. However, some individuals are not socially perceptive. They are not sensitive to social nuances in everyday living, and they may be unaware of how their actions and behavior are interpreted by others.

Many reading-disabled students are unable to accommodate themselves to another person's point of view. Because they fail to consider the needs of other people, their chances for successful social interaction with peers are reduced. The research of Wong and Wong (1980) showed that learning-disabled students, particularly girls, were less able than normal students to adopt an alternative point of view in judging a series of events suggested by cartoons. These authors suggest that role-playing games, in which a person is made to adopt the viewpoint of another person, may help to improve social relationships. A study by Bruininks (1978) showed that, in contrast to normal children, learning-disabled children overestimate their popularity. These students do not seem to be able to perceive their own social shortcomings. Thus, research evidence substantiates that students in remedial and special education programs often have difficulty relating to peers in a social setting.

The Cultural Environment

The population of North America is a composite of hundreds of different ethnic and cultural traditions. In today's society, we see ever-changing patterns of immigration and movement as new groups of people add their cultural diversity and richness to our schools. A few decades ago, it was assumed that Americans would all be assimilated into the "melting pot" of the dominant culture. Since then, we have witnessed a new awareness of the value of different cultural traditions and the importance of maintaining them. One of the greatest challenges of our schools has been the education of students from all cultures, whatever their geographical origin, socioeconomic status, or language.

Poverty can produce certain cultural effects. Since a significant portion of American families live below a specified poverty level, it is important for reading teachers to be aware of the effects of poverty on students' academic performances. Although individuals with incomes below the poverty level come from diverse backgrounds, they tend to have certain similarities. Because they are necessarily concerned with basic survival needs, parents are likely to have less energy to devote to their children's intellectual and cognitive development. As a consequence, children from these families often must learn to care for themselves at a very young age. In addition, these children often come to school with relatively limited background experiences.

Sometimes students reject the traditional values of the school. Instead, they may identify with subcultures in which values work against school learning. This trend is particularly evident when adolescents join "gangs." The values of a gang can conflict with successful school performance. The reading achievement of gang members is often substantially below that of other students, despite a high degree of verbal skills, leadership qualities, and intelligence (Labov et al., 1969). Cultural differences, particularly those arising from a culture of poverty, may lead to intense suspicion and discomfort with those individuals perceived to be in the dominant culture.

These generalizations do not, of course, hold true for all low income students. In many poor families, education is cherished, the values of the school are upheld, and family members are encouraged to read and achieve. The opportunity to progress from poverty to economic security is a fundamental promise of democratic nations such as Canada and the United States.

Assessing of Environmental Factors

Informal strategies that the teacher of reading can use to assess the environment include *behavioral observation*, the *interest inventory*, and *interviewing*. These methods are discussed below:

Behavioral Observation.   Systematic observation is a useful method of assessing student behavior and interaction with the environment. Even short observations can provide invaluable information, since they provide objective evidence to substantiate information from other sources. The key to behavioral observation is to identify and describe clearly behaviors that are being observed. The observation should not consist of value judgments, such as "Amy misbehaved." A written observation is a careful recording of what is actually observed; for example, "Amy walked up to Mary's desk and tore up Mary's spelling paper." The cumulative records of many observations provide a base for making diagnostic decisions and planning remediation.

Many different systems can be used for observing behavior (Wallace and Larsen, 1978). Three methods of observation are: time sampling, event sampling, and the anecdotal record.

1. *Time Sampling.* This method enables the teacher to observe the length of time a student persists in certain behaviors. Generally, one type of behavior is chosen for analysis. The teacher records the number of times the behavior occurs and the length of time it persists during the observation period. Table 3.1 illustrates a time sampling observation for Chet, a student whose attention in class was a matter of concern.

2. *Event Sampling.* Here, a specific type of event is chosen for recording. In event sampling, the observer tries to record the event in as much detail as possible each time it is observed. Table 3.2 illustrates event sampling for Billy, a student who was thought to have problems getting along with peers.

3. *The Anecdotal Record.* This method is also known as a continuous recording. Anecdotal recording is not limited to one type of event. The student is observed

Table 3.1 Time Sample Observation

Reason for observation:	Chet was thought to be inattentive during class lessons at school.
Setting:	Chet was observed during a group remedial lesson by a teacher aide.
Time frame:	Observed during two thirty-minute lessons, from 10:00 A.M. to 10:30 A.M.
Behavior observed:	Inattention to the teacher or to class lesson was noted.
Observations:	

Day 1 10:04–10:10 Chet looked around room.
        10:15–10:20 Chet talked to another student.
        10:25–10:28 Chet listened to his radio using an earphone.

Day 2 10:05–10:12 Chet wrote a note to another student.
        10:15–10:20 Chet talked to another student.
        10:25–10:29 Chet looked at his papers and "daydreamed."

Conclusion: Chet attended to less than half the lessons.

Table 3.2 Event Sample Observation

Reason for observation:	Billy was thought to be an aggressive student.
Setting:	Observed in the classroom by teacher.
Time frame:	One school day.
Behavior observed:	All conflict situations were noted and described.
Observations:	

8:45 A.M.   On way to classroom, Jimmy A. accidentally bumped Billy. Billy kicked him; Jimmy did not respond.

10:00 A.M. Bob made a face at Billy during group lessons; Billy returned it.

11:30 A.M. Billy kicked Lynn in the lunch line. Lynn says she did nothing. Billy says he doesn't know why he did it.

1:00 P.M.   (Report, not observation) Billy and Joe were reported for fighting. They said they had not been fighting.

2:00 P.M.   While standing in line, Bob called Billy "a rat" (overheard by teacher). Billy started to punch him.

Conclusions: Four hostile incidents were observed, and one was reported to teacher. They involved three boys and one girl and physical and verbal abuse. Billy seems to initiate some hostilities; other students initiate others.

throughout the day, and all incidents of particular interest are described in as much detail as possible. Many different types of activities can be recorded in the anecdotal record, since it is meant to give the "flavor" of a student's activities.

The Interest Inventory.   The interest inventory is a valuable tool for all remedial reading students. It serves to establish rapport with the student, it provides insight into the student's areas of interests, and it gives the teacher a way to motivate a desire to read. A negative attitude toward reading can often be overcome if the teacher captures the student's personal interests. A strong positive relationship has been found between student interests and reading preferences (Estes and Vaughan, 1973).

In an interest inventory, students respond to specific questions regarding their interests and activities. Topics include hobbies, play and sport preferences, television viewing, comics, computers, and movie attendance, as well as reading preferences. The sample interest inventory, given in Table 3.3, is a suggested format. The teacher may wish to modify the content depending upon the age, sex, and geographic location of the student. For example, a pupil in Colorado might be asked about an interest in skiing, whereas one in California might have an interest in surfing.

While the interest inventory can be administered at any time during the diagnostic procedure, it is usually given early. It can also be used during a long or strenuous testing period to provide a break or change of pace. The interest inventory may

Table 3.3   Sample Interest Inventory

Name: _____ Age: ___ Date: _____

  I. *Hobbies (circle the hobbies you pursue)*

photography	collecting postcards	knitting
painting	crocheting	carpentry
dancing	making models	raising plants
collecting stamps	collecting coins	collecting matches
acting	singing	sewing
raising animals (pets)	other _____	

What hobby do you think you would enjoy doing?

  II. *TV (circle the kind of TV programs you enjoy most)*

comedies	sports	news
cartoons	mystery	documentaries
monster shows	science fiction	movies
westerns	variety shows	adventure
other _____	police	war stories

What are the names of the TV shows you like best? _____
Least? _____

III. Sports (circle the sports you enjoy doing)

baseball	golf	handball
basketball	bowling	ice skating
football	volleyball	roller skating
jogging	soccer	swimming
bicycling	hockey	boxing
fishing	tennis	wrestling
other _____		

Now go back and put a check next to the sports you do not do yourself but you enjoy watching.

IV. Reading (circle what you like to read)

comic books	animal stories	magazines
mystery	humor	newspapers
romance	stories about people	"how to" books
adventure	history	other_____

What is the name of the best book you've ever read? _____
The worst book? _____ What is your favorite comic book? _____

V. Miscellaneous

1. How do you spend your time after school? _____
2. How do you spend your time on weekends? _____
3. What toys do you enjoy most? _____
4. What do you like to do best? _____
5. What do you like to do least? _____
6. Who is your favorite real-life hero? _____
7. Who is your favorite fiction/make-believe hero? _____
8. What is your favorite game? _____
9. What is your favorite movie? _____

VI. School

1. What is your favorite subject in school? _____
2. What subject do you like least in school? _____

VII. Interests (check things you would like to know more about)

_ auto mechanics	_ fairy tales	_ history	_ health
_ famous people	_ electricity	_ electronics	_ radio
_ television	_ woodwork	_ video games	_ aviation
_ art	_ music	_ adventure	_ dancing
_ mystery	_ foreign lands	_ poetry	_ current events
_ riddles	_ comic strips	_ cartoons	_ animals
_ insects	_ science	_ transportation	_ soap box derby
_ race cars	_ football	_ cars	_ baseball
_ basketball	_ other sports	_ cooking	_ monsters
_ stories about people	_ geography	_ myths and legends	_ jokes
_ comic books	_ Indians	_ reptiles	_ circus
_ detectives	_ zoo	_ nations	_ space travel
_ computers	_ astronomy	_ singers	_ other_____

be given in a written form to students whose reading level is sufficient to read the inventory and write the answers. For more disabled readers, it may be necessary for teachers to read the questions aloud and record oral responses. Teachers should be aware that some students hide their true feelings and misrepresent their actual interests. Those who are seeking approval answer questions in a way that they believe will be acceptable.

Information on interests can also be derived from several other sources: discussions with the student, the parent interview, and student observations. Frequently, further interests are revealed after reading instruction has begun and students have confidence that the teacher will be responsive to their preferences.

The importance of using a pupil's interests to plan the instructional program cannot be overemphasized. Often students have been exposed to years of unmotivating and difficult instruction. The use of student interests personalizes the reading program and assures students that their needs and concerns are important. Such assurance can be a powerful motivational tool.

The Interview. Interviews with informed and concerned people yield information about the student that cannot be obtained in any other way. The parent interview is usually part of the reading diagnosis. The personal and informal atmosphere of the interview encourages parents to share valuable information about their child. Interviews are best conducted by the teacher who will be responsible for the student's remedial instruction. The interview serves many important purposes:

1. An interview provides an opportunity for parents to express themselves freely to a sympathetic but objective party whose sole purpose is to help their child.
2. The interview reveals the parents' perceptions and attitudes about their child's reading problem.
3. The interview can also aid in the development of teaching strategies by rounding out the picture of the student. For example, if the interview reveals the student is interested in old cars, the lessons and materials can center on this interest.
4. The interview provides an avenue for obtaining information that would be difficult to discover through other evaluation techniques. Data about early illnesses, accidents, birth history, school history, family relationships, and developmental milestones can be collected readily. Parents often do not remember all the relevant information during the initial interview, but with continued parental contact, they may add additional background information at a later time. We have found that parents are usually eager to share information about their child.

Some basic procedures for successful interviewing are:

1. Begin by telling parents that this information will be used to help their child and will be kept confidential
2. Strive for an amiable, open atmosphere, yet one in which the conversation follows a directed plan.
3. Avoid indicating disapproval of parent responses or actions.

Since there are important legal and moral considerations involved in an interview, it must be kept confidential. If the teacher wishes to tape the interview, parents or guardians must give their consent. The presence of another individual during the interview also requires the consent of parents or guardians. Finally, information shared at an interview or any other part of the diagnostic procedure cannot be released to another agency without parental permission. A sample interview form is presented in Table 3.4 as a guide for questions that might be included. Teachers can copy this form in developing an interviewing instrument.

Although the interview often reveals intriguing information, the teacher should remember that the interview is only one source of diagnostic data. Interviewers should refrain from drawing conclusions until sufficient information is collected from several sources and integrated with the interview information.

EMOTIONAL FACTORS

Poor readers, particularly those with a long history of reading failure, often have accompanying emotional problems that impede learning. Weinberg and Rehmet (1983) found that 58 percent of the children referred for reading disorders had symptoms of depression. Emotional problems often increase as a youngster moves up through the grades and enters the teenage years.

It is difficult to know whether a reading disorder is the result of an underlying emotional disturbance or whether emotional problems develop because of a reading disorder. If the reading failure is caused by a preexisting emotional disturbance, then the treatment should focus on the interfering emotional problem. Such treatment may require psychotherapy, counseling, and the use of methods that build confidence, establish self-esteem, and capture the pupil's interest (Manzo, 1987). On the other hand, if the emotional problem is the consequence of a primary reading difficulty, treatment should focus on immediate teaching of reading. With successful reading experiences, the student's emotional problems are likely to lessen and, it is hoped, be overcome.

In most cases, even if the student displays some emotional distress, we recommend that teachers begin by teaching reading. At the same time, if they are sensitive to the emotional needs of the student, they can provide much support and understanding while teaching. Successful experiences in learning can be a kind of therapy in helping the child overcome emotional problems.

Emotional and Personality Factors That Affect
Reading Achievement

No one personality type describes all poor readers. Because students react to learning failure in different ways, the psychodynamics of failure lead to different types of responses. Some disabled readers evidence no emotional problems, others display a variety of disordered psychological behaviors (Cohen, 1986; Bryan, 1986a). What are some of the emotional reactions to reading failure observed by teachers?

Table 3.4   Sample Interview Form

Student's Name: _____ Age: ___ Grade: ___ Sex: ___
Birthdate: _____ Birthplace: _____
Home Address: _____
             Street   City   State   Zip

Telephone: _____
School: _____ School Address: _____
Interviewer: _____ Interviewee: _____
Date of Interview: _____

A. Members of Immediate Family in Present Home

	Name	*Age*	*Birthplace*	*Occupation*
Father	_____	___	_____	_____
Mother	_____	___	_____	_____

Siblings

1. _____   ___   _____   _____
2. _____   ___   _____   _____
3. _____   ___   _____   _____
4. _____   ___   _____   _____

Others in Home

1. _____
2. _____

Family Members Not in Home

1. _____
2. _____

Have any members of the family had reading or learning difficulties? _____
If yes, give details: _____
Languages Spoken at Home: _____

Previous Diagnoses of Student

Professional/Agency	*Date*	*Conclusions*
1. _____	_____	_____
2. _____	_____	_____

B. Educational History

1. Did student attend nursery school? _____ No. of years: ___ Age: ___
2. Did student attend kindergarten? _____ Age: ___
3. Age of entering first grade: ___
4. Has student repeated any grades? _____ If yes, indicated grades and reasons for retention: _____
   _____

5. Schools attended by student

Name and Location	Grades	Dates	Reasons for Withdrawal
_____	_____	_____	_____
_____	_____	_____	_____
_____	_____	_____	_____

6. Summer school private tutoring: _____
7. Special placement or special help in school: _____
8. Have there been periods of frequent or extended absence? _____ If so, give reasons: _____
9. How is student functioning in school at present? _____
   _____
10. Level of general achievement. Good: _____ Average: _____ Poor: _____
11. At what age did a reading problem develop? _____
12. What may have contributed to the development of this problem? _____
    _____
13. How does student do in academic areas other than reading? _____
    _____
    _____
14. Describe your child's school and classes. _____
    _____
    _____
    _____

C. Physical Health

1. Pregnancy, delivery, and early birth history: _____
   _____
2. General health: _____
   _____
3. Illnesses (include dates and temperatures): _____
   _____
4. Accidents (describe injury, whether unconscious, and give age): _____
   _____
5. Has student ever been unconscious? _____
   _____
6. First walked: _____ Talked (single words): _____ (sentences): _____
7. Disabilities (indicate age of initial observation and treatment):
   Speech problems: _____
   Hearing defects: _____
   Physical disability: _____
   Others: _____
8. Vision. When was student's vision last tested? _____ (results)
   Does student wear glasses? _____ If yes, how long? _____

D. Reading Environment

1. What are the reading materials in the home? _____
   _____

2. What are the attitudes of the parents toward reading?
   Father: _____
   Mother: _____

3. What are the reading activities in the home?
   Oral reading: _____
   Story telling: _____

4. What are student's attitudes?
   Toward reading: _____
   Toward school: _____

E. Environment

1. Describe the student's relationship with parents: _____
   _____

2. Describe student's relationship with siblings: _____
   _____

3. What are the student's interests? _____
   _____

4. How does student spend leisure time? (TV, hobby, work) _____
   _____

5. How does student get along with peers? _____
   _____

F. Emotional Climate

1. How does student feel about the reading problem? _____
   _____

2. Is there any evidence of emotional tension, fear, irritation, or lack of confidence
   in student's behavior? _____ If yes, please describe: _____
   _____
   _____
   _____

3. In comparison with other children of this age, would you describe the student's
   general development as average____, above average____, below average____.

4. List three (3) positive things or characteristics your child possesses: _____
   _____
   _____
   _____

From Reading Clinic, Northeastern Illinois University

Learning Block.   If learning has been a painful experience, the student may develop a block which prevents learning. The student builds a defense mechanism to keep pain and distress out of the reach of consciousness. Learning blocks often can be overcome when reading is taught in interesting and non-threatening ways and students begin to enjoy learning.

In one case, nine-year-old Maria developed an emotional block against books. Whenever the teacher brought out a book, her response was "I told you I can't read a book." In this case the teacher took all the words out of one picture book and taught them, one word at a time, without showing Maria the source. After all the words were mastered, the teacher presented the book to Maria who, of course, at first refused to read it. However, when the teacher demonstrated that Maria could read any word in the book, she overcame the learning block and went on to read that book, and others.

Hostility-Aggressive Behavior.   Reading-disabled pupils may become hostile and overly aggressive to compensate for feelings of inadequacy. Such students may appear to be tough, ready to fight, and even delinquent in their behavior. Actually, they may be seeking a sense of accomplishment that they are unable to find in the classroom setting.

Antisocial behavior can be a manifestation of students' anger and frustration experienced because of failure in academic areas, as well as the failure of others to understand them. Often such students display less hostility when they are taught in small groups, or individually, and when their problems receive earnest attention from teachers.

Learned Helplessness.   Avoiding failure can be the primary goal of some disabled readers. To make sure that they do not fail, students may refuse to try. Thus they avoid stress and the possibility of failure through withdrawal and apathetic behavior. They may deliberately choose not to complete assigned tasks, participate in class discussions, or engage in reading activities, claiming that they do not wish to read or that they do not need reading. In effect, the learner becomes emotionally unavailable. These students need to be encouraged to take risks (such as guessing at words they are not sure of) and to learn that a certain amount of failure is an unavoidable and acceptable part of living. When instructing such students, tell them what they will be learning and why they are learning it. Encouraging and rewarding students for "guessing" may also be helpful.

In some cases, poor achievers cannot accept personal credit for any successes that they have because they think that the teacher has been in charge of the learning situation and has caused the learning to occur (Bryan, 1986 a,b). These students need more personal involvement in the learning situation.

Low Self-Esteem and Depression.   Understandably, students who have been subjected to continual failure develop a low opinion of themselves. They display a negative self-image, poor ego development, and a lack of confidence. The problem often deepens when students become older and realize that they are not meeting society's expectations (Bryan 1986 a,b).

A self-defeating "what's the use" attitude may result in an overall depression. Such students need to know that they are accepted as they are, and that the teacher understands the problem and has confidence that the student can learn. Every instructional success must be emphasized for the student who displays low self-esteem.

Anxiety. Anxiety is another reaction to academic stress and failure in the learning situation. Anxious students are never sure of their abilities and are afraid of making a mistake and being reprimanded. A state of pervasive anxiety clouds their lives, which in turn drains the energy and ability to concentrate on learning. Anxious students need reassurance that they can learn; they need to feel comfortable in the learning situation.

Assessing Emotional and Behavioral Factors

By being aware of the student's emotional responses, the teacher can help the student read more effectively. Usually, informal assessment of emotional factors is sufficient for the purposes of the reading diagnosis. Occasionally, however, it is necessary to gather more information in this area. Formal tests of behavioral and emotional factors can be used and are described in Test Inventory 3.1 at the end of this chapter. In some cases, it may be necessary to make a referral for evaluation to mental health specialists (such as psychiatrists, psychologists, or social workers). Such referrals are most appropriate when emotional problems appear to be so severe that they interfere with reading progress, and the student has made little growth over a long period of instruction.

One useful informal diagnostic measure that can be used by a reading teacher is the sentence completion activity. In addition, information from the interview (described in the previous section) provides useful information on the child's emotional status.

The Sentence Completion Activity. The sentence completion activity is a series of beginning sentence fragments that the student completes. Examples are "I like to _____" and "Reading is _____." By completing these sentences, students often provide revealing insights into their thoughts and feelings. Like the interest inventory, the sentence completion activity can be administered in an oral or written fashion. A sample sentence completion form is given in Table 3.5. In interpreting the sentence completion activity, bear in mind that it is only an informal measure. While it may suggest ideas about student attitudes, these hypotheses should be verified further through interview, observation, and perhaps the administration of formal measures.

Table 3.5 Sample Sentence Completion Form

1. I like _____
2. Eating _____
3. I am happiest when _____
4. School is _____
5. My greatest fear is _____
6. I wish I could _____
7. There are times _____
8. My mother _____
9. My father _____
10. Sometimes I wish _____
11. I sleep _____
12. When I dream _____
13. My greatest ambition is _____
14. I am most annoyed _____
15. Sometimes I hope _____
16. I think I will never _____
17. Compared with other people, I am _____
18. My greatest asset is _____
19. I dislike _____
20. I feel sorry for people who _____
21. My mind _____
22. Most of the time _____
23. I try to _____
24. I think of myself as _____
25. My greatest regret is _____

PHYSICAL FACTORS

Many physical factors affect the student's ability to learn reading skills. These include hearing problems, visual problems, and neurological dysfunction, as well as other physical problems. Some students with reading difficulties may be receiving medical or biomedical treatment. Tests of physical factors are described in Test Inventory 3.2 (at the end of this chapter).

Hearing Impairment

Since the ability to acquire reading skills may be severely affected by even moderate or temporary hearing loss, it is recommended that pupils be screened for possible hearing impairment. It should be noted that the ability to *hear sounds* (auditory acuity) is different from the ability to *distinguish between sounds* (auditory discrimination). (See Chapter 13 for a discussion of auditory discrimination.)

Hearing loss has several causes: (1) childhood diseases, such as scarlet fever, meningitis, mumps, or measles; (2) environmental conditions, such as repeated exposure to loud noises; (3) congenital conditions, such as malformation of, or injury to, the hearing mechanism; (4) temporary or fluctuating conditions, due to allergies, colds, or even a buildup of wax in the ears; (5) maternal prenatal infection (including rubella); (6) middle ear infection or problems; (7) certain medications (such as *amino glycosides* and some *diuretics*).

Screening for Hearing Impairment. Hearing acuity is measured by testing the ability to hear in two dimensions: frequency and intensity. *Frequency* refers to the ability to hear different pitches or vibrations of a specific sound wave. The pitches are actually musical tones; and the higher the tone, the higher the frequency. Since different sounds of our spoken language have different frequency levels, a person may be able to hear sounds clearly at one frequency level but miss sounds at another.

Intensity refers to the loudness of a sound and is measured in terms of *decibels*. The louder the sound, the higher the intensity or decibel level. Hearing loss is measured in terms of decibels. How loud does the sound (or decibel level) have to be before the subject can hear it? A person who can hear soft sounds at 0 to 10 decibels, for example, has excellent hearing. If the student cannot hear sounds at a 30 decibel level, then he or she is likely to encounter some difficulty in school learning.

The audiometer is an electronic instrument for measuring hearing acuity. In screening for a hearing loss, students wear headphones and sit with their backs to the examiner. The examiner sounds tones and asks the subject to raise a hand when a tone is heard. For screening, the audiometer is set at one intensity level and the student is tested at several frequency levels. The right and left ears are tested separately. Also, several intensity levels can be tested at each frequency level.

An audiogram showing the results of an audiometric hearing test is illustrated in Figure 3.1. Students who cannot hear frequency sounds at the preset level of 30 decibels at one or more frequencies should be referred to a hearing specialist for further testing. The eight-year-old pupil whose audiogram appears in Figure 3.1 showed a 40 decibel loss at 2000 frequencies and 4000 frequencies in the right ear and was therefore referred to a hearing specialist.

If auditory screening indicates a hearing problem, students should be referred to an *audiologist* (a nonmedical specialist in hearing) or to an *otologist* or an *otolaryngologist* (medical specialists in hearing). Although the audiometer is an excellent device for screening for hearing loss, only a specialist trained in measuring and treating hearing difficulties can make a final determination of the extent and nature of the possible hearing impairment.

Symptoms of Hearing Problems. A teacher may suspect the student has a hearing impairment based on such symptoms as

1. Slurred speech, monotone speech, or articulation problems.
2. Frequent minor ear problems such as infections or pain.
3. Turning the head to one side when listening.

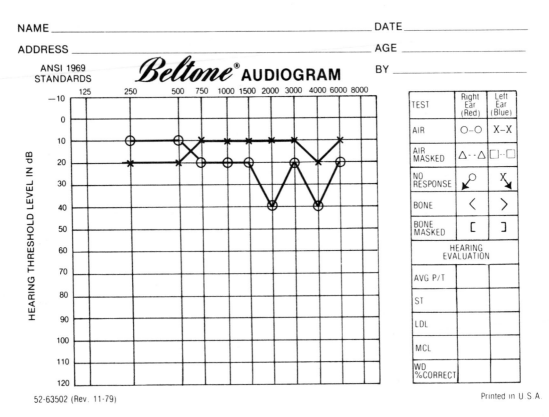

Figure 3.1   A Sample Audiogram.

Reprinted with the permission of Beltone Electronics Corporation.

4. Apparent inability to be attentive or to follow directions.
5. Frequent requests for repetitions.
6. Lack of response when being addressed.

Even moderate loss of the ability to hear may substantially affect the ability to learn reading. A hearing loss impedes effective communication with teachers and peers. It also places a burden on students when phonics methods are used because they have difficulty hearing certain sounds. A low-frequency hearing loss, of, for example, 500–1500 Hz (cycles per second) means that students may have difficulty distinguishing vowel sounds. High-frequency losses (2000–4000 Hz) indicate the student might have difficulty with consonant sounds that continue, such as *s, z, f, v, th, sh,* and *ch.*

Sometimes students pass the audiometric screening test, yet have hearing problems. For example, one little girl had a sporadic hearing loss due to allergies. Since her visits to the pediatrician came after the allergy season, the hearing problem was undetected for years. Although the hearing problem was eventually cleared up, she had a hearing impairment during much of her early reading instruction, and her difficulties in reading continued into the later grades.

The most devastating effect of a hearing loss is that it prevents normal language development. When children cannot hear adequately, they are deprived of the communication necessary for normal language acquisition and growth. Their vocabulary, grammar, and verbal thinking processes often remain poorly developed and their language skills may be inadequate to acquire higher-level reading skills.

Visual Impairment

The ability to see clearly is obviously critical to the reading process. However, the relationship between reading and vision is complicated. A particular visual impairment impedes reading development in one individual, while another person with a similar impairment may be able to read effectively.

Factors in Vision.   There are several types of visual impairment of concern to the reading teacher. These include myopia, hyperopia, astigmatism, binocular vision problems, and color perception.

1. *Myopia or nearsightedness.* This refers to the inability to see objects at a distance. Myopia is caused by an elongated eyeball that focuses visual images in an improper way. Although the problem of myopia has not been found to be highly related to reading difficulty (Robinson 1946), myopia can make it difficult to see objects that are far away, such as the blackboard. A substantial portion of the population is myopic, and the condition tends to begin between the ages of nine and twelve. Myopia is usually correctable with eyeglasses.

2. *Hyperopia or farsightedness.* This refers to the inability to see objects clearly at nearpoint (that is, 13 inches or less). In children, it is often caused by an eyeball that is too short to permit focusing in the proper place. Children are typically hyperopic until they reach the age of seven or eight; thus, primary-grade textbooks generally contain large print. If hyperopia is a continuing problem, it can be corrected with glasses. Since reading is done at nearpoint, hyperopia can affect the ability to read.

3. *Astigmatism.* Astigmatism refers to the blurring of vision because of irregularities in the surface of the cornea. This condition is generally correctable with eyeglasses.

4. *Binocular difficulties.* Binocular vision, the ability to focus both eyes on the same object, is one of the most complicated of visual functions. Both eyes focus together easily on an object that is far away, but as the object moves closer, the eyes must turn inward to maintain their focus. If the eyes cannot focus together, a double image (diplobia) may result. This condition is not tolerated well by the brain, and the image of one eye may be suppressed, possibly leading to a deterioration of that eye. In severe cases, the eyes appear to be crossed. Binocular vision problems may

blur vision and also cause the reader to become easily fatigued. Thus they can interfere with reading.

Unfortunately, binocular vision is not as easily correctable as are other visual problems. Three strategies are used to correct binocular problems: (1) surgery (often used to correct a "cross-eyed" condition), (2) corrective lenses in eyeglasses, and (3) visual exercises to strengthen eye muscles. Opinions differ among eye specialists about the value of visual exercises as a treatment in overcoming binocular difficulties.

5. *Color perception.* A small portion of the population is unable to perceive color. Males are more often affected by this condition, and the colorblindness may be limited to a few colors.

Screening for Visual Impairment.   Students with reading problems should be screened for possible visual difficulties. As with the hearing tests that are used by the reading teacher, the visual tests are intended only for screening purposes. Students who do poorly on the visual screening test should be referred to an *ophthalmologist* (a physician who specializes in eye problems) or to an *optometrist* (a non-medical eye specialist) for further testing. A description of the three most widely used visual screening tests is given in Test Inventory 3.2. The *Orthorater* and the *Keystone Vision Screening Test for Schools* are particularly useful for the reading specialist, since they test a variety of visual functions, including binocular vision.

Teachers can observe students for symptoms of possible visual problems:

1. Losing place while reading.
2. Avoiding close work.
3. Poor sitting posture and position while reading.
4. Positioning print at an unusual angle.
5. Holding reading material closer than normal.
6. Frowning excessively, squinting, scowling.
7. Excessive head movements while reading.
8. Tilting head to one side.
9. Rubbing eyes frequently.
10. Covering one eye during reading.

Neurological Dysfunction

All learning is neurologically based, including learning to read. The reading process is a complex human task, requiring an intact and well-functioning brain and central nervous system. It is not surprising that a dysfunction in the central nervous system can interfere with learning to read. The condition of *dyslexia* is a severe type of reading disability which is thought to be the result of a neurophysical anomaly. It is hypothesized that for an individual with dyslexia, the neurological dysfunction interferes with the ability to recognize words and to interpret what is seen visually or heard auditorily (Cruickshank, 1986).

It has been suspected for almost a century that dyslexia is caused by neuroanatomical abnormalities in brain structure (Galaburda, 1986). Over the years, the clinical experiences of many teachers and the evidence gathered by early neuroscientists strengthened the belief that atypical brain function is a factor in preventing individuals identified as dyslexic from acquiring reading skills (Galaburda, 1986). However, physical evidence to support this suspicion was lacking.

Today, knowledge about the brain and its relationship to learning is rapidly expanding. Discoveries made in the past ten years provide some evidence that the brain structure and brain function of dyslexics are atypical, differing from those of the normal person. This evidence is provided by several research sources in the neurosciences.

One source consists of the post-mortem (autopsy) studies, an on-going research project on dyslexia at Harvard Medical School. In these studies, neuroscientists are conducting autopsies to examine the brain tissues of deceased individuals who had been identified as dyslexic. Many of these dyslexics were young men who met sudden death in circumstances such as motorcycle accidents. In a few cases, dyslexic individuals made provisions in their wills to donate their brains to this project. The analysis of the brain tissues examined thus far (less than a dozen) shows that dyslexic individuals did have neuroanatomical abnormalities (Galaburda, 1986; Geschwind, 1986). The post-mortem studies revealed two types of anomalies in dyslexic brain tissue (Galaburda, 1986; Vellutino, 1987; The Orton Dyslexia Society, 1987). First, the researchers compared the two halves of the brain, the right and left hemisphere. In the normal brain, certain regions of the left hemisphere are more highly developed than the same regions of the right hemisphere. In the dyslexic brain, however, researchers did not find this differentiation. These findings are significant, for the left hemisphere of the brain controls language functions. Second, the researchers found a distortion in the language-related areas of the right hemisphere in the brains of the dyslexic individuals.

Studies showing a genetic basis for dyslexia are another interesting source. One study, conducted at the Institute for Behavioral Genetics at the University of Colorado at Boulder, identified the possible localization of a particular gene on chromosome 15 in members of families in which there was a history of reading disability (Lewitter, DeFries, and Elson, 1980). While this is a promising finding, the study has not yet been replicated (Vellutino, 1987).

The theory of a genetic sex-linked basis for dyslexia is supported by studies that show that more than four times as many boy as girls are impaired in reading (Vellutino, 1987). Familial and twin studies carried out over the years support the concept of an inherited basis of dyslexia. DeFries and Decker (1982), in an extensive study of 250 families and 1,044 subjects, found strong evidence that the tendency for reading disability has a genetic basis.

A potentially promising direction in brain research may be the examination of the living brain as the individual engages in reading. This research, which is in the very beginning stages, is made possible through recent technological advances in machines for brain measurement. These provide the means for more detailed study of the relationship between the central nervous system and human behavior (Duane, 1986). The new technology includes CT (computed tomography), an established radiological tool for visualization of the brain; MRI (magnetic resonance imaging), which enables neuroscientists to view multiple sections of the brain; and BEAM (brain electrical activity mapping), a procedure to monitor brainwave activity. With these new tools, neuroscientists can study brain activity as the individual is engaged in reading. Such information will greatly contribute to our understanding of both the normal reading process and of the neurological role in reading failure (Duane, 1986).

Sex Differences

For reasons that are not entirely clear, more boys than girls exhibit reading problems in American schools. In fact, boys commonly outnumber girls by more than four to one in remedial reading programs. At least three reasons have been proposed for the preponderance of boys in remedial reading: heredity, maturation, and the school environment.

(1) Heredity. As mentioned previously, reading disability may be caused by a sex-linked gene.

(2) Maturation. Since boys are less physically mature than girls at the age of beginning reading instruction, they may not have developed certain skills that aid in reading, such as the ability to pay attention and the ability to manage pencils and books.

(3) School environment. The school environment may affect boys and girls differently. The primary-grade classroom is traditionally female oriented, employing women teachers and rewarding behaviors such as being neat and quiet. In other cultures, boys actually exhibit superior reading ability (Preston, 1979; Gross, 1978), suggesting that sex differences may be due to cultural factors or other factors in instruction rather than to hereditary or maturational differences. Since more boys than girls are likely to be in remedial reading classes, it is important to make these boys feel welcome and happy in the reading environment.

Other Physical Problems

Good physical health is an important basic condition for learning. Learning is an active process that requires the student to be alert, energetic, and concentrated for long periods of time. The pupil who is listless, tires easily, and cannot maintain attention may have an underlying medical problem. Prolonged illness, especially accompanied by high fevers and long periods of absence from school, can also contribute to a reading problem. Concussions to the brain can affect school learning.

General Health and Nutrition. Nutrient deficiency in infancy or early childhood has been shown to result in anatomical and biochemical changes in the brain. Early malnutrition impairs growth, both of the body in general and the central nervous system in particular (Martin, 1980). Health concerns include problems of nutrition, rheumatic fever, asthma, lack of sleep, biochemical imbalances, and endocrine problems. A general physical examination is often recommended as part of a complete assessment for reading problems.

Medical and Biochemical Treatments. Some students with reading problems receive medical or medically related treatments, which are purported to alleviate their educational problems. Since teachers may be asked to provide feedback to physicians or parents about students, it is important to be aware of both the underlying conditions and the therapies.

1. *Hypoglycemia.* One theory of the cause of learning problems is a medical condition known as hypoglycemia. This condition is due to a deficiency in the level of blood sugar. Treatment consists of control of sugar in the student's diet (Runion, 1980).

2. *Allergy.* Allergies, which are caused by both the diet and the environment, are the basis of another theory of the cause of learning and reading difficulty. The treatment consists of the removal of the element causing the allergy (Crook, 1977; Rapp, 1979). The precise relationship of allergies to the learning process is yet to be determined.

3. *Drug therapy.* Many students with reading disabilities are prescribed medication intended to control their hyperactivity, increase attention span, and reduce impulsive and aggressive behavior. Widely used medications include Ritalin, Dexedrine, Librium, and Cylert. Levinson (1984) has suggested the use of anti-motion sickness medication. There is some difference of opinion about the effectiveness and safety of these drugs. It is very important to monitor their effects closely. Teachers are an important resource for providing essential feedback to physicians on the effectiveness of the medication and the behavior of the patient.

4. *Food additives.* The concept that food additives and some food substances can adversely affect learning and behavior is the basis for another medically related treatment. One of the most widely discussed and controversial theories on the effect of food additives is that of Feingold (1975), who points out that artificial flavors, colors, and preservatives are used increasingly in the American diet. Feingold's treatment consists of the control of diet and the removal of foods that contain additives, as well as certain natural foods. However, a panel of experts at the National Institutes of Health concluded that there was insufficient evidence available to recommend the defined diet treatment for childhood hyperactivity (Silver, 1986).

Silver (1986, 1987) reviewed many of the medical and biomedical treatments for learning problems and found their effectiveness to be unproven. He concluded that the treatment of choice for reading disabilities is the best educational instruction available, taught by a well-qualified and sensitive teacher.

SUMMARY

Correlates of reading problems are factors that are related to reading disability, but the precise cause and effect relationship cannot be specified. Correlates discussed in this chapter include environmental factors, emotional factors, and physical factors.

Environmental factors are the different environments in which a student lives and grows. The home environment is the child's first environmental system. The parents play a crucial role in the home environment. The school environment is another important system for the student, one that is often difficult for students with reading problems. Reading disabled students also have difficulty in their social environments. The cultural environment is another system that affects attitude and interest in reading. Methods for assessing environmental systems include behavioral observation, interest inventory, and the interview.

Emotional problems also influence reading achievement. Opinions differ about the need to treat emotional problems prior to the treatment of reading problems. Among the emotional problems exhibited by remedial readers are emotional blocks, hostility-aggressiveness, learned helplessness, low self-esteem and depression, and anxiety. Emotional factors may be informally assessed using the sentence completion activity. Interview data also provides emotional insights.

Physical factors are also related to reading disability. Hearing impairment, including a mild or temporary hearing loss, can affect language learning and learning to read. The audiometer is used to screen for a hearing loss. Teachers can also note symptoms of hearing problems by carefully observing students in the classroom.

Visual impairment is also related to reading disability. Visual problems include myopia, hyperopia, astigmatism, and poor binocular vision. There are several instruments for screening for visual impairment, and teachers can learn to observe symptoms of visual difficulty.

Neurological problems are another factor for some remedial readers. Central nervous system dysfunctions can impede the learning of reading. The relationship of brain psychology to reading is being intensively investigated.

Reading difficulties are more common in boys than girls. Causes may be genetic, maturational, or cultural.

Other physical problems related to reading are health and nutrition. Many disabled readers receive medical and medically related treatments, including drug therapy, control of food additives, and treatment for hypoglycemia and allergies. Teachers should be aware of such conditions and the students who are receiving such treatment.

Test Inventory 3-1.   Tests of Behavior and Emotional Factors

---

AAMD Adaptive Behavior Scale, School Edition

CTB/McGraw-Hill   *Ages 3–16*

Interview format assesses social and daily living skills and behaviors. Part I evaluates personal independence in daily living. Part II measures personality and behavior disorders. Factors covered: Personal self-sufficiency, communication self-sufficiency, personal-social responsibility, personal adjustment, and social adjustment.

Can be administered by trained teacher. Informant can be any person familiar with student. 30 minutes.

Children's Apperception Test (CAT)

C.P.S., Inc.   *Ages: 3–10 years*

Consists of a series of ten pictures of animals in various situations to which students react verbally. Personality disturbances are classified through assessment of such topics as relations to authority figures, sibling rivalry, relationship to parents, and fantasies about aggression. No norms are given.

Individual administration: 10–15 minutes. Usually given by a trained psychologist who interprets results. Also CAT-H in which children react to pictures of humans.

Devereux Adolescent Behavior Rating Scale (DASB)
Devereux Elementary School Behavior Rating Scale (DESB)

Devereux Foundation   *Ages: 5–12, 13–18 years*

Teachers rate individual students from 1 to 7 on forty-seven items broken into eleven factors: classroom disturbances, impatience, defiance, external blame, achievement anxiety, external reliance, comprehension, inattentiveness, irrelevant responsiveness, creative initiative, and dependence on teacher. Yields scores for factors, standard scores.

Individual test.

The Piers-Harris Children's Self-Concept Scale

Western Psychological Services   *Grades: 4–12*

Student reads such statements as "I am a happy person" and "I cause trouble to my family" and responds "yes" or "no" to each. Statements may be read by teacher. Six factors assessed include behavior, intellectual status, physical appearance, anxiety, popularity, and happiness. Yields percentile and stanine scores.

Group or individual test: 20 minutes.

The Pupil Rating Scale (Revised): Screening for Learning Disabilities

Grune & Stratton   *Grades: K-6*

Students rated 1 to 5 on several teacher-observed behaviors including auditory comprehension, spoken language, orientation, coordination, and social behavior. Yields verbal, nonverbal, and total learning scores.

Individual test: 10–15 minutes.

The Rorschach Psychodiagnostic Test

Grune & Stratton   *Ages: 3 years–adult*

Projective test has students reveal feelings by telling what they see in ten inkblot pictures. Used to assess personality disturbances.

Individual test: 1 hour. Must be administered and interpreted by psychologist.

Scales of Independent Behavior

DLM   *Ages: infant–adult*

Provides noncognitive measures of adjustment in the social, behavioral, and adaptive areas. The scales measure functional independence and adaptive behavior in motor skills, social and communication skills, personal living skills, and community living skills. This test can be used independently or as part of the *Woodcock-Johnson Psycho-educational Battery*.

Individual test: 1 hour. Can be administered by trained teacher. Informant can be subject, parent, teacher, or other person familiar with the subject.

Thematic Apperception Test (TAT)

Harvard University Press   *Ages: 14 years–adult*

Projective test has students reveal feelings by telling a story about each of nineteen pictures and one blank card. Used to assess personality disturbances. No norms.

Individual test administered in two sittings: 2 hours total. Trained psychologist must administer and interpret.

Vineland Adaptive Behavior Scales

American Guidance Service   *Ages: birth to adolescence*

Assesses social and independent living skills. Areas include daily living skills, socialization, and motor skills. Three versions are available: (1) interview edition, (2) interview edition—expanded, and (3) classroom edition. Yields age scores and social quotient.

Individual test: 30 minutes. Can be administered by trained teacher. Informant provides ratings on the major categories.

Weller-Strauser Scales of Adaptive Behavior

Academic Therapy   *Elementary Scales—ages 6–12*
                                                            Secondary Scales—13–18

Adaptive behavior of learning disabled students in four areas: social coping, relationships, pragmatic language, and production. Each scale has 35 items and examiner selects alternative that best describes student's behavior. Yields profile for each area.

Individual test: 30 minutes. Teacher can administer.

Test Inventory 3-2   Tests of Physical Factors

Audiometer

Beltone Electronic Corporation
Maico Hearing Instruments

Instruments screen a subject's hearing threshold for a series of tones, or frequencies, at various decibel levels. Left and right ears are tested separately. The subject raises a hand to indicate when a tone is heard. Both air and bone conduction can be tested. Hearing threshold is graphed on an audiogram in decibels of loss.

Individual test: 10–20 minutes.

Keystone Vision Screening for Schools

Keystone View Company

Instrument screens fourteen basic skills including eye posture and binocular imbalance, binocular depth perception, color discrimination, usable binocular vision, and near-point and farpoint acuity. Eyes can be tested separately. Ratings of unsatisfactory, re-test, and satisfactory are received.

Individual test: 10–15 minutes.

The Orthorater

Bausch and Lomb

Instrument contains twelve subtests that screen for the binocular action of the eyes, nearpoint and farpoint vision, depth perception, and color discrimination. Norms are available for job-related activity, and an adapted version may be used with children.

Individual administration: 15–20 minutes.

Snellen Chart

American Optical Company

A method of screening visual acuity using a wall chart consisting of rows of letters gradually decreasing in size in each descending row. The letters are to be read at a distance of twenty feet. The test is a limited visual screening method since it does not assess nearpoint (reading) vision or binocular vision. Only nearsightedness (myopia) is detectable.

Individual administration: 2–3 minutes.

Spache Binocular Reading Test (BRT)

Keystone View Company

Student orally reads passages from cards inserted into Telebinocular machine. Some words appear only to left eye, others only to right eye. By noting word omissions, examiner can see if one eye is suppressed during reading. Lower level contains pictures rather than words. Informal norms provide basis for visual referral.

Individual test: 2–4 minutes.

**A Teacher Rating Scale for Use in Drug Therapy
with Children (Hyperkinesis Index)**

Abbott Laboratories   *Ages: 6–12 years*

Questionnaire assesses the effectiveness of drug therapy. One set of questions is for the parent and one for the teacher. The questions cover behavior of child, group participation, attitude toward authority, and family. A rating of 1 to 3 is given to each item. Questionnaire is given before student is placed on drugs and again periodically to assess effects of drugs. No norms available. Scores obtained at different times are compared.

Individual administration: 10–15 minutes. No special training required.

4

CORRELATES
OF READING
DISABILITY II

Intellectual Potential
and Language Development

The previous chapter examined several correlates of reading. This chapter continues the discussion of factors related to reading.

INTRODUCTION

Two correlates of reading disability which should be considered in an evaluation are intelligence (the potential or capacity to learn) and language abilities. Both of these factors are critical elements for the initial stages of learning to read and in the ongoing reading process.

INTELLIGENCE: THE POTENTIAL FOR LEARNING

There is a strong relationship between intelligence and reading performance. The correlation is somewhat higher with verbal intelligence test scores (.60 to .85) than with nonverbal or performance test scores (.20 to .56) (Harris and Sipay, 1985; Moore and Wielan, 1981). However, the very concept of intelligence and its measurement is subject to many basic questions. These questions relate to the definition of intelligence, how intelligence is measured, and ways of using intelligence test information in the reading diagnosis.

Definition of Intelligence

For centuries, philosophers and scholars have attempted to define intelligence, yet the debate about its nature continues. As generally used, intelligence refers to one's aptitude for learning, to an individual's cognitive or thinking abilities, or to a child's potential for acquiring school skills. Wechsler's (1975, p. 139) definition of intelligence is often cited: "the capacity of an individual to understand the world about him and his resourcefulness to cope with its challenges."

Since a person's intelligence cannot be observed directly, what we call intelligence is inferred by observing the individual's behavior (usually in a test situation). These observations are used to explain intellectual differences among people in their present behavior and to predict differences in their future behavior.

Is a person's intelligence determined by heredity (the result of one's biological makeup) or by environment (the result of one's personal experiences)? This hotly debated question has been studied since intelligence tests were first developed at the turn of the century. Actually, both heredity and environment make significant contributions to a person's cognitive abilities. A complex sequence of interactions between heredity and environmental factors occurs during the development of an individual's intelligence. Although heredity may account for much of the variance in intelligence, the environment also contributes a substantial portion (Anastasi, 1976).

Moreover, research shows that a child's mental abilities can change significantly under favorable conditions. Environmental factors which influence an individual's intellect include the home, the school, social experiences, and the level of health care and nutrition (see Chapter 3). Recent studies of preschool at-risk children show that the intelligence test scores of preschoolers are highly modifiable and can increase substantially when they receive early intervention (Lerner, Mardell-Czudnowski, and Goldenberg, 1987). Studies also show that the cognitive functioning of adolescents can be modified (Feuerstein, 1979).

Basic to the teaching profession is the conviction that the human organism is open to modifiability at all stages of development. Teachers play a vital role in the teaching/learning process. What teachers do through the environment of the school can make a significant difference.

Measuring Intelligence

What do intelligence tests measure? Many different cognitive abilities make up intelligence, and full intelligence is much richer than what is actually measured by intelligence tests. Among the abilities that one might consider part of intelligence are: mechanical ability, street knowledge, creativity, and social skills. However, most intelligence tests simply predict whether an individual is likely to do well in school-work, especially in learning tasks with highly verbal content (Salvia and Ysseldyke, 1988). Therefore, intelligence tests can be best regarded as measures of scholastic aptitude.

Intelligence tests are sometimes referred to as "IQ tests." The letters, IQ, originally were an abbreviation for "intelligence quotient" (the result of dividing mental age by chronological age). Today, other techniques of obtaining intelligence test scores are usually used, and the term IQ now simply refers to the general score obtained in an intelligence test.

Any test is merely a sample of selected behavior at a certain point in time. The IQ score, in part, reflects the relationship between the kinds of questions asked on the test and the experiential background of the student. Since different questions are asked on different intelligence tests, a student's score often varies from one test to another. Intelligence scores are also affected by a student's attitude and general mood on the day of testing.

Since a person's IQ is not a fixed, unchanging measure, and is amenable to modification through environmental interventions—including educational experiences—we cannot predict with certainty what a child's true intelligence might be. Nor do we know how much a particular child might ultimately achieve. Intelligence tests only measure current potential for learning; future potential is unknown. In summary, while intelligence tests may be useful tools in the reading diagnosis, they must be used in a judicious manner.

Using Intelligence Test Information
in the Reading Diagnosis

The purpose of obtaining information on a child's cognitive abilities and aptitude for learning is to help the teacher better understand the reading problem. The intelligence test information can be used to: (1) assess a student's current potential,

(2) analyze a student's component cognitive abilities, and (3) observe the student's behavior during the testing situation. Each of these uses is discussed below.

Assessing A Student's Potential. Information from an intelligence test can help the teacher determine whether a troubled student has the potential to read better than he or she does at present. To illustrate this use, in evaluating Ellen, we find that her intelligence test score indicates a potential for reading which is much higher than her present reading achievement level. Thus, we conclude that Ellen's significant discrepancy between her potential and performance shows she has the cognitive ability to read much better than she does at present. In contrast, in evaluating Mark, we conclude that although he is reading poorly, he is actually doing fairly well in relation to his potential for learning. Mark, however, will still benefit from reading instruction suited to his individual needs.

When evaluating a child with suspected learning disabilities, federal law (PL 94–142) requires the evaluation team to consider if the child has a severe discrepancy between the potential for learning and the current level of performance. Various methods for measuring the discrepancy are discussed later in this chapter.

Analyzing a Student's Component Cognitive Abilities. Intelligence is more than a single general factor. The "component" theory of intelligence suggests that intelligence is comprised of many separate abilities (Sternberg, 1985). In addition to providing an overall general score (IQ score), many tests of intelligence contain subtests that measure different (or component) mental abilities and cognitive functions. These tests are particularly useful in the reading diagnosis because they help us analyze the student's disparities in various mental abilities. This analysis can reveal strengths and weaknesses in learning aptitude. Several methods are used in trying to detect characteristic cognitive patterns in students with reading and learning disabilities (Breen, 1986; Holcomb, et al., 1987.)

1. *Comparison of verbal and performance skills.* The *Wechsler Intelligence Scales* (including WISC-R, WPPSI, WAIS-R) classify subtests as either verbal tests or performance tests. This allows the diagnostician to compare abilities in language-based tasks with those in performance-based tasks.

2. *Evidence of subtest scatter and variability.* Some intelligence tests, such as the *Wechsler Intelligence Scales for Children-Revised* (WISC-R) and the *Woodcock Johnson Psychoeducational Battery - Cognitive Abilities* (WJPEB-CA), contain subtests which tap differing abilities. A significant scatter among subtest scores shows that the student did well in some subtests and poorly in others, suggesting variability in cognitive functioning. However, many test experts advise caution in the over-interpretation of subtest scatter (Taylor, Partenio, and Ziegler, 1983).

3. *Recategorization of subtest scores to ascertain unique cognitive patterns.* Some practitioners suggest that subtest scores be regrouped or clustered to provide insight into the child's cognitive functioning. Different methods for regrouping have been advocated. Bannatyne (1974) suggests regrouping the subtests of the WISC into

four areas: spatial ability, verbal conceptualization ability, sequencing ability, and acquired knowledge. Kaufman (1981) uses factor analysis to regroup WISC-R subtests into clusters of verbal comprehension, perceptual organization, and freedom from distractibility.

The scoring system of the *Woodcock-Johnson Psychoeducational Battery-Cognitive Abilities* enables the tester to group individual subtests to obtain general clusters of cognitive factors and scholastic aptitude. Clusters of cognitive factors include verbal ability, reasoning, perceptual speed, and memory. Clusters of scholastic aptitude include reading aptitude, mathematics aptitude, written language aptitude, and knowledge aptitude (Breen, 1986). The sixteen subtests of the *Kaufman Assessment Battery for Children* (K-ABC) can be regrouped into clusters of sequential processing and simultaneous processing (Stoiber, Bracken, and Gissal, 1983). Kaufman and McLean (1986) report a joint factor analysis of the K-ABC and the WISC-R showing these factors.

What do measurement experts say about the procedure of clustering of subtest scores? Kavale and Forness (1987) point out a number of problems in the research underlying such clustering. Although they view this type of research as promising, they suggest that more investigation is needed before clusters can be used with confidence.

Observing a Student's Behavior.   Testers have the opportunity to observe student's informally as they take intelligence tests. The tester can observe which activities the student enjoys, which activities are frustrating for the student, and how the student goes about solving problems. Techniques of observation are discussed in Chapter 3.

In interpreting intelligence tests scores, teachers should remember that the content of these tests and the validity of their scores have come under serious criticism. An IQ test provides much valuable information, but it cannot give a definitive or permanent rating of a student's mental ability. Thus, teachers should be alert to the many other sources of information about students, including behavior in class, independence in living, and interests and accomplishments outside the school setting.

Individual and Group Tests of Intelligence

Instruments that assess intellectual ability can be divided into two types: group tests and individual tests. Group tests are designed to be given to several students at a time, but can also be given to students individually. In contrast, individual tests must be given to one student at a time. In general, more credence is given to scores obtained from individual intelligence tests than those from group tests. Some individual intelligence tests must be given by a trained examiner, and often this person is the school psychologist. While other individual tests can be given by the teacher, these also require training in administration and scoring. In addition, there are informal ways to estimate the child's potential for learning, such as giving a listening test (discussed later in this chapter).

Group intelligence tests are sometimes routinely administered as screening devices to identify those pupils who are different enough from average to warrant a more thorough evaluation. They are used because they can be given quickly by teachers to large numbers of students. A drawback of group intelligence tests is that they often require students to read, making the IQ score dependent upon reading ability. In addition, they do not provide in-depth information (Salvia and Ysseldyke, 1988).

A listing and brief description of tests of intelligence and potential are presented in Test Inventory 4.1 at the end of this chapter. Some individual intelligence tests that are frequently used in a reading diagnosis are discussed below.

The Wechsler Intelligence Scale for Children - Revised (WISC-R). This is one of the most frequently administered intelligence tests. It is an individual test and must be given by a trained examiner, usually the school psychologist. However, in diagnosing a student's reading problem, teachers can make good use of the information obtained in the WISC-R by examining subtest scores, as well as the scores of the Full IQ, Verbal IQ, and Performance IQ. The test covers ages 6 to 16. (Other Weschler tests cover younger and older individuals; see Test Inventory 4.1).

The WISC-R is particularly useful for measuring component subskills of intelligence. The test yields a Verbal IQ score, a Performance IQ score and a full IQ score. There are twelve subtests: six verbal subtests and six performance subtests.

Verbal Scale

1. Information: answering informational questions.
2. Similarities: noting how two things are alike.
3. Arithmetic: solving timed problems.
4. Vocabulary: defining words.
5. Comprehension: dealing with everyday situations and abstract issues.
6. Digit Span: repeating digits forward and backward (supplementary).

Performance Scale

1. Picture completion: determining missing items.
2. Picture arrangements: sequencing pictures to "tell a story."
3. Block design: duplicating pictorial design with red and white blocks.
4. Object assembly: fitting puzzle pieces together.
5. Coding: matching and writing symbols with numbers.
6. Mazes: finding way through a maze (supplementary).

The WISC-R provides a score for each of the twelve subtests. By comparing the various subtest scores, the teacher tries to detect a pattern in the components of mental functioning. Students with learning problems are thought to exhibit more scatter than normal learners.

Kaufman (1981) reviewed a number of studies concerning the scatter of the subtest scores of the WISC-R. The studies indicated that although normal readers have scatter in their WISC-R subtest scores, the scatter produced by readers with learning problems was somewhat greater than it was for the normal population. In addition, students with reading problems tend to have higher scores in performance IQ than verbal IQ (Moore and Wielan, 1981).

"... I can't go bowling tonight, Freddie, I'm cramming for an IQ test tomorrow ..."

The Woodcock-Johnson Psychoeducational Battery-Cognitive Abilities (WJPEB-CA). The *Woodcock-Johnson Psychoeducational Battery* is an individual test, consisting of four parts: (1) Cognitive Abilities Subtests, (2) Achievement Subtests, (3) Interest Subtests, and (4) Scales of Independent Behavior. Our interest here is with the first part, the Cognitive Abilities Subtests. This part consists of twelve subtests that may be used to assess both cognitive ability and specific scholastic aptitudes. These subtests are:

Picture Vocabulary	Spatial Relations
Memory for Sentences	Visual Auditory Learning
Blending	Quantitative Concepts
Visual Matching	Antonyms-Synonyms
Analysis-Synthesis	Numbers Reversed
Concept Formation	Analogies

The WJPEB-CA can be given by teachers who have been trained to give the test. The teacher can obtain cluster scores, with weighted combinations of subtests. These cluster scores are used to analyze different abilities displayed by the student. A useful feature of this test is that the scores on the Cognitive Battery part can be readily compared to the scores on the Achievement Battery part. The first three parts of the *Woodcock-Johnson Psychoeducational Battery* were normed on the same population. The test can be used over a wide range, from preschool through adult. Studies show that the WJPEB-CA is a valid indication of general cognitive abilities, similar in interpretation to the full score of the WISC-R (Ipsen, McMillan, and Fallen, 1983).

Slosson Intelligence Test—Revised. The *Slosson Intelligence Test—Revised* (SIT-R) is frequently used in reading diagnosis. It is an individual test and can be administered by teachers, guidance counselors, principals, or psychologists. The SIT-R is a relatively short screening test and includes many items that appear in the *Stanford-Binet Intelligence Scale* (see Test Inventory 4.1). The test yields a single IQ score. It covers a wide age range and was standardized on people from 17 months of age to 17 years, 2 months.

Interpreting Intelligence Test Scores

Several technical terms used in reporting scores on intelligence tests are important for teachers to know. Two of the most important are mental age (MA) and intelligence quotient (IQ).

Mental Age. Mental age (MA) refers to the age-level score of a student's performance on an intelligence test when compared with the norm population. (The norm population is the large number of students who initially took the test to establish norms). For example, if a student receives an MA of 15 on an intelligence test, that student's performance is equivalent to the performance of the average fifteen-year-old subject. If the student receives an MA score of 7–6, this means that the student's performance was equivalent to that of the average student of age seven years, six months who took the test. Although early intelligence tests used the concept of MA scores extensively, recent tests use IQs based on deviation scores rather than on mental age.

IQ Scores. There are two ways to report IQ scores: (1) the ratio IQ and (2) the deviation IQ. In the *ratio* IQ, a ratio is taken between *mental age* and *chronological age*. For example, if a student has a mental age of eight years and a chronological age of ten years, an IQ score of 80 indicates that the student learns eight-tenths as fast as a student of similar age with a score of 100. As mentioned above, the ratio IQ is no longer commonly used.

The second type of IQ score is the *deviation* IQ. Here, the student is compared only with others of the same age who were in the norm group. The standard deviation

IQ score is based upon the concept of a normal curve, as shown in Figure 4.1. An IQ of 100 is designated as the mean for each age group. As shown in Figure 4.1, approximately 34 percent of the population will fall within one standard deviation below the mean and 34 percent of the population will fall within one standard deviation above the mean. To illustrate, on the WISC-R, one standard deviation is 15 points. Therefore, 34 percent of the population will score between 85 and 100, and 34 percent of the population will score between 100 and 115. Figure 4.1 illustrates the distribution of IQ scores on a normal curve.

Intelligence ranges for the WISC-R (Wechsler, 1974) are shown below. Teachers will find them useful for reporting results of this IQ test to parents. If tests other than the WISC-R are used, the test manual should be consulted for the IQ range for those tests.

130 and above	Very superior
120–129	Superior
110–119	High average (bright)
90–109	Average
80– 89	Low average (dull)
70– 79	Borderline
69 and below	Mentally deficient

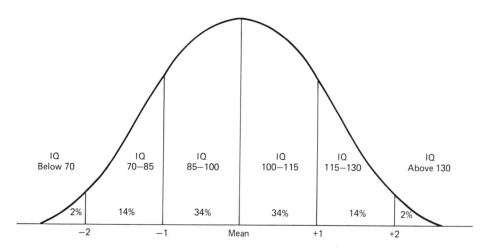

Figure 4.1   Distribution of IQ Scores on a Normal Curve*

*Scores are clustered around the mean, which is the tallest point. A standard deviation (SD) is a number (e.g., in the WISC-R it is 15). A child scoring one standard deviation above the mean, if the mean is 100 and the standard deviation is 15, would score 115. A child scoring two standard deviations above the mean would score 130. The percentages show what percent of the population is included in any standard deviation. For example, 34 percent of the people score between zero and one standard deviations below (or above) the mean. Two percent of the population scores between two and three standard deviations below (or above) the mean.

Determining the Existence of a Reading Disability

As noted in Chapter 2, a critical step in the reading diagnosis is to decide if the student actually has a reading disability. In the process of selecting students for remedial instruction, teachers often find that some students who have been referred do not, in fact, have a reading disability. In addition, more students are usually referred for special reading instruction than time and resources permit to be helped. Selecting students for special reading instruction is a complex and demanding task—one that entails serious consequences for the student. Criteria must be established for selecting students most in need of remedial instruction.

There are two ways to identify students with reading disabilities: the *practical* approach (which looks at how well the student functions in the reading environment) and the *discrepancy* approach (which compares intellectual potential to current reading achievement).

Practical Criteria for Determining a Reading Disability.   A practical way to select students for special reading instruction is to look at how well they are adapting academically to their school environments. In this approach, the teacher considers how students function in the school and with their peers. The teacher investigates the student's ability to cope within the classroom situation and also takes into account such factors as the degree of reading retardation in relation to the peer group and the student's need for special assistance in order to cope in the classroom. The following criteria may be considered.

1. *Students cannot function in school and reading activities as well as peers.* Disabled readers cannot function well academically with peers in the educational setting, and they are unable to participate fully in reading tasks with their age or peer group. This criterion suggests that "national" norms are not applicable to all segments of the population. To apply national norms without discretion is considered discriminatory and unfair to the students (Spache, 1981).

2. *Students have a consistent pattern of poor reading.* The disabled reader shows poor reading performance consistently over a period of time. That is, the reading problem is not temporary. Further, the disabled reader requires extensive intervention rather than a minor correction for a specific area of reading.

3. *The amount of reading retardation meets guidelines for the grade level.* The school can set guidelines to help determine the amount of reading retardation needed for eligibility for reading assistance. However, adjustments may be made for individual situations. We suggest the following guidelines:

Primary grades	Over 0.5 years
Intermediate grades	Over 1.0 years
Junior high school	Over 1.5 years
Senior high school	Over 2.0 years

Discrepancy Criteria for Determining a Reading Disability.   The second approach to deciding if a student has a reading disability is to use discrepancy criteria. The teacher determines if a significant discrepancy exists between reading expectancy (determined partially by the IQ score) and the student's current reading performance. That is, does the student read as well as predicted by measures of potential? The discrepancy concept of reading disability is widely accepted and used. For example, the American Psychological Association in *Diagnostic and Statistical Manual* (DSM III-R, 1987) describes a developmental reading disorder as reading achievement that is markedly below the expected level, given the individual's school experiences and intellectual capacity.

Steps in Determining a Reading Discrepancy.   There are three steps in determining a reading discrepancy. It should be noted that each has certain inherent problems that have been the source of professional debate and disagreement.

1. *Estimating reading expectancy.* This refers to a judgment of how well a student is potentially capable of reading. Methods of estimating reading expectancy use IQ, MA, listening levels, or arithmetic achievement grade level.
2. *Estimating current reading level.* This refers to the level at which a student is currently reading. Reading survey tests, individual reading tests, or oral reading tests are used to make this estimate.
3. *Determining the discrepancy between reading expectancy and reading achievement.* This refers to the size of the gap between the level at which the student is capable of reading and the level at which the student is currently reading. Guidelines for judging this discrepancy are given above.

Expectancy Formulas.   Determining the reading discrepancy requires that the teacher first estimate the student's reading expectancy. Several formulas have been developed to aid in this process. One of the most widely used methods for estimating reading expectancy is *the reading expectancy age method* (Harris and Sipay, 1985):

$$\text{REA (reading expectancy age)} = \frac{2\,\text{MA} + \text{CA}}{3}$$

In this formula, MA (mental age) and CA (chronological age) should be expressed in years and tenths (rather than years and months). The formula gives a reading expectancy age. To convert from an expectancy *age* to an expectancy *grade*, subtract 5.2.

To illustrate the reading age expectancy formula, Marion is 10–0 years old, and she has an IQ of 120 and a MA of 12.0 years. Using this formula, she has a reading expectancy age of 11.3 and a reading grade expectancy of 6.1 (11.3 − 5.2). If Marion's current level of reading is 3.0, she would have a 3.1-year discrepancy.*

*To obtain MA from the IQ, use the formula:

$$\text{MA} = \frac{\text{IQ} \times \text{CA}}{100}$$

$$\text{REA} = \frac{2(12.0) + 10.0}{3} = 11.3 \quad \text{REG (grade)} = 11.3 - 5.2 = 6.1$$

Another widely used formula is the *years-in-school formula* suggested by Bond, Tinker, Wasson, and Wasson, 1984:

$$\text{REG (reading expectancy grade)} = \frac{\text{years in school} \times \text{IQ}}{100} + 1.0$$

To illustrate, if Marion is now in the middle of the fifth grade, she has been in school 4.5 years (grades one, two, three, four, and half of the fifth). Using this formula, Marion has a reading expectancy grade of 6.4.

$$\text{REG} = \frac{4.5 \times 120}{100} + 1.0 = 6.4$$

If she has a current reading level of 3.0, she would have a discrepancy of 3.4 years.

As is apparent, these two methods give different estimates of reading expectancy, resulting in different estimates of discrepancy. These two formulas, along with several others, were studied by Dore-Boyce et al. (1975) to determine which best predicted reading achievement. Using forth and fifth grade students, their findings indicate that the years-in-school method was not as good a predictor of reading achievement as was the reading expectancy age method. Further they found that the reading expectancy age formula proved to be most useful with fourth and fifth graders who had IQs of 90 or better.

To avoid doing calculations in assessing reading expectancy, a table such as that shown in Table 4.1 is a helpful aid. If a teacher knows the IQ and CA of a student, the reading expectancy grade can then be found by noting the intersection of the chronological age with IQ. For students over fifteen years of age, use 15.0 as the chronological age. If the CA and IQ fall between two values on a table, use the closest value. Table 4.1 is based on the reading expectancy formula of Harris and Sipay. To aid the teacher, the expected *grade* level (rather than *age*) is reported directly.

LANGUAGE DEVELOPMENT

Reading can be thought of as language expressed in written form. The ability to express and receive thoughts through language is, therefore, fundamental to being able to read. The individual's underlying language structures profoundly affect the ability to acquire reading skills. It is not surprising that many disabled readers do have underlying language difficulties. As noted earlier, reviews of research on the *Wechsler Intelligence Scale for Children* show that pupils with reading problems have significantly more difficulties with verbal subtests than with the performance subtests (Spache, 1981; Moore and Wielan, 1981).

Table 4.1   Reading Expectancy Grade Table*

	IQ SCORE															
	70	75	80	85	90	95	100	105	110	115	120	125	130	135	140	145
6-0	—	—	—	—	—	—	—	1.0	1.2	1.4	1.6	1.8	2.0	2.2	2.4	2.6
6-3	—	—	—	—	—	—	1.0	1.2	1.5	1.7	1.9	2.1	2.3	2.5	2.7	2.9
6-6	—	—	—	—	—	1.1	1.3	1.5	1.7	2.0	2.2	2.4	2.6	2.8	3.0	3.2
6-9	—	—	—	—	1.1	1.3	1.6	1.8	2.0	2.2	2.4	2.7	2.9	3.1	3.4	3.6
7-0	—	—	—	1.1	1.3	1.6	1.8	2.0	2.3	2.5	2.7	3.0	3.2	3.4	3.7	3.9
7-3	—	—	1.1	1.3	1.6	1.8	2.0	2.3	2.5	2.8	3.0	3.2	3.5	3.7	4.0	4.2
7-6	—	1.0	1.3	1.6	1.8	2.0	2.3	2.6	2.8	3.0	3.3	3.6	3.8	4.0	4.3	4.6
7-9	1.0	1.3	1.5	1.8	2.0	2.3	2.6	2.8	3.1	3.3	3.6	3.8	4.1	4.4	4.6	4.9
8-0	1.2	1.5	1.7	2.0	2.3	2.5	2.8	3.1	3.3	3.6	3.9	4.1	4.4	4.7	4.9	5.2
8-3	1.4	1.7	2.0	2.2	2.5	2.8	3.0	3.3	3.6	3.9	4.2	4.4	4.7	5.1	5.3	5.5
8-6	1.6	1.9	2.2	2.4	2.7	3.0	3.3	3.6	3.9	4.2	4.4	4.7	5.0	5.3	5.6	5.8
8-9	1.8	2.1	2.4	2.7	3.0	3.3	3.6	3.8	4.1	4.4	4.7	5.0	5.3	5.6	5.9	6.2
9-0	2.0	2.3	2.6	2.9	3.2	3.5	3.8	4.1	4.4	4.7	5.0	5.3	5.6	5.9	6.2	6.5
9-3	2.2	2.5	2.8	3.1	3.4	3.7	4.0	4.4	4.7	5.0	5.3	5.6	5.9	6.2	6.5	6.8
9-6	2.4	2.7	3.0	3.4	3.7	4.0	4.3	4.6	4.9	5.2	5.6	5.9	6.2	6.5	6.8	7.2
9-9	2.6	2.9	3.2	3.6	3.9	4.2	4.6	4.9	5.2	5.5	5.8	6.2	6.5	6.8	7.2	7.5
10-0	2.8	3.1	3.5	3.8	4.1	4.5	4.8	5.1	5.5	5.8	6.1	6.5	6.8	7.1	7.5	7.8
10-3	3.0	3.3	3.7	4.0	4.4	4.7	5.0	5.4	5.7	6.1	6.4	6.8	7.1	7.4	7.8	8.1
10-6	3.2	3.6	3.9	4.2	4.6	5.0	5.3	5.6	6.0	6.4	6.7	7.0	7.4	7.8	8.1	8.4
10-9	3.4	3.8	4.1	4.5	4.8	5.2	5.6	5.9	6.3	6.6	7.0	7.3	7.7	8.1	8.4	8.8
11-0	3.6	4.0	4.3	4.7	5.1	5.4	5.8	6.2	6.5	6.9	7.3	7.6	8.0	8.4	8.7	9.1
11-3	3.8	4.2	4.6	4.9	5.3	5.7	6.0	6.4	6.8	7.2	7.6	7.9	8.3	8.7	9.0	9.4
11-6	4.0	4.4	4.8	5.2	5.5	5.9	6.3	6.7	7.1	7.4	7.8	8.2	8.6	9.0	9.4	9.8
11-9	4.2	4.6	5.0	5.4	5.8	6.2	6.6	7.0	7.3	7.7	8.1	8.5	8.9	9.3	9.7	10.1
12-0	4.4	4.8	5.2	5.6	6.0	6.4	6.8	7.2	7.6	8.0	8.4	8.8	9.2	9.6	10.0	10.4
12-3	4.6	5.0	5.4	5.8	6.2	6.6	7.0	7.4	7.9	8.3	8.7	9.1	9.5	9.9	10.3	10.7
12-6	4.8	5.2	5.6	6.0	6.5	6.9	7.3	7.7	8.1	8.6	9.0	9.4	9.8	10.2	10.6	11.0
12-9	5.0	5.4	5.8	6.3	6.7	7.1	7.6	8.0	8.4	8.8	9.2	9.7	10.1	10.5	11.0	11.4
13-0	5.2	5.6	6.1	6.5	6.9	7.4	7.8	8.2	8.7	9.1	9.5	10.0	10.4	10.8	11.3	11.7
13-3	5.4	5.8	6.3	6.7	7.2	7.6	8.0	8.5	8.9	9.4	9.8	10.2	10.7	11.1	11.5	12.0
13-6	5.6	6.0	6.5	7.0	7.4	7.8	8.3	8.8	9.2	9.6	10.1	10.6	11.0	11.4	11.9	12.4
13-9	5.8	6.3	6.7	7.2	7.6	8.1	8.6	9.0	9.5	9.9	10.4	10.8	11.3	11.8	12.2	12.7
14-0	6.0	6.5	6.9	7.4	7.9	8.3	8.8	9.3	9.7	10.2	10.7	11.1	11.6	12.1	12.5	13.0
14-3	6.2	6.7	7.2	7.6	8.1	8.6	9.0	9.5	10.0	10.5	11.0	11.4	11.9	12.4	12.8	13.3
14-6	6.4	6.9	7.4	7.8	8.3	8.8	9.3	9.8	10.3	10.8	11.2	11.7	12.2	12.7	13.2	13.6
14-9	6.6	7.1	7.6	8.1	8.6	9.1	9.6	10.0	10.5	11.0	11.5	12.0	12.5	13.0	13.5	14.0
15-0	6.8	7.3	7.8	8.3	8.8	9.3	9.8	10.3	10.8	11.3	11.8	12.3	12.8	13.3	13.8	14.3

Chronological Age (in years and months)

* This table gives reading expectancy grade level. If the intelligence score or chronological age falls between two values, use the closest one. For students over fifteen years of age, use the 15.0 chronological age value.

The Nature of Language

Teachers who deal with reading problems should have an understanding of the structure of language. Although it is easy to distinguish people who use language effectively from those who do not, it is difficult to define exactly what effective language usage is. A broad perspective of language includes both the oral form (*listening* and *speaking*) and the written form (*reading* and *writing*). These four components of language have an interdependent relationship.

Measures of oral language distinguish between receptive oral language (listening) and expressive oral language (speaking). Usually, people have greater abilities in receptive oral abilities than they do in expressive. That is, they understand more words than they use in speaking. This distinction is important in measuring the language skills of students. Sometimes teachers conclude erroneously that students have low-level language abilities because the students are observed to engage in little conversation or give one-word replies to the teacher's questions. However, measures of expressive language are influenced by factors such as the student's comfort in the classroom, clinic, or testing situation or conditions such as speech defects. These factors may only affect the student's expressive abilities, leaving receptive abilities functioning adequately. Therefore it is important to assess both aspects of oral language.

Components of Language

To help understand the nature of language, linguists identify several different systems: (1) phonology (the sounds of language), (2) morphology (meaningful elements within words), (3) syntax (the grammatical aspects of language), and (4) semantics (the vocabulary of language). Remedial readers may have difficulties with any of these language systems.

1. *Phonology.* The sound system of our language is called phonology. Language consists of a stream of sounds, one after the other. The sounds of English speech do not reflect directly the letters of the English alphabet. For example, the letter "c" represents two different sounds as in the words "city" and "cat." The sound "sh" is composed of two letters, but it represents only one English sound. Although English has only twenty-six letters in the alphabet, the average American English dialect contains forty-four sounds.

Each of the individual sounds is called a phoneme. There are major differences in the phoneme sounds of English and those of other languages. For example, the sounds "y" and "j" are pronounced differently in English as in "yellow" and "jello," but the Spanish speaker may hear them as the same sound and confuse these words. These differences between English and other languages make the mastery of English difficult for students whose native language is not English (just as Spanish or French is difficult for native English speakers).

Phonology refers only to the sounds produced in speech. The term "phonics," which is used by reading teachers, refers to the system that relates letters to sound equivalents in written language.

Young children have difficulty in producing certain phonemes. Not all English speech sounds have been acquired by the time the average child enters first grade. Late-maturing consonant sounds include *r, l, ch, sh, j, th* (*as in thy* and *thigh*), *s, z, v* and *zh* (as in *pleasure*).

In addition to *hearing* sounds, students must learn to *distinguish* sounds that are spoken by others. "Auditory discrimination," the ability to hear distinctions between phoneme sounds is an area of great difficulty for some disabled readers (Wiig and Semel, 1984).

Phonological awareness, the ability to recognize that words can be divided into sounds, is an aspect of phonological development which is closely related to success in beginning reading (Stanovich, 1985; Liberman and Shankweiler, 1985; Williams 1986).

2. *Morphology.* The term morphology refers to meaningful units (or morphemes) that are contained within words. For example, the word "walked" contains two morphemes: "walk" and "ed," a morpheme that signals the past tense. Other examples of morphemes are "s" (games) and "re" (*rewind*). Many students with reading disabilities have deficits in morphological development (Wiig and Semel, 1984; Vogel, 1974).

When pupils are tested on oral language abilities, they usually are tested on suffixes (which are attached to the end of a word). For example, the pupil is asked to make plurals or possessives. (Here is one dog. Here are two_____.) In the field of reading, morphology is referred to as structural analysis. (See Chapter 9.)

3. *Syntax.* Syntax (or grammar) refers to the principles that govern the formation of appropriate sentences in a language. The rules of English syntax tell us, for example, that a well-formed sentence has a subject and a verb (e.g., "Jane walks"). Further, we can combine sentences using conjunctions such as "Jane walks *and* Jane runs." The rules of English also tell us that we can delete certain elements; for example, "Jane walks and runs." Extensive study has gone into the description of the syntax of English and its acquisition by children. Psycholinguistic research indicates that children do not acquire syntactic ability passively. Rather, they recreate syntactic rules for themselves. Children who say "he goed" for the past tense of "go" are using the rule that the past tense is formed by the addition of "ed"; however, they are overgeneralizing this rule. Although most basic syntactic structures are acquired by the age of six, some growth in syntax continues through the age of ten. The development of the ability to understand very complex or difficult sentence patterns may continue even throughout the high school years. Since the development of syntactic abilities continues through the school years, teaching sentence comprehension is important to reading instruction. Table 4.2 presents examples of difficult sentence types.

4. *Vocabulary (semantics).* Compared with other languages, English has a very large vocabulary. An awareness of the historical development of English helps

Table 4.2   Difficult Sentence Types

Category	Example
Passive sentences: reversible°	John was given the pen by Mary.
Out-of-order time sequences*	Move a yellow bead, *but first* move a red one.
	Move a yellow bead *after* you move a red one.
Relative clause construction	John, *who is in the second grade*, is learning to read.
	The man *standing on the corner* is nice.
Appositives	Mr. Smith, *the postman*, is very nice.
Complement structures	*The fact that Steve is silly* worries Meg.
	Steve's being silly worries Meg.
	For Steve to be silly worries Meg.
	Steve asked Meg *what was worrying her.*
Delayed reference in sentences†	John promised Mary to go.
	John asked Mary what to feed the doll.
Anophoric, or reference, structures	John saw Mary and *he* said hello.
	John saw Mary and said hello.
Sentence connectives	*If* you don't do this, I will go.
	Unless you do this, I will go.

° The nonreversible sentence *The ball was dropped by the boy* would be easier.
* The construction *Move the yellow one and then the red* would be simpler because it occurs in time order.
† In these cases, *John* does the action of going or feeding the doll. In a sentence such as *John told Mary what to feed the doll, Mary* feeds the doll. The latter type of sentence is easier to comprehend.

to explain its complexity and variety. English vocabulary comes from two language roots: the Germanic and the Romance languages. The Germanic strand dates back to the original Anglo-Saxon language in old England. The Romance strain came to English when William the Conqueror brought French to England in 1066. The Romance strand was further enriched when many words were directly borrowed from Latin in the 1500s and 1600s. The complex and rich variety of English makes the mastering of English vocabulary a lifelong task.

In assessing vocabulary development, important considerations include

a. *Size of vocabulary.* This means the number of words that students can use or understand.

b. *Knowledge of multiple meanings of words.* For example, the words "plane" and "cold" each have several meanings.

c. *Accuracy of vocabulary meaning.* The student may overextend or underextend the meanings of words. For example, a small child may call all four-legged animals "dogs." Developing the accuracy of vocabulary is referred to as horizontal vocabulary growth (McNeill, 1970).

d. *Accurate classification of words.* For example, "red," "blue," and "green" all belong in the classification of "colors." The development of this system is referred to as vertical vocabulary growth (McNeill, 1970). Piaget (1926) also discusses the ability to classify objects into categories as an important aspect of language and cognitive development.

e. *Relational categories of words.* Relational words include prepositions (under, over, besides, to, from); comparative terms (good-bad, better-worse, lighter-darker); time elements (yesterday-today-tomorrow), and terms of human relationship (mother, father, aunt, uncle).

Limited vocabulary development can seriously hamper reading. In an extensive review of the literature, Anderson and Freebody (1981) found that vocabulary is highly related to reading achievement.

Language Problems and Reading

Since reading is based on language abilities, problems with language can affect the ability to read. In this section, two types of language problems are discussed: speech defects and language disorders.

Speech Defects.   There are three types of speech problems: (1) articulation problems (the inaccurate production of sounds), (2) voice disorders (improper pitch or intonation), and (3) stuttering (breath or rhythm problems). Although there is a somewhat higher incidence of speech defects among poor readers, speech defects do not necessarily lead to reading failure. However, students who exhibit speech difficulties should be referred to the speech-language specialist for further evaluation and therapy, if needed. In addition, since hearing impairment is a possible cause of speech defects, hearing acuity should be tested. It is important to remember, however, that the average child does not complete full articulation development until the age of about eight. Students with speech defects are often embarrassed when asked to read orally, and therefore oral reading should be avoided.

Language Disorders and Reading.   Language disorders refer to the slow or atypical development of receptive and expressive oral language. The child with a language delay is slow at talking, poor in vocabulary development, and may have difficulty in learning to formulate sentences. Language delay appears to be a forerunner of later difficulty in reading for many pupils (Vogel, 1974; Wiig and Semel, 1984). If the teacher suspects an underlying language disorder, the speech-language specialist can provide further evaluation and treatment.

Assessing Language Development

Impressions about students' oral language can be gathered by observing them during conversation. More objective methods are given below.

Tests of Language.   Some of the widely used tests that assess expressive and receptive language ability are described in Test Inventory 4.2 (at the end of this chapter). There are several problems in obtaining objective measures of language. If the pupil does not know the examiner, the student tends to produce less language and therefore scores poorly. Language output can be increased if the examiner strives to develop rapport before testing. This can be accomplished by talking to the student for a short period of time prior to the testing session. Another shortcoming of language tests is that many are not designed for students past age ten; there are relatively few oral language tests for older students.

Measuring Listening Level. The ability to comprehend what is heard is sometimes used as an informal measure of a student's receptive language abilities. If remedial students are reading below their listening comprehension level, this means that they are reading below their level of language comprehension. The listening level provides an idea of how well the student might read once the reading disability is overcome. If reading and listening levels are both low, further instruction for language development may be needed.

A student's listening level is sometimes used as a measure of potential for understanding the written word. Listening abilities can be compared with other estimates of a student's reading potential. The difference between instructional reading level and the listening level indicates the degree of reading disability. If a fifth-grader's instructional level is second grade and the listening level is fifth grade, the student can be estimated to have a three-year discrepancy between actual and expected levels. Of course, listening tests can be influenced by such factors as the ability to pay attention.

The procedure involved in determining the listening level consists of reading selections aloud to a student and then asking comprehension questions based on the material. Some commercial tests contain subtests which measure listening level.

1. *The Durrell Analysis of Reading Difficulty.* (Psychological Corporation) This test contains a subtest for measuring listening level. A graded story is read and comprehension questions are asked.
2. *Stanford Achievement Series.* (Psychological Corporation) This test contains a listening test for the primary I through the advanced levels.

In addition to these tests of listening, an informal reading inventory (IRI) can be used to evaluate listening level. (See Chapter 5 for a discussion of the IRI and Appendix D for a sample IRI.) After the frustration level of the IRI has been established, the teacher reads aloud passages at and above the frustration level and asks the student comprehension questions. The highest level at which the pupil can maintain a comprehension score of 70 percent is the listening level.

LANGUAGE DIFFERENCES AND READING

Many students in our schools use language forms that are different from the standard language of the textbook or of school instruction. These language forms are alternatives rather than deficit forms, and they are not inferior. However, because differences in language usage can affect reading instruction, teachers need to understand them. In this section, dialect-different students and bilingual (or second-language) students are discussed.

Students with Nonstandard Dialect

A dialect is a language pattern used by a subgroup of the speakers of a language. There are many dialects in American English. For example, speakers from New York City, Boston, Montreal, or certain Southern states often speak a characteristic regional dialect. Some students raised in certain specific cultural groups speak a dialect of English used in their environment, such as Appalachian or a dialect referred to as Black English Vernacular (BEV). To illustrate the differences between one such dialect of English and the dialect that is generally considered to be "Standard English," the features of BEV are given in Table 4.3.

American dialects have been studied by several linguists (McDavid, 1976; Wolfram, 1969; Labov et al., 1968). These linguists conclude that all dialects, regardless of their cultural associations, are logical, rule-based systems of English. They also have found that, while dialects may seem to be different, all English speakers share

Table 4.3 Features of Black English Vernacular

PHONOLOGICAL OR SOUND CHANGES

Category	Examples
When two or more consonants are at the end of a word, one may be omitted.	*Test* is pronounced like *tes.*
"R" may be omitted.	*Bump* is pronounced like *bum.*
"L" may be omitted.	*Fort* is pronounced like *fought.*
Short "i" and short "e" are pronounced the same before some consonants.	*Toll* is pronounced like *toe.*
	Pin is pronounced like *pen.*

SYNTACTIC OR GRAMMATICAL CHANGES

Category	Examples
The possessive may be omitted.	That's Molly('s) book.
The verb *to be* may be omitted.	He('s) downstairs; they('re) there.
The past-tense ending may be omitted.	He walk(ed) to the store yesterday.
The third-person-singular ending may be omitted.	She think(s) he is very nice.
Contractions signaling the future may be omitted.	He('ll) be there soon.
A "be" construction to indicate ongoing action may be inserted.	I *be* going there on Thursdays.

common underlying language forms. Students who speak nonstandard English can learn to read texts in standard English without changing their speech patterns.

When assessing and teaching students with reading difficulties who speak nonstandard dialects, teachers should be aware of some pitfalls. First, since reading is a language process, constant correction of the students' oral language may be very destructive. Such correction of dialect patterns makes students feel that their speech is unacceptable. If the student feels uncomfortable with the teacher, verbal output will be reduced in the classroom, and a barrier between the student and teacher can result. Second, dialect differences should not be mistaken for cognitive deficits or defective language development.

Students with Limited English Proficiency (LEP)

An increasing number of students in our schools cannot speak the language of instruction fluently. Often these students present reading problems and are placed in special reading or language programs. Although these students come from many different backgrounds and ways of life, they may be divided into two groups: (1) recent immigrants and (2) students whose families have been living in the country for several generations but maintain a separate language and cultural identity.

Among factors which influence a person's ability to learn a second language are the age of acquisition, the role of language in the culture, the exposure to a second language, and the relationship of the first and second language. These topics are each considered in the paragraphs that follow.

Second languages are usually learned better at earlier ages, with children showing more facility than adolescents and adults. The ability to acquire a foreign language with native fluency often disappears at about the age of fourteen. Before this, the language will be acquired fully; after this, the speaker will tend to have a "foreign accent."

Language learning is also influenced by cultural values. If a second language is perceived positively in the student's environment, learning will be enhanced. Unfortunately, this is not always the case. Often, a second language is only used in school and thus is of little value in everyday life. Or a second language may be associated with people who are hostile. The more knowledge and empathy a teacher possesses of a student's personal background and cultural heritage, the more effective second-language instruction will be.

Exposure to a second language is important. If students use it frequently, they will learn it more easily. We have observed that students tend to learn a second language more quickly when only a few of their classmates speak their native language. Students benefit most from exposure to people who communicate fluently and naturally in the language to be learned.

Finally, the relationship between the native and second language must be considered. If the two languages are related closely, the second language will be easier to learn. For example, learning English presents fewer problems to Spanish-speaking student than to a speaker of Cantonese. By knowing about the student's native language, teachers can anticipate possible difficulties in learning English. Because there are many Spanish speakers in our schools today, teachers may need to know about the differences between Spanish and English. These are presented in Table 4.4.

Approaches to Second-Language Learning

Three distinct approaches to second-language learning are (1) the TESL approach, (2) the bilingual approach, and (3) the immersion approach. Each is based on different assumptions, and each has certain advantages.

The acronym *TESL* stands for "teaching English as a second language." The TESL model is particularly useful when teaching students of many different language backgrounds. In some TESL methods, students learn by carefully controlled oral repetition of selected second-language patterns. The patterns are repeated, practiced, and memorized. This ensures exposure to good second-language models and helps students to avoid repeating language mistakes. However, the repetition method may emphasize the correct form of language at the expense of meaningful communication.

Table 4.4   Differences Between Spanish and English

PHONOLOGICAL OR SOUND CHANGES

In English there are five vowel sounds; in Spanish there are over fourteen; thus Spanish speakers may confuse some English vowels.
The following consonant substitutions may be made:

"j" may become	"ch" as in "chair"
"th" may become	"d" as in "dis" or "s" as in "sigh"

"Voiced" consonants may become unvoiced:

"z" becomes	"s"
"b" becomes	"p"
"d" becomes	"t"
"v" may become	"b"
"Use" and "yellow" may become	"juice" and "jello"
"W" in "way" may become	"guay"

SYNTACTIC OR GRAMMATICAL CHANGES

"Not" may become "no."	"He is no going."
Negative auxiliaries may be omitted.	"They no did that."
The progressive tense may become the present tense.	"I am going" becomes "I go."
"It" may be omitted from a sentence.	"It is Tuesday" becomes "Is Tuesday."
Sometimes "to be" is replaced by "to have."	"I have hunger." "I have twenty years."
"Does" and "do" may not be used to form questions.	"Does she have a job?" becomes "She has a job?"

A method known as Total Physical Response (TPR) has also been used to teach TESL. In this method students first learn to understand and to carry out motor responses to such commands as "stand up," "sit down," "throw the ball" (Krashen, 1983). TPR is active and highly motivating.

In the *bilingual* approach students use their native language for part of the school day and a second language for the remaining portion. An important aspect of bilingual programs is strengthening the native language so that it will provide a firm basis for learning a second language (Ortiz, 1986). Thus academic subjects are taught in the native language. For example, Hispanic students first are introduced to reading in Spanish, and the second language, English, initially receives only oral practice. Bilingual programs motivate students by respecting their native language and culture and by building upon the foundation of their native-language competence. However, the approach is only feasible where large groups of students share one native language and suitable teachers can be found. In addition, if students interact mainly with speakers of their native language, exposure to the second language may not be sufficient for mastery.

The progress that students make in bilingual programs appears to be related to the overall effectiveness of the school. Case studies from bilingual education in low-income areas show that the method can be highly effective if schools are characterized by high goals, active leadership, democratic staff decision making, and community involvement (Carter and Chatfield, 1986).

In the *immersion* approach, students are "immersed" in, or receive extensive exposure to, a second language (Genesee, 1985). In fact, even when there is no formal instruction, most individuals can learn a language through extensive and repeated exposure. Adults who wish to acquire a second language quickly often enroll in a commercial course where they must speak the language for several hours a day. The immersion approach was formalized as an instructional method for school children in Quebec, where it is used to teach French to English-speaking children by enrolling them in French-speaking schools. The immersion method is most feasible where there are only a few foreign-language speakers who can be exposed easily to fluent second-language speech. The method gives the language learner wide exposure in learning. The disadvantages of the immersion approach are that it may be uncomfortable for the student, it is often unstructured, and it does not incorporate the child's native language and culture. The immersion approach is currently under study as an alternative to the bilingual approach (Ramirez, 1986; Genesee, 1985).

Reading and Students with Limited English Proficiency (LEP).

As with all students in our schools, students who speak other languages are expected to learn to read the dominant language, English. Yet, since reading a language depends upon understanding it, teaching reading often presents many problems.

A distinction should be drawn between students who can read fluently in their native language and those who cannot. Students who are fluent readers simply need to learn English and then can transfer the reading knowledge they already possess to English. However, if students cannot read in any language, they must learn both to speak English and to read it. Students who come from countries where education is not universal often face these dual tasks.

Different opinions exist as to whether reading instruction should be done in the student's native language or in the second language. If students cannot read and do not speak English fluently, reading instruction is often done in the native language. This approach is used widely in bilingual programs. Advocates of the native-language approach feel that, since learning to read is a difficult process, it should first be done in the child's stronger language. After the student has learned to read, the knowledge can be transferred to the second language, resulting in a better long-term effects for academic learning in both languages. Many experimental studies have investigated this approach. Although, in general, teaching reading in the native language has shown positive effects, not all studies have supported this viewpoint. Relevant research is summarized by Orfield (1986) and Arias (1986).

In the immersion approach, students are given reading instruction in the second language. It is assumed that students do not need to be fully fluent in a second language in order to read it and that reading skills and language learning can reinforce one another. Although research on learning to read in this way is not extensive, some studies have shown immersion programs to have positive cognitive and educational effects (Gamez, 1979; Hornby, 1980).

Often, of course, the language of reading instruction is determined by available resources rather than by philosophy. Where there are many students from one language group, reading instruction in the native language is feasible. When students come from many different language backgrounds, or there are only a few foreign-language speakers, English is generally used for reading instruction.

Whatever language is used for instruction, authorities agree that students must have *some* understanding of a language before they can read it effectively. For example, in the immersion approach, students are provided with oral teaching of a second language for one year before it is used in reading instruction. Teachers of students who are learning to read in a second language can help to assure understanding by using words and sentences in conversation before students are asked to read them. Perez (1981) found that oral English activities prior to reading a selection significantly improved the reading achievement of students whose native language was Spanish.

It is also important to remember that there is a complex interaction between cultural identity and attitudes toward language. This interaction greatly affects the overall achievement of students who speak English as a second language (Matute-Bianchi, 1986).

Hough, Nurss, and Enright (1986) report that an old standby—story reading—is a successful technique for LEP children. Frequent reading of stories to small groups of LEP children helps them to acquire language and learn the structure of stories. It also guides the LEP child into reading in English. These authors suggest:

1. Read stories frequently (at least once per day) to small groups (5 to 7 children).
2. Use strategies to focus on the meaning while reading to maximize children's understanding.
3. Involve all the children in the story by asking questions appropriate to their individual levels of language acquisition.
4. Select predictable books (ones that have a repeated refrain, see Chapter 8) to read aloud, encouraging the children to repeat the refrain.
5. Select well-illustrated books (ones with many illustrations closely tied to the text).
6. Throughout the story, ask the children thought-provoking questions.
7. Read and reread favorite stories and let the children listen to them on tapes or records while following along in the book.
8. Provide related follow-up activities using a variety of formats and manipulative materials.

SUMMARY

Chapter 4 deals with two correlates of reading: intelligence and language.

Intelligence in the reading diagnosis means the potential for learning to read. Intelligence tests tend to measure scholastic aptitude.

One issue involving intelligence is whether it is most influenced by heredity or environment. The environment perspective is that intelligence can be dramatically influenced by environmental conditions. The heredity perspective is that intelligence is inherited and is not amenable to environmental modification. In general, the teaching profession assumes that the environment, including teaching, can make a difference.

Intelligence is composed of component or separate abilities. Some intelligence tests, especially the WISC-R *(Wechsler Intelligence Scale for Children-Revised)*, have subtests that are useful for gathering information about subabilities.

In interpreting intelligence test scores, several technical terms are used, including *MA* (mental age) and *IQ*. Two kinds of IQs are the *ratio IQ* and the *deviation* IQ.

Two ways of determining if a student has a reading disability and should receive special reading instruction are (1) the practical method and (2) the discrepancy method.

It is important to assess oral language ability in a reading diagnosis. Many disabled readers have poor language skills. Oral language includes two modes: oral receptive language (listening) and oral expressive language (speaking).

Linguists have identified four language systems: (1) *phonology* (the sound system of language), (2) *morphology* (the system of expressing meaning through word parts), (3) *syntax* (the sentence structure or grammatical forms of language), and (4) *semantics* or vocabulary (the words in language). Studies show that some students with reading disabilities have difficulty with one or more of these language systems.

Language problems that can affect reading include speech impairment and language disorders.

Language differences can also affect reading. These include both a nonstandard dialect as well as a different language. Language differences should not be interpreted as language inferiority. The approaches to teaching students a second language include *TESL*, *bilingual instruction*, and *immersion*. Some authorities feel that students should first learn to read in their native language.

Test Inventory 4.1   Tests of Intelligence and Potential

**AAMD Adaptive Behavior Scale
(Public School Version)**

American Association on Mental Deficiency   *Grades: 2-6*

Determines intellectual aptitude based on tests of total life functioning. Considered more accurate for determining mental deficiency or need for special placement than traditional IQ tests (WISC, Stanford-Binet). While interviewing an informant, an assessment is made of (1) development, including independent functioning, economic activity, domestic activity, and socialization; and (2) maladaptive behaviors, such as violence, withdrawal, and odd mannerisms. Percentile scores allow for comparison of students in five different school placements.

Individual administration: 15–20 minutes.

Cognitive Abilities Test (CAT)

Riverside Publishing Company   *Grades K–12*

Group test of cognitive abilities. Levels include: Primary I (K–1), Primary II (Grades 2–3), Multilevel (Grades 3–12). Provides a variety of tasks. 3 batteries: verbal, quantitative, nonverbal.

Group test: 1 hour.

Culture-Fair Series 1, 2, 3

Institute for Personality and Ability Testing   *Ages: 4–adult*

Scale 1 tests relationships of shapes and figures for ages 4–8. Scales 2 and 3 are group nonverbal tests of pencil and paper tasks. Designed to be free of verbal fluency and emotional factors.

20–30 minutes.

The Goodenough-Harris Drawing Test

Psychological Corporation   *Ages: 3–15 years*

Nonverbal test in which mental ability is assessed through an analysis of the characteristics included in three student drawings: a man, a woman, and a self-portrait. Yields standard scores and percentile ranks.

Group test: 10–15 minutes.

Hiskey-Nebraska Test of Learning Aptitude

The Hiskey Nebraska Co.   *Ages: 2.5–18.5 years*

Nonverbal test of mental ability often used with mentally retarded, speech-handicapped, bilingual, and deaf students. Two sets of norms, one for pantomimed directions with deaf subjects. Yields learning age scores and learning quotient.

Individual test: 45–60 minutes.

Illinois Test of Psycholinguistic Abilities (ITPA).

University of Illinois Press   *Ages: 2.6–10.0*

Twelve subtests. Auditory, visual, and motor areas.

Individual administration: 1 hour.

Kaufman Assessment Battery for Children (K-ABC)

American Guidance Services   *Ages 2.6–12.6*

Individual test of intelligence and achievement. Yields four major scores: Sequential Processing, Simultaneous Processing, Mental Processing Composite, and Achievement.

Individual administration: 1 hour.

Kuhlman-Anderson Tests

Scholastic Testing Service   *Grades: K–12*

Multiple-choice format used to measure IQ. Scores given for verbal, quantitative, and total intelligence. Eight levels available.

Group test: 50–75 minutes.

The Leiter International Performance Scale (LIPS)

C. H. Stoelting Company   *Ages: 2–18 years*

Nonverbal test where student places items on a tray to correspond with picture on stimulus card. Assessment includes the ability to judge the relationship between two events, spatial imagery, and immediate recall. Yields MA score.

Individual test: 1–1½ hours. Training needed in administration.

The McCarthy Scales of Children's Abilities (MSCA)

Psychological Corporation   *Ages: 2½–8½ years*

Particularly appropriate for young children. Test contains eighteen subtests grouped into six categories: (1) verbal scale, (2) perceptual-performance, (3) quantitative scale, (4) memory scale, (5) motor scale, and (6) general cognitive index. Yields scaled scores and general cognitive index or IQ.

Individual test: 45–60 minutes.

Otis-Lennon School Ability Test (OLSAT)

Psychological Corporation   *Grades: 1–12*

Multiple-choice measures of verbal, figural, and numerical reasoning abilities. Two forms (R and S) and five levels are available. Yields an age percentile, stanine score, and a School Ability Index, which has the same statistical properties as an IQ score.

Group test: primary levels, 80 minutes; 4 upper levels, 45 minutes.

Peabody Picture Vocabulary Test-Revised (PPVT-R)

American Guidance Service   *Ages: 2½–40 years*

Tests verbal ability. Examiner says a word and subject chooses one of four pictures that represents that word. Test yields standard score (distributed as is done for IQ score), age equivalent, percentile, and stanine.

Individual test: 10–20 minutes.

Raven Progressive Matrices
STANDARD PROGRESSIVE MATRICES
COLOURED PROGRESSIVE MATRICES
ADVANCED PROGRESSIVE MATRICES

Psychological Corporation   *Ages: 8–65 years*

Nonverbal tests assessing mental ability through problem solving using abstract figures and designs. The subject is asked to complete visual patterns. The Standard Progressive Matrices are for ages 8–65 years; the Coloured Progressive Matrices are for ages 5–11 years and mentally deficient adults; the Advanced Progressive Matrices are for adolescents and adults. Set I is for average ability and Set II is for above-average ability. All tests yield percentile scores.

Group or individual administration: approximately 30 minutes needed.

Slossen Intelligence Test-Revised (SIT-R)

Slossen Educational Publishers   *Ages: 2–adult*

Based on Stanford Binet IQ Test. A cognitive test that can be administered by teachers. Verbal and some performance items; no reading required. Yields a deviation IQ score.

Individual test: 20–40 minutes.

Stanford-Binet Intelligence Scale, fourth edition

Riverside Publishing Company   *Ages: 2–adult*

An adaptation of the first individual test of intelligence. Consists of 15 subtests grouped in four areas: verbal reasoning, quantitative reasoning, abstract/visual reasoning, short-term memory. Test yields Standard Age Scores. One form.

Individual test: 60–90 minutes. Need specialized training to administer.

System of Multicultural Pluralistic Assessment (SOMPA)

Psychological Corporation   *Ages: 5-11 years*

An assessment "system" rather than a test. Determines intellectual level and functioning based on a wide variety of measures. Separate norms available for black, Hispanic, and white American students. There are two main parts: the parent interview and the student assessment: The interview contains (1) Sociocultural Scales (information about the family); (2) Adaptive Behavior Inventory for Children (ABIC) (questions about the student's activities); and (3) Health History Inventories. The assessment contains (1) Physical Dexterity Tests, (2) the Bender Visual Motor Gestalt Test, (3) the Wechsler Intelligence Scale for Children-Revised, (4) Weight by Height, (5) Visual Acuity, and (6) Auditory Acuity.

Individual administration: about 3 hours. Specialized training required for administering some parts.

Vineland Adaptive Behavior Scales

American Guidance Services   *Ages: 1 month–adult*

Assesses individual's level of social maturity, competence, and independence.

20–90 minutes.

Wechsler Intelligence Scales

WECHSLER PRESCHOOL AND PRIMARY SCALE OF INTELLIGENCE (WPPSI)	*Ages: 4–6½*
WECHSLER INTELLIGENCE SCALE FOR CHILDREN-REVISED (WISC-R)	*Ages 6–16*
WECHSLER ADULT INTELLIGENCE SCALE-REVISED (WAIS-R)	*Ages: 15–adult*

Psychological Corporation

These scales, along with the Stanford-Binet, represent the most widely used tests of intelligence. Each of the three levels is divided into a verbal and a performance scale. These two scales combine into a total scale. Three scores are available, verbal, performance, and total IQ.

WISC-R: AGES 6–16 YEARS—See text for subtests
WAIS-R: AGES 16–74 YEARS

       Verbal scale: Same as WISC-R with all six tests required.
Performance scale: Same as WISC-R but mazes omitted.

WPPSI: AGES 4–6½ YEARS

       Verbal Scale: Same as WISC-R but digit span is replaced with sentence repetition.

Performance scale: 1. Picture Completion, Block Design, and Mazes are the same as on the WISC-R.
2. Animal Houses—matching the color of the animal's house to the animal.
3. Geometric Design—duplicating a design on paper.

Items in arithmetic and all performance subtests are timed. Each subtest is scored individually, allowing for patterns of development to be obtained if manual directions on interpretation are followed. Tests yield IQ scores.

Individual administration: about 45 minutes. Special training needed for administration.

Woodcock-Johnson Psychoeducational Battery-Tests of Cognitive Ability

DLM   *Ages: 3–80*

Evaluates cognitive level through twelve subtests: (1) picture vocabulary, (2) spatial relations, (3) memory for sentences, (4) visual-auditory learning, (5) blending, (6) quantitative concepts, (7) visual matching, (8) antonyms and synonyms, (9) analysis synthesis, (10) numbers reversed, (11) concept formation, and (12) analogies. Only tests 1 through 6 are used at preschool level. The battery also contains ten achievement subtests and five interest subtests. Yields expected achievement score.

Individual test: 1 hour for cognitive tests; complete battery about 2 hours.

Test Inventory 4.2   Tests of Language Development

Carrow Elicited Language Inventory

DLM   *Ages: 3-7 years*

Grammatical structures are measured by sentence repetition. Errors are tallied according to type (substitutions, omissions, reversals) and grammatical category. Age equivalents, percentiles, and mean are obtained.

Individual test: 10–15 minutes. Usually administered by speech or language therapist.

Clinical Evaluation of Language Fundamentals (CELF)

Psychological Corporation   *Grades: K-12*

Consists of a screening test and a diagnostic battery. The screening test has an elementary (K–5) and an advanced (5–12) level. It measures productive and receptive (called "processing") language. Elementary format is adaptation of "Simon Says"; advanced uses playing cards. Diagnostic battery contains thirteen tests, including word association, model sentences, and spoken paragraphs. The test yields a percentile rank only.

Individual administration: screening test 15 minutes; diagnostic tests 1½ hours.

Goldman-Fristoe Test of Articulation

American Guidance Service   *Ages: 2–16+ years*

Articulation test measuring sound production in (1) words, (2) sentences, and (3) repetition format. Concentrates on consonant sounds. Yields percentile scores.

Individual test: 10–15 minutes. Usually administered by speech or language therapist.

Northwestern Syntax Screening Test (NSST)

Northwestern University Press   *Ages: 3–7 years*

Test consists of two parts: receptive and expressive. Yields percentile score.

Individual test: 15 minutes. Usually administered by speech or language therapist.

Picture Story Language Test

Grune & Stratton   *Ages: 7–17 years*

A developmental scale for written language. Students write a story about a picture and are scored for productivity, syntax, and abstraction of word meanings. Yields mean age score.

Group or individual administration: 20–30 minutes.

Test of Language Development (TOLD)

Pro Ed   *Ages: 4–12 years*

Five tests assess semantics and syntax in receptive and expressive language. Two supplementary phonology tests assess word discrimination and word articulation. Test yields a language age, scaled score, and linguistic quotient. Primary and Intermediate Levels.

Individual administration: 40 minutes.

Utah Test of Language Development (UTLD)

Communication Research Associates   *Ages: 2–14 years*

Test includes receptive and expressive language and some perceptual skills. Yields a language age equivalent and a language quotient.

Individual administration: 30–45 minutes.

Woodcock Language Proficiency Battery
ENGLISH FORM
SPANISH FORM

DLM   *Ages: 6-13*

This test assesses oral language, reading, and writing. The English test contains eight subtests of the *Woodcock Johnson* (see Test Inventory 5.2). These tests have also been translated into Spanish, and if both the English and Spanish tests are administered, provisions are made for determining the student's dominant language. The subtest can also be used diagnostically. The three oral language subtests are picture vocabulary, antonyms-synonyms, and analogies.

5

ASSESSING READING
ACHIEVEMENT I
Informal Assessment

Ways of collecting information about reading can be divided into two broad classifications: informal measures (discussed in this chapter) and formal measures (discussed in Chapter 6).

INTRODUCTION

This chapter deals with informal measures of reading assessment. We devote a major portion of the chapter to the informal reading inventory, and the many insights it gives into both general and specific reading diagnosis. In addition, we discuss other informal measures of reading, including reading miscue analysis, observing reading in the classroom, assessing comprehension through the cloze and retelling techniques, assessing the student's views and concepts of reading, curriculum-based assessment, and diagnostic teaching.

As we explore these assessment tools, remember that the ability to read, in any situation, depends upon the interactions among the reader's background and interest, the nature of the text, and the context of the reading situation. Thus, reading ability is not fixed for a student, but varies depending upon many factors.

A TWO-PHASE FRAMEWORK FOR ASSESSING READING

The use of a two-phase framework helps teachers to organize diagnostic information. As noted in Chapter 2, two important components of a complete reading diagnosis are (1) general reading assessment and (2) specific reading assessment. In the first phase, we gather general information about the student's reading performance. In the second phase, we seek in-depth diagnostic information. This two-phase framework is illustrated in Table 5.1.

General Reading Assessment

The purposes of the general reading phase are (1) to assess a student's current reading level and (2) to identify the student's general areas of reading strengths and weaknesses. General areas of reading include: word recognition, comprehension,

Table 5.1 Two Phases for Assessing Reading Abilities

	PHASE 1	PHASE 2
	General Reading Assessment	Specific Reading Assessment
Type		
Purpose and: Information Gained	Student's Reading Level General Areas of Reading Strengths and Weaknesses	Knowledge and Use of Strategies and Patterns within Specific Areas of Reading

meaning vocabulary, study strategies, and reading rate. In addition, readiness for reading, language development, and informational background (or schema) may be evaluated. Thus, general assessment provides information about the level at which the student reads and also identifies the major areas of reading difficulty. For example, the general assessment for Steve, an eighth-grade student, tells us that he is reading at the sixth-grade level. In addition he demonstrates strength in word recognition and meaning vocabulary, but weakness in reading comprehension and study strategies.

Specific Reading Assessment

The purpose of the specific reading assessment is to gather in-depth information in order to develop an effective teaching plan. Knowledge obtained in the general reading phase guides the information gathering in the specific phase. In the case of Steve, during the specific phase, the teacher would probe his comprehension abilities in greater depth. The teacher would also try to detect the strategies that Steve is using to study.

Although general and specific assessment are presented here as two distinct phases of the diagnosis, often a single assessment tool, such as an informal reading inventory, yields both kinds of information. The framework of general and specific assessment provides an orientation for the discussion of informal measures (in this chapter) as well as formal measures (in Chapter 6).

OVERVIEW OF INFORMAL ASSESSMENT MEASURES

Informal measures refer to various ways, other than standardized tests, of collecting information about a student's reading.

Characteristics of Informal Measures

There are two key differences between formal and informal measures. (1) Informal measures have not been normed on large populations of students, as have formal tests. Therefore informal tests cannot be used to compare one student's performance with that of other students. To make such comparisons, we must use formal tests. (2) Informal measures are flexible and can be adapted to serve the specific needs of the diagnostic situation. This flexibility is a key advantage of informal measures. Because of this flexibility, many reading specialists consider informal measures to be the cornerstone of the reading diagnosis.

Interactive Assessment of Students, Texts, and the Context of the Reading Situation

Informal measures may be structured and modified so that they can give an accurate picture of the three components that interact to form the reading process for all students: (1) the student, (2) the text, and (3) the context of the reading situation. The flexibility of informal measures allows the teacher to do an interactive diagnosis (Lipson, et al., 1984; Wixon and Lipson, 1986; Wixon, 1987). Thus, the teacher can gather information on how *students'* abilities, backgrounds, and interests prepare them to read various types of *texts* in the context of many school *situations*.

Informal tests allow us to personalize diagnosis to the needs of the *student*. Students come to reading with different backgrounds, interests, and attitudes. For example, a student may have a detailed knowledge of and considerable interest in athletics, but little in history. When asked to read about sports, this student would achieve a considerably higher instructional level than when asked to read historical passages. Informal diagnosis allows teachers to note such differences and to use them in planning instruction.

Informal diagnosis also enables the teacher to adjust to students' differing attitudes and abilities in reading. Certain students are shy, and may need considerable teacher probing and encouragement before they can supply answers to questions. Other students behave differently from day to day, and teachers may need to read-minister measures several times in order to gather accurate information. Since informal measures have not been standardized, teachers can feel free to make modifications in test procedures, or to administer informal measures several times. In this way, teachers probe a student's responses.

Informal measures also enable the teacher to see how students perform on a variety of *texts*. Using informal measures, teachers can ascertain how students cope with a chapter or book, rather than the one-page selections that are often given in formal tests. They can also see how students read both informational texts and stories.

Finally, informal testing allows us to observe reading in a variety of *situations*. The tasks students must perform in formal tests are often limited to word and paragraph reading. However, using informal measures, teachers can assess tasks similar to the ones that students are performing in their classrooms. Thus, a resource teacher might ask a sixth-grade student to read silently an entire social studies chapter and answer the questions at the back of the chapter in writing. This teacher might also want to observe the student reading in the regular classroom. Information obtained in varied situations gives the complete picture of reading which will help resource teachers to plan effective instruction.

To summarize, informal measures allow teachers the flexibility to adapt assessment so that it gives maximum information about students, texts, and situations, and how these three factors interact to affect reading. In this way, teachers can best determine how students can meet the demands of school reading.

INFORMAL READING INVENTORIES

Informal reading inventories (IRIs) provide one of the best clinical tools for observing and analyzing reading performance and a wide range of reading strategies. The IRI is an individual test that can either be purchased or constructed by teachers.

In 1946, Betts observed many inadequacies of existing formal reading tests. He found that scores on these tests did not give enough information for a comprehensive reading diagnosis. In addition, the existing tests did not permit the teacher to observe pupils reading the types of reading materials used in classrooms. To overcome these inadequacies, Betts suggested using an informal reading inventory.

In an informal reading inventory, a student reads actual material from textbooks at different grade levels. Thus, a teacher can see how the student functions in classroom material. This information is often more useful and realistic than the results of a standardized test. In addition, the IRI enables teachers to answer specific instructional questions efficiently and to understand the nature of the student's reading (Johnson, Kress, and Pikulski, 1987).

The IRI is an individual measure. Since the teacher gives it to one student at a time, there is much opportunity for observation. The test is extremely useful in providing information for both the general and specific phases of diagnosis. In the *general* phase, a teacher can determine the student's level of reading—how the student functions while reading actual instructional material. Using instructional materials, the teacher determines three levels of reading: independent, instructional, and frustration. In addition, in the general phase, the teacher can compare performance in major areas of reading. In the IRI, a student both reads passages orally and answers comprehension questions. These procedures make it possible to compare the student's word recognition with the level of comprehension. In addition, the IRI requires a student to listen to stories as well as read them. This allows the teacher to compare listening and reading comprehension, giving teachers insight into the student's language abilities.

In the *specific* phase, the IRI provides information about the strategies a student uses for word recognition by analyzing oral reading in depth. Diagnostic insight in comprehension may be gained through comparing oral and silent reading comprehension, and by seeing how a student responds to different types of questions.

Finally, during the administration of an IRI, a teacher has many opportunities to observe students' attitudes toward reading: Do they read eagerly? Do they see reading as a meaning-gaining process? Do they become frustrated easily? The insights that teachers can gain through the administration of this measurement are of great value.

However, IRIs, like other assessment tools, have some limitations. Examiners, especially untrained ones, can miss oral reading miscues (Pikulski and Shanahan, 1982). In addition, a student's performance on a passage may be greatly affected by interest in the subject, background knowledge, and text organization (Caldwell, 1985, Lipson, et al., 1984). Some teachers administer several passages at each level to obtain a fuller view of the student's reading abilities.

To obtain the greatest diagnostic value, teachers need to prepare carefully for administration of the IRI. They need to use professional observation and judgment to translate effectively IRI results into instructional decisions. In short, the IRI is only a tool for your use in gathering diagnostic information.

Administering and Scoring
the Informal Reading Inventory

The steps for conducting, scoring, and analyzing the informal reading inventory are illustrated in Figure 5.1.

The informal reading inventory consists of a series of graded reading selections. Briefly, the student reads from sequentially graded selections until the material becomes too difficult. Often the test is constructed so that the student reads two passages at each grade level, one orally and one silently. After each passage is read, the teacher asks the student to answer comprehension questions. Starting with easy selections and continuing on to increasingly difficult passages, the student finally reaches a frustration level. This is the level at which oral reading becomes difficult or the student can no longer answer the comprehension questions satisfactorily. Throughout the test, the teacher records (1) any differences between the student's oral

Figure 5.1   Flow Chart for Administering and Scoring the Informal Reading Inventory

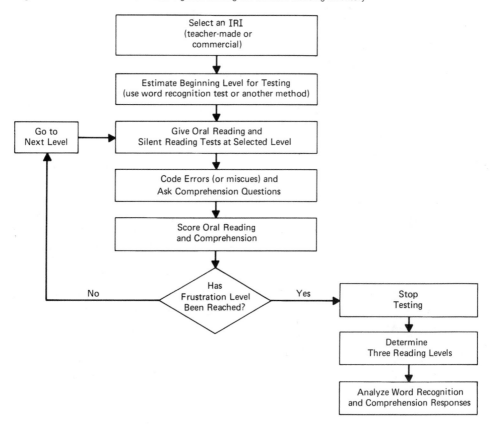

reading and the words in the text and (2) the student's responses to the comprehension questions.

There are many different types of IRIs. Some are published as separate tests; others are available with basal reading series; teachers may also construct their own IRIs. Whatever type you choose, remember that an IRI is informal, and the teacher can make adaptations to meet changing purposes and needs. The directions we give for administration are based on the IRI in Appendix D. Field testing (Kushner and Stecker, 1987) shows these directions to yield dependable results with this IRI and with other teacher constructed inventories. However, most commercial IRIs provide directions for administration, and these may vary in some details from the ones in this book.

To give the IRI, select a period of about an hour to work with an individual student. To avoid fatigue, testing may be divided into two periods. Seat the student across from you. The student will read (both orally and silently) from the student's copy of a passage. As the student reads orally, you record the student's performance on another copy. To keep the coding from being noticed, use a testing easel or place the scoring pad against or below the table. Since the reading inventory is different from other tests, prepare students by explaining that they will read selections both orally and silently, that they will be asked questions on the material, and that the selections will become more difficult as they go along.

Word Recognition Test. A word recognition test is often given prior to the reading of the IRI passages as a quick way to estimate the student's reading ability and to determine where to begin the testing of the reading passages. The student reads from word lists, which are graded lists of words. There is one word list for each level, from the preprimer level through grade six. (Directions for constructing word lists are given later in this chapter.)

Students read from these word lists, starting with the easiest list. Words can be exposed one at a time by covering the list with a blank sheet of paper and moving the paper down as the student reads. The teacher records the responses on the teacher's copy. The graded word lists are administered until the student scores below 60 percent on any list (for example, eight errors out of twenty words). However, the teacher uses the highest grade level at which the student performs at about 80 percent correct to indicate where to begin testing on the reading passages.

Performance on the word list can give the teacher much diagnostic information. Table 5.2 shows a sixth grade boy's performance on a second grade word recognition list. The complete recording of each response provides a basis for diagnostic information. An examination of the scored test (Table 5.2) shows that this student makes use of phonics but relies only on the beginnings of words as clues to identification. Some teachers find it very helpful to separate performance on the word recognition test into two columns: one column is used to record performance on instantly recognized words (sight words) and one column is used to record performance on words recognized after analysis.

Table 5.2   Scored Word Recognition Test

SECOND GRADE LEVEL	INSTANT RESPONSE	ANALYSIS RESPONSE
field	C	
banana	C	
mine	C	
awoke	away	c
sidewalk	C	
chocolate	C	
twenty	C	
week	C	
skin	C	
drop	drape	drew
cage	C	
bicycle	C	
yesterday	C	
splash	splat	splash
till	C	
between	C	
coal	C	
what	C	
policeman	poleman	postman
frighten	C	
% Correct	80 % instant	85 % Total

Reading Passages.   A first task in administering the reading passages test is to decide where to start testing, that is, the appropriate difficulty level of the beginning reading passage. This level can be determined in several ways: (1) give a word recognition test (as described); (2) use the information from previous achievement test scores; or (3) begin testing two levels below the student's present grade level. If the student performs very poorly on the first passage, testing should continue at an easier level.

At each reading grade level, the student reads a passage orally and then another passage silently. Before each reading, the student is given a brief introduction to the subject (e.g., "This is a story about a circus"). During the reading, the teacher records any differences between the text and the student's oral reading on a duplicate copy of the passage. Some reading specialists also time the reading with a stopwatch, a procedure appropriate for students of intermediate grade level or higher. If the student appears to be nervous about the timing, use a watch with a second hand or a digital watch. After reading each oral and silent passage, the student is asked comprehension questions. The test proceeds with increasingly difficult selections until the frustration level is reached.

Coding Oral Reading. It is important to write all of the student's variations from the text (or miscues) so that it will be possible to look back at the protocol at a later time and reconstruct the student's performance. Some teachers find it helpful to use a tape recorder so that they can later verify their coding. Even experienced examiners sometimes make inaccurate transcriptions of student's oral reading (Page and Carlson, 1975). Students can be put at ease when a tape recorder is used if they are asked to help the teacher operate the machine.

Commercial Informal Reading Inventories (IRIs) generally provide their own coding system. For teachers who construct their own IRIs, or use the one in Appendix D, we suggest the following coding system.

1. *Omissions:* circle ⟨on the table.⟩   *little*
2. *Additions:* insert word added above a caret   *on the ˄ table*
3. *Substitutions, mispronunciations:* write the word the student says above the word in
   toast
   the text and underline the substituted word: *on the <u>table</u>.*
4. *Repetitions:* draw a wavy line below the words   *on the table.*
5. *Reversals:* same as substitutions.
6. *Examiner aid:* if the student hesitates for more than ten seconds and cannot continue, tell the student the word and write "P" above the word for "pronounced." (Note: pronouncing the word for the student might inflate the comprehension score. Therefore, many authorities suggest that the examiner should not supply the word during the administration of the IRI.)

For a more complete transcription, some teachers add the following coding symbols:

- Words pronounced correctly, but with hesitations:
- Words that have been corrected spontaneously:
- Lack of punctuation: *I saw Mary. She was . . .* (This indicates the student ignored the period.)

An example of a coded IRI passage is shown in Table 5.3.

Scoring Oral Reading. Y.M. Goodman (1976) points out that some miscues (or differences between the text and a student's oral reading) actually show that the student is comprehending the passage. For example, in Table 5.3, the substitution of *sunny* for *light* showed that the student obtained the correct meaning.

We believe that the method of scoring oral reading should take into account the fact that the ultimate goal of reading is meaning. Therefore, miscues that do not affect the meaning of the passage (or minor miscues) should count less heavily than those that do affect meaning (or major miscues). For example, in the sentence "Those boys will not be permitted to go," a minor miscue would be substituting "these" for

Table 5.3 Sample IRI Passage

First grade level, oral passage
81 words
From:
MacMillan, *Lands of Pleasure*

Introduction: Did you ever go to the Food Fair at Carnival time?
                 We're going to read a story about two boys who will
                 be going to another kind of fair.

On the day of the fair, Ben got up as soon as it was light. After he had
something to eat he ran to the barn. He had to get his calf ready for the fair.
Tommy wanted to sleep, but he got up as soon as Ben did. He went with Ben
to the barn.
The boys looked in the barn. Ben's calf was not there! The two boys told their
father that Big Twin was not in the barn.

                                                    81 words

                                                    6 errors

                                        93% oral reading score

Scoring System: ◯   for omission   for repetition ᷍᷍᷍
                       ⋏   for insertion   for examiner aid *P*
        write word for substitution   corrected C

"Ready for the Fair" adapted from *The Little Twin* by Grace Paull. Copyright 1953 by Grace Paull. Reprinted by permission of Doubleday & Company, Inc.

"those." A major miscue would be substituting "permanent" for "permitted." The first does not affect comprehension as seriously as the second. We suggest that major miscues be counted as one full error and minor miscues be counted as one-half error.

Based on field testing of Kushner and Stecker (1987), we suggest additional criteria. The repetition of an entire phrase should be counted as one-half error if the phrase is continuous, and a one-word repetition should not be counted as an error at all. Also, if the same mispronunciation is made over and over, it should only be counted twice. In sum, we suggest the following criteria:

	MAJOR MISCUE (AFFECTS COMPREHENSION)	MINOR MISCUE (DOES NOT AFFECT COMPREHENSION)
Substitutions	1 Error	$\frac{1}{2}$ Error
Omissions	1 Error	$\frac{1}{2}$ Error
Additions	1 Error	$\frac{1}{2}$ Error
Reversals	1 Error	$\frac{1}{2}$ Error
Repetitions	—	$\frac{1}{2}$ Error (2 or more words)
Aid by examiner	1 Error	—

Some miscues should never be counted as errors. These include mispronunciations which are due to dialect differences, speaking English as a second language, immature speech patterns, or speech impediments. For example, a student who speaks a dialect other than Standard English might pronounce the word *tests* as *tes*. In such miscues, readers are simply recoding the written words into their own pronunciation. Pupils should not be penalized for such recoding.

Three other types of miscues should not be counted as errors: (1) spontaneous corrections (2) repetitions of only a single word (3) disregard for punctuation and hesitations. However, all three types of miscues should be noted for diagnostic analysis.

As the student reads, the teacher records each deviation from the printed text on a duplicate copy of the passage. After the reading selection is completed, the full errors and half errors are totaled. The percentage of correct words in the passage is computed to find the oral reading score. In the coded and scored passage in Table 5.3, there are 81 words, 6 errors, and 75 correct words. The percentage correct is therefore 93 percent.

$$\frac{75 \text{ (Words correct)}}{81 \text{ (Total words)}} \times 100 = 93\%$$

Table 5.4 presents a convenient way for finding the percentage of words correct in an oral reading passage. Simply find the intersection between the number of words in the passage and error count. For example, if the passage contains 150 words and the error count is 15, then the percentage correct is 90 percent.

Scoring Comprehension. After the student reads each passage, the teacher gives the student questions to check comprehension. If the answer is incorrect, the teacher writes the exact student response. A percentage-correct score is obtained for both oral and silent reading. For example, if the student answers 3 of 4 comprehension questions correctly, the comprehension score would be 75 percent on that selection. The oral and silent comprehension scores may be averaged to compute the average comprehension score at each level. The testing continues until the student reaches a frustration level. Table 5.5 gives the percentage correct scores for different numbers of comprehension questions.

Table 5.4 Table for Oral Reading Accuracy Score (each number indicates percentage correct)

NUMBER OF ERRORS

Words in Passage	1	2	3	4	5	6	7	8	9	10	11	12	13	14	15	16	17	18	19	20	21	22	23	24	25	26
28– 32	97	93	90	87	83	80	77	73	70	67	63	60	57	53	50	47	43	40	37	33	30	27	23	20	17	13
33– 37	97	94	92	89	86	83	80	77	74	72	69	66	63	60	57	54	52	49	46	43	40	37	34	32	29	26
38– 42	98	95	93	90	88	85	82	80	78	75	72	70	68	65	63	60	58	55	52	50	48	45	42	40	38	35
43– 47	98	96	93	91	89	86	84	82	80	78	76	73	71	69	67	64	62	60	58	56	53	51	49	47	44	42
48– 52	98	96	94	92	90	88	86	84	82	80	78	76	74	72	70	68	66	64	62	60	58	56	54	52	50	48
53– 57	98	96	95	93	91	89	87	85	84	82	80	78	77	75	73	71	69	67	66	64	62	60	58	56	55	53
58– 62	98	97	95	93	92	90	88	86	85	83	82	80	78	77	75	73	72	70	68	67	65	63	62	60	58	57
63– 67	98	97	95	94	92	91	89	87	86	85	83	82	80	78	77	75	74	72	71	69	68	66	65	63	62	60
68– 72	99	97	95	94	93	92	90	88	87	86	84	83	82	80	79	77	76	74	73	72	70	69	67	66	64	63
73– 77	99	97	96	94	93	91	90	89	87	86	85	84	83	81	80	79	77	76	75	73	72	71	69	68	67	65
78– 82	99	98	96	95	94	92	91	90	89	88	86	85	84	82	81	80	79	78	76	75	74	72	71	70	69	68
83– 87	99	98	96	95	94	93	92	91	89	88	87	86	85	84	82	81	80	79	78	76	75	74	73	72	71	69
88– 92	99	98	97	96	94	93	92	90	89	89	88	87	86	84	83	82	81	80	79	78	77	76	74	73	72	71
93– 97	99	98	97	96	95	94	93	91	90	90	89	88	86	85	84	83	82	81	80	79	78	77	76	75	74	73
98–102	99	98	97	96	95	94	93	92	91	90	89	88	87	86	85	84	83	82	81	80	79	78	77	76	75	74
103–107	99	98	97	96	95	94	93	92	91	90	89	88	87	86	85	85	84	83	82	80	79	79	78	77	76	75
108–112	99	98	97	96	95	94	93	92	92	91	90	89	88	87	86	85	84	83	82	81	80	79	79	78	77	76
113–117	99	98	97	96	96	95	94	93	92	91	90	89	88	87	86	85	85	84	83	82	81	80	80	79	78	77
118–122	99	98	98	97	96	95	94	93	92	91	90	90	89	88	87	86	85	84	84	83	82	81	81	80	79	79
123–127	99	98	98	97	96	95	94	94	93	92	91	90	90	89	88	87	86	85	84	84	83	82	82	81	80	79
128–132	99	99	98	97	96	95	94	94	93	92	92	91	90	89	88	87	87	86	85	84	84	83	82	82	81	80
133–137	99	99	98	97	96	95	95	94	93	93	92	91	90	90	89	88	87	86	85	85	84	83	83	82	81	81
138–142	99	99	98	98	97	96	95	94	94	93	92	92	91	90	89	88	88	87	86	85	85	84	83	83	82	81
143–147	99	99	98	98	97	96	95	95	94	93	93	92	91	90	90	89	88	87	86	85	85	84	84	83	82	82
148–152	99	99	98	98	97	96	95	95	94	94	93	92	91	91	90	89	88	88	87	86	86	85	84	84	83	83
153–157	99	99	98	98	97	97	96	95	94	94	93	92	92	91	90	89	89	88	87	86	86	85	85	84	83	83
158–162	99	99	98	98	97	97	96	95	95	94	93	93	92	91	90	90	89	88	88	87	86	86	85	85	84	84
163–167	99	99	98	98	97	97	96	95	95	94	94	93	92	91	91	90	89	88	88	87	87	86	86	85	84	84
168–172	99	99	98	98	98	97	96	96	95	94	94	93	92	92	91	90	90	89	88	88	87	86	86	85	85	85
173–177	99	99	98	98	98	97	96	96	95	95	94	93	93	92	91	91	90	89	89	88	87	87	86	86	85	85
178–182	99	99	98	98	98	97	97	96	95	95	94	94	93	92	92	91	90	90	89	88	88	87	87	86	86	85
183–187	99	99	98	98	98	97	97	96	96	95	94	94	93	93	92	91	91	90	89	89	88	88	87	87	86	86
188–192	99	99	98	98	98	97	97	96	96	95	95	94	93	93	92	92	91	90	90	89	88	88	88	87	86	86
193–197	99	99	98	98	98	97	97	96	96	95	95	94	94	93	92	92	91	91	90	89	89	88	88	87	87	86
198–202	100	99	98	98	98	97	97	96	96	95	95	94	94	93	93	92	91	91	90	90	89	89	88	88	87	87
203–207	100	99	99	98	98	97	97	96	96	95	95	94	94	93	93	92	92	91	90	90	89	89	88	88	87	87
208–212	100	99	99	98	98	97	97	96	96	95	95	94	94	93	93	92	92	91	91	90	89	89	89	88	88	87
213–217	100	99	99	98	98	97	97	96	96	96	95	95	94	94	93	92	92	91	91	90	90	89	89	88	88	87
218–222	100	99	99	98	98	97	97	96	96	96	95	95	94	94	93	93	92	92	91	90	90	89	89	88	88	88
223–227	100	99	99	98	98	97	97	96	96	96	95	95	94	94	93	93	92	92	91	91	90	90	89	89	88	88
228–232	100	99	99	98	98	98	97	97	96	96	95	95	95	94	94	93	92	92	91	91	90	90	89	89	89	88
233–237	100	99	99	98	98	98	97	97	96	96	95	95	95	94	94	93	93	92	92	91	91	90	90	90	89	89
238–242	100	99	99	98	98	98	97	97	96	96	96	95	95	95	94	94	93	93	92	92	92	91	90	90	90	89

NUMBER OF WORDS IN PASSAGE

Table 5.5   Table For Comprehension Accuracy Score (each number indicates a percentage-correct score)

NUMBER OF CORRECT RESPONSES

		1	2	3	4	5	6	7	8	9	10	11	12
NUMBER OF QUESTIONS	1	100											
	2	50	100										
	3	33	67	100									
	4	25	50	75	100								
	5	20	40	60	80	100							
	6	17	33	50	67	83	100						
	7	14	26	43	57	71	86	100					
	8	12	25	38	50	62	75	88	100				
	9	11	22	33	44	56	67	78	89	100			
	10	10	20	30	40	50	60	70	80	90	100		
	11	9	18	27	36	45	55	64	73	82	91	100	
	12	8	17	25	33	42	50	58	67	75	83	92	100

Reading Levels Obtained from the Informal Reading Inventory

In the general phase of reading assessment, discussed earlier, the teacher determines the level of a student's reading. The IRI readily provides this information by giving three different levels of reading—independent, instructional, and frustration. Each of these is expressed in terms of a grade level (from preprimer through eighth grade). By knowing the student's functional levels of reading, the teacher can select reading materials for various purposes. Thus, a unique and valuable assessment feature of the informal reading inventory is that the scoring system can be translated directly into guidelines for selecting classroom materials. Remember, however, that reading levels may vary, depending upon, for example, how familiar a student is with the subject matter of a specific passage.

Reading levels are based on performance on the reading passages and do not include scores from the word lists. Levels are based on (1) the oral reading score and (2) the average comprehension score (of oral and silent passages). Field testing (Kushner and Stecker, 1987) shows that the criteria given below most closely agree with teacher placement for disabled readers when miscues are scored according to the procedures we have given.

Criteria for Three Reading Levels

READING LEVEL

	Oral Reading		Comprehension
INDEPENDENT	95–100%	and	90–100%
INSTRUCTIONAL	90–95%	and	70–90%
FRUSTRATION	Less than 90%	or	Less than 70%

Independent Reading Level. The reader can handle material at this level easily and independently, without assistance from the teacher. This is the level to be used for free or recreational reading.

Oral reading: 95–100 percent
and
Average comprehension: 90–100 percent

Instructional Reading Level. At this level, the reader makes some errors and requires instructional aid to benefit from the reading. The teacher anticipates the difficulties and plans appropriate instruction. Students should be placed in instructional level materials for most work with a teacher.

Oral reading: 90–95 percent
and
Average comprehension: 70–90 percent

Frustration Reading Level. At this point, the material becomes too difficult for the reader, even with assistance. This level should be avoided because effective learning cannot occur. (The reading teacher can provide a real service to classroom and subject area teachers by finding books at the student's instructional level.)

Oral reading: below 90 percent
or
Average comprehension: below 70 percent

When administering an IRI, it is sometimes difficult to determine when a stable frustration level has been reached. If a student falls only slightly below the frustration criteria, teachers should continue testing to make sure the frustration level has been reached.

Listening Comprehension Level. In addition to the three reading levels, the IRI enables the teacher to obtain an assessment of the student's listening level. After the three reading levels have been determined, the teacher reads passages aloud to the student, starting at the frustration level, and then asks comprehension questions about the passages. The highest level at which the student gets 70 percent or more of the answers correct is the listening level. This listening level provides a rough estimate of the student's level of understanding language (receptive language). It is used by some diagnosticians as one measure of the potential for reading. If we find that a student's listening level is higher than the reading level on the IRI, we may conclude that this student's current language potential is higher than the level at which he or she is now reading. The listening level and its interpretation also are discussed in Chapter 4.

Other Criteria for Determining Reading Levels.   The original criteria for determining reading levels suggested by Betts (1946) were

	ORAL READING	COMPREHENSION
Independent level	99%	90%–100%
Instructional level	95%	75%–90%
Frustration level	below 90%	50% or below

We suggest that the Betts criteria be modified for two reasons. (1) Using the Betts criteria, the student's reading level is unclear when oral reading falls between 90 and 95 percent or when comprehension falls between 50 and 75 percent. (2) The Betts criteria are quite stringent because he suggested that students read a passage silently before reading orally, a practice that is not currently in use. Certain modifications for the criteria were suggested by Powell (1970). The criteria we suggested in this text (given in the previous section) combine both elements of Betts and Powell, and reflect our research in developing an informal reading inventory with disabled students (Kushner and Stecker, 1987).

Interpreting the Scores
of the Informal Reading Inventory

The summary page (shown in Figure 5.2) is useful for recording the IRI scores for word recognition, oral reading accuracy on passages, oral reading comprehension, silent reading comprehension, average comprehension (the average of oral and silent passages), and listening level. (A blank form of the IRI summary page is provided in Appendix D.) Teachers can use this summary sheet and the exact recording of the student's reading to obtain many different types of information from an informal inventory.

General Diagnosis.   The case of Deepika illustrates how to obtain general diagnostic information. Deepika is a sixth-grade student whose IRI is summarized in Figure 5.2. In terms of reading levels, her independent level is 3, her instructional level is 4, and her frustration level is 5. (These levels may vary somewhat depending upon the type of material Deepika is reading and her reading situation.)

The general phase of Deepika's diagnosis also includes an assessment of language development through her listening level. Deepika's current language potential (or listening level) on the informal reading inventory is grade 6, her grade placement level. Thus, her language level is two years above her current instructional level, which is 4.

Since Deepika both read orally and answered comprehension questions, we can compare the relationship of two major areas of reading, word recognition and comprehension.

	Used to Compute Reading Level		Used to Compute Reading Level			
Level	(1) Word Recognition Scores		Passage Scores				(6) Listening Level
	(Instant) / Total	(2) Oral Reading Word Accuracy	(3) Oral Comprehension Score	(4) Silent Comprehension Score	(5) Average Comprehension Score	
PP	(100) 100					
P	(90) 90					
1	(85) 90					
2	(80) 85	100%	100%	100%	100%	
3	(60) 65	99%	90%	90%	90%	
4		99%	70%	80%	75%	
5		98%	50%	40%	45%	80%
6						70%
7						50%
8						

Estimated reading levels:
Independent level _____3_____
Instructional level _____4_____
Frustration level _____5_____
Listening level _____6_____

Figure 5.2   IRI Summary Page for Deepika

Figure 5.2 shows that Deepika's oral reading of passages (column 2), is nearly perfect and always at the independent level (95–100%). In contrast, many of the comprehension scores in columns 3 and 4 are at the instructional level (70–90%) or at the frustration level (below 70%). This shows that Deepika's oral reading, or word recognition skills, are stronger than her ability to comprehend.

Specific Diagnosis: Word Recognition.   An analysis of a student's oral reading in passages reveals the strategies that the student is using. Miscues, that is, mismatches between the text and what the student says, provide diagnostic opportunities to analyze a student's reading strategies.

Some miscues show that the student is using meaning, or contextual clues. A student might substitute a word that makes sense in the context, for example, "kleenex" for "handkerchief." As we know, readers bring a vast store of knowledge and competence to the reading act. When students use contextual clues, they are bringing meaning to reading. The use of contextual clues often shows a positive effort to preserve comprehension (K.S. Goodman, 1965; Goodman and Gollasch, 1980-81; Y. Goodman, 1976).

Other miscues show that the student is using phonics clues to attempt to recognize words. In this case, the words substituted contain many of the same sounds as the words that are in the passage. However, the miscues often do not make sense in context. In fact, sometimes they are not even real words. Students who are overly dependent on phonics may laboriously sound out words, hesitating so long that they lose the meaning of the passage.

An exact recording of oral reading can be analyzed to see which strategies a student tends to use. In the example below, the first student is using contextual clues, while the second is using phonics.

Example 1. *Use of Context Clues*

~~On~~ the day of the fair, Ben ~~got~~ up as soon as it was light. After he had something to eat,
<small>a</small> <small>woke</small> <small>sunny</small> <small>good</small>

he ran to the barn. He ~~had~~ to get his ~~calf~~ ready for the fair.
<small>wanted</small> <small>cow</small>

Example 2. *Use of Phonics Clues*

On the day of the ~~fair~~, Ben got up as ~~soon~~ as it was light. After he had ~~something~~ to eat,
<small>far</small> <small>sun</small> <small>somebody</small>

he ~~ran~~ to the ~~barn.~~ He had to get his ~~calf~~ ready for the ~~fair.~~
<small>runs</small> <small>bank</small> <small>cat</small> <small>far</small>

"Ready for the Fair" adapted from *The Little Twin* by Grace Paull. Copyright 1953 by Grace Paull. Reprinted by permission of Doubleday & Company, Inc.

It is important that students learn to employ both contextual and phonics clues so that they can effectively recognize unknown words and read with comfort and efficiency.

There are several other aspects of oral reading that may be noted when analyzing an IRI.

1. *Substitutions, mispronunciations.* These are the most frequent types of miscues. They may reflect the use of contextual or phonics clues. Barr (1972) found that students taught by phonics methods tended to produce nonsense substitutions using phonics. Those taught by sight word methods produced real words.
2. *Omissions.* Some omissions, particularly those of word endings, may be due to language differences. These should not be counted as errors. In addition, students who

do not read carefully may skip over some words; these are not serious errors if meaning is kept intact. Other students who have trouble with longer words may simply pronounce the first syllable, indicating a need for instruction in word analysis skills. Students who tend to omit whole lines or sections may need a visual examination.

3. *Additions.* Words added to the text often represent an attempt to smooth out the meaning of the passage. If students have misread one word, they will often add additional words so that the entire sentence will be grammatical.

4. *Reversals.* Most beginning readers (of any age level) tend to make reversals. In fact, reversals are a hallmark of a primary reading level. However, if reversals seriously hamper reading progress, the teacher may need to try to eliminate them (see Chapter 9).

5. *Repetitions.* Repetitions may indicate that the student is attempting to work out words. If readers are having trouble with one word, they may repeat an entire phrase to check the meaning in context. Because this is a desirable process, repetitions are not considered a serious error. Sometimes repetitions are due to nervousness.

6. *Aid by examiner.* This is the most serious type of miscue. A student who relies on aid has an inadequate sight vocabulary and possesses few other strategies for analyzing unknown words. Sometimes, students who rely on teacher aid actually possess word recognition skills (such as phonics or context) but they have not learned to use them during reading. Other students have simply become psychologically dependent on the teacher.

7. *Hesitations, spontaneous corrections, and disregard of punctuation.* Although these miscues are not counted as errors, they do indicate some difficulty with the reading process. Hesitations and corrections show that the reader does not recognize words instantly. Disregard of punctuation and expressionless reading often indicate severe discomfort with the passage or show that the student does not see reading as a meaning-gaining process.

When analyzing oral reading, keep in mind that the ultimate goal of word recognition is the ability to read fluently, so that the reader can focus attention on comprehension. Thus, if a student often hesitates, repeats words, or shows signs of discomfort, he or she is probably reading at too difficult a level, even if the student eventually recognizes all of the words. Such students need instruction and practice in reading fluency if they are to read at higher levels. Only when word recognition becomes automatic and comfortable will students be able to concentrate on comprehension.

Finally, when analyzing oral reading miscues, it is not desirable to include passages which are at the student's frustration level. Kibby (1979) found that including frustration level miscues in an analysis can give a distorted view of the reader's strategies. However, teachers may choose to analyze miscues from frustration-level passages separately.

Specific Diagnosis: Comprehension. The IRI can provide many insights into a student's reading comprehension processes. First, inventories that contain both oral and silent passages enable the teacher to compare oral and silent comprehension. Many remedial students have particular problems with silent reading. This may indicate that the student's reading is at such a low level that this student needs the feedback that oral reading provides. Or it may reflect a lack of practice in silent reading, perhaps because the classroom reading instruction is done orally.

Many IRIs provide a variety of types of comprehension questions, including factual questions, central thought questions, vocabulary questions, and so forth. A teacher may obtain a comparison of some of the components of comprehension by noting the types of questions that a student answers correctly. For example, a student who performs well only in factual questions demonstrates a need for understanding the nonliteral information (such as inferences and main thoughts) which may be obtained from text. However, due to the limited numbers of questions of each type and the difficulty of dividing comprehension into different skills, we must remember to view this analysis as tentative (Schell and Hanna, 1981).

Interactive Diagnosis and the IRI. As noted earlier, informal diagnosis is flexible enough to allow us to see how the three crucial factors in reading, the reader, the text, and the context of the reading situation, interact. When interpreting a student's performance on an informal reading inventory, we should note how the interaction of these three factors may have affected the results.

In terms of the *reader*, the examiner should consider the student's familiarity and interest in the subject of a passage, for these can markedly affect results. For example, if a student's comprehension is particularly low in one or two passages, try to determine the student's background information by asking a few questions. In a passage dealing with the topic of mining, ask the student what mining is, and what types of things are mined. If the student cannot answer these general questions satisfactorily, the teacher can provide some information about mining to determine if giving this background knowledge enables the student to comprehend the passage. Alternately, the teacher can substitute a passage, at the same grade level, on a topic with which the student is more familiar. The use of an alternate passage would give a more generous assessment of the student's reading abilities.

The nature of the *text* is important to reading. In fact, for any given student, it is often useful to think of a *range* of instructional levels, which depends upon the student's interest and knowledge of the text being read. This is supported by Newcomer (1985), Klesius and Homan (1985), and Lipson et al. (1984) who find that different commercial IRIs often place students at widely varying reading levels. Some passages contain literary words and intricate syntactic constructions which cause remedial reading students much difficulty. Scores obtained reading such texts should be interpreted with caution.

The *context* of the reading situation (or task) is also an important factor in reading. For example, we have found that when students are able to reexamine passages after reading, they are sometimes able to formulate the answers to difficult inferential questions. Other students will recognize more words correctly when the teacher reminds them to "sound it out" or "to use the meaning." Thus, through modifying the standard procedure of not allowing students to reexamine material or not giving them prompts, we gain considerable diagnostic information.

Through thoughtful analysis, the teacher can determine how the student, text, and situation interact to affect the results of an informal reading inventory. Sometimes, an alteration in the informal reading inventory procedure can yield useful information. The flexibility of the IRI allows the teacher to analyze and modify it to gain a broad picture of reading ability.

Commercial Reading Inventories

Several commercial reading inventories are available. These may be published separately or may accompany a basal reading series. There are several features to consider when selecting a commercial inventory. (1) Since the literary quality of the passages is the heart of an inventory, be sure to read the passages and decide if they are well written. (2) In the middle and upper grades, there should be expository (informational) as well as narrative (story telling or fictional) passages, since students of this age are required to read both types of material. (3) The passages should require only background information that students would reasonably be expected to know. (4) Finally, passages should be long enough to permit some meaningful comprehension to develop.

It is also helpful to have more than one passage at each level. This permits the testing and retesting of both oral and silent reading. IRIs that provide worksheets for teacher analysis are also convenient, as are those that permit materials to be photocopied.

Some commercial IRIs contain special features. For example, *The Bader Reading and Language Inventory* (see Test Inventory 6.1) contains a retelling measure of comprehension as well as questions. Many IRIs now provide readability formula information on the passages; some have been extensively researched with students having reading difficulties. (The IRI found in Appendix D also has both of these characteristics.)

Widely used commercial IRIs are listed in Test Inventory 6.1.

Constructing an Informal Reading Inventory

Informal reading inventories can be constructed readily by using a basal reading series. The chief advantages of developing one's own IRI are that it can be based upon materials the student is using, and that it is relatively inexpensive. Disadvantages are that constructing an IRI takes a great deal of time and requires a fair amount of technical knowledge.

To construct the IRI, the teacher must first select a basal reading series. It will be necessary to (1) select words for the graded word lists, (2) select passages for oral reading and silent reading, and (3) develop comprehension questions for the oral and silent reading passages.

Word Lists. The word lists contain twenty words selected randomly from new words for each difficulty level through grade six. Proper nouns (names, places) are excluded. It is usually unnecessary to test sight recognition beyond grade six. Selections can also be made from other available graded word lists.

Reading Passages. Each selection should be preceded by a motivational statement designed to orient the student to the subject of the passage. Two reading passages are selected at each reading level, one for oral reading and one for silent reading. The selections should become gradually longer as they increase in difficulty. The following guidelines for length are suggested: preprimer, 25–35 words; primer, 35–60 words; grade one, 75–100 words; grades two and three, 75–150 words; grades four and five, 160–220 words; grades six through ten, 200–400 words. Each selection should be able to stand alone, apart from the story from which it was taken, and still make sense and convey meaning. The teacher may wish to vary the kinds of samples selected to include narrative and expository material. Teachers should also keep students' background knowledge in mind when selecting passages.

The reading grade level for each selection on the IRI can be checked by using a readability formula. A readability formula is a method for checking the difficulty level of a passage. For reading materials at grade levels one through four, the Spache formula is often used (Spache, 1953). For reading materials at grade levels four or over, the Dale-Chall formula is useful (Dale and Chall, 1948). A convenient way to determine readability level is the Fry Chart, as shown in Figure 5.3 (Fry, 1968). To use the Fry Chart, the teacher finds the intersection of the number of syllables and the number of sentences in a 100-word passage.

Comprehension Questions. After reading each selection, the student is asked a series of comprehension questions. The questions should be of various types (facts, main idea, inference, vocabulary, sequence). As a guide, passages from grades preprimer and primer should contain four to five questions; passages from grades one to two should contain five to eight questions; passages from grades three and up should contain ten questions.

Questions with two-choice answers (such as yes/no, either/or) should be avoided since the student has a 50:50 chance of guessing correctly. Questions should be clear. For example, in a story in which a child awakens, dresses, eats breakfast, and leaves for school, the question, "Tell me what Bobby did after he got up," is not clear. The student could give a partial answer. A better question would be, "Name three things that Bobby did after he got up." The answer to the questions should depend upon reading the passage rather than upon prior knowledge.

READING MISCUE ANALYSIS

Reading miscue analysis is an assessment procedure which focuses on the student's miscues during reading in order to determine the underlying language processes that the reader is using. This procedure is carefully detailed in the *Reading Miscue Analysis* (RMI), Goodman, Watson, and Burke, (1987, see Test Inventory 6.1).

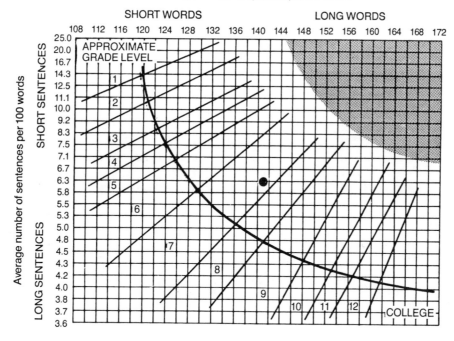

Average number of syllables per 100 words

Source: Edward Fry, reprinted from the *Journal of Reading*, April 1968, and *Reading Teacher*, March 1969. Reproduction permitted; no copyright.

Figure 5.3   Fry Readability Chart

From Edward Fry, *Reading Instruction for Classroom and Clinic* (New York: McGraw-Hill, 1972), p. 231).

The assessment procedure in the RMI is similar to the Informal Reading Inventory in some ways, but different in others. IRIs focus both on how well a student reads and on the processes the student uses to read. In contrast, the RMI focuses particularly on the process of reading.

In the *Reading Miscue Inventory*, the student is given one story of considerable length to read orally. To encourage production of miscues, the story should be at a level that is difficult enough to produce some reading deviations. As the student reads orally, the teacher marks all the miscues on a duplicate copy of the passage, using a coding system. The *Reading Miscue Inventory* contains passages and scoring sheets to help teachers put this procedure into practice (see Figure 5.4). After reading the selection, the teacher asks the student to retell the story. The story is scored for accuracy and completeness.

An essential part of the reading miscue procedure is the analysis of oral reading miscues. Goodman, Watson, and Burke (1987) suggest that six questions be asked about each miscue.

1. Does the miscue occur in a structure that is *syntactically* acceptable in the reader's dialect? (Syntactic acceptability)
2. Does the miscue occur in a structure that is *semantically* acceptable in the reader's dialect? (Semantic acceptability)

Partial reproduction of text and reader's miscues:

Ⓡ Ⓒ so 1
* "Why don't you do my work some day? I''ll
2 start house 3 keeping 4
stay home and keep house," said the woodman.

*The words "why don't you" were repeated.

Questions for reading miscues:

*READER	TEXT	1 SYNTACTIC ACCEPTABILITY	2 SEMANTIC ACCEPTABILITY	3 MEANING CHANGE	4 CORRECTION	See 2, 3, 4 MEANING CONSTRUCTION: No Loss	Partial Loss	Loss	See 1, 2, 4 GRAMMATICAL RELATIONSHIPS: Strength	Partial Strength	Overcorrection	Weakness	5 GRAPHIC SIMILARITY: H	S	N	6 SOUND SIMILARITY: H	S	N
so	some	P	P	–	Y	✓			✓				✓				✓	
start	stay	P	P	–	N		✓					✓	✓				✓	
house	home	P	P	–	N		✓					✓	✓				✓	
keeping	keep	P	P	–	N		✓					✓	✓			✓		

Figure 5.4 Miscue Analysis

*Coding sheet and passage from Goodman, Watson, & Burke, 1987.

3. Does the miscue result in a change of meaning? (Meaning change)
4. Is the miscue corrected? (Correction)
5. How much does the miscue look like the text? (Graphic similarity)
6. How much does the miscue sound like the expected response? (Sound similarity)

These questions help the teacher assess the student's reading strategies. For example, if the answers to questions 1 and 2 are yes, the student is probably making use of context and meaning clues in reading. On the other hand, if questions 5 and 6 are positive, the student is probably making use of phonics clues.

The results of the miscues' semantic acceptability (question 2), meaning change (question 3), and correction (question 4) are synthesized into categories which reveal how fully the student is constructing meaning from the text. Questions 1 (syntactic acceptability), 2, and 4 show how well the student is obtaining grammatical relationships. An analysis might show, for example, that the student is reading too cautiously. If the student self-corrects (question 4) a miscue that was syntactically appropriate (question 1) and semantically appropriate (question 2), then the correction was unnecessary, if reading is viewed as a meaning-getting process.

To illustrate miscue analysis more completely, a partial reading is given in Figure 5.4, and the student's miscues are presented along with an analysis.

The RMI is an excellent testing instrument for teachers who want an in-depth view of reading strategies on a long, difficult passage. The retelling comprehension check reveals comprehension strategies for recall and organization. However, teachers should remember that the RMI will not give a placement in instructional materials.

OBSERVATION OF READING

One of the most useful methods of assessing a student's reading behavior is through informal observation. Day-by-day observations by teachers who can respond immediately to the strengths and difficulties they observe are often as effective and even more practical than elaborate test batteries. Observation provides a way to assess many areas of reading not measured by tests, such as pupil interest, resistance to distractibility, and the ability to work independently.

Strang (1968) recognized the crucial importance of observation when she encouraged teachers to be "child watchers." Teachers should learn to observe students because through observation they can obtain valuable diagnostic information that can be put to immediate use. To observe successfully, teachers should have knowledge of behaviors and conditions associated with reading difficulties. They should also be familiar with techniques for gaining accurate, insightful observations. Finally, it is important to understand and be able to interpret the behavior observed in students.

The student can be observed on many occasions during the day: during testing sessions, teaching lessons, free time and playground periods, group activities, and independent work periods. Although observations are not always recorded, it is helpful at times to have a systematic recording of significant student behaviors. Such a record can be useful to the teacher, the student, or the parent. Records may be kept through anecdotal observations that are dated, recorded, and filed. (See Chapter 3.) Another way of recording observations is through a checklist. A sample observational checklist is given in Table 5.6.

Observation also provides the opportunity to learn about how the student actually is using reading and language in the classroom. This type of observation is strongly recommended by Y. Goodman (1978), who refers to it as "kid watching." Two types of information can be gathered:

1. Does the student use reading in the classroom? Does the student read signs and directions in the classroom or depend on others? Does the student read for pleasure? Is the student reading in an increasing number of situations?
2. Does the student apply language skills to reading? A student who substitutes the word "car" for "vehicle" is using language skills in reading.

Table 5.6   Observation Checklist

AREA	ADEQUATE	SOMEWHAT ADEQUATE	INADEQUATE	COMMENTS
General Observations				
Quality of classwork _____				
Independent working habits _____				
Impulsivity _____				
Response to teacher questions _____				
Following directions _____				
Participation in class _____				
General health and nutrition _____				
Interaction with peers _____				
Reading Attitudes				
Willingness to participate _____				
Willingness to read orally _____				
Willingness to read silently _____				
Willingness to read outside of lessons ___				
Reading Ability				
Oral reading fluency _____				
Ability to figure out unknown words ___				
Comprehension _____				
Ability to read longer selections _____				
Ability to use reading in content areas ___				
Rate of reading _____				

Teachers can also observe how students use writing and listening. For example, do students write independently? Do they like to write? "Kid watching" enables the teacher to observe the student's integrated use of language—including reading.

It is also important for resource teachers and clinicians to understand what reading activities are required of students in the regular classroom. Resource teachers should try to schedule regular sessions with the classroom teacher to discuss the class demands and student progress. It is helpful to ask for samples of a student's classroom assignments and work so that all teachers can better coordinate their programs. This information helps resource teachers to anticipate difficulties that the student may experience in the regular classroom and to provide supportive instruction (Allington and Shake, 1986).

CURRICULUM-BASED ASSESSMENT

Curriculum-Based Assessment involves a careful analysis of the student's daily work in the class based on direct and frequent measures of students' performance in an instructional curriculum (Tindal and Marston, 1986). Curriculum-Based Assessment (CBA) involves keeping detailed and continuous records of how well students are performing the tasks required of them in their classrooms. Through these records, resource and classroom teachers can make informed decisions about the appropriateness of the curriculum, and the student's progress.

For example, Deno, Mirkin, and Chiang (1982) used five curriculum-based measures to assess reading. Each of the measures was drawn from the student's basal reader. The five measures were (1) reading word lists orally, (2) reading excerpted passages aloud, (3) defining word meanings, (4) providing words deleted from passages (the cloze procedure), and (5) reading underlined words in excerpted passages.

DIAGNOSTIC MEASURES OF READING COMPREHENSION

Two useful methods of obtaining diagnostic information about reading comprehension are the retelling technique and the cloze procedure.

The Retelling Technique

By asking a student to retell a story or selection, the teacher can obtain many diagnostic insights into comprehension processes. Tierney and Pearson (1983) state that, when people read, they actually develop a text in their own minds which is parallel to the text that the author is presenting. As readers, we develop expectations, constructing a text in our own minds just as the author has constructed a text on the page. Good readers are able to construct a full, accurate text. Teachers can determine how well remedial readers construct a text by asking them to retell the story.

When asking a remedial student to retell a story, we encourage the student's active participation in the assessment process (Hittlemen, 1978; S.L. Smith, 1979). This contrasts with teacher-formulated comprehension questions, which require a short response, perhaps only one word. Further, when teachers formulate questions, they find out only whether the student knows what adults consider important in the story. Using the retelling technique, however, we find out what the *student* considers important.

Thus, retelling offers a unique opportunity to observe comprehension in action. It allows us to see how a student organizes a selection and what information in the text the student remembers.

However, since few objective guidelines for retelling have been developed, the retelling technique is more useful for gaining insight into the comprehension process than for determining an instructional level.

To obtain the fullest value from retelling, a student should be asked to read a full story or complete text selection. This will provide enough text structure to make the retelling worthwhile. The material should be read silently, not orally. In this way the student will be telling the story to a teacher who (presumably) does not know it already (S.L. Smith, 1979). The student first reads the story or selection and then retells it. The teacher should not interrupt as the story is told. When the student has finished, however, the teacher may prompt the retelling by asking the student to tell more about certain things. This is important, since problem readers often know more about a story than they will produce in free recall (Bridge and Tierney, 1981; Barr and Sadow, 1985). Students who are more practiced with the procedure will produce better retellings.

When assessing a retold story, remember that children's concept of story structure is developmental in nature and does not fully mature until the teen years. Since even normally achieving younger readers do not produce sophisticated retellings, the young remedial reader may have great difficulty with this task. Nevertheless, some guidelines may be given for judging retelling.

In stories (or narrative texts), teachers should look for

the presence of the major character(s)
the defining characteristics of the characters (eg., good, bad, curious)
the problem presented by the story
the solution to that problem (or the end)
events presented in sequential order
the ability to present important events at the expense of events not important to the story

Informative selections (expository text) may be used with intermediate and upper grade students. When dealing with expository material, look for

the main topics of the selection
the important facts about these topics

The Cloze Procedure

Cloze refers to rewriting a passage with words deleted, and asking students to fill in the deleted words.

The cloze procedure requires students to make use of their language system, especially their syntactic and semantic cue systems, to comprehend written language. Based on the Gestalt idea of closure, the cloze procedure capitalizes on a person's impulse to complete a structure and make it whole by supplying a missing element. By omitting every "*nth*" word (that is, every fifth word, or seventh word, or tenth word) in a printed passage, the reader is invited to complete the passage and supply missing words. The advantage of this technique is that the reader must bridge gaps in both language and thought to supply the missing elements. A sample cloze selection is shown in Table 5.7. Try to fill in the missing words.

Table 5.7   Cloze Selection

Often when people go _____ the movies, they find _____ a taller person is _____ in front of them. _____, they can't see over _____ person's head. If this _____ to a child, who _____ grown to full height, _____ or she may take _____ in the fact that _____ day they may be _____ tall adult. But for _____, who will grow no _____, the frustration of only _____ able to see half of _____ screen is permanent.

(Answers: to, that, sitting, sometimes, the, happens, hasn't, he, comfort, one, a, adults, taller, being, the).

If you correctly filled in nine blanks (which corresponds to 60 percent) you are reading at your independent level! As we can see from the experience of doing a cloze passage, it is highly unlikely that anyone will be able to supply correctly all of the blanks.

We recommend using cloze as an assessment tool only with intermediate and older students, since primary children will find the procedure extremely frustrating. Cloze has two advantages for assessment: it can easily be administered to a large group, and it frees the teacher from the difficulty of having to compose questions.

The cloze technique can be used for three purposes. (1) It can determine whether or not a student or group of students can read a particular book or selection. (2) It can give diagnostic insight into comprehension processes and needs. (3) It can be used as a teaching tool. (This third use will be covered in Chapter 10.)

To use cloze in order to see if students can read a certain book or selection, follow this procedure:

1. Choose at random two or more samples from each selection of graded material to be included using the following criteria:
   a. Begin at the beginning of the paragraph.

    b.   Use a continuous context.
    c.   Select passages containing at least 250 words.
  2. Delete every fifth word and replace the words with underlined blanks of uniform
      length.
  3. Duplicate the paragraphs and present them to the students. Instruct them to write
      the word that they think is appropriate in each blank. If the test is administered
      individually, the student may simply say the word.
  4. Score responses as correct when they exactly match the deleted words, disregarding
      minor spelling errors (as suggested by Bormuth, 1968).

These are general procedures, not fast and firm rules. Opinions vary about
how the cloze procedure is to be conducted. Among the suggested variations are leaving the first sentence intact and beginning word deletions with the second sentence.
The passage length may be shorter for younger students.

What do the scores on a cloze mean? A score of 44 percent means that a
student is on the instructional level, and can read this material with a teacher's guidance. A score of 57 percent correct means that the student can read the book independently (Bormuth, 1969).

Cloze Score	*Reading Level*
below 44 percent	Frustration Level
44 percent	Instructional Level
57 percent	Independent Level

Cloze tests generally take only one class period to administer and can help you to
choose instructional materials.

The cloze procedure can also be used to gain diagnostic insight into comprehension. When using it in this manner, feel free to vary the procedure. Two examples
will help to show how cloze can help teachers diagnose problems.

Dimitrius, a third grader, did not use word endings in his reading. His teacher
reproduced a page from his reading book, and simply crossed out five word endings
(not the entire word). She then asked him to read the page orally, supplying the word
endings when they were omitted. Dimitrius was able to do this successfully. This
showed his teacher that he did have an underlying oral language understanding of
word endings, and that his problem with word endings was due to lack of attention
while reading.

A seventh grade teacher wanted to determine how much preparation for
reading a group of remedial children would need to read their social studies chapter
effectively. He selected several difficult terms from the chapter and located some sentences containing these words. Then he wrote the sentences on the board, omitting
the words. None of the students could supply the words. When the teacher then supplied the words for them, most of the students could not use the sentence context to
approximate the meanings of the words. This variation on the cloze procedure revealed that much background and vocabulary work would have to be done before the
students could read the chapter effectively.

Tailoring the cloze procedure to student needs, provides many diagnostic insights. Cloze can also be used for instruction (see Chapter 10).

ASSESSING STUDENT PERCEPTIONS OF READING

As part of the diagnostic process, it is useful to determine what the student thinks about reading. We present techniques for assessing two areas: student view of reading and concepts about print.

Attitudes toward Reading

The function that reading serves in our lives dramatically affects our motivation to read. Some remedial students view reading as something that takes place only during school reading time, or as an oral performance done for a teacher. Not surprisingly, such students develop little motivation to read. Good readers know that reading is an enjoyable activity that can serve many functions.

Harste and Carey (1979) suggest that reading takes place within three life settings or contexts.

1. A print context. This refers to the material the student is reading. For example, students usually react differently to a set of directions, a basal-reader school book, and a comic strip.

2. A situational context. Students react differently to a reading lesson than to reading for pleasure. They react yet another way when they are reading a note passed from a friend.

3. A cultural context. Reading assumes varying degrees of importance in different cultural contexts. The student may come from a subculture which does not value reading, or one that values it highly. The classroom is also a cultural context for reading. Teachers who display many books and reading materials, and who set aside a time and a place for reading, form classroom cultures that value literacy.

How may we best assess students' views of reading and the functions it serves in their lives? One way is simply by observing the student. Over a period of time, the teacher can note the presence of freely chosen books, newspapers, writing material, and other literacy material. Teachers will also be able to see if the student is willing to read, enjoys reading, and can gain meaning from reading.

Another informal diagnostic tool is simply to ask a student a series of questions about reading. The questions which follow were taken from Goodman and Burke (1980, p. 46), from Paratore and Indrisano (1987), and from Richek (1983–89).

How do you pick something to read?
How do you get ready to read?
When you come to a word you don't know, what do you do?
What is something you read that you liked?

What is the first thing that you read this morning?

What is the longest thing that you read yesterday?

Name something that you enjoyed reading. Why did you enjoy it?

Name something that you read at home.

Do you know adults who read? What do they read, and why do they read those things?

Do you like to read in class? Why?

Such questions reveal much about how students view reading. If students give narrow answers, or are unable to answer many of these questions, teachers should help them to broaden their perceptions of reading by bringing in varied and motivating types of reading materials. These can include notes, horoscopes, advice columns, form letters, parking tickets, directions, and many other materials that show how many ways reading functions in modern lives.

Concepts about Print

The research of Marie Clay (1966, 1979) shows that many young children who are at risk for reading failure lack the concepts that underlie an understanding of how printed materials work. Concepts such as reading from left to right, locating the front of a book, and distinguishing a letter from a word are necessary for successful reading acquisition. Clay's test *Concepts about Print* (Clay, 1985) assesses these basic concepts. In the Clay procedure, children take a book specifically written for the test (entitled either *Sand* or *Stones*, see Test Inventory 6.1) and respond to the teacher's requests for "help" as the teacher reads the book to them. The teacher asks the child twenty-four questions dealing with: (1) knowledge of the orientation of a book (front and back); (2) knowledge that the story is contained in the print rather than the pictures; (3) knowledge that we scan lines from left to right and follow them back down to the left; (4) knowledge of concepts such as word and letter; (5) knowledge of punctuation marks; and (6) ability to match capital and lower case letters.

If you are working with young children (five, six, and seven year olds) at risk, the *Concepts about Print* test is a valuable tool. Alternatively, some informal probing using a picture book will help to give you an approximate idea of a child's orientation to print.

First, hold up the book with the spine facing the child, and ask him or her to find the front of the book. Then, after opening the book, ask the child to point to what you will be reading, and see if the child points to the words or the pictures. After reading a few pages to the child, turn to a new page, and ask the child where you should start reading, where you should go next, and (at the end of a line) where you should go. This will tell you whether the child can consistently track from left to right, and down. Next, see if the child can point to the words of one line, word by word, as you read. Finally, ask the child to show you one word and one letter in the book. These procedures will give some indication of the child's knowledge of print conventions.

DIAGNOSTIC TEACHING

Teachers can obtain useful diagnostic information about students through simply teaching them and observing how they respond. For example, if a teacher wanted to select a word recognition method for a remedial student who was just beginning to read, the teacher could do some *trial teaching* to determine how the student best learned. The teacher could present several rhyming words which use the common phonics element *ay*, (*say, may, day*) and another set of words taken from the student's language experience story (a student-dictated story). The student's response to this trial teaching would help the teacher select the more effective and enjoyable teaching method. This method would then be used for instruction.

In another form of diagnostic teaching, the teacher could use a *school-based task* (or work sample). The teacher gives the student tasks similar to ones that form everyday school reading. This procedure allows the reading teacher to assess how a student functions in an everyday classroom environment. When doing a school-based task, follow the procedures that the classroom teacher actually uses. If the chapter is read silently in class, for example, use this reading mode in the diagnostic task.

To illustrate the school-based task, Ms. Silver wanted to observe how Manuel, a seventh-grade remedial student, functioned in history. Choosing a chapter he was about to begin in class, Ms. Silver first assessed background by asking Manuel what he knew about the topic. Then she asked Manuel to read the first section of the chapter silently and write out answers to the questions in the text (the procedure used in class). When Manuel finished, Ms. Silver asked him to summarize the section orally.

Ms. Silver then did some additional follow up. She asked Manuel to find two pieces of information in the text, noting how he located the information (eg., did he use headings, did he search for key words?). Next, to assess Manuel's word recognition fluency, Ms. Silver asked him to read two paragraphs from the chapter aloud. Finally, presenting two important terms from the text, she asked him to define them.

This school-based task revealed that Manuel's ability to recognize words, answer specific questions in writing, and locate information were well developed. However, in order to cope more effectively with history, he needed help in gaining background knowledge, summarizing material, and defining important terms.

In summary, through diagnostic teaching, the reading teacher offers instruction in order to see how students will respond. By being alert to the student's reactions, the instructor gains invaluable diagnostic clues for planning instruction.

SUMMARY

Reading assessment may be divided into general and specific levels. In the general phase, we assess a student's current reading level and identify major areas of reading strength and weakness. In the specific phase we determine more in-depth information of knowledge and use of reading strategies.

Reading assessment measures may be divided into formal and informal. Informal measures have not been normed on large populations (as have standardized tests) and may be used flexibly enough to gather information on the interactions among the student, text, and reading situation.

The informal reading inventory (IRI) consists of a series of graded reading selections. The student reads increasingly difficult material until a frustration level is reached. Many IRIs measure both oral and silent reading. Three levels of reading are obtained: the independent level, the instructional level, and the frustration level. These levels are based on the student's oral reading accuracy and ability to comprehend passages. Assessment of oral reading accuracy should take into account the fact that the goal of reading is to gain meaning. A listening level, which is one measure of language understanding, is also obtained from an IRI.

Informal reading inventories permit teachers to measure reading in school-like passages and to observe the student closely. However, the student's performance on IRI passages is influenced by prior knowledge and interest.

Commercial reading inventories are available, or teachers may construct their own inventories. To construct an IRI it is necessary to develop word lists, select passages for oral and silent reading, and develop comprehension questions for both oral and silent reading.

Reading miscue analysis focuses on the student's miscues (or deviations from print) during reading, analyzing the processes which underlie them.

Observation of reading is a valuable way to obtain diagnostic information. Resource teachers should try to observe students in their home classrooms.

In curriculum-based assessment (CBA) direct and frequent measures of students' daily work are used to formulate decisions.

Two informal methods for assessing reading comprehension are the retelling technique and the cloze procedure. Retelling requires a student to retell a story after it is read. In the cloze procedure, students must replace words that have been deleted from a passage.

Students' perceptions of reading are also important. Attitudes toward reading help to show how students use reading. Concepts about print help to determine if beginning readers understand how printed materials, such as books, words, and letters, work.

Diagnostic teaching uses the teaching session to obtain assessment information.

6

ASSESSING READING ACHIEVEMENT II
Formal Assessment

This chapter continues the discussion of methods for assessing reading achievement. In the previous chapter, we described informal reading measures. In this chapter we discuss formal reading tests.

INTRODUCTION

An overview of formal reading tests is presented first in this chapter. Then tests of general reading assessment and tests for diagnosing specific reading problems are presented. Next, guidelines are given for combining formal assessment with informal probing. The chapter concludes with guidelines for interpreting both norm-referenced and criterion-referenced tests.

OVERVIEW OF FORMAL READING TESTS

By formal tests, we mean commercially prepared, formally developed instruments. Many of these tests are *norm-referenced* or "standardized" tests. By using norm-referenced tests, the scores of a student being tested can be compared with the scores of the sample of students who were used to standardize the test (the "norm sample"). Norm-referenced tests have generally been developed carefully with a large number of students who are representative of the general population. To assure that a student's scores can, in fact, be compared with the norm sample, it is essential that procedures for test administration, scoring, and interpretation be followed strictly.

Other formal instruments are called *criterion-referenced* tests, and these are constructed from a different theoretical base. Rather than comparing students with one another, a criterion-referenced test determines whether a student has mastered certain competencies. Criterion-referenced tests are generally used to assess student mastery of specific reading skills.

There are several types of formal reading tests, each offering a different type of information. To obtain an accurate picture of the pupil's abilities, it is desirable to use a variety of assessment procedures, including formal as well as informal methods (Farr and Carey, 1986). Information obtained from one source can corroborate, check, or supplement that obtained from another. The diagnostician's skill consists of analyzing and coordinating all of the assessment data to formulate a coherent set of diagnostic conclusions and recommendations.

In formal testing, the teacher tries to assess the student's reading performance as accurately as possible. In contrast, informal testing is flexible, concentrating upon observation and the determination of reading strategies. In Chapter 5, we introduced a two-step framework for the phases of assessing reading: (1) *general reading assessment,* which determines the student's reading level and the general areas of reading strengths and weaknesses and (2) *specific reading assessment* which assesses strengths and weaknesses within a specific area, such as word recognition. In this chapter, formal tests are divided as follows: (1) formal tests that are used to assess *general* reading abilities (group survey tests, individual survey tests, normed oral reading tests, and literacy tests) and (2) formal tests that are used for *specific* or *diagnostic* reading assessment (diagnostic reading batteries and diagnostic tests of specific areas).

TESTS OF GENERAL READING ASSESSMENT

Tests of general reading assessment are used to assess a student's general level of achievement as well as to determine the general areas of reading strengths and weaknesses. Types of tests that are used in the general reading assessment phase include (1) group survey tests, (2) individual survey tests, (3) normed oral reading tests, and (4) literacy tests.

Group Survey Tests

Survey tests are norm-referenced tests that are used to assess the student's reading level. Both group survey tests and individual survey tests are used for this purpose.

Group survey tests are often used by classroom teachers to assess reading (as well as other academic areas) at the end of the year. Examples of group survey tests include the *Stanford Achievement Test,* the *Iowa Test of Basic Skills,* and the *Gates-MacGinitie Reading Tests.* Although they are designed for group testing of developmental readers, they also can be used for testing remedial readers in individual settings. The remedial reader's scores on the group survey test can be compared with those of the norm sample.

The total score on the group survey reading test is usually computed from at least two subtests: (1) a measure of reading vocabulary and (2) a measure of paragraph comprehension. Scores on these subtest sections may be compared to determine the major areas of reading difficulties. For example, a comparison of 12-year-old Katie's vocabulary grade equivalent subtest score of 6.1 with her comprehension subtest score of 3.2 shows a weakness of comprehension in relation to vocabulary. Survey tests for advanced students also measure study skills and reading rate.

A useful feature of most survey tests is that they have more than one form (e.g., Form A and Form B). The two forms are normed similarly and therefore can be compared readily. Progress can be monitored by giving Form A during the diagnosis and Form B after a considerable amount of instruction is completed.

Despite their excellent statistical properties, survey tests have some limitations for use with remedial readers. (1) Generally, the survey test given varies with the grade level of the student. Since most remedial readers read well below grade level, it is difficult to know which level of the survey test to give. For example, should an eighth-grader reading at a third grade level receive the eighth grade level test or the third grade test? This problem is solved to an extent by the "out-of-level" norms provided by some publishers. (2) Some research indicates that scores on group survey tests tend to overestimate the student's reading ability by six months to a year (Sipay, 1964;

Jones and Pikulsky, 1974; Bradley, 1976). (3) Survey tests contain tasks, such as reading single words and short paragraphs, that do not reflect the longer tasks children must do at school.

Some group survey tests contain unique features. The *Degrees of Reading Power* (DRP) is a group survey test which matches a student's abilities to the difficulty of text. The test, designed for students reading at grades three and above, contains a single subtest. Students are given short passages with deleted words (a cloze format), and then instructed to fill in the missing word from choices. This format helps insure that students have to read the passages in order to obtain the answer and, thus, are not answering a question correctly simply from background knowledge.

The student's score on the DRP is recorded as a number, or degree of reading power, ranging from approximately 35 to 90. In addition, many textbooks and other reading materials have been assigned a degree of reading power (or reading difficulty) which is scaled in the same way as the student's DRP test score. If the DRP of the student matches, or exceeds, the DRP of the text, the student can read the text comfortably. If not, the text is too difficult for the student. The DRP is unique in this direct matching of student ability and reading material difficulty. The College Board estimates that a DRP of 67 is a common standard for adult-level material (*News for Counselors*, 1985).

The DRP is a unique and valuable test. There have been, however, criticisms of it. Carver (1985) contends that it underestimates student ability at the lower grades, and overestimates ability at upper high-school and college levels.

Another group survey test which is useful for remedial readers is the *Stanford Diagnostic Reading Test* (SDRT). Since this is intended for use with low achievers, it contains more easy items than most achievement tests at the same levels. The four levels of the test cover reading levels from the end of grade one through grade eight. They are also suitable for older readers at low reading levels. The SDRT contains many subtests in decoding, vocabulary, comprehension, and rate. It is designed both as a general measure of reading ability and as an instrument for pinpointing specific strengths and weaknesses. The SDRT is both norm and criterion referenced.

Individual Survey Tests

Individual survey tests are used widely in assessing the reading level of remedial students. These achievement tests usually consist of one form, which is suitable for a wide range of reading abilities. Since an individual test might cover levels 1 through 9, it would be suitable for an older reader who is reading at a primary grade level. Individual survey tests are usually standardized and permit valid comparisons with the norm sample.

Administering an individual survey test also allows the teacher to observe the strategies that a reader uses when arriving at answers. For example, in a test of word recognition, the teacher can note whether the student hesitates or recognizes words instantly and whether words are sounded out. Thus, an individual test enables the teacher to gather some diagnostic information in the process of the general reading assessment.

The actual reading tasks that students are asked to perform vary greatly from test to test. Often, test authors use considerable ingenuity to make their tests shorter or to make them conform to a multiple-choice format. Unfortunately, the resulting tests may not actually measure the ability to read. Before using a test, the teacher should inspect the actual items to determine exactly what the student is asked to do. The name of a test, or of its subtests, may not reflect the content.

The three most widely used survey tests are the *Wide Range Achievement Test Revised* (WRAT-R), the *Peabody Individual Achievement Test* (PIAT), and the *Woodcock Reading Mastery Test, Revised* (WRMT-R). The WRAT-R contains a reading test consisting of a graded list of words for oral reading. A grade placement level is determined by having the student read this list. Although short and convenient to administer, this subtest does not present a comprehensive assessment of reading abilities. The WRAT-R also measures mathematics and spelling.

The reading sections of the *Peabody Individual Achievement Test* (PIAT) measure word recognition and comprehension. Word recognition is measured through oral reading of a list; in the reading comprehension subtest, students choose a picture that describes a reading paragraph. The PIAT also measures mathematics, spelling, and general information.

The *Woodcock Reading Mastery Tests, Revised* (WRMT-R) is an individual survey test which contains many diagnostic features. The test measures individuals from a beginning reading level through that of an advanced adult. It is available in two forms, and both forms can be jointly administered. The WRMT-R contains four basic subtests, (1) word identification, (2) word attack, (3) word comprehension, and (4) passage comprehension. These may be combined to obtain a full-scale reading performance assessment.

In the word identification subtest the student reads single words. In word attack, the student sounds out nonsense words. The word comprehension test requires the student to perform three separate tasks with vocabulary: provide antonyms, provide synonyms, and complete analogies to a word pair (e.g., *day* is to *night* as *up* is to _____). The vocabulary areas are divided into general reading, science and mathematics, social studies, and humanities. In the passage comprehension subtest, the student orally fills a missing word into a paragraph.

In addition, form G contains two subtests for beginning readers: (1) a visual-auditory test, taken from the *Woodcock-Johnson Psychoeducational Battery* (see Chapter 4) in which children are assessed on their ability to associate words to picture-like symbols and (2) a test of letter identification.

The WRMT-R also permits comparison with other tests authored by Woodcock. Detailed directions for scoring and interpretation are available, including computer-assisted scoring systems and audiotapes for teacher training.

The *Woodcock Reading Mastery Tests-Revised* contain many useful features and teacher aids. However, only in the reading comprehension subtest is the ability to read in context measured. Figure 6.1 details the structure of the test.

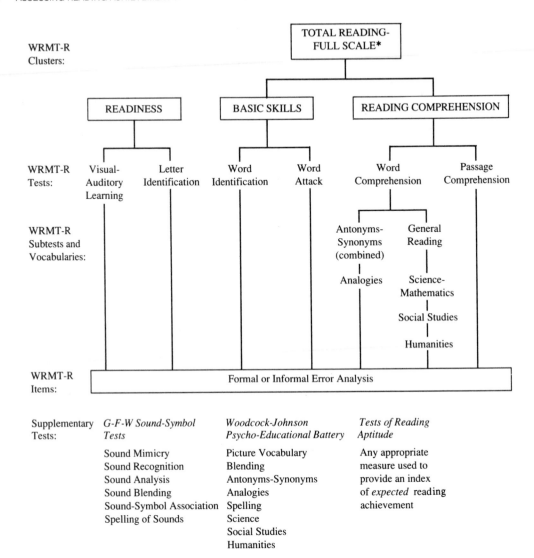

WRMT-R
Clusters:

TOTAL READING-
FULL SCALE*

READINESS   BASIC SKILLS   READING COMPREHENSION

WRMT-R
Tests:

Visual-
Auditory
Learning

Letter
Identification

Word
Identification

Word
Attack

Word
Comprehension

Passage
Comprehension

WRMT-R
Subtests and
Vocabularies:

Antonyms-
Synonyms
(combined)

General
Reading

Analogies

Science-
Mathematics

Social Studies

Humanities

WRMT-R
Items:

Formal or Informal Error Analysis

Supplementary
Tests:

*G-F-W Sound-Symbol
Tests*

Sound Mimicry
Sound Recognition
Sound Analysis
Sound Blending
Sound-Symbol Association
Spelling of Sounds

*Woodcock-Johnson
Psycho-Educational Battery*

Picture Vocabulary
Blending
Antonyms-Synonyms
Analogies
Spelling
Science
Social Studies
Humanities

*Tests of Reading
Aptitude*

Any appropriate
measure used to
provide an index
of *expected* reading
achievement

*Total Reading--Short Scale consists only of Word Identification and Passage Comprehension.

Figure 6.1   Structure of information included in the total interpretation plan for the *Woodcock Reading Mastery Test*-Revised.

Normed Oral Reading Tests

Normed oral reading tests, like informal reading inventories (IRIs discussed in Chapter 5), contain graded passages for oral reading. However, unlike IRIs, normed oral reading tests include statistical norms. These tests provide another way to obtain a general reading assessment.

Several normed tests of oral reading are available commercially. These include the *Gilmore Oral Reading Test* and the *Formal Reading Inventory*. Some diagnostic reading batteries also contain normed oral reading subtests. The analysis of oral reading and the rich diagnostic insights it provides were discussed in Chapter 5. Test Inventory 6.1, which is located at the end of this chapter, includes a description of several tests of oral reading.

Literacy Tests

Literacy tests are often used for the general reading assessment of older remedial readers who read at low levels. An increasing awareness of the problems of adolescent and adult illiterates has resulted in a number of tests that measure the ability to read functional material for everyday living. Material on these tests measure such skills as reading traffic signs, menus, and bills. These tests are often used in assessing minimal competencies for graduation requirements.

Some literacy tests are norm referenced; others are criterion referenced. Criterion-referenced tests are appropriate for use when the teacher wishes to determine whether or not a person possesses the specific skills to function in society. Literacy tests are described further in Test Inventory 6.1 at the end of this chapter.

TESTS FOR DIAGNOSING SPECIFIC READING PROBLEMS

Diagnostic reading tests yield more specific information than general reading tests. They provide a more detailed analysis of specific reading strengths and weaknesses and often permit the teacher to assess student strategies in reading. Two kinds of diagnostic tests described in this section are (1) diagnostic reading batteries and (2) diagnostic tests of specific areas.

Diagnostic Reading Batteries

A diagnostic reading battery consists of a group of subtests, each of which assesses a different component of reading. It is therefore useful for obtaining a profile of the remedial student in several areas.

Diagnostic reading batteries evaluate such areas as oral reading, phonics, and sight vocabulary. Some, such as the Spache *Diagnostic Reading Scales* contain complete oral reading tests, enabling the teacher both to administer an oral reading inventory and to assess a variety of other components of reading. Areas such as spelling may be covered as well. While most batteries are individual tests, some are group tests (e.g., the *Botel Reading Inventory*).

Although these batteries sample several components of reading, they are often more comprehensive in the areas of readiness and word recognition than in comprehension and word meaning. Typically, diagnostic batteries are more suitable for beginning readers.

In addition, many diagnostic reading batteries generally test skills in isolation, containing few subtests that enable us to see how students actually use these skills while they are reading. For this reason, we recommend that diagnostic reading batteries be used in conjunction with instruments containing actual reading and measures of comprehension.

Some additional cautions must be used when giving a diagnostic battery. Like any other measure, these tests cannot substitute for teacher observation and analysis of the reading problem. Teacher judgment is also important in choosing the parts of the test to administer. The teacher may not wish to administer an entire test, but just to give the sections relevant to a particular student. Finally, the teacher should examine the items on the subtests to ensure that they are actually testing the skills that are named in the test.

Some diagnostic batteries are normed, whereas others (e.g., the *BRIGANCE®* *Diagnostic Inventory*) are criterion referenced. While norming is useful, the norms for diagnostic batteries are seldom constructed as carefully as are those of survey tests. Thus, teachers should inspect the norming procedures of batteries carefully before placing confidence in them.

The *Gates-McKillop-Horowitz Reading Diagnostic Test* is an illustration of a diagnostic battery. The eight distinct parts of the test are illustrated by the scoring sheet reproduced in Figure 6.2. The battery contains an oral reading inventory, several tests of word recognition and readiness, and an assessment of spelling and writing. The oral reading test consists of one continuous passage that increases in difficulty, and there are only thirty words on any specific grade level. The grade placement score is based solely on oral reading, for no comprehension questions are asked. The many tests of sight vocabulary, phonics, and readiness require diverse tasks. Some involve primarily listening skills (such as the test of spoken vowel sounds); others assess reading skills. The inclusion of spelling and writing subtests reflects new trends toward viewing reading in a broader context. This battery was normed on only 600 students, a small sample compared with most survey tests.

The BRIGANCE® Inventories are another widely-used set of diagnostic batteries. They are criterion referenced. There are five different batteries (see Test Inventory 6.1). We will describe the *Brigance Diagnostic Inventory of Basic Skills* (Grades PreK-6).

The *Brigance Diagnostic Inventory* is a criterion-referenced test containing no norms. It covers a wide range of skills in readiness, reading, language arts, and math. The topics covered by the reading section are reproduced in Figure 6.3. Section B contains graded oral reading passages in the form of an IRI.

A student's performance on any subtest of the *Brigance Diagnostic Inventory* can be *directly* translated into an instructional objective. For example, if students do not "pass" the Long Vowel Subtest of the *Brigance Diagnostic Inventory*, the test provides a specific objective for them to master.

> When presented with one syllable words having the patterns "consonant, vowel-consonant, and final e" or "consonant, double vowel, consonant," the student will

PUPIL RECORD BOOKLET

Gates • McKillop • Horowitz
READING DIAGNOSTIC TESTS

SECOND EDITION

ARTHUR I. GATES
Professor Emeritus of Education

ANNE S. McKILLOP
Professor of Education

ELIZABETH CLIFF HOROWITZ
Adjunct Assistant Professor of Education

TEACHERS COLLEGE, COLUMBIA UNIVERSITY

Pupil's Name _____ School _____ Date _____

Age____ Birthday_____ Grade_____ Examiner_____ Teacher_____

Age, Grade, Intelligence				READING AND OTHER TEST SCORES			**1** Raw Score	**2** Grade Score (	**3** Ratings)|( )
Chronological Age		_____							
Grade Corresponding to Chronological Age		_____		Name of Test		Date Given			
Actual Grade		_____		1 _____					
Intelligence Testing: Name of I.Q. Test	_____			2 _____					
Date Administered	_____			3 _____					
I.Q.	_____								

READING DIAGNOSTIC TESTS

	Raw Score	Grade Score	Ratings ( ) ( )		Raw Score	Grade Score	Ratings ( ) ( )
Oral Reading				**Knowledge of Word Parts: Word Attack**			
Analysis of Total Errors				Syllabication			
Omissions				Recognizing & Blending Common Word Parts			
Additions				Reading Words			
Repetitions				Giving Letter Sounds			
Analysis of Mispronunciations				Naming Capital Letters			
Directional Errors				Naming Lower-Case Letters			
Wrong Beginning				**Recognizing the Visual Form of Sounds**			
Wrong Middle				Vowels			
Wrong Ending				**Auditory Tests**			
Wrong in Several Parts				Auditory Blending			
Accent Errors				Auditory Discrimination			
Total Mispronunciation Errors				**Written Expression**			
Reading Sentences				Spelling			
Words: Flash				Informal Writing Sample			
Words: Untimed							

Figure 6.2 Scoring Sheet for the Gates-McKillop-Horowitz Reading Diagnostic Test

II. READING

Test | **Title**

A. Word Recognition

A-1 Word Recognition Grade Level
A-2 Basic Sight Vocabulary
A-3 Direction Words
A-4 Abbreviations
A-5 Contractions
A-6 Common Signs

B. Reading

B-1 Oral Reading Level
B-2 Reading Comprehension Level
B-3 Oral Reading Rate

C. Word Analysis

C-1 Auditory Discrimination

Test | **Title**

C-2 Initial Consonant Sounds Auditorily
C-3 Initial Consonant Sounds Visually
C-4 Substitution of Initial Consonant Sounds
C-5 Ending Sounds Auditorily
C-6 Vowels
C-7 Short Vowel Sounds
C-8 Long Vowel Sounds
C-9 Initial Clusters Auditorily
C-10 Initial Clusters Visually
C-11 Substitution of Initial Cluster Sounds
C-12 Digraphs and Diphthongs
C-13 Phonetic Irregularities

Test | **Title**

C-14 Common Endings of Rhyming Words
C-15 Suffixes
C-16 Prefixes
C-17 Meaning of Prefixes
C-18 Number of Syllables Auditorily
C-19 Syllabication Concepts

D. Vocabulary

D-1 Context Clues
D-2 Classification
D-3 Analogies
D-4 Antonyms
D-5 Homonyms

©1976, 1977 Curriculum Associates, Inc.

Figure 6.3 BRIGANCE® Diagnostic Inventory of Basic Skills—Reading Sections

pronounce the vowel(s) with a long sound. He will be able to perform this task for _____ (quantity) of the five vowels. (Brigance, 1977, p. 54).

Thus, performance on a subtest may be immediately transferred to a specific goal. This feature makes the *Brigance Diagnostic Inventory* valuable for writing the Individual Education Programs (IEPs) required for special education students. It also helps reading teachers to formulate direct instructional goals.

Despite the convenience of this test, it should be remembered that it has no developed norms or studies of reliability and validity. Thus, while the *Brigance Diagnostic Inventory* is diagnostically useful, the teacher cannot assume that it will place students at appropriate grade levels. In addition, the *Brigance,* like many other tests, measures most elements of reading in isolation, with only modest provision for determining how students apply these in a reading context.

Diagnostic Tests of Specific Areas

Unlike diagnostic reading batteries, tests of specific areas concentrate on the in-depth evaluation of a specific reading area. The tests are particularly useful in gathering very detailed information about one area of reading, such as phonics. Diagnostic tests of one area may be group or individual, norm or criterion referenced. Tests of specific areas include, for example, the *Sipay Word Analysis Test* and the *Phonics Knowledge Survey.*

More recently, tests focusing upon the area of comprehension have been published. For example, the *Test of Reading Comprehension* (TORC) is based on a psycholinguistic view of reading. It analyzes several different aspects of the reading comprehension process. The four core subtests measure general vocabulary (the ability to choose words related to a common concept), syntactic similarities (identifying grammatically different sentences that have similar meaning), paragraph reading, and sentence sequencing (the ability to arrange five sentences in order). Supplementary tests include three vocabulary tests (math, science, social studies) and understanding written directions. Scores are reported as Reading Comprehension Quotients (distributed like IQ scores).

COMBINING FORMAL ASSESSMENT WITH INFORMAL PROBING

A formal test may be administered and scored according to directions, but then informally probed to obtain additional information. By doing informal probes of formal tests, the sensitive teacher is able to gain new perspective on the student's performance.

To illustrate the use of informal probes, we will describe two methods of probing a standardized achievement test (specifically, the *Gates MacGinitie Reading Test-Third Edition*) to answer additional diagnostic questions.

(1) Does a time limit affect a reader's performance? Eric, a fifth grader, took the *Gates MacGinitie Reading Tests-Third Edition*, level D (for grades 4–6) according to standard directions. However, his teacher noted that he was a slow worker, and wondered what would happen if the test were administered under untimed conditions. To find out, the teacher did not stop Eric after time had run out for formal testing. Instead, she simply noted Eric's place in the test at the time limit and let him continue until he finished. This resulted in two scores (1) the formal timed score, assessed from the items Eric had answered correctly within the time limit and (2) the untimed score, from the total number of items Eric had answered correctly. A comparison of the scores showed that the untimed scores were considerably higher than the timed scores, indicating that time had been a major inhibiting factor.

(2) Is the student's lack of word knowledge due to problems in word recognition or problems in meaning vocabulary? The teacher was also interested in whether Eric's problems stemmed from poor word recognition or poor meaning vocabulary. To find out, Eric was first given the vocabulary subtest, a 45-item test which required Eric to read silently in order to match a word to its synonym when presented with four choices. After Eric had taken the vocabulary test using this standard administration, the teacher then orally read the subtest to Eric. If Eric's ability to recognize words had been interfering with his original score, he would have improved his score when the subtest was read to him. Since Eric did not improve his score, the teacher concluded that his problem was with word meanings, rather than with recognizing words.

These informal probing procedures show how formal tests may be first administered to obtain information from norms, and later informally probed to obtain additional diagnostic information.

INTERPRETING SCORES ON READING TESTS

The manuals of formal tests provide important information. This includes tables of test scores, information about the development of the test, and data about its standardization, validity, and reliability. Formal tests may be divided into norm-referenced tests and criterion-referenced tests.

Norm-Referenced Tests

As stated earlier, norm-referenced tests are standardized on representative samples of students. Using a norm-referenced test, a student's performance can be compared with other students of the same grade or age level.

Raw scores are converted into meaningful scores for interpreting reading performance. Scores on norm-referenced tests are reported in several ways. Types of scores include the reading grade score, reading age score, percentiles, and stanines. In addition, norm-referenced tests generally report standardization, validity, and reliability.

Reading Grade Score.   This score indicates how well the student reads in terms of grade level. For example a score of 4.5 (fifth month of the fourth grade) indicates that the student correctly answered the same number of questions as the average pupil in the fifth month of the fourth grade. The International Reading Association (1981) warns about the misuse and misinterpretation of grade equivalent scores. Reading grade scores do not indicate an absolute performance; rather, they indicate how the student performed in relation to the students in the norm sample population.

Reading Age Score.   This score is similar to a reading grade score except that the norms are developed according to the *age* of the pupils in the normed sample (rather than their grade levels). A score of 8-10 indicates that the student answered correctly the same number of questions as the average student of eight years, ten months of age in the norm sample.

Percentiles.   Percentile scores, sometimes called centiles, describe the scores of the student in relation to the scores of others in the same age or grade. Percentiles can be understood as ranks in groups of 100, expressed in numbers from 1 to 99. A percentile score of 57 shows that the student scored higher than 57 percent of the comparison group and lower than 42 percent. The fiftieth percentile is the average, or median, for the age or grade group to which the student is being compared. The higher the percentile (the highest is 99) the better the student's performance.

Equal distances in percentiles, however, do not indicate equal differences in raw score points. Since many scores center near the mean, the difference between the 50th and 60th percentiles may be only a few raw score points, whereas the distance between the 80th and 90th percentiles may be a great many raw score points on the test. (See Figure 6.4.)

Normal Curve Equivalent Scores (NCE).   NCE scores are similar to percentiles in that they have a range from 1 to 99 and a mean of 50. They differ from percentile scores because they have been transformed into equal units of reading achievement. For example, the difference between the 50th and 60th NCE and the 80th and 90th NCE is the same in raw point scores. The distribution of NCE scores is compared to percentiles in Figure 6.4.

Stanines.   The stanine score ranks pupils of a given age or grade from 1 to 9. The lowest stanine score is 1, the median stanine is 5, and the highest is 9. Stanine scores are assigned so that the result represents a normal distribution. Thus, in an average class, most students will receive stanine scores of 4, 5, or 6, and few will receive stanine scores of 1 to 9.

The name "stanine" is a contraction of "standard nine" and is based on the fact that the score runs from 1 to 9. Stanines are normalized standard scores with a mean of 5 and a standard deviation of 2. Figure 6.4 shows the percentage of students in each stanine, in each 10 NCE units, and compares these with percentiles.

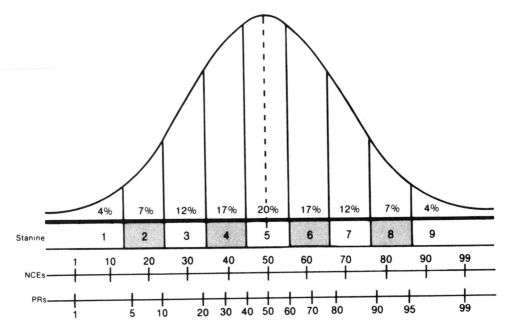

Figure 6.4 Relation between stanines, NCEs, and percentiles (PRs). Reproduced from Gates-MacGinitie Reading Tests, Manual, Form D, Riverside Publishing Co., 1978 by permission of publisher.

Standardization. Teachers are often called upon to choose tests for remedial readers. Among the factors to be considered in judging the value of a norm referenced test are the test's standardization, validity, and reliability.

To standardize a test, it is given to a large representative group of students (the norm sample). Based on data derived from this norm sample, then, inferences are made about other students who take the test.

In making a judgment about the value of the test, the teacher can consider the characteristics of the individuals who comprised the norm sample. Was the sample size adequate? Was the makeup of the sample representative of the students who are being tested? If the norm sample population is not considered representative, some school districts develop their own local norms. The student being tested can then be compared with other students in the school district.

Validity. Validity refers to whether a test measures what it is supposed to measure. There are at least two types of validity: (1) content validity and (2) criterion validity. Content validity involves inspecting the test to see if the items are valid for the testing purposes. For example, a valid reading comprehension test would probably contain paragraphs with questions. A comprehension test that required the student to match words would have questionable content validity.

Criterion validity refers to how the test compares with some other aspect of achievement. Most norm referenced reading tests provide information about the comparison of performance on the reading test with some aspect of school achievement (for example, grade point average). The comparison is usually done in the form of a statistical correlation. This correlation may range from + 1.0 (a very positive correlation to − 1.0 (a very negative correlation). For acceptable criterion validity, the correlation should be high (generally above .70).

Reliability.   Reliability refers to the constancy and stability of test scores. There are two forms of reliability (1) test-retest reliability and (2) internal reliability. In test-retest reliability, the test is given to a group of students two times. Then the scores are correlated to determine if individual students perform about the same on the first and second administrations.

In internal reliability, items within a test are compared with each other. In one form of internal reliability, split-half reliability, a group of students' scores on one half of the test items is correlated with performance on the items from the other half. Internal reliability may also be calculated by Kuder-Richardson internal consistency formulas (1937), which compare all items within a test to each other.

For all types of reliability, the reliability coefficient on an acceptable test should be above .70.

Out-of-Level Testing.   Remedial readers often must be given tests that are appropriate for their reading level but not for their age level. For example, George, an eleven-year-old student in the sixth grade, was given a third grade test because he could not read the sixth grade test. The problem encountered in "out-of-level" testing is that the third grade test was normed on an eight-year-old population (not with the scores of eleven-year-olds). George's score shows how he compares with eight-year-olds, not with eleven-year-olds. This is more of a problem for group tests, which usually use different forms for different grade levels, than it is for individual tests, which usually use one form to test a wide range of grade levels. Publishers of some group tests, such as the *Gates McGinitie Reading Tests*, provide tables for out-of-level norms, if requested.

Criterion-Referenced Tests

In contrast to norm-referenced tests, which compare students with a normed sample of other students, criterion-referenced tests offer a measure of the student's mastery of specific reading skills. For example, can the student recognize "ing" endings? Can the student find the main idea in a paragraph? To develop a criterion-referenced test, the test author must designate a hierarchy or ordered set of specific developmental reading skills. The student's reading ability is judged by how many of these sequential reading skills have been mastered.

An analogy can be drawn to another area of learning—swimming. In norm-referenced terms, a child can be tested in swimming and judged to swim as well as the average nine-year-old. In criterion-referenced terms, a child is judged as being able to do certain instructional tasks, such as putting one's face in the water, floating on one's back, and doing the crawl stroke. In other words, criterion-referenced tests measure mastery rather than grade level, or they *describe* rather than *compare* performance.

Criterion-referenced tests are useful because they provide a means of accountability. While it is often difficult to show that a student has improved in terms of percentiles, stanines, or even grade level scores, the teacher can show that the student has learned certain specific skills in terms of mastery of criterion-referenced measures.

Criterion-referenced tests have been criticized on the grounds that (1) they require a great deal of time in terms of record keeping, (2) students may pass the various skill tests but be unable to transfer the skills to reading situations, (3) there is no agreed-upon sequence of reading skills, and (4) they encourage the instruction of discrete skills rather than encouraging extended reading in context.

SUMMARY

Formal reading tests are commercially prepared instruments. They may be divided into norm-referenced tests (which compare students with a representative sample of other students) and criterion-referenced tests (which measure mastery of specific skills).

Many kinds of tests can be used for general reading assessment, including group survey tests, individual survey test, oral reading tests, and literacy tests. Tests for diagnosing specific reading problems include diagnostic reading batteries and diagnostic tests of specific areas.

When interpreting test scores, it is important to distinguish between norm-referenced and criterion-referenced tests.

The kinds of information reported in the manuals of norm-referenced tests include reading grade scores, reading age scores, percentiles, stanines, and normal curve equivalent scores. Validity and reliability statistics give the user information on the value of the test. Validity refers to whether a test measures what it should be measuring. Reliability refers to the constancy of test scores. Out-of-level testing refers to cases in which poor readers take tests that are appropriate for their reading level, but are intended for students of other age levels.

Several formal tests of reading ability are criterion-referenced.

Test Inventory 6.1 Tests Commonly Used in the Reading Diagnosis

The tests listed have been identified according to the following categories.

- Survey test
- Oral reading test
- Informal reading inventory
- Diagnostic battery
- Diagnostic test: Specific areas

- Literacy test
- Reading Miscue Inventory

If a test fits into more than one category, this is indicated.

Adult Basic Learning Examination (ABLE)
Psychological Corporation

Literacy Test
Ages: Adult

For adults with limited reading skills. Measures oral vocabulary and reading comprehension. Also measures problem solving, spelling, and arithmetic computation. Two forms (A, B). Three levels: I, achievement, grades 1–6; II, grades 3–9; III grades 9–12.

Analytical Reading Inventory (Second Edition)
Merrill

Informal Reading Inventory
Grades: 1–9

Contains word recognition test (P–6) and oral reading passages for primer through grade nine. Six to eight comprehension questions following each passage: main idea, fact, terminology, cause and effect, inference, conclusion. Yields independent, instructional, frustration reading levels, listening, analysis of miscues, comprehension analyses. Longest passage is 339 words.

Individual test: 20–30 minutes. Three equivalent forms in one spiral notebook.

Bader Reading and Language Inventory
Macmillan

Diagnostic Battery (with oral reading test)
Grades 1–12

Reading assessed on sets of graded passages, pre-primer through grade 12. Retelling included in passages. Also includes word lists, fourteen word analysis subtests, spelling tests, cloze tests, visual and auditory tests, an interest inventory, measures of receptive language, handwriting, arithmetic.

Individual test.

Basic Reading Inventory
Kendall/Hunt

Informal Reading Inventory
Grades: PP–8

Contains word recognition lists (PP–8) and reading passages from preprimer to grade eight. Five to eight comprehension questions following each passage: literal, critical, main idea, vocabulary. Uses facets of psycholinguistic miscue analysis in scoring. Yields independent, instructional, and frustration reading levels. Longest passage is 100 words.

Individual test: 20–30 minutes. Three forms.

Boder Test of Reading-Spelling Patterns
Grune and Stratton

Diagnostic: Specific Area
Grades: All

Reading and spelling subtests consist of lists. Test used to identify four types of disabled readers: (1) dysphonetic, (2) diseidetic, (3) dysphonetic and diseidetic, and (4) nonspecific.

Individual test.

BRIGANCE® Diagnostic Inventory of Basic Skills

Curriculum Associates

Diagnostic Battery
(with oral reading test)
Grades: K–6

Contains 141 criterion-referenced subtests for reading, readiness, and reference skills as well as for math, handwriting, spelling, and grammar. Used for assessing skill levels between grades Pre-K–6 for remedial students. Subtests include twenty-four for readiness, six for word recognition, three for reading (oral reading level, comprehension, and oral reading rate), nineteen for word analysis, five for vocabulary, and nine for reference. Contained in easy-to-administer binder with student's copy and examiner's on opposite pages. Yields ratings of satisfactory/needs to improve for given grade level. Subtests coordinated with IEP rating system.

Individual test: 15–90 minutes. One form. (Also *Brigance Diagnostic Comprehensive Inventory of Basic Skills* grades pre K–9; *Inventory of Early Development*, ages 0–7; *Inventory of Essential Skills* grades 6–adult; and *Diagnostic Assessment of Basic Skills, Spanish version*, grades K–9.)

Classroom Reading Inventory (Silvaroli)

William C. Brown

Informal Reading Inventory
Grades: 1–8

Contains graded word lists (PP–8), graded oral paragraphs with five comprehension questions for grades preprimer to eight, and optional graded spelling survey. Yields independent, instructional, frustration reading levels, hearing level, rate, and analysis of oral reading errors. Longest passage 174 words.

Individual test: 12–20 minutes. Three forms in one spiral notebook.

Computer-Based Reading Assessment

Kendall-Hunt

Informal Reading Inventory
Grades: 1–8

Passages followed by eight multiple-choice questions. Available in Spanish and English versions. Computer scoring system available.

Individual test: two forms.

Concepts about Print

Heinemann

Diagnostic: Specific Area
Ages: 4–7

Test requires *The Early Detection of Reading Difficulties*, by Marie Clay, supplemented by specially printed paperback books *Sand* and *Stones*. As examiner reads book, child answers questions about orientation of book, letters, words, and other concepts needed for reading.

Degrees of Reading Power

College Board

Survey Test
Grades: 3–14

A Degree of Reading Power (DRP) is given to each student, based on the ability to choose cloze deletions from passages, when given multiple choice format. Student DRP can be matched to that of textbooks, which also have been measured by the DRP scale. Levels PA and PB-8 (grades 3–5); PA and PB-6 (5–7); PA and PB-4 (7–9); PA and PB-2 (9–12); CP-1A and B (12–14).

Group test; two forms at each level.

Diagnostic Reading Scales (Spache), Revised   *Diagnostic Battery*
CTB/McGraw-Hill   *(with oral reading test)*

Samples word recognition, passage reading, comprehension, and phonics knowledge through three graded word lists and two sets of graded selections containing eleven passages from levels 1.4 to 7.5, each followed by comprehension questions. Twelve supplementary tests of word analysis: initial consonants, final consonants, consonant digraphs, consonant blends, initial consonant substitutions, auditory recognition of initial consonant sounds, auditory discrimination, short and long vowels, "r"-controlled vowels, vowel dipthongs and digraphs, common phonograms, and blending. Phonics tests use nonsense words to fourth grade, then real words. Oral reading level called "instructional" level; silent reading level is higher and considered "independent." Yields independent (silent), instructional (oral), and frustration reading levels, listening level, and grade equivalent for phonics tests.

Individual tests: 20–30 minutes. Two forms of reading passages in one binder.

Diagnostic Word Patterns
Tests 1, 2, 3   *Diagnostic Test: Specific Area*
Educators Publishing Service   *Ages: 3–Adult*

Three tests of 100 words each can be used as a dictated spelling test or as a test of word recognition. Each test concentrates upon different phonics, structural analysis, and sight-word patterns. No norms; diagnostic analysis provided.

Group test for spelling; individual for reading: 20–45 minutes.

Doren Diagnostic Reading Test of Word Recognition Skills   *Diagnostic: Specific Area*
American Guidance Service   *Grades: 1–4*

Measures twelve specific areas for remedial readers. Each skill is arranged from simple to complex. Subtests include letter recognition, beginning sounds, whole word recognition, words within words, speech consonants such as the difference between "ch" and "sh," ending sounds, blending, rhyming, vowels, discriminate guessing, spelling, and sight words. Criterion referenced with overlay correcting form for scoring. Remedial activities presented in manual. Individual skill profiles contain ratings for satisfactory/not satisfactory for each area.

Group test: 60–180 minutes. One form.

Durrell Analysis of Reading Difficulty   *Diagnostic Battery (with oral reading test)*
Psychological Corporation   *Grades: 1–6*

Contains (1) eight short, progressively harder paragraphs for oral reading from which rate and comprehension (using questions) are determined, (2) eight short paragraphs for silent reading from which reading rate and free recall are determined, (3) six paragraphs to determine listening comprehension, (4) two sets of isolated word lists to analyze instant recognition (tachistoscopic) and word analysis, (5) other subtests including listening vocabulary, visual memory for words, identifying sounds in words, sounds in isolation, phonic spelling of words, prereading phonics abilities, and spelling ability. Subtests administered vary. Yields grade equivalent scores.

Individual test: 30–60 minutes. One form.

Ekwall Reading Inventory

Allyn & Bacon

Informal Reading Inventory

Grades: 1–9

Contains word recognition test (PP–9) and passages for oral and silent reading from preprimer through grade nine. Comprehension questions following passages: literal, inference, vocabulary. Oral and silent reading are presented alternately at each level. Testing continues in one mode if frustration level is reached in the other. Yields independent, instructional, frustration reading levels. Also contains El Paso Phonics Survey. Longest passage 202 words.

Individual test: 20–30 minutes. Four forms available in one binder.

Formal Reading Inventory (FRI)

Pro-Ed

Oral Reading Test

Grades: 1–12

Measures oral reading, silent reading, and comprehension through thirteen graded passages followed by five multiple-choice completion questions for each passage. Forms A and C require silent reading; forms B and D require oral reading. Silent reading quotient is derived. Scores are standardized. In addition, forms are provided for an analysis of miscue types (meaning similarity, function similarity, graphic/phonemic similarity, use of multiple clues, self correction).

Individual test; 20–40 minutes. Four forms in one binder.

Gates-McKillop-Horowitz Reading Diagnostic Tests

Teachers College Press

Diagnostic Battery
(with oral reading test)

Grades: 1–6

Tests oral reading, sight knowledge, phonics, spelling, and writing. Contains (1) continuous set of graded short oral reading paragraphs; (2) four reading sentences with regular words; (3) flashwords presented with tachistoscope; (4) untimed word list for sight recognition or analysis; (5) tests of word attack using nonsense words: syllabication, recognizing and blending word parts, reading words, letter sounds, and naming capital and lowercase letters; (6) test of identifying spoken vowel sounds; (7) test of auditory blending and discrimination; and (8) spelling test and informal writing sample. Yields grade equivalent scores and informal ratings. Also analysis of oral reading errors, phonics.

Individual test: 60–90 minutes. One form.

Gilmore Oral Reading Test, New Ed. (GORT)

Psychological Corporation

Oral Reading Test

Grades: 1–8

Tests oral reading using ten graded paragraphs each followed by five comprehension questions. Yields grade equivalent, stanines, and percentiles for oral reading, comprehension, and rate.

Individual test: 15–20 minutes. Four forms, each in separate booklet.

Gray Oral Reading Tests-Revised

Pro-Ed

Oral Reading Test

Grades: P–12

Revision of the classic test by Gray and Robinson. Measures oral reading through thirteen timed, graded passages, each followed by five comprehension questions. Passage score is derived from the rate and errors in reading. In addition, there are standard scores for oral reading comprehension and a total reading score. Miscue analysis form is also provided.

Individual test: 15–20 minutes. Two forms in one binder.

Group Assessment in Reading   *Diagnostic Battery*
Prentice Hall   *Grades: 1-12*

Includes a series of graded passages (grades 1–12) for silent reading, cloze tests, comprehension tests (for measuring word meaning, literal comprehension, inferential comprehension, and critical reading), locating information, (reference sources, use of pictures and graphic clues, organizing information), and attitude and interest inventory. Gives reading levels and diagnostic assessment.

Group test; one to two hours administration. One form.

Group Phonics Analysis Test   *Diagnostic: Specific Area*
Jamestown   *Grades: 1-3*

Criterion-referenced test assessing basic phonics skills that are presented in developmental order. Covers number reading, letter reading, consonant sounds, alphabetizing, recognizing long and short vowels, and the use of vowel sound rules. No norms.

Group test: 20–30 minutes. One form.

Informal Reading Inventory (Burns, Roe) 2nd ed.   *Informal Reading Inventory*
Houghton Mifflin   *Grades: 1-12*

Informal reading inventory provides passages from grades 1 to 12. Yields reading levels and diagnostic assessment. No norms provided.

Individual test: 20–40 minutes. Two forms in single binder.

Instrumento Para Diagnosticar Lecturas Para Computadora

This is a Spanish version of Computer-Based Reading Assessment instrument.

McCarthy Individualized Diagnostic Reading Inventory   *Informal Reading Inventory*
Educators Publishing Service   *Grades: 2-12*

Contains reading passages from primer through twelfth, followed by questions itemized into specific skills and an optional survey of basic phonics skills. Yields inventory of student strengths and weaknesses.

Individual test: 60–90 minutes. One form.

Monroe Diagnostic Reading Test   *Diagnostic Battery*

C.H. Nevins   *Grades: Remedial students, any grade*

Analytic tests include alphabet reading, word recognition, and oral reading as well as recognition of orientation, mirror reading, mirror writing, number reversals, word discrimination, sounding, and "b," "d," "p," "q," "u," "n" tests. Yields profile of errors.

Individual test: untimed. One form.

Nelson Reading Skills Test   *Diagnostic Battery*

Riverside   *Grades: 3–9*

Assesses level of reading and reading strengths and weaknesses. Subtests include word meaning, reading comprehension, word parts (sound/symbol choices and identifying root words), reading rate, and an optional syllabication test. Yields grade equivalent and percentile rank for vocabulary, comprehension, and total. Rate given in words per minute. Item analysis provided.

Group test: 60 minutes. Two forms, three levels in each for grades 3–4a, 4b–6, and 7–9.

Peabody Individual Achievement Test (PIAT)   *Survey*

American Guidance Service   *Grades: K–12*

Has five subtests in math, reading recognition, reading comprehension, spelling, and general information. Easel provided for easy administration. Yields grade equivalents and percentiles.

Individual test: 30–40 minutes. One form.

Performance Assessment in Reading (PAIR)   *Literacy Test*

CTB/McGraw-Hill   *Grades: 7–9*

Measures minimal competency through printed materials encountered in school, home, and community. Seventy-two items, divided into two parts, include warning signs, street maps, card catalogues, encyclopedia entries, telephone directories, and bus schedules. Vocabulary, comprehension, and location/study skills emphasized. If junior high students master the PAIR skills, they should demonstrate proficiency on senior high competency tests required for graduation. Instructional prescriptions of individual needs and student grouping guidelines given. Criterion-referenced: passing/not passing.

Group test: untimed. One form.

Reading/Everyday Activities in Life (REAL)   *Literacy Test*

Westwood Press   *Ages: 10 years and above*

Assesses functional literacy for adults at basic education levels. Nine real-life reading selections are used in test (eg., signs, schedules). Directions and questions are on cassette tape, which is student controlled. Criterion-referenced: 80 percent correct indicates functional literacy.

Individual or group test: 50–90 minutes.

Reading Miscue Inventory   *Reading Miscue Inventory*
Richard C. Owens   *Grades 1–8*

Provides information on the strategies used by a student during oral reading. Student reads a four-page (or longer) selection. Passage should be difficult enough to generate miscues. Reading is taped and miscues are analyzed to determine use of langauge processes in reading. After reading, student retells story. Yields analysis of miscues (for syntactic acceptability, semantic acceptability, meaning change, correction, graphic similarity, sound similarity, meaning construction, and grammatical relationships) and retelling score. Detailed curriculum development guidelines included.

Individual test; 20–40 minutes.

Rosewell-Chall Diagnostic Reading Test
of Word Analysis Skills
(Revised and Extended)   *Diagnostic: Specific Area*
Essay Press   *Grades: K–4*

Assesses skills in developmental order, including single consonants, consonant combinations, short vowels, rule of silent "e," vowel combinations, and syllabication. Yields ratings of competence/deficiency. Useful for diagnostic patterns.

Individual test: 5–10 minutes. Two forms.

Senior High Assessment of Reading Performance (SHARP)   *Literacy Test*
CTB/McGraw-Hill   *Grades: 10–12*

Measures minimal competency in reading skills necessary for everyday life. Used as a posttest measure of a competency-based education program for basic reading skills. Thirty displays represent forms and written materials encountered in daily living such as social security cards, telephone directory, charge account agreement, newspaper article, and so on. A new form published each year to minimize test security problems for schools using the test as a graduation requirement. Criterion-referenced (passing/not passing) and scaled scores.

Group test, untimed. One form.

Sipay Word Analysis Test   *Diagnostic: Specific Area*
Educators Publishing Service   *Ages: 6–adult*

Measures visual analysis, phonic analysis, and visual blending through seventeen subtests pinpointing specific strengths and weaknesses. Each subtest has four components: a "Mini-Manual," a set of test cards, an answer sheet, and an individual report. A manual covers topics not in Mini-Manual. Uses nonsense words and requires oral responses; no writing. Yields ratings of skill strengths and weaknesses.

Individual test: 10–15 minutes per subtest, 160–200 minutes entire test. One form.

Slosson Oral Reading Test (SORT)   *Survey*
Slosson Educational Publications   *Grades: P–high school*

This is a test of word recognition. Students are asked to read aloud twenty graded lists of words ranging from primer to high school. Yields reading grade level.

Individual test: 3–5 minutes.

Standardized Reading Inventory (SRI)   *Oral Reading Test*
Pro-Ed   *Grades: 1–8*

Contains ten graded passages from preprimer to eighth grade. On each passage, oral and silent reading are assessed, followed by comprehension questions. Scores are standardized and, in addition, test yields an independent, instructional, and frustration level.

Individual test: 20–40 minutes. Two forms.

Stanford Diagnostic Reading Test   *Diagnostic Battery*
Psychological Corporation   *Grades: 1–12*

Identifies strengths and weaknesses with an emphasis on low achievers. Subtests, which vary from level to level, include auditory vocabulary, auditory discrimination, phonetic analysis, word reading, vocabulary, word parts, and comprehension. Yields percentile ranks, stanines, grade equivalents, and scaled scores.

Group test: approximately 2 hours. Two forms for each of four levels: Red (Grades 1.5–4.5); Green (3.5–6.5); Brown (5.5–8.5); Blue (7.5–13.0).

Test of Reading Comprehension (TORC)   *Diagnostic: Specific Area*
Pro-Ed   *Grades: 2–12*

Tests silent reading comprehension through general vocabulary (words related to a common concept), syntactic similarities (understanding of sentences similar in meaning but syntactically different), paragraph reading (answering questions related to paragraphs), sentence sequencing. Also vocabulary in math, science, social studies, and reading schoolwork directions. Yields scaled score for each subtest and basic comprehension quotient.

Group test: 1–1½ hours.

Wide Range Achievement Test (WRAT)-Revised   *Survey*
Jastak   *Age: 5 years–adult*

A quick measurement of achievement in reading, spelling, and arithmetic. Contains two levels: level I, ages 5–11.5; level II, ages 12.0–adult. Reading section includes recognizing letters and orally reading graded word lists. Yields standard scores, percentiles, and grade ratings.

Individual test: 25–40 minutes.

Woodcock-Johnson Psychoeducational Battery (WJPEB)   *Diagnostic Battery*
DLM   *Ages: Preschool to adult*

Four subtests of this 27 subtest battery test involve reading directly. They are: letter-word identification, word attack, passage comprehension, and reading interest. (See Test Inventories 3.1 and 4.1 for more information.)

Woodcock Reading Mastery Tests-Revised (WRMT-R)   *Survey and Diagnostic Battery*
American Guidance Service   *Grades: 1–adult*

Four basic tests include word identification, word attack of nonsense words, word comprehension (with antonyms, synonyms, and analogies subtests), and passage comprehension (a cloze completion exercise). Norms yield grade placements, percentiles, and other scores for total reading and subtests. Supplementary tests include letter identification and auditory-visual association. Extensive diagnostic analysis available for several subtests. Materials presented in stand-up easel kit for easy administration.

Individual test: 30–40 minutes. Two forms separately bound.

Word Discrimination Test   *Diagnostic: Specific Area*
Miami University Alumni Association   *Grades: 1–8*

Tests visual discrimination in reading confusable words. Each row contains one real word and four similar groups of letters. The student identifies the real word. Yields grade equivalents.

Group test: untimed but requires approximately 15 minutes. Two forms.

7

OVERVIEW
OF REMEDIAL
INSTRUCTION

In Part III of this book we deal with strategies for successfully teaching students with reading problems. Chapter 7 outlines effective principles and overall plans for teaching of remedial reading. Chapter 8 presents techniques useful for teaching students fluent recognition of words through sight and word analysis strategies. Chapter 9 treats more advanced word recognition topics and word meaning. Chapter 10 focuses attention on reading and listening comprehension. Chapter 11 addresses reading and studying expository (or informational) texts. Chapter 12 considers the essential role of writing and other language-arts areas in acquiring and maintaining literacy.

INTRODUCTION

In this chapter we present an overview of remediation. This overview includes a discussion of the role of reading in remedial classes, principles of remedial teaching, components of the lesson, building rapport, and the instructional setting. In addition, we discuss two special populations of learners: adolescents and adults.

THE ROLE OF READING IN REMEDIAL INSTRUCTION

Providing the student with opportunities to read is the key ingredient of remedial teaching. Reading, like any other skilled activity, must be practiced in order to be learned. In fact, a common way that children reading on level acquire their good reading skills is simply by doing copious amounts of reading.

Abundant Reading Experiences

Since students with problems are so in need of reading experiences, one would expect their teachers to plan for extensive reading. Unfortunately, however, remedial readers actually do little reading. In a study of third grade classes, Allington (1984) found that children in low reading groups did much less reading than children in average and above-average groups. McDermott (1977) found that poor readers spent one-third less time actually reading than good readers. In another study, Allington (1977) found that remedial readers in grades two through eight read an average of only forty-three words per reading session!

Such findings have been duplicated by research in special education. Haynes and Jenkins (1986), studying learning disabilities resource rooms, found that "overall the amount of reading instruction was remarkably low" (p. 161). Leinhardt, Zigmond, and Cooley (1981) found the same trend for self-contained learning disabilities classes.

What are students doing if they are not reading? Much instructional time is spent on skills and drills and on worksheets. Johnston, Allington, and Afflerbach (1985) asked children in Chapter I classes to name their most frequent activity. They overwhelmingly cited filling out worksheets. Rather than being supplementary to reading, completing worksheets apparently makes up most of the program.

Yet no student learns to read by filling out worksheets. To read, students must spend much time applying their knowledge to printed text. They must *read, read, read* in order to see how main ideas, consonant sounds, and predicting actually work when they are applied to reading material. We may think of learning to read as something like learning to swim. Many people have taken swimming lessons, given at the side of the pool, which concentrate on breathing, kicking, arm strokes, and so on. However, after people learn these skills, they are still not swimmers. They become swimmers when they swim. They must learn to apply these skills *as they are swimming*. In the same way, students can only learn to read by applying what they are learning about reading as they are *actually* reading.

Using Reading Strategies

Effective remedial instruction concentrates on teaching students reading strategies. In a strategy, students learn *how* to read *as* they *are* actively reading. Students become strategic readers by learning to control internally their own reading process. Thus, a strategy has two characteristics. First, it is done within the context of a reading situation. Second, it teaches students to control their reading processes.

How is teaching a reading strategy different from merely teaching a reading skill? An example serves to illustrate this difference. When a student merely fills out worksheets identifying the main idea of short paragraphs, this is skills instruction. Since this activity is not connected to other reading that the student does, the student might mistakenly think that finding the main idea is a useful skill by itself, and might not use it while reading. Clearly, however, the function of finding a main idea is that it serves to simplify actual reading.

To change this skill instruction to a strategy lesson, the students and teacher should jointly explore the purpose of being able to abstract main thoughts (or ideas). The students might think about personal experiences in which finding a central thought in reading helped them to classify and remember. Then, students might brainstorm about ways to find the main idea, establishing student control over the learning process. The teacher might model additional ways. Next, students should learn to hypothesize the central ideas, using texts like the ones they use in their classrooms (eg., history, health). Throughout several examples, students formulations of the central thought should be discussed and evaluated.

Pacing and Encouraging Reading

The more text children read, the better they achieve (Barr and Dreeben, 1983). Barr (1988) finds that it is not useful to hold low achieving first-grade pupils back in a reader until they have mastered every word. Rather, reading can best be fostered by moving, at a faster pace, to the next story and exposing children to new material. At the same time, to maintain a faster pace for remedial readers, additional time may need to be spent in reinforcement of the material read, through rereading, word study, and so forth. Barr recommends that an additional daily period be provided for children with reading problems.

Leading remedial students to do extensive reading is not an easy task. Stanovich (1986b) discusses a "Matthew effect," a process by which low-achieving students progressively become worse. This negative cycle occurs in the following manner: First, students who are not skilled readers tend to avoid reading. Then, because they have not practiced reading, they become less skilled. In turn, because they are not skilled, they tend to further avoid reading, and so on. This continues until, tragically, students are doing almost no reading.

As teachers, we need to prevent the "Matthew effect" from occurring. Our greatest challenge is to foster the desire to read, so that children will, ultimately, make learning to read a self-sustaining process.

PRINCIPLES OF REMEDIAL TEACHING

As just described, the overriding principle of remedial teaching is to *provide extensive opportunities to read.* In addition, the principles given in this section will help to translate a diagnosis into an effective teaching plan.

Begin Instruction at an Appropriate Level

Use Material that Students Are Able to Read Effectively.   We can determine the appropriate level for a student's instructional materials from the diagnosis. For example, one student in our clinic, Tiku, was a seventh grader who had a fourth-grade instructional level. In his classroom, all of Tiku's materials were at the seventh-grade level, which was so high that it was frustrating. On the other hand, in his Chapter I class, Tiku used a second grade book, which was too easy for him, and thus he wasted valuable instructional time. In our clinic, we located materials on the fourth grade level, Tiku's instructional level. Working with these appropriate materials, we were soon able to improve his reading.

The appropriate level of material can vary somewhat, depending upon the subject of the text, and interest and motivation of the reader. Reading is an interactive process, one to which reader, text, and the context of the reading situation all contribute. Teachers should remember that a reader's background and interest can often motivate him or her to handle material that would otherwise be too difficult. Joshua, a twelfth grader, was able to read only fifth grade materials, except when the subject was fishing. On fishing, his background knowledge and interest were so extensive that he could successfully read advanced newspaper and magazine articles.

Support Instruction in the Regular Classroom

Teach What Is Needed to Help the Student Succeed in the Regular Classroom.
One purpose of supplementary instruction is to provide a scaffold that will enable
students to function better in regular classes. To provide supportive supplementary
instruction, remedial teachers need to be familiar with the curriculum of the student's
regular classroom. The classroom teacher and the resource teacher must jointly decide
how best to help the student through collaborative planning and teaching (Allington
and Broikou, 1988).

We remember, with horror, a situation in which a first-grade student was
confused by three conflicting forms of reading instruction. In his regular classroom,
he received instruction in a basal reader. In his Chapter I room, he was taught the
DISTAR system (see Chapter 13), which used a regularized alphabet. In his learning
disabilities resource room, he used the Gillingham method (see Chapter 13). Each
teacher was unaware of what the others were doing. The student, who could barely
master one method of learning to read, was bombarded with three different methods
every day! If teachers do not communicate with each other and coordinate their programs, the result will be, as it was for this student, confusing and at cross purposes.
In fact, research shows that having too many supplementary programs can actually
decrease achievement (Glass and Smith, 1977).

Guidelines for coordinating Chapter I resource room instruction with classroom basal reader instruction are given by Beebe, Feeney, and Hill (1987). They suggest that elementary school resource teachers need to do four things:

1. Communicate with regular classroom teachers.
2. Become familiar with the basal reader children are using in the home classroom.
3. Use the same management system as the home classroom. (For example, if children
   take an end-of-unit basal reader test, Chapter I instruction should help them prepare
   for this test.)
4. Group children for Chapter I instruction by the levels they are grouped in basal
   reader instruction.

Some school districts have programs in which supplementary instruction is
done only in regular classrooms. For example, in Orange County, Florida, middle-
school and high-school reading resource teachers actually go into departmental classrooms (U.S. history, biology) to teach students useful reading and study strategies
that aid in the transition to reading regularly assigned expository (or informational)
textbooks. These generic reading strategies can be used across all areas of the secondary curriculum (Reading Resource Specialist Handbook, 1985; Monahan, 1987). The
reading resource teachers demonstrate and start to implement the strategies, and departmental teachers continue to teach them. Soon students start to assume ownership
of the strategies, and to use them independently. This helps ensure that reading instruction will assist students on a continuing basis in organizing information for learning and remembering. Thus, reading instruction supports ongoing learning as resource teachers, departmental teachers, and students become partners.

Use Time Effectively

Use the Limited Time for Remedial Instruction Wisely.   A number of studies have shown that a great deal of school time is not spent "on task" but, rather, on noninstructional activities (Fisher et al., 1978a, b). Time that has been allocated to reading instruction may actually be spent in activities such as taking students to and from class and passing out papers. Berliner (1979) reports on second-grade classrooms where students actually received less than one hundred hours of instruction in reading and math combined during an entire school year.

Many remedial readers have problems controlling their behavior, and their teachers must spend precious instructional time on discipline and other management procedures (Gaskins, 1988). McDermott (1978) found that students in a top reading group spent three times as much time on task as did students in the bottom group. Time is wasted on activities such as calling on students to read orally, which often becomes a complex negotiation for readers in low-achieving groups.

What can a remedial teacher do to utilize instructional time effectively?

1. Streamline noninstructional procedures by establishing firm routines for coming to class and settling down to work.
2. Call on specific students to increase their attention. Often, teachers tend to avoid calling on low-achieving or inattentive students, yet these are precisely the students who tend to be "off task."
3. Do not allow supplemental reading instruction to replace reading in the classroom. Supplemental instruction should be given *in addition* to classroom reading. (In fact, this is specified in current federal Chapter I guidelines.)

Increase the Complexity of Instruction

Guide Instruction toward Longer and More Difficult Tasks.   Teachers should always be alert to opportunities for moving students to the more complex tasks that will help them function independently in their classrooms. Try to move students progressively to more difficult materials, for example, from a second to a third grade instructional level. In addition, try to increase the length of materials that students read.

Unfortunately, remedial students can get caught in a "rut," simply proceeding through one workbook until they finish it. Remedial students are already behind their peers and, unless they improve as quickly as they can, they will fall further and further behind. For example, we once observed a seventh grader doing weeks of practice in choosing the main ideas in paragraphs. This instruction continued through an entire skills book, long after he was proficient at it. At the same time, in history, he and his classmates were studying whole chapters and taking written tests on them. This student should have been exposed to increasing complexity in his reading instruction. For instance, he might have progressed from finding main ideas in workbook paragraphs, to dealing with one- or two-page selections, and finally to locating the main ideas in chapters. This strategy would have helped the student to meet the demands of his history class.

Give Students Control and Independence

Plan for Students to Assume Responsibility for Their Instruction. Human beings learn better when they are involved in instruction and have invested in the learning. Research shows that students with reading and learning problems tend to be passive, and do not take responsibility for their own learning (Jenkins et al., 1986; Johnston, 1984; Schumaker et al., 1986). Students must learn how to initiate and control their own reading if they are to function independently. They must be directly involved in reading rather than feeling that it is an activity that is done for thirty minutes a day, simply to please the teacher. There are many ways that teachers can foster such control.

1. Help students to become conscious of the aims of their instruction. They should be aware of *what* they are learning, *why* they are learning it, and *when* it is most appropriate to use this knowledge (Wixon and Lipson, 1986; Paris, 1986; Paris, Cross, and Lipson, 1984). For example, a teacher might explain that students are learning to use a study system so that they can learn more effectively when they study U.S. history.
2. Help students to become actively involved in instructional activities. For example, rather than the teacher writing words of two syllables on a list, students should be allowed to collect their own words while reading, and write their own list.

   Student writing encourages active involvement. Through writing, students come to see how the things they read are created. We have often observed that students who write regularly come to feel a sense of control over both reading and writing, and to approach reading with more interest. (Chapter 12 gives many writing ideas.)
3. Give students opportunities to choose their own reading and learning materials. This choice fosters a sense of control over learning. To help build bridges to reading enjoyment, teachers should make trade books (children's literature books) available in class, and encourage children to read them.

Remedial readers can search their home environments for reading materials. Valuable reading and study strategies can be learned from television guides, newspapers, baseball and football programs, record jackets, popular magazines, and manuals. The use of these materials shows students that reading is directly connected to their lives. One remedial reading teacher wanted to show primary students the many reasons for reading. She asked each student to bring in something that one of their parents read. The resultant display and reports on college texts, telephone books, and memos was a highly motivating experience for the children.

Use Silent and Oral Reading Appropriately

Employ Each Reading Mode According to the Needs of Your Students. Silent reading is very effective for teaching students to control their own reading processes. In reading silently, students are able to control their own pace, review material as they need to, and form deeper personal reactions to reading. Unfortunately, research shows that children with reading problems do not often read silently. Comparing children in the same classes who were in a high-achieving reading group with those in the "low group," Allington (1984) found that good readers read about three times the amount that poor readers read silently. At the first grade level, the low-achieving group averaged only five words of silent reading per day! In an observational study of compensatory classes, Quirk et al. (1975) found that only 2 percent of time was spent on silent reading.

How may we encourage silent reading? In some schools and classes, time is set aside (perhaps twenty minutes, three times per week) when everybody, including students, teachers, administrators, lunchroom staff reads silently. The model of adults "practicing what they preach" about silent reading is a powerful one. This activity is often called Sustained Silent Reading.

Another strategy to encourage silent reading is to have students engage in it as soon as they walk into class. Since the first moments of a class are often wasted with arrangements, students may enjoy some private time to read silently while others are dealing with lunch money, attendance, etc.

While silent reading is the more desirable reading mode, some oral reading activities are also useful for increasing fluency and comfort. Many remedial students, especially those who are reading within the primary grade levels, will need to do some oral reading. Oral reading may be done individually, through choral reading, or with the assistance of a teacher (as further explained in Chapter 8).

Studies show that teachers tend to over-interrupt remedial readers who make miscues when they read orally, even when the interruption is harmful. For example, Allington (1980) compared what happened when first and second grade children in both low groups and high groups read orally in comfortable material. During this reading, when students came to the occasional word that they could not pronounce immediately, teachers interrupted the children in the high group only 31 percent of the time. In contrast, they interrupted the children in the low group 74 percent of the time. The contrast between the two patterns of interruption shows that teachers were not allowing the low-group children to figure out the words for themselves, and thus were limiting their independence.

Allington also found that poorer readers were interrupted often, even when their miscues made sense. Thus when high-group students made a miscue such as substituting "a" for "the," the teacher stopped them only 10 percent of the time. When low-group students made such a misreading, teachers stopped them 56 percent of the time. In this way, teachers were allowing good students to realize that reading is getting meaning, but unintentionally conveying to less able students that reading is *word perfect performance*.

Furthermore, when high-achieving students missed a word during oral reading, they were encouraged to figure it out for themselves. In contrast, low-achieving readers were often immediately supplied the word by the teacher (Allington, 1980). Hoffman et al. (1984) found that supplying the word to students (which they called "terminal clues") was associated with the least gain in reading performance.

To encourage independence, teachers should try to limit interruptions of remedial students. If mistakes do not affect the meaning of what they are reading, do not stop students. When you do need to interrupt, try *not* simply to give them the word. Instead, ask students to reread the sentence, and perhaps concentrate on the first letter or syllable of the unknown word.

At the same time, stress to other students in the group that interrupting oral reading to call out words is impolite. The student who is reading needs time to figure out words independently. If the student is stuck, and wants assistance, he or she may hold up a finger, indicating "help me."

Of course, these guidelines for oral reading must be used sensibly. The teacher should assist students when they can read no further or have lost the meaning of the material.

COMPONENTS OF THE REMEDIAL LESSON

Most remedial sessions last from thirty to forty-five minutes. What should the teacher be sure to include during this time? We will discuss the following components of a lesson: (1) instructional reading, (2) focused instruction, (3) review, and (4) independent reading.

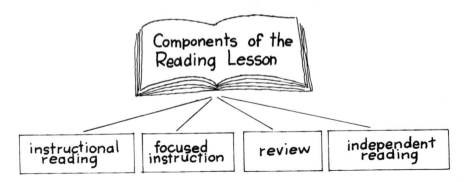

Instructional Reading

As we have emphasized, the most important activity for students is reading. In instructional reading, students read from a text at their instructional level (see Chapter 5). At this level, they will encounter some new words and concepts, but are under the guidance of a teacher, who anticipates difficulty and helps them to master the material.

Instructional reading can be used to teach or model a specific reading strategy or can simply be used to provide reading practice and enjoyment. In either case, it is important to give comprehension follow-up. Students should always be able to share their personal reactions, summarize the story, answer teacher questions, make up their own questions, or pursue the many other activities that foster comprehension.

Focused Instruction

Depending upon the students' needs, teachers may choose to devote a small amount of time to focusing directly on some specific facet of reading. This instruction helps students to focus on an aspect of reading that they are experiencing difficulty with, and to use it in a controlled context.

One example of focused instruction is a group of students reading together orally, with a teacher. This activity helps students to focus on reading fluency.

Students may also focus on a reading strategy. For example, students may discuss how to best summarize a story, or they may focus on how to predict when reading a story.

Finally, specific skills can also be presented during focused instruction. For example, if students are having trouble with words containing two syllables, the teacher may concentrate on instruction in syllabication patterns. However, the teacher must make sure that this specific skill instruction is followed by ample opportunities to apply these skills during instructional reading.

Review

Since remedial readers often have difficulty remembering what they have learned, teachers may want to devote a short time to review. Review can focus on difficult *material*, such as vocabulary words or text. Review of material is particularly important for beginning learners, for whom the reading act is unfamiliar. They can readily profit from reading a story over, or reviewing words containing a certain phonics pattern. Older readers may need to review word meanings.

Review can also emphasize *strategies*. For example, students might review with the teacher how to preview before reading a textbook. A review of strategies helps to establish them firmly in students' minds and to give students control over their own reading processes.

Independent Reading

To establish permanent reading habits, students must find reading interesting, informative, and enjoyable. Students should be encouraged to choose their own reading materials. They should be encouraged to choose books that are at their independent level, an easier level than that used for instruction. They can read these easy books on their own, without teacher help.

As they read, students find that reading is not limited to textbooks, for independent reading provides a perfect opportunity to peruse such favorites as *Harry the Dirty Dog* (by G. Zion), *Amelia Bedelia* (by P. Parish), *Soup* (by R. Peck), and *Sweet Valley High* (by F. Pascal).

Independent reading of easy material is particularly important for pupils who have mastered beginning reading skills because it provides the practice they need to consolidate gains (Allington, 1986). Berliner (1981) found wide reading on levels that were very comfortable fostered student achievement.

Discussing the reading selection can add to enjoyment, but discussions should not become testing sessions. Help the student to enjoy the story!

Types of Reading Materials

A wealth of different types of materials can be used to help students with reading problems. The major types of materials are listed below. Lists of specific materials are given in Appendix A.

1. *Remedial reading series books.* These are series of graded books containing stories or articles, sometimes accompanied by comprehension questions and practice exercises. These series are designed to supplement classroom reading instruction, for example in a basal reader. Remedial reading series books are controlled for difficulty level; however, new words from one story tend not to be repeated in another. In addition, topics within the books are generally not related to each other. Thus, the teacher may prefer to use these books with students who have acquired some reading fluency and who can cope with many different subject matters. Examples of these series are *High Action Reading Series* and *Reading for Concepts.*

2. *Easy reading books.* Often called "high-interest–low-vocabulary books," these concentrate on enjoyable reading experiences rather than direct instruction. Thus, they generally do not include exercises for skill development. They contain either several stories or one continuous story. Some easy reading books, such as the *First Reading Books* (formerly the Dolch books) provide reading practice throughout 75 to 100 pages with a total vocabulary of 200 to 500 words. Since this enables a student to practice sight words several times, we recommend these books for remedial students at primary reading levels.

Other easy reading books are controlled for reading level but do not contain specified word lists or repeat a limited number of words. These books may be used effectively to foster wide reading for somewhat more advanced students. Examples are *Attention Span Stories* and *The World of Sports.* Such high-interest–low-vocabulary books are often geared to match student interests (sports, rock stars, teenage problems) and are highly motivating.

3. *Basal readers.* These books are used for developmental reading and are the materials many remedial readers use in their classrooms. Supplementary reading instruction should foster success in reading the classroom basal.

Sometimes older remedial readers use basal readers intended for younger children in their remedial reading classes. Careful pacing and consistent practice make these materials useful for readers who can only acquire sight words with difficulty. However, using a low-level basal may remind older students of past failures; or the child-like style and content of the reader may be demeaning.

Some sets of basals have been designed for use with remedial students. These series contain books which look like at-level basal readers, but are written at lower reading levels. For example, a book designed to be used with sixth graders might contain selections with a fourth-grade readability. Examples of such series are *Focus* (Scott Foresman), *Key Text* (Economy), *Quest* (Scholastic), *New Directions in Reading* (Houghton Mifflin), and *The Reading Connection* (Open Court).

There are also basal readers written in Spanish, and published in the United States, for use in bilingual classes. These readers enable Spanish-speaking children to learn to read first in their native language.

4. *Content area texts.* These are texts used in students' social studies, health, and science classes. Reading teachers may help students cope better in school by teaching them to use effective comprehension and study strategies with these texts.

5. *Trade books.* These are books published for children's free reading. Trade books are extremely useful for remedial readers, particularly in their independent reading. Nonfiction books containing factual information open up worlds of experience. Literature books help remedial students appreciate stories.

6. *Real-life materials.* This refers to the abundance of material that surrounds us, such as newspaper articles, captions of pictures, magazines, manuals, and advertisements. These materials can be used to practice reading and sight words. The interest of such real-life material makes vocabulary control a matter of secondary interest. Some instructional series, such as the *Basic Life Skills*, also concentrate upon students' abilities to perform real-world tasks, for example, using a checkbook and reading job ads.

BUILDING RAPPORT

The value of a successful teacher-pupil relationship cannot be overestimated; it may be far more important than the methods or materials that are used for instruction. Several principles serve as guidelines for building rapport.

Acceptance

Students should feel that teachers accept them as individuals. Often, poor readers are caught in a vicious cycle of reading failure and negative teacher reaction. By the time they have reached the need for special attention, behavioral problems tend to invite rejection by the teacher. Students may understand that they need help in reading, yet it is important to make them feel that, in total, they are likable people. Each remedial student should be accepted as a valuable and promising human being.

Success

Remedial students are in desperate need of experiencing success. Too often, their lives have been filled with unrelenting failure. If the tasks presented in the remedial lesson can be accomplished successfully, this goes a long way to establishing a solid relationship between the student and teacher.

Security

Remedial students also need to feel a sense of security in the instructional setting. One way to foster this is to start each instructional session in the same way, giving students a sense of routine.

Security may also involve a sense of personal space. Eleven-year-old Janet resisted coming to her special reading lesson because of her fear of a new environment. However, when the teacher made a "place" for her by covering the top of her desk with specially patterned paper, she felt she had a special location and became more willing to come and settle down for instruction. If desks are shared with students who come at other times, movable name cards can be used.

Emotional security is very important. Pupils need to become secure enough to be able to take such risks as attempting difficult material and unknown words. They need to feel confident skimming material for information without having to read every word. If teachers provide a secure environment, in which students are not penalized for taking risks, remedial students will learn to take the kinds of instructional risks that are needed to become good readers.

Charting Progress

It is important to provide students with a sense of accomplishment. For example, evidence of progress can be charted easily by displaying a list of words that students have learned. When students enter a room in which several attractive sets of words are displayed on posters, they often try to read these posters, thus multiplying the learning effects. Displays of new words also serve as sight word practice for students at lower reading levels and as meaning vocabulary practice for those at upper levels.

In another example of charting, eight-year-old Samantha enjoyed her personal "bookworm" that the teacher displayed on the wall. Each segment of the worm represented a book she had read. For a group of teenagers who were working to improve reading rate, the teacher charted the progress of each student every day so that they could see how their rate of reading was improving.

When charting progress, however, it is important to remember that publicly displayed charts may embarrass the student who is making few or no gains. For some students, records of progress should be kept private. Chapter 8 provides many ideas for making charts.

Bibliotherapy

Bibliotherapy is a method of using books to help students work out personal problems. By identifying with the characters in the book and overcoming the problem along with the character, students are helped to deal with their own situations (Dreyer, 1985). For example, a student who is faced with the death of a member of the family could read a book about how another individual dealt with a similar problem. The reading experience helps the student to work out his or her own feelings and understand that others have faced and survived such hardships. Three important steps in bibliotherapy are: (1) determining the student's needs, (2) choosing the right book, and (3) discussing the student's feelings. Teachers should recognize that bibliotherapy undertakes to deal with intensely personal feelings and should use this method cautiously.

THE SETTING

The teacher can organize certain elements of the environmental setting, such as (1) choosing individual or group instruction; (2) providing an inviting environment; (3) eliminating overstimulation for distractible students; and (4) establishing the frequency and duration of instruction.

Group and Individual Instruction

Students with reading problems may be instructed individually or in groups. For students with very severe difficulties in reading, individual instruction is often preferable. Individual attention allows the teacher to closely monitor instructional needs. In addition, students can avoid the embarrassment of exposing problems to their peers.

However, for most students, group instruction has considerable benefits. Since reading and writing are communication, the more people we share and use these experiences with, the more we broaden our literacy (Barnes, 1975).

Group instruction enables students to learn from each other. As students listen to the reactions of others to a story, their own comprehension deepens. Sometimes students can explain concepts to their peers that the teacher has difficulties transmitting. They can observe others figuring out words in context or demonstrating comprehension of text, and can use the models of their classmates to help them succeed. They can also share background knowledge. Even if no single student knows much about a topic, if several students pool their knowledge, they will, in total, often provide a good background for reading.

In *cooperative learning* students form small groups, and each group is responsible for the joint learning of its members. Cooperative learning fosters a sense of solidarity among students and often increases the enthusiasm as well as subject-area mastery of all the students.

Group instruction also provides an opportunity to interact and to share literacy experiences. A small group can participate in choral reading and readers' theater (for materials, see Gilford, 1967; Thane, 1967). Pupils can also write to each other.

Sharing reading with others also helps students to become more active readers. They may ask each other questions about material, share and discuss predictions about what will happen next in their reading, and study with each other.

Although group instruction can be highly effective, groups should not be allowed to become too large. Two studies suggest that reading groups up to six individuals are more effective than larger groups (Steirnagle, 1971; Cashdan, Pumfrey, and Lunzer, 1971).

Peer tutoring is a special type of group work in which students teach each other directly. Generally, one student is assigned to another as a teacher. Older students are often used to teach younger ones (cross-age tutoring), or the tutor and learner may be the same age. A noteworthy finding is that students who act as tutors often gain more in reading skills than do the students they are teaching (Sheenan, Feldman, and Allen, 1976). With careful teacher supervision, peer tutoring has proven to be worthwhile for both the tutor and the learner.

The Learning Environment

Teachers should provide a welcoming learning environment. Your classroom should be rich in literacy materials, with trade books, magazines, and pamphlets invitingly displayed so that students will be motivated to pick them up and read. For primary students, plastic letters and laminated cards containing words stimulate literacy activities.

We like to display student-made materials. It is delightful and motivating to walk into a room decorated with student writings, word charts, artwork, and lists of favorite materials. In one class, the teacher constructed a "Book of Our Favorites" from a blank artist's sketchbook. As students read books independently they could enter them on a blank page in the king-sized book and could describe why they were favorites. Other students could go to the book to get ideas for reading.

Displaying books invites children to read them. Books placed on racks or on a table are more accessible than shelved materials. A corner with low chairs or a carpet surrounded by books within reach encourages free reading.

In the same way, a "writing corner" with supplies and collected samples of writing encourages students to record their thoughts and feelings. Writing materials, including pens, pencils, crayons, magic markers, and paper should also be available. If you think about making reading and writing materials accessible to students, you will develop an environment in which it is hard *not* to read and write.

Modifying the Environment for Distractible Students

Remedial reading instruction should adapt to the needs of all students, including the occasional severely disabled reader who is highly distractible. A sheltered physical environment may be needed for this student. Strauss and Lehtinen (1947) advocate providing a private setting. They suggest reducing stimuli by modifications such as having students work in cubicles, covering windows, using a soft voice, and avoiding brightly colored clothing and jewelry.

One teacher reduced the disruptive behavior of a very distractible group by facing their desks away from the door instead of toward it. Thus visitors entering and leaving the classroom were not in the sight line of the students. Another teacher built a three-sided cubicle out of a cutup cardboard box for an extremely distractible boy. The cubicle rested on his desk and gave him—and his neighbors—privacy.

Frequency and Duration of Reading Instruction

One of the most important decisions that a teacher must make concerns the frequency of remedial instruction. Should a student receive instruction three times per week, or should the remedial sessions be limited to once per week? Spache (1981) suggests that frequent instructional sessions in reading facilitate learning for younger students, whereas longer, but fewer, sessions are appropriate for older students. Students with low-level reading skills typically need frequent teaching, since learnings in beginning reading are easily forgotten from session to session. Further, since severely disabled readers can do little reading on their own, they need frequent sessions to practice newly acquired skills. Students who have acquired some proficiency, however, may need less frequent teaching. More advanced students require time to absorb material and to transfer strategies to their class situation. A teaching session held on a weekly basis may suffice for encouraging the development of higher-level comprehension strategies or refining meaning vocabulary.

The duration of the special reading program must also be considered. Should students be kept in a program only long enough to get a "start," or should they be kept in as long as possible? In general, research suggests that remedial readers will profit from instruction that is continued over a long period of time. Spache (1981) reviewed forty studies of reading programs of varying duration and concluded that most students progress at the rate of about two months for each month of remedial instruction. On the other hand, short, intensive programs (5 to 15 weeks) appear to bring the greatest initial gains, (3.4 months' gain for every month of remedial instruction). Guthrie, Siefert and Kline (1978) found that students needed at least fifty hours of instruction to make permanent gains.

Although students continue to improve in reading proficiency while they are enrolled in remedial programs, they tend to fall back to their former rates of reading gains after special instruction has terminated. Measures can be taken to help students maintain remedial gains. Balow (1965) found that, when remedial reading teachers continued to have some contact with students after instruction had stopped, the students continued to maintain high reading gains.

Rennie, Braun, and Gordon (1986) found that students who are encouraged to read and write extensively in remedial instruction remembered these activities, and maintained gains long after remedial instruction had ceased. This indicates that a concentration on reading and writing activities in remediation has a marked instructional payoff.

TEACHING ADOLESCENTS AND ADULTS

The numbers of adolescents and young adults receiving help in reading has increased in the past several years, as society has become more aware of the needs of older students. This section details some of the issues encountered when teaching reading to older students.

Adolescents

Emotional and behavioral problems tend to increase as pupils reach adolescence. Junior and senior high school students often have encountered failure on a daily basis for many years. The school provides little opportunity to escape from failure, so the student may skip school or drop out to avoid facing the instructional situation. But while an adult may choose to change a job if conditions become intolerable, or may choose to remain on the job because of the monetary reward, the failing adolescent has no socially acceptable alternatives to school.

While adolescence has always been a trying time in the human growth process, it seems to have become even more difficult in today's society. Problems such as the rates of school nonattendance, academic disability, mental illness, school violence and vandalism, unemployment, sex-related problems, and drug abuse reach into the lives of adolescents throughout the nation (Cullinan and Epstein, 1979; Rossman, 1980). The ranks of the unemployed are swelled with adolescents who are illiterate or semiliterate. The problem of learning to read is intertwined with all these social, cultural, and personal problems. The ability to read, however, may provide the way out for a troubled teenager.

Adolescents vary widely in their receptivity to different methods of instruction. For example, two adolescent boys (Mark, 17, and Jeremy, 18) recently attended the reading clinic conducted by one of the authors. Both boys were reading at approximately the second grade level and had severe word recognition problems. Mark decided that, because of his severe problems, he would like to read easier material and was given second grade level materials. Although the books were geared toward the interests of younger children, Mark recognized that they helped him to learn the skills he needed for reading. Jeremy, however, wanted nothing to do with these materials. Instead, he wanted to pursue his interest in history. His reading materials were short newspaper articles and picture captions dealing with the life of former U.S President John F. Kennedy. The needs of both adolescents were fulfilled in an acceptable way.

Disabled adolescent readers also have many similarities. In contrast to younger children, they tend to have a keen awareness of their reading problem. Teenagers may also be embarrassed about their inability to read, knowing that they face the possible ridicule of their peers. A limited amount of school time remains to help the reading-disabled adolescent. Each adolescent faces the reality of soon entering the adult world.

There are several different kinds of instructional programs for adolescents. Some are designed to prepare teenagers for further schooling; others are intended to prepare them for the world of work. A survey of approaches being used with learning-disabled adolescents by Alley and Deshler (1979) revealed that five predominant program options are used:

1. *Basic skills remediation.* This approach attempts to improve basic academic skill deficits by providing remedial instruction. Students receive instruction at their current reading level. Stress is placed on improving deficit reading skills. A survey showed that 51 percent of the high-school programs sampled use this approach.

2. *Tutorial curriculum approach.* This approach provides instruction in academic content areas. That is, the teacher helps students with problems they are having in content-area classes, such as English, social studies, or science. The approach tends to be used with readers who have mild to moderate problems. Roughly 24 percent of the programs surveyed used this approach.

3. *Functional curriculum approach.* This approach is designed to help students function in society. They are taught survival skills, that is, skills that will enable them to get along in the world outside of school. These skills include consumer education, completion of application forms, banking and money skills, and life-care skills. About 17 percent of the programs surveyed used this approach.

4. *Work-Study Model.* This approach teaches the adolescent job- and career-related skills by providing on-the-job experience. Students in the program typically spend half the day on the job and the remainder of the day in school. The survey showed that 5 percent of the respondents were using this approach.

5. *Cognitive learning strategies approach.* Alley and Deshler (1979) suggest the use of a "learning strategies" model. The objective of this approach is to teach adolescents how to learn, rather than to teach specific content. In short, this is "learning how to learn." The remaining 3 percent of the adolescent programs in the survey consisted of this type of approach.

Adults

Adults are reentering the learning situation in increasing numbers. Some are relatively young adults who have dropped out of school and now find themselves blocked from employment. Others, particularly women, have been out of the work force for many years and wish to reenter. Still others are currently employed but want to advance in their jobs or enhance their personal skills.

Many adults in reading programs were denied an opportunity for education in their youth. They may have lived in countries where free education was not provided, or perhaps they were forced to work in order to help support their families. Many adult learners are concerned with learning to speak and write the English language.

Characteristics of Adult Learning. Adult learners have many characteristics which set them apart from children and adolescents. The wise teacher takes these into account when planning a program.

1. *Adults need to view learning as useful.* Adults soon lose patience when they do not understand the usefulness of what they are learning. Unlike children and adolescents, adults have returned voluntarily to the learning situation. If learning does not serve their purposes, however, they will not continue. Adults of any learning level are goal oriented about their education. That is, they go to school for a specific purpose—learning to drive, learning skills for employment, or learning to read the newspaper. The teacher must ascertain what purpose the adult has for education, and then address it in instruction.

2. *Adults have a wealth of life experiences.* It is important to respect the fund of information and knowledge which all adults have accumulated. Adults may be remedial *readers*, but they are not remedial *people*. Each of the adults the authors have instructed has some area of expertise—be it knowledge of another country, politics, dancing, or playing a musical instrument. This knowledge needs to be respected. Often adult students can share expertise with each other and with the teacher, resulting in rich and varied classroom experiences.

3. *Adults have many life constraints.* Adult learners are often employed or have families. Thus, many constraints are placed upon their lives. These responsibilities may prevent even the well-intentioned person from attending some instructional sessions. Teachers need to be sympathetic and understanding of such situations. Often they can help by allowing adults to bring small children to class.

4. *Adults may view their reading difficulties as permanent.* An adult who is out of the school situation may come to view a reading disability as a fixed, non-changing condition. Thus, adults often place little hope in the instructional situation, and it is difficult to persuade them to enter remedial instruction, put forth effort, or attend regularly. Because of an adult's often lengthy history of failure, the emotional aspects of learning become very important. Adults may be unwilling to face the negative emotions associated with learning. For these reasons, it is important that the

teacher of adults maintain a positive attitude and be hopeful about the future. Many adults improve their skills considerably through instruction.

Programs for Adults. There are many different types of programs for adults with reading needs. These include, of course, remedial reading instruction. In addition, there are other types of programs available.

1. *ABE and GED Programs* These two programs provide (1) Adult Basic Education—at elementary levels through eighth grade, and (2) high school level education. A person passing the GED examination is awarded a high school equivalence degree. Such programs are funded by the government and require group instruction. In Illinois, a minimum of twenty registrants is required for any program.
2. *Literacy Volunteers of America* This private organization trains volunteers to work with disabled adults in an individual setting and provides materials for tutoring. Programs are aimed toward the illiterate and semiliterate adult. A component for teaching English as a second language is also available.
3. *The Laubach Program* Frank Laubach, a missionary, developed a program for teaching literacy to millions of people worldwide. Materials include initial instruction in a pictorial alphabet. Laubach literacy materials are available through New Readers' Press (see the newspaper *News For You*, Appendix A).

SUMMARY

Providing students with abundant reading experiences is the key element of teaching remedial reading. Students with reading problems often do not read enough to become competent. Instruction should concentrate upon teaching students to become strategic readers by controlling their reading processes.

In addition to providing students with abundant reading experiences, other principles of effective instruction are (1) use material at student's instructional level; (2) support instruction in the home classroom; (3) use time for instructional purposes; (4) increase instructional complexity; (5) plan for students to assume responsibility for their own learnings; (6) encourage silent reading, supported by appropriate oral reading. Teachers should not over-interrupt students' oral reading.

The components of the reading lesson are (1) instructional reading, in which students read at their instructional level; (2) focused instruction, in which students focus on some specific learning; (3) review; and (4) independent reading.

Instructional materials for remedial reading include remedial reading series books, easy reading books, basal readers, content area texts, trade books, and real-life materials.

In building rapport, the teacher should make students feel accepted, facilitate and notice successful experiences, make the student feel secure, and carefully keep records that demonstrate progress. In bibliotherapy, students work out personal problems by reading about people with similar problems.

The setting of remedial instruction can be varied in several ways. Individual instruction assures close attention to severe reading problems; group attention helps students to share excitement and to learn from each other. The learning environment should be rich in literacy materials. Remedial students experience gains during special instruction. After remediation is terminated, however, students often have trouble maintaining gains.

Adolescents pose a special challenge to the teacher because they are very aware of their disability, may present emotional problems, and will soon enter the adult world.

Adults need to view reading as useful. Each adult has a wealth of life experiences. Teachers should recognize the many life constraints of adults. Adults may view their reading difficulties as permanent.

8

IMPROVING BASIC WORD RECOGNITION ABILITIES

This chapter is concerned with providing students basic methods of recognizing words. It must be remembered that learning words is only a means to an end—its purpose is to facilitate reading for meaning. We discuss several cue systems to word recognition: (1) using contextual meaning (context clues), (2) recognizing words by sight (sight words), (3) using phonics, and (4) employing structural analysis. Both phonics and structural analysis are parts of word analysis. Each type of word recognition clue is defined below:

1. *Context clues.* The recognition of words through the meaning of the rest of the passage. Readers make primary use of their language knowledge and experience.
2. *Sight word clues.* The immediate or instant visual recognition of words.
3. *Phonics clues.* The use of the predictable relationships between letters and sounds to recognize words.
4. *Structural analysis clues.* The use of meaningful subunits of words for identification. Subunits include prefixes, suffixes, compound words, etc.

INTRODUCTION

How do young beginning readers normally develop word recognition abilities? First graders who are developing reading ability in a normal fashion quickly build a sight vocabulary of words that they can easily recognize. They use this core of words to do wide reading of stories and books. The wide reading, in turn, helps them to acquire additional sight vocabulary. Soon these primary children are reading for fun, showing off their newly acquired skills to teachers, parents, and adoring aunts and uncles. Within a couple of years, they are able to recognize words quickly and efficiently, and to shift their concentration to the meaning of the reading passage.

In contrast, children with reading problems often continue to struggle with recognizing words, and have little energy left to concentrate on comprehension (Goldman and Pellegrino, 1987; LaBerge and Samuels, 1974). Our goal is to help remedial students acquire fluent word recognition so that they can concentrate on meaning and enjoyment.

For students with reading problems, recognizing words quicky and fluently is not an easy task. Research shows that, as a group, remedial students have deficits in the automatic processing skills that facilitate word recognition (Stanovich, Cunningham, and Feeman, 1984). For example, poor readers tend to take more time than normal achievers to recognize flashed words. In addition, remedial readers are likely to have trouble understanding the alphabetic nature (or sound system) of English. To overcome these obstacles, and to achieve fluent word recognition, they need much reading practice.

USING CONTEXTUAL MEANING IN READING

Contextual meaning (or context clues) refers to the recognition of words through the meaning of the passage and the reader's world knowledge. As we emphasize throughout this book, learning to recognize words is best done in the context of actual reading.

By having remedial students consistently read stories and books, they will naturally learn to make use of context clues.

However, in addition, some students need further instruction with strategies that focus attention on using context. Three such teaching strategies are (1) reminding students to use context clues early in the reading process, (2) encouraging students to monitor for meaning, and (3) using the cloze procedure.

Reminding Students to Use Context Clues First

Students need to be reminded that, when they encounter unknown words in reading, they should use context clues *first*. The meaning of the surrounding context is by far the most powerful tool for decoding an unknown word. Yet many remedial readers use meaning as a *last* resort, only after laboriously trying to "sound out" the word. By stressing the importance of using meaning first, teachers will greatly improve their students' word recognition abilities.

Encouraging Students to Monitor for Meaning

Too often remedial students proceed blithely along through text long after it has ceased to make sense. Such students need to be refocused on the meaning. The teacher might stop students during reading and ask them to (1) tell if there is anything that they do not understand, (2) summarize what they have read so far, or (3) discuss what they are thinking about as they read the text. Stopping students periodically as they are reading and asking questions of this type helps remedial students monitor their reading. It guides them to understand that they must employ contextual meaning to achieve understanding.

Using the Cloze Technique

The cloze technique teaches the use of context and enables students to focus on specific words and syntactic structures. In the cloze technique (also described in Chapter 5) certain words are deleted from material, and students try to supply these words using the sense of the surrounding text. A short example of a cloze exercise is given below.

> Mary saw Bob as he passed by the grocery_____. She waved to him and she called out "Hello."_____he came over to see her and asked her_____she was doing.
> (Answers: store, then, what)

Students may work alone or cooperatively to supply words. After they are finished, it is worthwhile to go over the cloze exercise orally with a teacher. In this way, students discuss the rationale for their choices.

There are several ways to construct a cloze exercise. Words may be deleted in a regular fashion (ie., every tenth word), or the teacher may choose to delete key words that will focus attention on a specific element (such as adjectives). Choices may be provided for deleted words, or students may be asked to insert any word they think fits.

Although cloze is a worthwhile activity, students sometimes find it frustrating. Teachers can make cloze easier by deleting fewer words or providing hints for word completion (such as a first letter).

Several commercial materials are available for teaching cloze (see Appendix A). There are also many variations of the cloze technique, including zip cloze and confirming, which will be discussed later in this chapter.

Diagnostic Teaching of Contextual Meaning

Through teaching context clues, instructors will gain many diagnostic insights. For example, as the teaching of context clues progresses the teacher may notice that children start to use clues without teacher prompting. Another sign of progress is seen when children independently start to reread a sentence that contains an unknown word. Finally, students may spontaneously start to use context clues before phonics, as is suggested earlier. All these indications show advances in learning to use contextual meaning—the reader's most powerful word-recognition tool.

In the remainder of this chapter, we will continue to stress the role of meaning, or context clues, as the most useful way to figure out unknown words during reading. We suggest techniques for combining context clues with the strategies of sight word recognition and word analysis.

FOSTERING THE FLUENT RECOGNITION OF WORDS BY SIGHT

Sight words are recognized instantly, without additional analysis. In this section we present ways for improving the ability to recognize words quickly so students can read fluently. Useful teaching techniques include: (1) using predictable books, (2) assisted reading, (3) the language experience approach, and (4) focusing on individual words. Most of these strategies teach word recognition directly in the context of reading. They also help students to become active learners, providing opportunities for them to choose books and to communicate through writing. The section on sight words concludes with a description of the "Curious George" method, which combines several of the elements of other strategies into a comprehensive program.

Using Predictable Books

Predictable books, or pattern books, contain refrains which are repeated over and over. Many are based on folk tales and fairy tales. For example, you may remember the refrain of *The Little Red Hen* (by P. Galdone), a classic predictable book. As the little red hen asks for help, the other animals reply:

"Not I," said the dog.
"Not I," said the cat.
"Not I," said the mouse.
"Then I will," said the little red hen.
And she did.*

Predictable books are invaluable for fostering word recognition for two reasons. (1) The repeated refrains in the books provide extensive support for word recognition, allowing children to build a mastery of the material. (2) Since many predictable books are based on classic tales, their rich content interests and motivates children (Holdaway, 1979).

Predictable Trade Books. Many predictable books are published in the trade book market, that is, they are intended as children's literature. *The Little Red Hen* (by P. Galdone) and *Fortunately* (by R. Charlip) are examples of such books. Such books may be used for either independent or instructional reading. The work of Peterson (1988) in the Reading Recovery in Ohio Project (1987) has been useful in establishing the difficulty of predictable trade books. Peterson has found that predictable trade books offering maximum support to beginning readers have these characteristics: illustrations that closely describe the action of the text, much repetition of predictable refrains, few different refrains, familiar oral language patterns, content common to personal experiences, and story lines of simple events narrated with little description. In contrast, as books become more difficult, they tend to have: illustrations that do not describe the action, less repetition of refrains, "literary" language, content of fantasy or new information, and more extensive development of plot and characters.

Table 8.1 gives a list of predictable books that are particularly useful at different levels (Peterson, 1988). Peterson emphasizes, however, that levels can only be approximate; the ultimate test of a book's difficulty is a child's response to it.

How can teachers use predictable trade books? It is important to create an environment rich in these books. If possible, buy several books and display them on a table or a rack.

To foster a love of predictable books, teachers should read them to students. This exposes children to the way that the book sounds in fluent reading. After the book has been read to them, invite the children to accompany you in rereading the book, perhaps joining in at the refrain. Experiences with joint readings foster confidence and fluency. Finally, students in a group situation often like to dramatize the stories, each taking a part. After presenting a predictable book in this fashion, leave it in a conspicuous place so that students will be able to pick it up and read it.

Predictable trade books can form the basis of a high-interest, supportive program that gives children with problems the practice they need to become fluent readers. They can also lead to writing. For example, nine-year-old Jeanette, a student in our clinic, wrote several verses based on her favorite predictable book *Brown Bear* (by B. Martin).

*From *The Little Red Hen*, Paul Galdone, Houghton Mifflin, 1973.

Table 8.1 Predictable Trade Books*

AUTHOR	TITLE AND PUBLISHER
	Very Easy Books—through beginning first grade level
Burningham, J.	*The School* (Thomas Y. Crowell)
Lindgren, B.	*Sam's Ball; Sam's Cookie; Sam's Lamp; Sam's Teddy Bear; Sam's Wagon* (Morrow)
Martin, B.	*Brown Bear, Brown Bear* (Holt Rinehart Winston)
Shaw, C.	*It Looked Like Spilt Milk* (Harper & Row)
Wildsmith, B.	*Cat on the Mat; Toot; All Fall Down, Toot* (Oxford Press)
	Easy Books—middle first grade level
Brown, M. W.	*Goodnight Moon* (Harper & Row)
Burningham, J.	*The Blanket; The Baby; The Cupboard; The Dog; The Snow* (Thomas Y. Crowell)
Carle, E.	*The Very Busy Spider* (Philomel)
Hutchins, P.	*Rosie's Walk* (Greenwillow), *Titch* (Macmillan)
Kraus, Robert	*Herman the Helper* (Windmill)
Kraus, Ruth	*The Carrot Seed* (Scholastic)
Tolstoy, A.	*The Great Big Enormous Turnip* (Pan)
West, C.	*Have You Seen the Crocodile?; "Pardon?" Said the Giraffe* (Harper & Row)
Wheeler, C.	*Marmalade's Nap; Marmalade's Snowy Day; Rose* (Knopf)
	More Difficult Books—late first grade level and above
Burningham, J.	*Mr. Gumpy's Outing; Mr. Gumpy's Motorcar* (Puffin)
Carle, E.	*The Very Hungry Caterpillar* (Puffin)
Charlip, R.	*Fortunately* (Four Winds Way)
Emberley, E.	*Drummer Hoff* (Prentice Hall)
Galdone, P.	*The Little Red Hen; The Three Bears; The Three Little Pigs* (Scholastic)
Hutchins, P.	*Goodnight Owl; Happy Birthday Sam; The Wind Blew* (Puffin)
Kraus, Robert	*Leo, the Late Bloomer* (Windmill)
Lobel, A.	*Mouse Soup, Mouse Tales; Frog and Toad are Friends; Frog and Toad Together* (Harper & Row)
Sendak, M.	*Where the Wild Things Are* (Harper & Row)

Adapted from Peterson, 1988.

*Although this table divides trade books into only three levels, the categories mirror the twenty levels used by Reading Recovery to categorize books. Very Easy Books, listed above, cover levels 1–5; Easy Books cover 6–12; More Difficult Books cover 13–20. (See section on Predictable Instructional Books.)

In addition to their use with primary and lower intermediate grade students, predictable trade books also appeal to older students who read on a primary level. Often we encourage older students to read these books to younger children (see Chapter 9).

Predictable Instructional Books. A second type of predictable book, designed to be used in instruction, is suitable for children at the beginning stages of reading. These books are finely graded into many levels, starting from the reading of pictures

A STRATEGY SNAPSHOT: USING PREDICTABLE BOOKS

The use of predictable books is illustrated in a two-week program done in a resource room. Each of the eleven second graders was reading at the primer level or below. The program introduced them to free reading and fostered word recognition. We introduced two books each session. First we read them to the children. Next the children read them twice in unison with us, and finally, the children acted out the ones that lent themselves to dramatization. The eight books used were *Henny Penny* (P. Galdone), *Too Many Lollipops* (R. Quackenbush), *The Good Thing, The Bad Thing* (K. Thomas), *The Little Red Hen* (P. Galdone), *The Carrot Seed* (R. Kraus), *Harry, the Dirty Dog* (G. Zion), *The Very Hungry Caterpillar* (E. Carle), and *Leo the Late Bloomer* (R. Kraus). In the following sessions, individual children identified their favorite books, and read them aloud with our help. Next, each child chose a book which he or she wanted to "write." The child dictated a personal version of the story and we wrote it in a blank book, signing the child as an author. This transformed the children into composers and provided eleven new books for the reading environment. Both the standard books and the child-made books were read avidly.

Because the children were starting to memorize the refrains, we made dittos for them which presented variations and required them to refine their methods of recognizing words. For example, one part of the *Little Red Hen* ditto read:

The mouse said, "Not I."
"Not I," The dog said.
The cat said, "Not I."
"Then," said the little red hen, "I will."
And she did.

We labeled these "The New Little Red Hen," and the children eagerly joined in the fun of reading them. This two-week exploration of predictable books greatly fostered the children's ability and enthusiasm for reading.

with single words and continuing to the reading of fairly complex text at the second grade level. The materials combine high interest with careful gradations of predictability.

Predictable instructional books were first developed in New Zealand, and are used there both as a basic reading program and in the Reading Recovery Program for children with reading problems. At the present time, several sets are being distributed in North America. These include *The Story Box*, distributed by the Wright Group, *Ready to Read*, distributed by Richard C. Owens publishers, and several sets distributed by Rigby publishers (see Appendix A). The New Zealand instructional system, devised by Marie M. Clay (1979, 1982, 1985), divides books into twenty levels of beginning reading. A portion of the book *Mrs. Wishy Washy*, (from the *Story Box*) considered to be level 8, is shown in the accompanying illustration.

"Oh, lovely mud,"
said the cow,

and she jumped in it.

"Oh, lovely mud,"
said the pig,

and he rolled in it.

When introducing books of this type to beginning readers, teachers can go through the book with the children, first reviewing pictures and predicting the story line. During this instruction, the teacher may choose to pronounce and use some of the more difficult story words in speech. Then children and teacher may read the book in unison, or children may read the book with the teacher helping at troublesome points. This assistance should focus on what makes sense (context clues), what would fit the repeating patterns of the book (context clues), and the way in which words begin and end (phonics clues). Readers will probably need (and want) to review books several times to foster fluency.

Many of these books also are available as big books, which reproduce the text and pictures in a much bigger format (usually 23 inches by 15 inches). These big books enable groups of children to see from afar and enable teachers to reinforce some important readiness and orientation to print concepts (see Chapter 5). Moreover, children find big books tempting enough to approach and read with great frequency.

The New Zealand Reading Recovery Program (Clay 1979, 1982, 1985), which uses many of these materials, has been implemented in North America throughout the state of Ohio, centered at Ohio State University (Lyons et al., 1986; Reading Recovery in Ohio, 1987). In this program, first graders in the lowest 20 percent of their classes are identified and tutored individually in a structured 30-minute daily lesson by a teacher trained in the Reading Recovery system. This tutoring is supplemental to regular classroom work. The lessons use predictable books covering the twenty reading levels mentioned above. The daily format includes (1) reading several easy, familiar books to build fluency, (2) composing and writing a sentence or short story which is later used for reading, and (3) the introduction and practice of a new book. Reading Recovery teachers are specifically trained to foster the integration of all reading clues within a reading situation. Letter recognition, awareness of the English sound system, and orientation to print are also included at very beginning stages of reading. Children are tutored for about fifteen to twenty weeks. Results of this program show that more than 80 percent of children are able to function in the middle group of their classroom after completing the Reading Recovery Program (Reading Recovery in Ohio, 1987).

Assisted Reading

In assisted reading (Hoskisson, 1975), students read material together with a fluent reader. A teacher might read material orally with students, students might repeat (or echo) the material a teacher has read, or students might read along with a tape.

There are many advantages to assisted reading. (1) It makes reading less threatening, for the teacher is there to support the student. Thus, reading becomes a cooperative venture rather than a test-like exhibition. (2) It provides students with the opportunity to read a book fluently. Because disabled students have to work hard to recognize words, they have little experience with fluently reading a whole book or story to enjoy it. (3) It gives a model of fluent reading, thus children are exposed to the way that a story should sound, and have a model to work towards.

The goal of assisted reading is to make children into independent readers. Thus it is important that the teacher gradually provide less and less support. Teachers might start by reading an entire book along with students. After a few readings, however, they should only assist when pupils are having problems. Soon, students should be reading the book independently and, if possible, silently. Gradually, the teacher's role in even the *first* reading of a new book should be reduced, so that students learn that they can read a new book on their own.

There are several different versions of assisted reading, including simultaneous reading, echo reading, choral reading, simultaneous listening-reading, and the group oral reading technique. Each is described in this section.

Simultaneous Assisted Reading.   In this technique, the teacher simply reads along with students. With individuals or small groups, the teacher can hold up a single book, which students and teacher read together. With a large class or a more mature group, individual students can each handle their own book or a "big book" can be used. The technique is most effective when material is repeated a few times. Independence is fostered because in each subsequent reading the teacher participates less and less.

Echo Reading.   In echo reading, the teacher reads a few lines or a page of text orally to the students, and the students "echo" this text (B. Anderson, 1981). Echo reading is particularly well suited for primary children, and it may be done profitably as a supportive technique to help children in the readers they are using in their home classrooms.

Choral Reading.   In choral reading, a group of children read material together in order to perform it. Students with reading problems enjoy this activity because it gives them the satisfaction of giving a well-rehearsed, expressive performance, and helps to develop expression in oral reading. Through choral reading, students come to appreciate the fact that reading is fun and a medium for entertaining others. Use material that is intended for performance, such as poems or nursery rhymes.

Simultaneous Listening/Reading.   In this technique, sometimes called *auding*, students listen to tape recordings of material while, at the same time, following along with the book. Simultaneous listening/reading has been used successfully with primary level children (Chomsky, 1978). By listening to a story on an audiotape, students can appreciate story line and language, and are motivated to learn to read the story. Auding is further discussed in Chapter 9.

Group Oral Reading Technique.   Developed by Hoffman (1985, 1987) and further refined by Morris (1986) and Nelson and Morris (1986), this technique is particularly effective for helping primary students to read their basal readers (Morris, 1986). It is a group technique in which children gain needed practice by reading material in several ways. The method usually involves presenting or reviewing a story over three days.

Day 1 - Presentation/reading phase. Children echo read a story, following the teacher's reading. At the end of each page, they predict what will happen next in the story. (This prediction technique, also called DLTA, is further explained in Chapter 10.) Even if the children have read the story before, we have found that the prediction process will be fun and profitable.

Day 2 - Practice/rehearsal phase. Each child is assigned a partner. The story is then reread with the partners changing pages. For example, if a child read pages 20, 22, and 24 the first time, he or she would read 21, 23, and 25 the second time. Children will eagerly listen to a partner's reading.

Day 3 - Performance/recitation stage. The children read independently in order to perform the story. The story may be dramatized, with children taking parts as they read. We have found it profitable to have the children perform twice, changing parts. If the story cannot be dramatized, it is read orally and expressively by the children.

The Language Experience Approach

In the language experience approach, students compose personal stories, which are then used for their reading instruction. Generally, students dictate their stories to the teacher, who records them in writing. Because students have actually produced these stories, they are anxious to read them. In addition, students can see the direct relationship between speech and reading, for language experience stories are "talk written down." Although the language experience approach is used most widely with younger children, it is also very effective with older students who are at lower reading levels.

Many teachers make permanent records of language experience stories. For an individual student, the stories may be printed or typed and collected in a notebook. For groups, the stories may be duplicated so that all students in the group have a copy. Older students often prefer to print (or type) their own stories.

The flexibility of the language experience approach enables it to serve many purposes for different types of students. In her book *Teacher* (1963), Sylvia Ashton-Warner described teaching culturally disadvantaged Maori children in New Zealand. She had children bring in "key words" that they chose to learn. Often, the student selected words that were packed with emotional content, such as *kiss* and *knife*. The freedom that these students felt in bringing in such words pointed to their comfort with the instruction.

To be most effective, the stories should be about experiences that are exciting and of personal interest. A recent first-hand experience such as a field trip, an exploratory trip around the school, an unusual event, a good book that has been read to them, or an exciting television program provides the opportunity to develop a language experience story.

Language experience stories may be used for individual teaching, or they may be used for teaching groups. With groups, the entire group of students can dictate stories, or the students can dictate stories individually and exchange them.

One problem that arises in using this method for remedial instruction is that students with reading disabilities have some difficulties composing a story. The student may have a language disability or may simply be unused to talking in a school situation. Students who encounter this difficulty may be helped to develop stories that they enjoy.

Many "wordless" picture books contain amusing stories related without words. Students can "read" and caption books such as *Frog and Toad are Friends* and its sequels (by M. Mayer) and *Alligator's Toothache* (by D. de Groat).

The visual humor in comic strips can also inspire language experience stories. Teachers may eliminate the dialogue "balloons" of the strips, or cut the words out of the strips and have children provide them. Or the dialogue might be retained, with children asked to summarize the story after they have read the strip.

The arts can be used as tools to express feelings and to respond to particular situations. A drawing of an object, for example, can lead children to see that there are many words to describe the object and many ways to picture it. These responses can be used to build a story (List, 1982).

The language experience approach also fosters reading growth by making children actively participate in literacy through composing. In Chapter 12 we will give two examples of effective reading/writing programs that used the language experience approach, one in an elementary school setting, and another in a secondary setting. The microcomputer has also proven to be an effective way to write language experience stories (see Chapter 14).

Despite its motivational value, there are some students for whom the language experience approach is not effective. Since words for language experience stories come from oral vocabulary, these words may accumulate faster than students can learn to read them. For example, Alonzo, a severely disabled thirteen-year-old reader, had to give up learning to read by this approach because his inability to read his own experience stories eventually frustrated him. Instead, the teacher had to use a method recommended for severely disabled readers (see Chapter 13).

Focusing on Individual Words

Students with reading problems can best learn to recognize words by practicing them in a reading context. In addition, to reinforce the recognition of words, and to gain a sense of control and focus over learning, remedial readers may need to record and practice individual words. While especially useful for children just beginning to read, this activity is also helpful for reinforcing sight word vocabulary that more advanced students are encountering in their classroom readers.

Lists of frequently used words can help the teacher select words for focus. Table 8.2 shows high frequency words based on a study of the Dolch Basic Sight Vocabulary updated by Johnson (1971). Table 8.3 shows common picture words. (These tables are located at the end of this chapter.)

Keeping Records of Progress. Remedial students should be aware of the progress that they are making. This can be accomplished by keeping records of the words that they have learned, or are learning. Because children do much reading, not every word will be chosen for record keeping. Children and teachers might want to choose their favorite new words, or words that present particular difficulty.

There are many ways to keep records of words. The word bank pictured below made from a shoe box can be used as an alphabetical file for new words. Children can also use it for writing with their words. Each reader may have an individual word bank and personal cards.

Sean, who was entering the second grade, had only a few words in his sight vocabulary. His tutor taught him several words from a book he enjoyed listening to. Sean put these words in his word bank and used them to make sentences and to match phrases in his book.

Readers may make colorful displays of their progress in learning words. For example, Eugene's chart, pictured below, recorded his words as "hats," in honor of his favorite book, *The Cat in the Hat.*

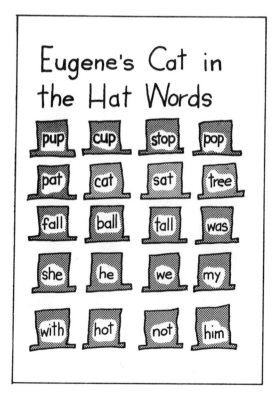

Martin recorded his favorite new words on a Spider-man chart

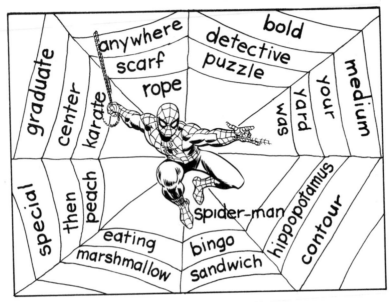

Retaining the words learned is a problem for some remedial readers. For example, Robert, a severely disabled reader, had much difficulty remembering sight words. His retention was facilitated by a consistency chart, where Robert reviewed his word learnings during each tutorial session.

Robert's Word Web

	3/3	3/5	3/7	3/10	3/12
airplane	★	★	☆	★	★
bell	☆	☆	☆	★	☆
box			☆	★	★
cap				★	★
doll		☆	☆	★	★
eye	★	☆	★	☆	★
fire		★	★	★	★
hen		★	☆	★	
money			☆	☆	★
mother		★	★	★	☆

Practicing Words.   Although most facility with word recognition comes from reading extended text, students can also profit from some review of individual words that they are learning.

Word cards provide one way to practice sight words. The teacher can simply ask students to read word cards, or students can select specific words from word cards set before them. Many students enjoy forming sentences from their cards. Readers can be asked to find the word card which correctly fills in a missing word in a sentence. In another activity, the student classifies word cards into sensible groups, such as animals. For variety, many students also enjoy a "switch," in which the student asks the teacher to identify words. Finally, teachers can give a student a personal pack of sight word cards to practice at home with a parent or friend. Make sure, however, that you retain a duplicate copy.

Games provide another way to practice sight words. They are easily made and can be designed for individual students. One type of game uses a "trailboard" such as that illustrated below.

The gameboard is made from a 2' × 3' piece of cardboard, laminated or coated with clear adhesive paper for durability. The words to be used are supplied by word cards that are piled on the board, enabling the practice cards to be changed easily. The student rolls dice (or one die), picks up a word from the pile, and moves the number of spaces indicated, if the word can be read correctly. The card is then moved to the bottom of the pack. A few cards, such as "You have been lucky today and may move two spaces," add spice and suspense to the game. These games can be played with a teacher and a student or several students who may wish to practice words independently.

Another game for practicing words is Bingo. Cards are prepared containing the words, and each space is covered as the word is called. If a student (rather than the teacher) calls out the words, the student must then say the word aloud as well as recognize it. Bingo is suitable for group instruction.

In the game of Fish, words are written on cards with a small magnet attached to each and placed in a container such as a fishbowl or empty coffee can. The student is given a small "fishing pole" with a magnet "hook," which is used to fish out a word and say it. The student with the biggest "catch" is the winner.

The "language master" is a type of recorder that is very useful for practicing sight words independently. Specially prepared cards have a sight word printed on the top of the card and an audiotape of the word on the bottom. The student reads the word from the card and then checks the reading by inserting the card through the language master, which plays back a recording of the word.

Mastering Function Words. Because the recognition of function words may be particularly troublesome for remedial students, they deserve special attention. Function words are the highly frequent but abstract words of English such as *if*, *but*, and *there*. They are distinguished from content words, which consist largely of nouns, adjectives, and verbs.

Function words are extremely frequent in text, but despite this frequency they are often difficult to master. These words tend to have irregular sound/spelling relationships and therefore must be mastered as sight words, since phonics rules often do not apply. In addition, function words can be confusing visually. Consider the words *there* and *them*. Because function words are so abstract in meaning, many students do not realize that words such as *the* and *what* actually *are* words (Cunningham, 1980). Such words cannot be easily pictured by remedial students.

Perfect mastery of all function words is not necessary for efficient reading (K.S. Goodman, 1967). Nevertheless, function words appear so frequently that if they present difficulty, reading will become uncomfortable. Function words are best learned through extensive experience in reading meaningful text. Thus, students who have difficulty should be given much reading at an easy level. This will provide the support of enabling them to predict some function words simply by using the context. The many variations of assisted reading will also help students to recognize function words.

Many students do not realize that context clues can help with function words. In fact, fluent readers use context frequently, often simply skipping function words during reading. Zip cloze (Blachowicz, 1977) is a strategy that helps students to use context clues to recognize function words. In zip cloze, a passage is given to students either on an overhead projector or on the board. However, several of the function words are covered with tape. Students read the passage through once, saying "zip" for every word that is covered. Then, they read the passage again, trying to predict what the missing "little words" might be. After they predict, the tape is "zipped off" and students see if their predictions have been confirmed.

Another strategy for practicing function words is highlighting them in text. Teachers can underline or highlight (using yellow magic marker) the function words in a meaningful passage, and then ask students to read it, first silently, and then aloud. Several passages should be used to give students extended practice in recognizing function words over a period of time.

An occasional remedial reader will require so much practice in function words that these words must receive intensive focus. When doing this, remember that each function word should be accompanied by a sentence, since function words contain little meaning by themselves. Students can use individual word cards with sentences written on the back to practice recognizing words individually.

Word wheels can help students overcome visual confusion of individual function words. Words are written around the circumference of a circular piece of paper that is mounted on cardboard. This paper is then covered with an equal-sized piece of paper that leaves space to expose only one word at a time. The student turns the word wheel to reveal different words.

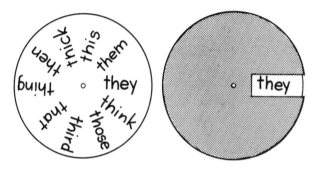

Certain students who find a few particular words to be very difficult may enjoy the "star word" approach. Here, one word is printed on a large star containing some room for little silver stars. The word is then introduced as the "star word" of the day. During a teaching session, it is called to the student's attention at periodic intervals. Each time it is pronounced correctly, a little tinsel star is placed on the big star.

Teaching Reading with Trade Books:
The Curious George Strategy

The interest created by a captivating book sometimes enables students successfully to read material that is above their previously determined instructional level, and to progress more rapidly in overcoming difficulties. A technique we call the "Curious George" strategy has helped children overcome barriers to reading. The method is most useful for small groups of children in the primary grades; it is designed for children who are reading at a low level or who have not yet achieved a reading level. Using children's natural enthusiasm for *Curious George* (by H.A. Rey) and its sequels, and employing many of the techniques described earlier (assisted reading, language experience, and focus on individual words), we have been able to achieve dramatic gains in reading level and enthusiasm.

The "Curious George" strategy has been used informally many times (Richek, 1983–89). A documented field study was reported by Richek and McTague (1988). At the end of an eighteen-day period, the experimental Curious George group had, when compared to a control group, increased their comprehension 25 percent and decreased their miscues 65 percent on passages from an informal reading inventory. These differences were statistically significant, and teachers also noticed a jump in enthusiasm for reading and ability to write independently.

A description of the strategy in action is given below.

A STRATEGY SNAPSHOT: THE CURIOUS GEORGE TECHNIQUE

Instruction is divided into four day segments of about 30 minutes each. On the *first* day of instruction, the teacher enthusiastically reads *Curious George* to the children, while holding the only copy of the book. Next, asking the students to help in reading the book, the teacher and students read together the first 16 pages, in an assisted fashion. Generally, the context enables students to supply many words and to read with some fluency. Next, there is a focus on individual words. Each child chooses five words, and the teacher writes them on pieces of construction paper. Each child should be given a different color. Finally, each child is handed a paperback copy of *Curious George* to take home with his or her five cards, and told to bring the cards and book back the next day.

On the *second* day of instruction, children "show off" their cards to others, reading them if they can. The teacher then gathers the children, and continues with the assisted reading of *Curious George*, pages 17–32. Since they have had the book overnight, the children have generally gained considerable fluency. Next, the children choose five more words, and the teacher writes them down on individual cards. They again take their personal cards and words home, and are instructed to return them.

On the *third* day of instruction the procedures of the second day are repeated, but the children complete the assisted reading of the book, reading pages 32–48.

On the *fourth* day of instruction, the teacher presents the children with a blank yellow "book" made from construction paper. Each page contains a picture cut out from a copy of *Curious George*. Children take turns dictating a text to accompany one picture, and thus make their own *Curious George* book.

After completing four days of *Curious George* instruction, the children read sequels, including *Curious George Goes to the Hospital, Curious George Takes a Job,* and *Curious George Flies a Kite,* in the same manner. Initially, the process of completing a book will take four days, but as children become more confident, they will take less time, perhaps three days. It is important to let children control their own reading process. For example, at a certain point, they may tire of word cards, and prefer to spend their time simply reading books to others or to themselves. As children move toward more independent reading, supply additional books about Curious George. Children will also enjoy playing games with *Curious George* words. Writing activities can also be included. Children enjoy writing letters to *Curious George,* or writing books with such titles as "Curious George and Charita" or "Curious George Joins the Army." Since expression, rather than writing mechanics, is of primary concern, a teacher need not correct the spelling and punctuation in this writing.

Curious George is read in an assisted manner.

Diagnostic Teaching of Fluent
Sight Word Recognition

There are many ways to assess if instructional techniques are helping children. First, we suggest that teachers periodically make individual tapes of children reading orally, say, a passage or two from an informal reading inventory or a book used in instruction. These should be made at two- to three-month intervals. If instruction in sight word recognition and reading fluency is succeeding, tapes made at later dates will have fewer miscues, take less time to read, and sound more comfortable. If a student does not make progress on such recordings, reassess instruction. Perhaps, despite a teacher's best efforts, a student may not be reading enough, and the amount of reading should be increased. Or further efforts might be needed to integrate remedial instruction with home classroom demands.

A reader's enthusiasm may also serve as a diagnostic tool. Disabled students who show little interest for reading often need other methods of instruction or materials that more nearly suit their background knowledge and interest.

Finally, an occasional child making no progress during instruction might be severely disabled and need the more intensive methods outlined in Chapter 13.

TEACHING WORD ANALYSIS

Phonics (or sound symbol relationships) and structural analysis form the cue systems we use to analyze the internal parts of words. Phonics refers to the relationship between printed letter sequences and the sounds in our languages. For example, the letter *b* represents the first sound in the spoken word "boy." Structural analysis refers to meaningful word parts, for example, the *ed* in *walked* or the individual words *cow* and *boy* in *cowboy*. In this section, we will first discuss phonics and then consider the structural analysis elements necessary to acquire basic word recognition abilities.

The Role of Phonics in Remedial Reading

Phonics is one cue system that may be used to recognize words. When combined with context clues, phonics can provide a powerful aid. Students with reading problems must learn to monitor their meaning-getting processes as they use phonics.

There is ample evidence to suggest that sound/symbol relationships of English provide valuable clues to reading (Chall, 1983; Anderson et al., 1985; Pflaum, et al., 1980). Children who can use phonics abilities *in context while they are reading* have a valuable set of strategies. They will be able to decode phonically regular words and to deal with words that are exceptions to phonics rules.

However, overconcentration on phonics in isolated drills robs students of precious instructional time to do the actual reading that will teach them to *apply* their skills. It is easy, but ineffective, to give children many worksheets. It is more difficult, but effective, to help them learn to use phonics while reading.

We know many remedial readers who have spent years with phonics work-sheets and short answer exercises, and still cannot use phonics to read. While good readers tend to learn independently how to apply phonics in reading, problem readers must be systematically taught to do this.

Readiness for Phonics—
Developing Awareness of Sounds

Like most teachers, we have encountered students who could not learn or retain phonics relationships. Research shows that many such students have not devel-oped phonological awareness; that is, they do not perceive that spoken words contain component sounds (Liberman et al., 1977; Williams, 1980; Stanovich, 1986a,b; Vellutino, 1987; Tunmer, Herriman, and Nesdale, 1988). Thus, they cannot under-stand the alphabetic nature of the English writing system, in which letters represent sounds.

Students may not understand that words can be orally segmented into sounds, and that these sounds can be separately represented by letters (or sets of letters). For example, they may not recognize that the word *man* can be separated in speech into three sounds *M-A-N*, and that each of these sounds corresponds to a letter.

Phonological awareness forms the basis of understanding phonics. Research shows that if children are taught the nature of the English sound system, they will be better able to grasp phonics (Williams, 1980; Bradley and Bryant, 1985). Children should first be taught that words can be segmented into sounds, and that one sound can be represented by one letter. After mastering these principles, they can begin to learn phonics.

We have adapted and used a manipulative procedure known as sound count-ing, or phonematic hearing (Ollila, Johnson, and Downing, 1974), very successfully with disabled children. The materials can easily be made. Teachers need (1) several sound counters (popsicle sticks or tongue depressors) for each child in a group and (2) two sets of pictures (sets A and B) mounted on index cards for each child (as described below). The steps in the procedure follow:

1. First choose concrete words with three and four letters that contain the same number of sounds as letters. Draw or find pictures of these words and place them on index cards. We have used the words: lamp, pin, bed, sled, spot, bag, flag, mop, jump, sink, plum, top, desk, drum, hop, sun, mild, hand, list, cot, plum, hat. For seven of the words, write the word underneath the picture (Set A). For the other words (Set B) do not write words under the pictures.

2. Give each child a pack of Set A cards and five sound counters. Working with one card at a time, ask the students to say the word slowly with you and to put a counter in place each time they hear a sound.

3. After they have mastered step 2, present students with the Set B cards, containing pictures but no words. Again, working with individual cards, students say the word orally and place a marker for each sound that they hear. This stage is very difficult, since there are no words accompanying the pictures. It requires considerable practice over a period of three to seven days.

4. Combine the sound counting with spelling. The students continue with Set B cards, but now each student receives a set of twenty sound counters with an individual letter written on each. (The words we have listed will require sound counters with the letters: a, b, c, d, e, f, g, h, i, j, k, l, m, n, o, p, r, s, t, and u.) Students select cards, and spell the words by placing the markers correctly. This stage is optional for teaching the concept of sound segmentation. It is useful, however, for reinforcing knowledge of short vowels, consonants, and consonant blends.

This inexpensive but effective program will help students to learn the regularities of the English sound system so that they can more easily learn and retain phonics.

There are also some commercial programs available for teaching segmentation concepts, including the Lindamood Auditory Discrimination in Depth (see Appendix A).

Teaching Phonics

A working knowledge of the sound patterns of English will greatly help students to analyze words. For reference, we give a list of common phonics patterns in Table 8.4. A short, informal test of phonics principles is given in Table 8.5. (These tables can be found at the end of this chapter.) This test requires students to pronounce nonsense syllables, a procedure which estimates phonics knowledge only in isolation.

When assessing or teaching phonics, allow students to pronounce words in their own speech patterns. For example, pupils with immature speech may pronounce *ride* as *wide*. If the student knows what the word means, however, there is no need to "correct" the pronunciation. This principle also holds true for pronunciation variations due to dialect and language differences.

Introducing and Practicing Phonics Patterns. We recommend that teachers focus on recognizing phonics patterns through groups of words rather than having children memorize rules. Children find thinking of patterns (such as *make, cake, rake*) easier than remembering the complex rules that govern long vowels.

Patterns need to be introduced and practiced so that children can internalize regularities. Examples of some instructional aids we have used are given below. In addition, this section gives some tips for teaching phonics effectively.

SINGLE CONSONANTS (as in bed)

1. Students can look for magazine pictures that begin (or end) with consonant sounds. Labeling these pictures with the actual words they represent reinforces learning.
2. A picture dictionary may be constructed showing pictures beginning with the consonant sounds.
3. Charts can be made using pictures that either begin or end with a certain letter sound (say *l*). The letter should be printed at the top of the chart. Students can be asked to attach a clothes pin to the left of the picture if it begins with the target letter and to the right if it ends with the letter.
4. *Tip:* Consonants provide more powerful clues to word recognition and are more dependable in sound than vowels. Therefore, consonants should be taught before vowels.

CONSONANT DIGRAPHS AND CONSONANT BLENDS
(as in shop and bread)

1. A familiar object (such as a *ship*) can be cut out of paper with the word written on it. The word (*ship*) can be changed by pulling a paper strip which exposes new consonant digraphs and blends (*trip, flip*). The ship below is for practicing blends and digraphs; the mouse helps with single consonants.

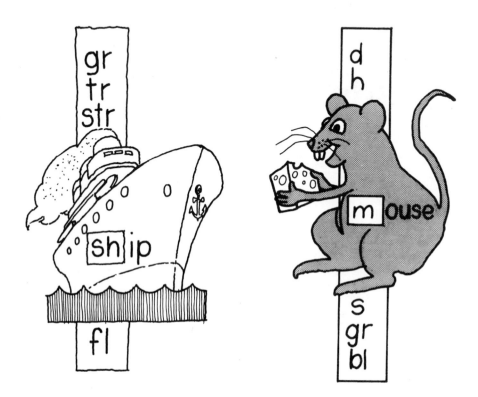

2. Bingo may be adapted using words that contain consonant digraphs and blends.
3. *Tip:* Because consonant digraphs are easier to pronounce than are blends, digraphs should be taught first. Students need not learn how many sounds the digraph or blend represents, nor should they be required to pronounce them in Standard English.

LONG AND SHORT VOWELS (as in cape and cap)

1. A "silent *e* teapot" can be made, and words can be pulled through one side (see picture). The other side contains a paper tab. When the student pulls it, an *e* is exposed and a word containing a long vowel can be read. When the *e* is not exposed, a short vowel sound is used in the word.
2. A cardboard circle can be constructed that has both long and short vowel words around the circumference. A metal pointer can be attached. When the pointer is spun, the student reads the word to which it points (see picture).

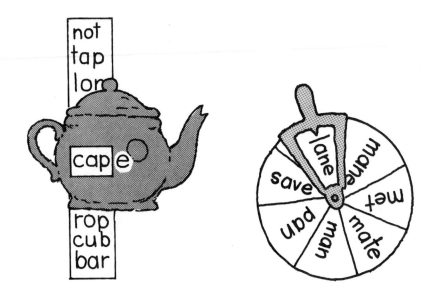

3. Cubes containing single vowel phonograms (with and without final *e;* for example, *ake, at, et, ape*) may be combined with consonants cubes to make words. These cubes can be bought commercially or adapted from Scrabble games. Students enjoy seeing how many words they can make in a two- or three-minute time span. Model word choices may be given by the teacher so that students do not have to spell words.

4. *Tip:* Remedial students will master sounds better when the long and short sounds of each vowel are contrasted with each other (e.g., short and long "a"). This procedure avoids teaching the short vowel sounds, which are very similar to each other, together. In addition, by teaching the long and short sound of a vowel at the same time, teachers can demonstrate how they alternate in such words as *rat, rate; pin, pine.*

R-CONTROLLED VOWELS AND VOWEL COMBINATIONS
(as in fir and food)

A double flip chart, consisting of two sides, either of which can be flipped, may be constructed (see picture). On one side, consonants are presented. On the other side, word endings using vowel combinations are given. The student can flip either side to see how many word combinations can be made. Meaningful words can be written down.

HARD AND SOFT C AND G (as in cat and city)

Students can look for long words containing *c* and *g*. Words can be collected giving students one point for each word up to seven letters, and two points for each word of eight letters or more. Some teachers give an extra point for any word which is an exception to the *c* and *g* rules.

SILENT LETTERS (as in know)

In check-a-match, a checkerboard is constructed with each square containing a silent letter word. The players move the checkers on the board according to rules. However, to stay on any square, they must pronounce the word written on it. Rules for checkers should be simplified.

After introducing children to a phonics pattern and having them practice it, develop their working knowledge by teaching them to transfer their phonics knowledge to a reading context. Students must remember to monitor their phonics application for meaning, especially when meeting the many words that form exceptions to phonics rules. These strategies will help students to transfer a knowledge of phonics elements to reading.

Making Analogies. When students come across a word that they cannot decode, teachers can ask them to think of an analogous word. For example, if a student were not able to decode the word "bay" the teacher might ask "Can you think of a word that ends like this word? (this would be an analogy). If the child could not supply an analogy, the teacher might then say "Think of the word 'day.'" After the child completes reading, the teacher can review the "ay" pattern, demonstrating it with words like "day, may, say." Focusing children's attention on analogous words will help to build up a pattern of phonics correspondences which they can use while reading. However, students with reading problems do experience some difficulties in making analogies (Ackerman, Anhalt, and Dykman, 1986), so learning to use them requires considerable teacher support.

Collecting Word Patterns. Students will also profit by making their own lists of words containing phonics patterns that they encounter in reading. Marcello, a fifth grader reading at a third grade level, was having difficulty understanding the principles involved in long and short vowels. He began to keep a list of words from his reading in which the "a" sounded like the one in *cat*, and a list, on the opposite page, of words where the "a" sounded like *cane*. As he gathered this list, Marcello came to notice patterns that usually determined the letter sound. Soon he began to look for these patterns when decoding words. After *a* words, Marcello went to *e* words, and then to *i* words. He never got to *o* and *u*, for by this time, he had mastered the principle. While making his book, Marcello encountered some exceptions to the principles he formulated. To help remember these words, he wrote down sentences that would help him use context clues.

Using the Confirming Procedure. The confirming procedure (Holdaway, 1979) helps students combine phonics and context. In this strategy, a teacher progressively reveals the words of a text to children, and children form hypotheses about what the next word might be. Often, the teacher reveals only the initial consonant or consonant blend of a word. To do this, the teacher might put a text on an overhead projector or might simply uncover the words in a text that an individual child is reading. Maximum instructional effectiveness will be gained if teachers use an entire short selection or story. The students read up to the word which is covered, and then predict the word. To enable the students to confirm their predictions, the teacher uncovers the first letter, or group of letters. For example, one set of students saw this sentence:

He opened the_____.

They hypothesized that the covered word was probably *door, package, present,* or *drawer.*

Next, the teacher uncovered the first two letters.

He opened the pa _____.

The children then started shouting "package, package." This was confirmed when the teacher showed the next letter, and finally revealed the entire word.

He opened the pac _____.

He opened the package.

Confirming helps students with reading problems to gain proficiency in combining initial phonics clues with context.

Using Meaningful Reading
to Foster Phonics Strategies

In order to master phonics, students need materials which are not only motivating and meaningful, but also present many phonically regular words (Anderson et al., 1985). Materials written using a high percentage of phonically regular words can be unmotivating. Fortunately, many such books are enjoyable for children.

Dr. Seuss (T. Geisel) wrote several madcap tales, such as *The Cat in the Hat, One Fish, Two Fish,* and *Green Eggs and Ham* that help children practice regular phonics patterns. Other trade books that will help children practice phonics patterns while enjoying a good story are *I Can't Said the Ant* (by E. Cameron), *Drummer Hoff* (by E. Emberley), *Rum Pum Pum* (by M. Duff), and *Bam Zam Boom* (by E. Merriam).

In focusing on phonics, teachers sometimes select sets of instructional readers that are phonics based (see Appendix A for examples). In these books, children are systematically introduced to phonics patterns and then practice them in stories which contain a high number of regularly-spelled words.

When deciding whether to select a phonics reader, consider the student's overall program. If, for example, the regular classroom does not use a phonics reader, it might be confusing to the student to use such a book in a resource room. In addition, some of the readers designed around phonics sacrifice good text and interest in their efforts to include phonically regular words.

Structural Analysis for Basic Word Recognition

Structural analysis refers to the process of recognizing words by identifying the meaningful parts within the words. For example, upon encountering the unknown word "playground," the reader might recognize that it is composed of two smaller words—"play" and "ground." By breaking the word into parts, the whole word is identified.

The structural analysis elements most used for basic word recognition are (1) compound words, (2) contractions, and (3) inflectional suffixes (or word endings). (More advanced word elements, including prefixes, roots, and most suffixes, are discussed in Chapter 9.)

Compound words are formed from two words (e.g., *cowboy*, *steamboat*, and *railroad*). Compound words are an excellent introduction to structural analysis skills and may be taught to very beginning readers.

Contractions are two words that have been abbreviated into one by the use of an apostrophe. Examples are *can't* and *I'm*. The student must learn to recognize that a contracted form has the same meaning as the full form. Since contractions are more common in speech than full forms, they generally are not difficult to teach and may be taught at early reading levels. Contractions that signal the future (such as *I'll* and *we'll*) and contractions with *would* (such as *he'd*) may be more difficult.

A suffix is a group of letters added to the end of a word. Inflectional suffixes (which include *s*, *ed*, *er*, *est*, *'s*) are quite common in spoken and written language and are generally taught at the primary-grade reading levels. However, they may present problems for speakers of nonstandard dialects or bilingual students. Since these students may not use inflections consistently in their speech, they may have trouble reading them. When working with such students, the teacher should point out the meaning signified by these inflections, but not be overly concerned about the student's pronunciation. If the student pronounces the word *Mary's* as *Mary* when reading orally, no correction should be made. Rather, the teacher should make sure that the student understands the meaning of the suffix (Labov, 1967). For example, the teacher might ask a student to identify the suffix and tell how it changes the word, *Mary*. Inflectional suffixes include

1. *The plural.* Examples: boys, parties.
2. *The past tense.* Examples: jumped, wanted.
3. *The possessive.* Examples: Mary's, dog's.
4. *The comparative.* Examples: faster, fastest.
5. *The third-person singular.* Example: he sings.
6. *The progressive.* Example: I am going.

As in learning phonics, students need to become aware of structural elements as they are reading. After they finish reading, they can go back to a selection to identify and perhaps list the structural elements.

Diagnostic Teaching of Word Analysis

The most important guide to assessing students' progress in their mastery of phonics and structural analysis is to see whether they are using these cue systems while reading in context. In the previous section on diagnostic teaching, we suggested that teachers make periodic tape recordings of students' reading. These tapes can also be used to assess mastery of word analysis in reading. The teacher can determine whether children are using their context clues and phonics skills jointly to recognize words. They can also see what word analysis patterns children still need to learn.

Two readings of the same text were done by Yolanda at three-month intervals. In the second reading, she could recognize more words and read more fluently, indicating progress with all aspects of word recognition. She showed more use of meaning, as seen by such meaningful substitutions as *home* for *house*. In terms of word analysis, at the first reading Yolanda had trouble with initial consonant blends. At the second reading, she had mastered these. However, her problems with words of more than one syllable remained at the second reading, and these now received focus.

The methods and materials we have suggested in this section are recommended for teaching word analysis in a meaningful context to almost all children with reading problems. There remain, however, a small set of disabled readers who need more intensive approaches. These approaches and their use are detailed in Chapter 13.

SUMMARY

Strategies that are useful in recognizing words are (1) the use of contextual meaning; (2) the instant recognition of words by sight and two-word analysis skills; (3) phonics, the use of sound-symbol relationships; and (4) structural analysis, the use of meaningful word parts.

Context clues involve the recognition of words through the meaning of the passage and the reader's world knowledge. Students need to use context clues first when they encounter an unknown word. Encouraging students to monitor for meaning helps them to use context. The cloze procedure, in which students replace words deleted from passages, also helps develop contextual analysis abilities.

Sight words are recognized instantly. Readers need to recognize words quickly so that they can read fluently. Predictable books, books with repeated refrains, help develop sight vocabulary. In assisted reading, a teacher reads the book with students. Variations of assisted reading include simultaneous assisted reading, echo reading, choral reading, and the group oral reading technique. In the language experience approach, students dictate stories which they then learn to read. Focusing on learning individual words is sometimes necessary for remedial readers. Function words (such as *the, to*) are often difficult to learn.

The goal of phonics is to help students recognize unknown words when they are reading. When combined with context clues, phonics is a powerful word recognition system. Students need to develop an awareness of the sound structure of spoken speech before learning phonics. Phonics learnings may be applied to reading in context through the use of analogies to known words, collecting word patterns in reading, and the use of the confirming procedure. To become useful, phonics must be applied in reading materials.

Structural analysis elements that beginning readers must master are compound words, contractions, and inflectional suffixes.

Table 8.2 Basic Sight Vocabulary Words

PREPRIMER	PRIMER	FIRST	SECOND	THIRD
1. the	45. when	89. many	133. know	177. don't
2. of	46. who	90. before	134. while	178. does
3. and	47. will	91. must	135. last	179. got
4. to	48. more	92. through	136. might	180. united
5. a	49. no	93. back	137. us	181. left
6. in	50. if	94. years	138. great	182. number
7. that	51. out	95. where	139. old	183. course
8. is	52. so	96. much	140. year	184. war
9. was	53. said	97. your	141. off	185. until
10. he	54. what	98. may	142. come	186. always
11. for	55. up	99. well	143. since	187. away
12. it	56. its	100. down	144. against	188. something
13. with	57. about	101. should	145. go	189. fact
14. as	58. into	102. because	146. came	190. through
15. his	59. than	103. each	147. right	191. water
16. on	60. them	104. just	148. used	192. less
17. be	61. can	105. those	149. take	193. public
18. at	62. only	106. people	150. three	194. put
19. by	63. other	107. Mr.	151. states	195. thing
20. I	64. new	108. how	152. himself	196. almost
21. this	65. some	109. too	153. few	197. hand
22. had	66. could	110. little	154. house	198. enough
23. not	67. time	111. state	155. use	199. far
24. are	68. these	112. good	156. during	200. took
25. but	69. two	113. very	157. without	201. head
26. from	70. may	114. make	158. again	202. yet
27. or	71. then	115. would	159. place	203. government
28. have	72. do	116. still	160. American	204. system
29. an	73. first	117. own	161. around	205. better
30. they	74. any	118. see	162. however	206. set
31. which	75. my	119. men	163. home	207. told
32. one	76. now	120. work	164. small	208. nothing
33. you	77. such	121. long	165. found	209. night
34. were	78. like	122. get	166. Mrs.	210. end
35. her	79. our	123. here	167. thought	211. why
36. all	80. over	124. between	168. went	212. called
37. she	81. man	125. both	169. say	213. didn't
38. there	82. me	126. life	170. part	214. eyes
39. would	83. even	127. being	171. once	215. find
40. their	84. most	128. under	172. general	216. going
41. we	85. made	129. never	173. high	217. look
42. him	86. after	130. day	174. upon	218. asked
43. been	87. also	131. same	175. school	219. later
44. has	88. did	132. another	176. every	220. knew

From Dale D. Johnson, "The Dolch List Reexamined," *The Reading Teacher*, 24 (February 1971), pp. 455–456. The 220 most frequent words in the Kucera-Francis corpus. Reprinted with permission of Dale D. Johnson and the International Reading Association.

Table 8.3 Eighty-five Picture Sight Words*

1. farm	23. telephone	45. mouth	67. ear
2. clothes	24. hat	46. nose	68. rollerskates
3. money	25. window	47. garden	69. sled
4. water	26. television	48. hand	70. radio
5. grass	27. car	49. snow	71. clown
6. fence	28. cookie	50. rain	72. bread
7. stoplight	29. apple	51. fire	73. tree
8. bus	30. school	52. dish	74. mirror
9. balloon	31. book	53. hair	75. bag
10. cake	32. chicken	54. children	76. pumpkin
11. duck	33. nurse	55. lion	77. flag
12. barn	34. store	56. world	78. candle
13. street	35. door	57. watch	79. castle
14. hill	36. doctor	58. picture	80. jewel
15. man	37. teacher	59. shoes	81. bicycle
16. house	38. egg	60. bed	82. baby
17. woman	39. rabbit	61. chair	83. sock
18. airplane	40. flower	62. table	84. horse
19. train	41. sun	63. spoon	85. ring
20. boat	42. cloud	64. fork	
21. dog	43. shadow	65. truck	
22. cat	44. eye	66. bird	

*Compiled from a survey of widely used basal readers.

Table 8.4 Useful Phonics Generalizations

1. *Single Consonants*: Reading grade level 1
Generally, consonants are dependable in sound. They include *b*, *d*, *f*, *h*, *j*, *k*, *l*, *m*, *n*, *p*, *r*, *s*, *t*, *v*, *w*, *x*, *y*, and *z*. C and g have two common sounds (see item 7).

2. *Consonant Digraphs*: Reading grade level 1
These refer to two consonants that, when together, make one sound. Common digraphs are *sh*, *ch*, *ck*, *ph*, and *th* (as in *thy* and *thigh*). Qu is sometimes considered a digraph.

3. *Consonant Blends*: Reading grade level 2
These are two or three consonants blended together for pronunciation. Beginning blends include *st*, *gr*, *cl*, *sp*, *pl*, *tr*, *br*, *dr*, *bl*, *fr*, *fl*, *pr*, *cr*, *sl*, *sw*, *gl*, *str*. Ending blends include *nd*, *nk*, *nt*, *lk*, *ld*, *rt*, *nk*, *rm*, *rd*, *rn*, *mp*, *ft*, *lt*, *ct*, *pt*, *lm*.

4. *Single Vowels, Long and Short Vowels*: Reading grade levels 2–3.
Long vowels are sometimes called "free" or "glided" forms. Short vowels are called "checked" or "unglided." Examples are:

VOWEL	SHORT SOUND	LONG SOUND
a	apple	pane
e	egg	teeth
i	igloo	ice
o	pot	home
u	run	use, tuba

Long vowels occur (a) when a vowel is followed by a consonant and an *e*, the *e* is usually silent (e.g., *rate*), and (b) when a vowel ends a word or syllable (e.g., *be*, *begin*). Short vowels occur when a single vowel is followed by one or more consonants (e.g., *rat*). Words like *rate* are often contrasted to pairs such as *rat*.

5. *"R"-Controlled Vowels:* Reading grade levels 2–3
These include *ar* (car), *er* (her), *ir* (stir), *or* (for), *ur* (fur). Note that *er*, *ir*, and *ur* sound alike.

6. *Vowel Combinations:* Reading grade levels 2–3
Dependable combinations include *oa* (boat), *ai* (raise), *ee* (bee), *oi* (boil), *aw* (saw), *ay* (say), *ew* (blew), *ou* (loud). Less dependable combinations are *ea* (seat, bear), *ow* (cloud, low), *oo* (boot, look).

7. *Hard and Soft "C" and "G":* Reading grade level 3
Hard and soft sounds are

LETTER	SOFT SOUND	HARD SOUND
c	city	cut
g	general	gold

Generally, soft sounds are followed by *e*, *i*, and *y*. Hard sounds occur elsewhere. These principles are more dependable for *c* than for *g*.

8. *Silent Letters:* Reading grade levels 3–4
When consonant combinations cannot be pronounced together, the second is *usually* pronounced (as in *know* and *would*). However, when the second consonant is *h*, the first consonant is pronounced (as in *ghost*).

Table 8.5   Words for Testing Phonics Generalizations

These nonsense "words" can be used to test phonics mastery. They should be typed in a large typeface or printed neatly and presented in a list format or on individual cards. Students should be warned that they are not real words, when asked to pronounce them.

1. SINGLE CONSONANTS

bam	fep	dif
dup	jit	hak
sut	rez	jer

2. CONSONANT DIGRAPHS

shap	chep
thip	quen
nack	

3. CONSONANT BLENDS

sput	streb	pind
crob	plut	gart
flug	grat	rupt
dreb		

4. SINGLE VOWELS: LONG AND SHORT

mab	sote	vo
mabe	lib	vom
sot	libe	

5. "R"-CONTROLLED VOWELS

dar	tor
ser	snir

6. VOWEL COMBINATIONS

toat	doil	geet
vay	roub	rood
zew		

7. HARD AND SOFT "C" AND "G"

cit	cam	gast
cyle	ges	

8. SILENT LETTERS

knas	wret
gnip	ghes

9

IMPROVING ADVANCED WORD RECOGNITION AND TEACHING WORD MEANINGS

This chapter focuses on strategies for teaching the recognition of more difficult words and for helping students learn word meanings.

INTRODUCTION

As students reach the intermediate grade reading levels, they must start to deal with longer and more difficult words. This chapter presents techniques for decoding long words, including strategies for syllabication and making use of advanced structural analysis. In addition, a four-step technique to teach students how to combine all of their word recognition strategies in recognizing difficult words is given.

Techniques are also given for fostering fluency in older readers and for dealing with some common problems that remedial readers have in word recognition, including finger pointing, lip reading, reversing letters and words, and difficulty reading silently.

The last part of the chapter is devoted to helping remedial students to learn word meanings.

RECOGNIZING MULTISYLLABIC WORDS

Many students who can recognize one-syllable words such as *cat* and *kite* falter when presented with longer and more complex words, such as *assisted* or *lilac*. To recognize such long words, readers can divide them into syllables (syllabication) and use structural word parts, such as *ing* and *tion* (structural analysis).

Why do students have problems recognizing long words?

1. *Students do not combine phonics and context clues.* Even if the student has mastered phonics generalizations, many long words contain exceptions to rules. Therefore, students should use context clues in decoding long and complex words. In this way, students can check the words they are trying to decode against the sense of the sentence. Together, phonics and context skills are powerful partners in recognizing long words.

2. *Students are overwhelmed by the reading situation.* Since long words typically occur in difficult reading material, the material, as a whole, may overwhelm and confuse the students. To avoid this, teachers need to assure that students are reading material which is at an appropriate level.

3. *Students do not know the meaning of the word.* Because remedial students may not have encountered certain words in speech, they are unfamiliar with their meaning. For example, Jeremy, a fifth grader, encountered the word *dysentery* in a book about Albert Schweitzer. Even though Jeremy could pronounce the word, he was not sure that he was correct, for he had never heard of *dysentery*. Teachers need to be alert to the need for introducing word meanings.

Remedial students often encounter problems with all aspects of recognizing longer words (pronouncing them, dealing with the words in context, and knowing word meanings) at the same time.

Syllabication Strategies

An awareness of syllabication guidelines (or rules) helps students to recognize long words. For your reference, a list of these guidelines can be found in Table 9.1. It is also useful to give a simple diagnostic test to check the student's ability to use syllabication principles and structural analysis principles in isolated words. Such a test is found in Table 9.2. Note that nonsense words are used so that we are certain students do not recognize words by sight.

Phonics guidelines do not work for many multisyllabic words. The *schwa*, a sound found in many multisyllabic words, creates many inconsistencies. The *schwa* is a reduced vowel that is found in words containing unstressed syllables, such as so*fa* or cott*on*. Students are confused because when they apply syllabication principles they get full vowel sounds, but the correct pronunciation of the word uses the unstressed sound. For example, students might try to pronounce the word *soda* as *so-dāy'*.

The types of sound-symbol inconsistencies shown by the *schwa* suggest three important principles for teaching multisyllabic words:

1. Teach students syllabication in a reading context. Then if the word does not perfectly follow syllabication guidelines the context helps the reader to arrive at a word that sounds similar and also makes sense in the sentence.
2. Introduce words that fit the same syllabication pattern together so that students, through practicing patterns, will unconsciously learn to use regularities. The goal is to have students *use* their knowledge, not recite it, to recognize word patterns rather than to memorize long rules.
3. Do not overburden remedial students with technical terms. It is unnecessary, for example, to learn the definition of a *schwa*. What students *do* have to know is that when the syllabication rules will not lead to a perfect pronunciation of a word, it may be necessary to adjust the sounds.

Table 9.1 Syllabication Guidelines

1. In a compound word, each small word is usually a syllable (e.g., cow-boy).
2. Structural word parts are usually syllables (e.g., re-wind; slow-ly).
3. Vowel combinations and "r"-controlled vowels usually retain their own sounds (e.g., taw-dry).
4. When a single vowel occurs in a multisyllable word:
   a. If it is followed by two consonants, it is generally given its short sound. This pattern may be referred to as VCC: "lit/tle," "ap/ple," "res/cue," "pic/nic". Teach this rule first with double consonants ("lit/tle, "ap/ple"). Then teach different middle consonants ("res/cue," "pic/nic").
   b. If it is followed by only one consonant, (1) the vowel may have its long sound (VCV, as in "li/lac," "tu/ba," "so/lace"), or (2) the vowel may have its short sound (VCV as in "ben/efit," "sev/eral," "mim/ic"). Students should try the long sound first, then the short sound.
5. The letters "le" at the end of a word are pronounced as in "rattle."

Table 9.2   Informal Test for Syllabication Abilities

Students may be asked both to divide these words into syllables using paper and pencil and to pronounce them.

1. COMPOUND WORDS	2. STRUCTURAL WORD PARTS
playdog	stipment
freeday	gaiter
	repainly

3. VOWEL COMBINATIONS	4a. VOWEL FOLLOWED BY ONE CONSONANT
tainest	waman
bayter	sowel
stirler	fomub
	setin

4b. VOWEL FOLLOWED BY TWO CONSONANTS	5. *LE* COMBINATIONS
mattel	rettle
fuddot	sontle
sandot	
dembin	

The strategies given below focus on helping students recognize patterns in longer words, and to use these patterns to decode words while they are reading.

Recognizing Syllables in Speech.   Some students are unaware that syllables are separate entities, and such students are often unable to decode multisyllable words. The strategy of "clapping syllables" is enjoyable and helps students develop awareness of syllables in speech. First, read a sentence containing some words with one, two, and three syllables. Then repeat the sentence word by word. After each word, ask students to clap once for each syllable that they hear. If they do not hear syllables clearly, repeat the word, and model the clapping pattern. It is fun to incorporate students' names into these sentences. An example might be:

Annabelle (3 claps) likes (1 clap) to (1 clap) listen (2 claps) to (1 clap) wonderful (3 claps) stories (2 claps).

Reading Multisyllabic Word Patterns in Sentences.   Remedial students often need direct, focused instruction with multisyllable words to see the patterns of regularity. In the teaching sequence which follows, words containing common syllabication patterns are given and then used in sentences, so that students can combine syllabication principles with meaning to try to figure out words in context. Note that the words in the example below have been chosen to be within most remedial students' meaning vocabularies.

1. *Double Consonant Patterns.* First concentrate upon words, such as *matter,* which contain double consonant patterns. (This pattern will also help students to master words ending with *er* and *le.*) Students should read sentences and try to decode these words:

    matter. My mother wanted to know what was the *matter* with me.
    little. I have only a *little* bit.
    manner. You should speak to people in a nice *manner.*
    bubble. I want to buy some *bubble* gum.
    pattern. My mother likes to use a *pattern* to sew.

    After completing such an exercise, students examine all of the double consonant words together, note the vowel sounds, and determine where these words are divided into syllables. They should also note that each syllable contains one vowel or group of vowels. Students can think of examples of other such words, or find them in their textbooks.

2. *Vowels controlled by two different consonants.* In the next lesson, students concentrate on words containing a vowel followed by two consonants that are different (such as *content*). With this set of words, the teacher starts to introduce three-syllable words (such as *tendency*).

    concert. I went to a rock *concert.*
    publish. I would like to *publish* a book.
    pencil. You can write with a *pencil.*
    tendency. I have a *tendency* to sleep late.

3. *Vowel followed by one consonant.* The instruction of the next lesson focuses on words in which a vowel is followed by only one consonant. In pattern 1, the first vowel has the long (or glided or unchecked) sound and ends the syllable; in pattern 2, the first vowel has the short sound and the first syllable ends with the consonant. First introduce these sentences:

Pattern 1.
    lazy. A *lazy* child likes to stay in bed.
    decide. I must *decide* if I will go out to play.
    music. I like to hear *music.*
    total. The *total* of two and two is four.

    After students note the pattern 1 sentences, give the students pattern 2 sentences.

Pattern 2.
    animal. A dog is an *animal.*
    finish. A person should *finish* his work.
    principal. The *principal* of the school rang the bell.

Comparing pattern 1 words with pattern 2 words teaches remedial students that they must be flexible in recognizing multisyllable words. Many teachers like to spend an extra day on these two sets of words, asking students to classify the words into two piles, depending upon the sounds (long or short) of the first vowel. To do this, place each word on an index card which contains the word *and the sentence* so that the students can check meaning.

4. In the next lesson, take *all* of the words that have been introduced so far, and ask students to sort them into patterns that help them to pronounce the words. Students' proficiency in doing this will help determine if they need some review of these patterns.

5. *Exceptions to regular word patterns.* As a last step, words will be introduced that do not conform to regular patterns.

The following words have special vowel sounds.

organ. Our heart is an *organ* in our bodies.
persuade. I tried to *persuade* my mother to give me a a gift.
author. An *author* writes books.
country. There are many trees in the *country.*

The next group of words are irregular, and conform to no pattern. Tell students that, while these words are irregular, they can probably figure them out by using some decoding skills and the context.

money. I would like to earn *money.*
chorus. The *chorus* sang a song.

This direct instruction in multisyllabic word patterns gives students a model for using syllable skills flexibly and for dealing with exceptions. Although this sequence provides students with a start in syllabication, they will need much more practice reading multisyllabic words in context before they become fluent in recognizing them. The strategies which follow give practice opportunities.

Reading Multisyllabic Words in Passages.   Students can gain experience recognizing long words by reading short selections. To focus attention, the teacher can underline several multisyllabic words in a short selection. The student silently reads the selection, combining syllabication principles and context into decoding the underlined words. A short sample of a passage follows:

"We want you to give up this *experiment.* You can't *afford* to go on." Charles looked at his friends for a moment. Then he shook his head. "I can't afford to stop," he said. "Some man will *succeed* in finding a way to use *rubber.*"

After reading the passage, the teacher asks students to identify each underlined word. For words they cannot identify, the teacher models the strategy of combining context and syllable division.

We suggest that students read complete short passages, rather than excerpts. After students read, they should focus on comprehension of the passage. Use this strategy for an extended period, perhaps using ten to fifteen passages in all.

Practicing Long Words in Instructional Reading.   Remedial students need additional practice in decoding long words in their general reading. To maintain the focus on multisyllabic words, ask students to note words that they have difficulty with as they are reading classroom or free reading material. To remember the unknown words, students can (1) lightly underline or check these words in their books, (2) use page markers to locate the words later, or (3) write words (with the page number) on a separate sheet of paper. After reading, have students go back and list the difficult words so that they can discuss them with the class or teacher. It is important that this activity not overwhelm students or keep them from enjoying reading. We usually limit students to just a few, very important or interesting, words per story. For even more focus, students can classify their lists by the way that the first syllable is divided.

Using Structural Analysis

Structural analysis elements refer to meaningful parts of words, such as *al* in the word *national* or *milk* and *shake* in *milkshake.* Since so many long words contain structural analysis elements, they are very useful in word recognition. For example, most readers will recognize the word *unending* by breaking it apart into the elements *un, end,* and *ing.*

Structural analysis can be divided into five different categories.

1. *Compound words.* Two root words are combined to form a new word (e.g., *cowboy*).
2. *Contractions.* Two words are put in reduced form (e.g., *cannot* becomes *can't*).
3. *Suffixes.* These are attached to the end of the word (e.g., *ed* in jumped, *ly* in actively).
4. *Prefixes.* These elements are attached to the beginnings of words (e.g., *un* in untie).
5. *Roots.* These form the main or central portion of a word (e.g., *end* in unending).

Although the mature reader is aware of all categories of structural analysis, each is especially useful at a different stage of the reading acquisition process. Contractions and compound words are most useful at the beginning stages of reading (see Chapter 8). Prefixes, roots, and most suffixes are used to identify longer words.

Suffixes.   Suffixes, or word endings, are very common in written English, and they provide valuable clues to recognizing long words. In running text, more than half of the words of more than one syllable contain suffixes. However, since many suffixes are more common in written language than in oral language, students may lack conscious awareness of them (Ives, Bursuk, and Ives, 1979). Remedial students often ignore word endings and need to practice focusing on them. Suffixes are fun and fairly easy to teach; a relatively small amount of effort can markedly increase a student's ability to recognize long words.

Many suffixes change the part of speech of a word. Examples of this are *identify—identification* (verb becomes a noun) and *comfort—comfortable* (noun or verb becomes an adjective).

Table 9.3 lists some of the most common suffixes in English and their approximate grade levels (Richek, 1969). Since almost all remedial readers have a subconscious awareness of them, it is not necessary to teach suffixes one at a time. Instead, it is more productive to teach students to be aware of suffixes as they read in context.

Three activities are useful for helping students to use suffixes.

1. Select a short text, and ask students to underline each suffix that they find. Provide the hint that some words contain two or even three suffixes. (We find words like ill-ness-es and publish-er-s in third and fourth grade materials.) Once students have completed this task, review it with them. Few remedial students catch *all* of the suffixes, and they will enjoy finding out about the less obvious ones. This activity also gives the teacher a chance to help students become aware of spelling changes (such as the relationship of *hurried* to *hurry*).
2. In a slightly more difficult task, students listen to (rather than read) a text read by the teacher. Each time they hear a suffix, they tap a table. For some words, they must tap two or three times. Since this requires intense attention, it deepens students' understanding of suffixes. Our older students often enjoy using newspaper articles for this activity.
3. Select one word and see how many different words students can make from it using suffixes. For example, from the word *sleep* they may make *sleeping, sleepily, sleepless*, etc.

Students can also increase their facility with suffixes by collecting words with suffixes and keeping notebooks of suffixed words that they meet in reading. To do

Table 9.3 Graded List of Suffixes

FIRST GRADE		SECOND GRADE	
er, est*	bigger, biggest	able	serviceable
s, es (plural)*	ponies	al	seasonal
s (possessive)*	Jane's	ing	singing
s (third person)*	she dances	ly	slowly
ed (past)*	waited	ness	bigness

THIRD GRADE		FOURTH GRADE		FIFTH GRADE	
y	cherry	ish	childish	ance	insurance
tion	relation	ive	impulsive	ity	serenity
ist	violinist	ful	beautiful	ent	excellent
ic	angelic	ency	presidency	age	postage
ize	idolize	ery	slavery	an	musician
ment	contentment	ous	famous		
		ate	activate		

*These are inflectional suffixes. Other suffixes are derivational.

this, students put a different suffix on the top of each page of a blank notebook. Then, as they encounter words with this suffix, they simply enter them in the notebook. Below, a list made by Ramireo, a fifteen-year-old remedial reader, is given.

Ramerio encountered these suffixed words in his reading.

Entire classes can keep joint lists. One intermediate-grade Chapter I group decided to hunt for a word containing as many suffixes as possible. Over several weeks, three suffixed words were succeeded by four suffixed words, and finally, someone found a word with five suffixes!

Prefixes and Roots. In addition to suffixes, structural analysis includes prefixes (word beginnings) and root words (the main part of the word). Many prefixes and roots used in English descend from Greek and Latin. Because both prefixes and roots contribute basic meaning to the words they form, remedial students can use them for vocabulary building. Examples of prefixes which affect word meaning are *pre* (before) and *trans* (across); examples of such roots are *port* (to carry) and *script* (to write). Students who know the meaning of a root such as *script*, for example, can more easily learn the meanings of *postscript, prescription, scribe,* and *inscription*. A list of useful roots and prefixes (Richek, 1969) is given in Table 9.4.

Table 9.4 Useful Prefixes and Roots

PREFIXES			ROOTS		
anti	antifreeze	against	astro	astrology	stars, heavens
aqua	aquarium	water	auto	automation	self
ante	antedate	before	micro	microscope	small
endo	endoderm	inner	aque	aqueduct	water
ex	exoderm	outer	bio	biosphere	life
ex	ex-president	former	dent	dentist	teeth
geo	geography	earth	dict	dictate	word
im	impossible	not	equi	equivalent	equal
non	nonparallel	not	itis	bronchitis	illness
post	posttest	after	graph	biography	write
pre	pretest	before	ling	linguistics	language
re	rewind	again	mid	amid	middle
semi	semisweet	sort of	ortho	orthodontist	straight
sub	subterranean	below	phobia	claustrophobia	fear
tele	television	far	phon	phonics	sound
trans	transistor	across	polit	political	politics
un	undo	not	script	scripture	writing
			sonic	resonant	sound
			spec	spectator	sight
			therm	thermometer	heat
			viv	vivid	life
NUMBERS					
mono, uni	1		oct	8	
di, bi	2		non	9	
tri	3		dec	10	
quadr, tetr	4		cent	100	
quint, penta	5		milli	1/1000	
hex, sex	6		kilo	1000	
hept, sept	7		hemi	1/2	

Reading Words through the Four-Step Strategy

Often remedial readers have received instruction in strategies for word recognition, yet do not know how to combine these strategies during reading. In contrast to good readers, readers with problems tend to overuse phonics clues and underuse meaning clues.

The four-step strategy for word recognition (Richek 1983–1989) combines the use of several different ways to recognize unknown words. The technique teaches remedial readers how to use clues in the sequence that more efficient readers employ. Readers are shown how to use meaning clues first, and then to check these with phonics and structural analysis.

We have found that this technique is successful in showing baffled readers how to integrate and apply their word recognition skills. Our intermediate and older students have found the four-step procedure to be particularly helpful.

1. If you don't know a word, first reread the sentence and try to figure it out (context clues).
2. If that doesn't work, sound out the first syllable and then reread the sentence (phonics clues).
3. If you still don't know it, look for word endings and try to figure out the base word (structural analysis clues).
4. If you still haven't figured it out, sound out the whole word. Remember, you may have to change a few sounds to make the word make sense (phonics clues).

The teacher should model the use of the four-step strategy over a period of a few days. Then students can practice using it independently in their reading. Our students sometimes list the words they have figured out after step 1, after step 2, etc. The four-step technique is designed to be used throughout the year. The procedure can become a reminder if put on tagboard for permanent display and reference in your classroom.

Diagnostic Teaching of Multisyllabic Words

It takes many years to become proficient in recognizing multisyllable words. Because improvement comes slowly, teachers must look for signs that indicate progress. A first indication, paradoxically, is when students realize that they cannot recognize long words. Typically, when remedial students have great difficulties with longer words, they simply overlook them, without even attempting recognition. As students start to demand more meaning from text, they realize they do not know a word, and ask the teacher about it.

The following procedure helps to determine whether students are aware of words that they do not know. First, ask students to read a short passage to themselves. Then ask if there were any words that the students did not know, and note these words. Next, locate a few *other* words in the passage, and ask the student to read them. If the students are able to read these other words, this is a promising sign that control is being gained over unknown words. In contrast, if the students cannot read the other words you chose, they still need more experiences to become more aware of the words in the reading environment.

Another indication of progress toward the recognition of unknown words is the student's ability to separate the first syllable of a word from the rest of a word (Barr and Sadow, 1985). If you note that students are showing more ability to do this, they are making progress in recognizing long words.

Some students cannot recognize long words because they do not know the meaning of these words. In order to determine knowledge of word meaning ask the student to define the word or to use it in a sentence.

FOSTERING FLUENCY IN OLDER READERS

Remedial readers functioning at the intermediate and upper grades often need to continue to work toward fluent reading. Abundant reading practice helps to develop the fluency they need to free them from focusing on words and enable them to concentrate on meaning (Samuels, 1988). In addition, we recommend the following strategies for intermediate students, adolescents, and adults.

The Neurological Impress Method (NIM)

This is a read-along technique that involves the teacher and student reading simultaneously (Heckelman, 1969.) This method is particularly effective with reading disabled adolescents. The underlying theory is that a new learning process, a neurological memory trace, is established when pupils see the words in print and hear both the teacher's and their own voices saying the words. Heckelman suggests that students who are permitted to make mistakes without hearing the correct versions of text become imprinted with incorrect responses that are later difficult to eradicate. The neurological impress method exposes students to accurate, fluent oral reading while enabling them to contribute to the reading process.

In this technique, student and teacher try to read as much continuous material as possible. Students should begin reading with material that is approximately at their independent level and that may have been read before successfully. Students are told to not be concerned about reading accuracy, but to try to read fluently, without looking back. Pictures are to be disregarded.

In the neurological impress method, the teacher and student both hold the material. The teacher is seated slightly behind the student, so that the teacher's reading goes directly into the student's right ear. Teacher and student read the material jointly. At first, the teacher reads slightly louder and faster, to imprint the correct responses in the student. As the student gains fluency and confidence, the teacher begins to read more softly and may start even to lag slightly behind the student.

However, if difficulty is encountered, the teacher should rescue the student in a loud, firm manner.

When beginning this procedure, teachers should follow the text along with their finger at the pace of the reading. As the student gains confidence, he or she can begin to assume the responsibility for following the reading. Students should not be stopped for correction during reading. Use of this method may improve oral reading very quickly. If no improvement has resulted after six sessions of instruction, the method should be discontinued.

Our experience shows that this method will work for some students but not for all. One fifth grade student, who enjoyed the method and was excited enough to ask for it several times, improved markedly in reading fluency. On the other hand, a seventh grade boy had a negative reaction, and we discontinued NIM. Teachers can decide whether the method is working based on their students' willingness to do it and the improvement in fluency.

Repeated Readings

The repeated readings technique is another individualized method for improving fluency (Samuels, 1979). Give the student a short reading passage of 50 to 200 words. The passage may be part of a story or a separate self-contained narrative. The student reads the selection, and the teacher records the reading speed and any deviations from the text. Then the student practices the selection until he or she feels capable of reading it fluently at a rate you have both selected. The student next reads the selection orally a second time, and both the reading rate and word recognition deviations are again recorded. This process is repeated until a predetermined criterion rate has been acheived. At this point, the student moves on to another reading selection.

The student's improvement is charted in both the areas of oral reading rate and accuracy. This graphic evidence of improvement provides positive reinforcement and encouragement.

Reading to Younger Children

When remedial students read to younger children they obtain needed reading practice and a sense of helping others. In preparing stories, older remedial readers must learn to read them fluently so that young children will enjoy and benefit from the reading performance. Reading the stories over and over gives remedial pupils the practice that enables them to read fluently. Predictable books (discussed in Chapter 8) are excellent for this activity.

One middle school Chapter I class, for example, practiced reading easy books so that students could perfect their babysitting skills and earn money. At another school, remedial students regularly went into the kindergarten class to read stories.

In another form of this activity, remedial students tape stories for younger students and record their name as narrator. Charles, a seventh grader in our clinic, taped-recorded *Curious George* (by H.A. Rey) for a second grader. In doing so, Charles practiced reading a third grade level book, which he would have been too embarrassed to read for himself. Yet, *Curious George* was an ideal independent-level book for Charle's low third grade reading level. When the second grader who listened to the tape recorded a "thank you," Charles was thrilled.

SPECIAL PROBLEMS IN WORD RECOGNITION

In this final section dealing with word recognition, we discuss common problems and offer guidelines for dealing with them. The problems include (1) reversal of letters and words, (2) the habits of finger pointing and lip moving, and (3) difficulty reading silently.

Reversals

Remedial readers with skills at the first, second, and third grade reading levels tend to reverse certain letters and words while reading. For example, they may substitute *b* for *d*, or *no* for *on*, or *saw* for *was*. In fact, it is not uncommon for poor readers at this level to produce backward "mirror writing." The tendency to reverse letters and words has sometimes been interpreted as a symptom of deep-seated problems in reading or brain dysfunction (Orton, 1937; Johnson and Myklebust, 1967). However, in most cases, reversals simply indicate a lack of experience with reading material. They are seen often in normally achieving children reading at primary-grade levels. In fact, learning-disabled students have been found to make no more reversal errors than normal readers when both groups of students are reading in equally comfortable material (Adams, 1988). Reversals also may occur in teenagers and adults who are just learning to read. Krise (1949) found that reversals could be induced in postcollege graduate students if an artificial language was used.

One reason that students make reversals is that reading is the only process in which symbols change because of their directional orientation. Thus, the only difference between the letters *b* and *d* is that one faces right and the other left. On the other hand, a real-life object, such as a chair or a dog, maintains its identify regardless of its orientation in space. A student beginning to read may not yet realize that the orientation of letters and words makes a difference in reading.

When a remedial reader exhibits reversals, the teacher must decide whether to provide special instruction to eliminate them. If the reversal is only occasional, no special instruction is warranted. If, on the other hand, reversals are frequent and interfere with effective reading, then special instruction to overcome them is needed.

To correct reversals of single letters, concentrate on one letter at a time. For example, to correct a *b* to *d* reversal, first concentrate on *d*. Teachers can make a large *d* chart that contains the letter *d*, a memory word (e.g., *dog*), and pictures that start with *d*. Accompanying this, several words that begin with *d* can be learned by sight. One teacher cut out a 2' × 3' felt *d* and pasted it on a board. The student reinforced the *d* concept by tracing over the letter (kinesthetic method). After the concept of *d* has been mastered thoroughly, wait a while before introducing the letter *b*. This "divide and conquer" method is very effective for remedial readers. Other methods are the following:

1. Flashcards may be made containing confused words and students may practice with these cards.
2. The first letter of confusable words may be underlined or written in a color other than black.
3. The pupil can trace the confusable letter or word on a large card and then write it from memory.
4. The student can manipulate letters on a felt or magnetic board to form words that are frequently reversed.

Finger Pointing and Lip Moving

Teachers often ask what to do when students point to words using their fingers or move their lips as they read silently. Sometimes finger pointing and lip moving can act as an aid that makes halting readers more comfortable and facilitates word recognition. These behaviors are characteristic of, and normal for, primary-grade-level readers. In addition, if material is too difficult, individuals of any reading level may point their finger or move their lips. Thus these behaviors are one indication that reading material is frustrating. If you feel that students need to finger point and move their lips in order to feel comfortable, then it is wise not to interfere with these habits. As students become more fluent readers, these actions will usually disappear.

Extensive finger pointing is one symptom of visual difficulties. Students who need to finger point in order to keep their place in reading should be referred for a visual examination. However, if the student simply lip reads or finger points from force of habit, these behaviors can be discouraged. First and most effective, the student should be made aware of the habits, told how they are inhibiting reading, and asked, respectfully, to eliminate them. This simple procedure, plus an occasional reminder, often rectifies the problem. Finger pointing can also be eliminated more slowly by providing a marker to replace the finger and gradually eliminating the use of the marker. For lip moving, students may be asked to consciously close their lips while reading.

Difficulty Reading Silently

The mature reader reads silently almost exclusively. Indeed, when called upon to read orally, most adults realize how extensively their oral reading skills have atrophied. To facilitate mature reading, silent reading should be used in remedial instruction as much as possible. Yet even the most cursory survey of instructional situations shows an extensive amount of oral reading. This is true for three sets of reasons.

1. Beginning readers form their first conceptions of reading from oral language. As a result, they are most comfortable when reading is related to language through oral reading. In fact, it is sometimes impossible for remedial readers at beginning stages to read silently. While we recognize the legitimacy of these needs, remedial students should be moved into silent reading as soon as they are at all comfortable with the reading process.

2. Many teachers are comfortable with oral reading because they feel that both students and teacher are "doing something" during the instructional time. Teachers often feel that oral reading provides continuous diagnosis and monitoring of unknown words. While this is true, teachers must weigh the advantages of diagnosis against the disadvantages of forming dependent reading habits in their students.

3. Many students have simply become used to reading orally. These students think that the aim of reading is to put on a performance rather than to learn new information and concepts. Such students must be convinced that silent reading is valuable and that it is "adult." One effective method is to ask them to go out and observe five adult readers to see whether they are reading silently or orally. This procedure generally convinces them that silent reading has merit.

To stress the importance of silent reading, have students read material silently *before* they read it orally. It is helpful if the oral reading that follows only serves a very specific purpose, such as finding information in a text, proving a point, or dramatizing a play. Often students need not reread the entire passage orally. Finally, students should be given direct motivation for reading silently. The teacher should stress the information that the student will find in the text. If teachers follow silent reading with questions and discussions, students will be helped to see it as meaningful.

LEARNING WORD MEANINGS

Learning word meanings and the concepts that words represent are critical elements in remedial reading instruction. Word knowledge is highly correlated with a student's ability to comprehend (Anderson and Freebody, 1981), and words themselves embody important concepts that students will meet in reading.

Two different approaches to the teaching of meaning vocabulary are incidental and direct. In *incidental* vocabulary learning, students simply learn words by being exposed to them. In *direct* instruction, word meanings are deliberately taught (Richek, 1987).

Incidental Learning of Word Meanings

Most of the words that we know were acquired through incidental methods, unconsciously, by simply listening to them spoken by others or by reading them in books. In fact, there is evidence that students who encounter unknown words in reading learn the meanings of some of them (Jenkins, Stein, and Wysocki, 1984; Nagy, Herman, and Anderson, 1985).

However, for several reasons, remedial readers are at a disadvantage for incidental learning. (1) Since they tend not to read in their spare time, they are not exposed to the vocabulary words that normally achieving students meet. (2) When remedial students do read, they tend to read easy material, which does not contain the types of words that foster vocabulary growth. (3) Remedial readers are sometimes at a disadvantage because many are not exposed to rich vocabularies and language usage in their homes.

We suggest two methods for increasing incidental vocabulary growth.

Reading to Students.   A teacher should read orally to children with reading difficulties. Since written material contains more difficult language than speech, reading to children is an excellent way to expose them to new words in a nonthreatening fashion. Try to read to students at least a few times per week. When reading orally, choose materials that would be too difficult for students to read by themselves.

Although some teachers simply invite students to enjoy their listening time, it is also possible to provide more focus. One sixth grade teacher asked her students to take out a pencil and paper, and, as they listened to the reading, to write down some words they enjoyed and would like to learn. Students were limited to no more than two words per day. Of course, the students' spellings were approximate, but in this way the teacher fostered an interest in words. We give other suggestions for reading to students in Chapter 10.

Modeling Difficult Words in Speech.   A second way to foster incidental vocabulary growth is for teachers to share their vocabularies with remedial students by using high-level oral language with them. People learn words from the language of those around them. If teachers consciously try to use "million dollar words," students will unconsciously absorb them. Employ words that challenge students to expand their vocabularies. Encourage them to ask the meanings of these words and, thus, to take control of their own vocabulary learning. For example, in a noisy fourth grade Chapter I class, the teacher said, "I find this noise onerous and burdensome." The children immediately quieted down, were fascinated by the words, and requested their meanings. The teacher wrote the words on the board and discussed them. Teacher use of challenging vocabulary takes little additional time, yet it is valuable, for it exposes children to many words.

Direct Learning of Word Meanings

Direct teaching of words is more structured than the incidental approach. Direct teaching effectively improves student's meaning vocabularies (Stahl and Fairbanks, 1986). A first task in teaching word meanings directly is to decide which words the student should learn. There are several sources for words.

1. Since remedial students usually find words from their basal readers, class reading, and content area reading overwhelming, we suggest selecting words from these sources for direct instruction. This practice offers direct support to classroom instruction.
2. Students can supply words. Ask your remedial students to find words from television,

newspapers, billboards, musical scores, or any other source. One teacher encouraged students by bringing in an empty cereal box and showing the pupils *nutrition* and *riboflavin*. Some teachers have the class study a student-supplied "word of the week."

3. The use of a theme (or conceptually connected instruction) for remedial instruction (see Chapter 10) is another way to find new words. In the theme approach, pupils study one subject in depth. For example, thirteen-year-old Ryan was interested in mysteries, and learned such words as *sleuth, accessory, culpable,* and *blood type.* Because the words are interconnected, Ryan was able to build sophisticated background concepts. For Ryan, the teaching of vocabulary was integrated with extending concepts and experiential background.

4. Word books and word lists may be used to teach meaning vocabulary. For young readers, we recommend the many word books that feature pictures. R. Scarry's *Best Word Book Ever* is one such book.

A thorough introduction to a word will make students feel more comfortable with it. The following procedures can be used to introduce a word.

1. Pronounce the word and then have the students pronounce it.
2. Provide a simple definition, using as few words as possible.
3. Use the word in a sentence. The sentence can be kept on the board throughout reading so that students can refer to it.

Some words are more difficult to learn than others. Words that involve unfamiliar concepts are particularly difficult to master. A word such as *furious* can be learned easily, for most students already have a concept for *anger.* However, recently we tried to teach a group of remedial fifth graders the unfamiliar word, *soberly.* At first, thinking that this word meant *seriously,* they came up with sentences such as *She was soberly ill.* Since soberly is not a synonym for *seriously* in all contexts, but adds a new concept, the teacher had to use the word many times before pupils could understand it.

Strategies for Introducing Words Found in Text

There are many specific techniques for introducing students to the words contained in the selections they are reading. We will present predict-o-rama, knowledge rating, possible sentences, and using context clues.

Predict-o-rama. By trying to classify words according to story grammar, remedial students become actively involved in word meanings and receive an orientation to text reading. To do the predict-o-rama, list the new words in a story, and then ask students to predict whether each word will be used as part of the setting, the actions, the character, the ending, or in another way. As they read, students can see if these words are used in the way they predicted (Blachowicz, 1986).

Knowledge Rating. In this method, the teacher lists the new words for a story and students think about whether they know the words. Each student places the words into one of three categories: (1) I know this word, (2) it sounds familiar, and (3) I don't know this word. Students then read the selection, keeping the words in mind and, after reading, the words are reviewed again (Blachowicz, 1986).

Possible Sentences.   This is a useful way to introduce intermediate and upper-grade students to new vocabulary in content area texts, such as social studies and science texts (Moore and Arthur, 1981). First give the title of the chapter that the students are about to read. Then write the new words on the board, for example *molecule, proton, atom, electron, neutron.* Next, have students think of sentences that possibly might be in the chapter. Each sentence must contain at least two words. An example would be "A *molecule* has two *atoms.*" Students develop expectations of the chapter as they go through this activity. Then have students read the chapter. Next, using the knowledge they have gained from reading the chapter, students evaluate the possible sentences they have written to see if they are true. They then change the sentences that need to be changed, and add other sentences which they know to be true. This simple strategy combines learning vocabulary with the learning of content material.

Using Context Clues.   Most good readers use the sense of the surrounding sentence, or context clues, to learn new words, and remedial readers will also profit from using context. While the context will not always define the word thoroughly, it will give many clues to meaning. Gipe (1980) experimented with several methods of teaching third and fourth grade students new vocabulary and found that learning words from context was the most effective method. However, the process of gaining meaning from context is not easy for many remedial readers. To build vocabulary in this way, they must be encouraged to take risks and to make "intelligent hypotheses." (We often use these very words to encourage our students).

To help students to use context clues, we use a strategy that makes them feel comfortable with context. We put words in a sentence context, and ask students to read them and think about the underlined word. An example might be: Because John *dawdled,* he arrived late. We then ask students to hypothesize what this word might be. Finally, one student looks the word up in the dictionary to determine the exact meaning.

Josel (1988) dramatically demonstrated to her remedial eighth graders that they used context clues to determine meaning. First, she gave them a list of words (taken from a novel) to match to definitions. Since the list contained words such as *etesia* and *clamorous,* few students could match any word and definition correctly. Next, she presented sentences from the book that contained these words (such as "We are sailing before the *etesia,* which blows from the northwest") and asked students to define the words. Students were able to define the majority of the words. This activity demonstrated the helpfulness of context clues in determining word meanings.

After students have become comfortable with context clues, ask them to use context clues as they are reading. First, list new words on the board from a selection students are about to read and ask students to think about what the words might mean as they encounter them in the selection. Then have students read. When they finish reading, go back to the words, asking students what meanings they hypothesize from the context. It is handy for the teacher to write down the location of the words in the text, so that the class can easily find the words for discussion. If questions remain, the class can consult the dictionary to clarify meanings. This procedure models the way that good readers combine context clues and dictionary skills.

Remedial students can also be taught that, when they come to a word they don't know, they should substitute a word or phrase that makes sense. The word or phrase that they substitute is likely to be the definition of the unknown word. For example, in the sentence, "Because prices were going up, we decided to *defer* buying a car until next year," many students would substitute the phrase "put off" or the word "delay." These are, in fact, approximate definitions of "defer."

Reviewing Word Meanings

Extended practice is needed before remedial students achieve ownership over words.

Conversations with Target Words.   Using words in conversations can help students to deepen meanings. One college remedial teacher conducts a conversation period each week with her students. During this time, they may discuss anything, but each student must use at least one of the target words.

Word Cards and Lists.   Students can make personal word cards. On the front, the word card should have only the target word; on the back should be a definition and an illustrative sentence. A pronunciation guide may also be included. Once a word has become comfortable for the student, it should be placed in a "words I know" file.

In other activities, classes can develop dictionaries and alphabetized books containing new words. To spark interest, students can employ creative ways to keep records of their words.

Displaying Words.   Placing words on public display can motivate students to learn them. Marvin displayed his words on a colorful ship honoring his interest, Viking conquests. In one seventh grade learning disabilities classroom, all of the words from one unit in the children's reader were placed on individual small cards which could be flipped up. Each student was given two cards, each containing a word. In the front, the pupil wrote his or her name, to establish ownership. On the back the student had to write a definition and a sentence for the word, both of which had to be approved by the teacher. The student who had signed his or her name to the word was an "expert consultant" on the word. All of these word cards were put on display on the bulletin board. When children wanted to review the words, they simply went to the board, read the word, and flipped up the chart to check the definition. As

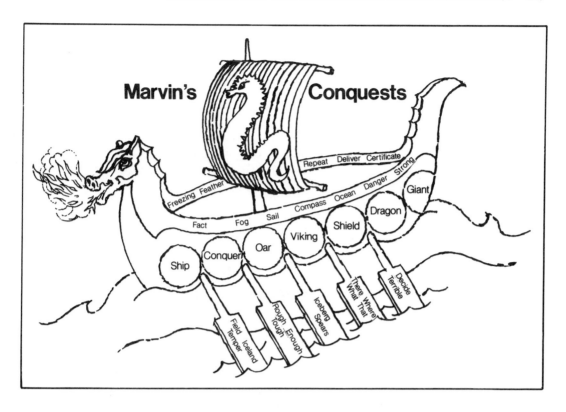

words were mastered, they were removed from the board, and replaced with other words.

Personal Clue.   Carr and Wixon (1986) suggest a modification of word cards to help students personalize words that are difficult to remember. As students learn a word, they associate any clue that helps them to remember it. For example, if the word is *delectable*, the student might think of chocolate cake, a food that the student thinks is *delectable*. To make a personal clue word card, the student lists vertically:

1. the word
2. the personal clue, and
3. the definition of the word

When reviewing, the student first looks at the top line and tries to remember the definition. If the definition has been forgotten, the personal clue is uncovered and serves as a reminder of the definition. The personal clue serves as a bridge between the student and the word.

Developing Images.   Students can also personalize words by forming images in their minds. Each student develops a personal image for a word and tries to remember it when reviewing the words.

Semantic Maps.   Semantic maps (or semantic webs) provide one way to develop rich associations for a word and deepen learning of important concepts. For example, students might need to develop a thorough understanding of the key concept "food" for a health class. The students name all of the words they can associate to the word *food*. Then students discuss how they might classify these words. The result is made into a semantic map (see below), which forms a rich organization of associations to the word "food."

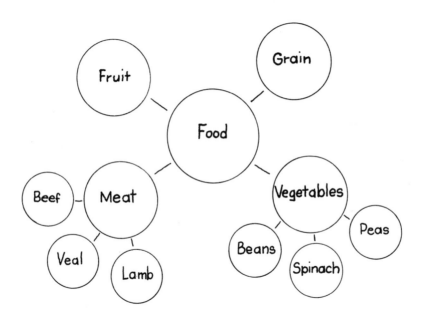

Developing Automaticity.   To fully master words, students need to be able to recognize them quickly and automatically. Spending a few minutes a week on having students say words quickly, rapidly supply definitions for words, or think of a sentence as quickly as they can are good ways to foster automaticity. In one study designed to improve vocabulary, Beck, Perfetti, and McKeown (1982) had students quickly answer "yes" or "no" to statements containing vocabulary words. Examples were:

A philanthropist steals money.
A hermit lives by himself.
A novice is still learning.

Using the Dictionary

The dictionary gives students independence in learning word meanings; however, it should not be overused as an instructional tool. Remedial students tend to find looking up word meanings tedious, and if they can learn words through other means, they should be encouraged to do so. Although dictionaries do supply definitions, they are not geared for instruction in correct usage. Sentences using words and discussions of words should accompany dictionary study.

In the same way, teachers should feel free to tell students word meanings when they ask. If teachers repeatedly tell students to look up words in the dictionary, students will come to see the dictionary as punishment, and will become reluctant to ask what words mean.

The dictionary does have many uses, even though it does not provide a complete vocabulary program. The dictionary provides definitions, offers a means to distinguish among definitions, gives a key for pronunciation, and supplies the different forms of a base word. There are several levels of dictionary usage. Dictionary skills, organized from less advanced to more advanced are:

1. Alphabetizing words. The use of the first letter in a word is taught first, followed by second letter, third letter, and so on.
2. Locating words. This includes opening the dictionary to the correct half or quarter to locate a word and learning to use key words to determine if a word is on a page.
3. Using the dictionary pronunciation key.
4. Determining the correct dictionary entry for different word forms. For example, the word *slowly* should be looked up under the word *slow*.
5. Determining which of several definitions should be used in a particular context.
6. Determining the historical origin of a word.

Some interesting games will help students to learn to use the dictionary effectively; these follow.

1. Making dictionary sentences. Students can open the dictionary to a given page and try to construct the longest sentence possible using words from that page (Moffett and Wagner, 1976). Words such as "the," "and," "is," "if," and "I" may have to be added.
2. Younger remedial readers can make pictures of words that they find in dictionaries. They can record the page where they found the word and the picture, and other pupils must then find the word in the dictionary.
3. Older remedial readers can see who can locate a word in the dictionary using the fewest opening "cuts." This exercise helps the students to locate words quickly.

Other Areas in Word Meaning

There are many additional ways to teach meaning vocabulary to remedial readers. Some special topics and resources that may help your students follow.

Synonyms and Antonyms. Synonyms (words with the same meaning) and antonyms (words with opposite meanings) may be used to enrich word meanings as well as to extend them. These can be taught to remedial readers to help them see the many different words in our language and how they relate.

One group of disabled fifth grade readers played a "synonym spot" game. They stuck round spots onto a paper leopard. Spots with words that meant the same thing (e.g., pretty, beautiful) were put together. Another teacher made pictures of a boy sitting, walking, and running. In order to encourage students to list as many synonyms as they could for these three activities, the pictures were kept up for several days. Another group of students played the "but" game for antonyms. For example,

I am happy but he is sad.
I am cold but he is hot.
I am XXXXX but he is XXXXX.

Adolescent remedial readers like the "overused word" game. Since these students tend to use certain "in" expressions repeatedly (e.g., cool, bad, right-on), the game requires them to think of as many synonyms as they can. In a similar vein, students can think of synonyms for common words. One upper-level teacher asked remedial classes to read the sports page of the newspaper to determine how many synonyms could be found for *win* (e.g., *beat, top, clobber*) (Mozzi, 1980).

The connotations, or implied meanings, of words can be taught by using synonyms. Some words have similar meanings, but different implications. For example, to be a *moral person* is positive, but to be a *goody-goody* is negative. In the same way, it is desirable to be *slender* but not to be *skinny* or *scrawny*. Finding words such as these is an amusing way to add to meaning vocabulary.

A thesaurus is an excellent tool for teaching synonyms and antonyms. Students use the thesaurus to find words of similar meanings. Several excellent thesauruses are published for students at different levels (see Appendix A).

Homonyms. Homonyms are words that sound alike but are spelled differently and, of course, have different meanings. Examples are *to, too, two* or *way* and *weigh.* Homonyms can also be used to enrich vocabulary. Several excellent children's books dramatize the meanings of homonyms. These include *Amelia Bedelia,* and *Come Back, Amelia Bedelia* (by P. Parish).

Multiple Meanings. Words in English often have several meanings. The study of multiple meanings of words is another way to enrich vocabulary. Many students find unknown meanings of common words that they use to be fascinating. A high school remedial reading class found that the word *loaded* was used frequently in used car ads. Discussing the multiple meanings of this word, they determined that it could also be used to describe a rich person or an intoxicated one. One of our remedial readers was astonished to learn in a social studies class that a concession could be something other than a hot dog stand! One practice activity requires students to find several meanings of common words such as hot and cold. Or students may be asked to match a definition with a sentence.

It was cold outside — without a show of emotion
She treated him coldly — having a low temperature

History of Words.   A study of the historical development of words frequently stimulates interest. The words *guy, sandwich,* and *lynch* all represent names and events in history.

As noted in Chapter 4, English has two language roots: one similar to German and one similar to Spanish, French, and Italian. Pairs of words exist in English, stemming from both of these roots (e.g., *deer-venison, calf-veal, father-paternal*). This means that many English words have cognates in foreign languages. Students, particularly those with bilingual backgrounds, may be interested in knowing about these cognates. Spanish and English have many similar words; for example, *furious, advice,* and *diary* have Spanish cognates.

Word history may also lead to the study of word parts (structural analysis). For example, the word part *uni* is descended from Greek, and the many words that incorporate *uni—unicycle, universe, unity, unicorn*—are all derived from Greek.

In addition, many remedial readers are fascinated with Greek and Roman mythology and the colorful stories of gods and goddesses. The words for many of the planets of the solar system are named after these deities (e.g., Venus, Mars, Pluto, Neptune). I. Asimov's book *Words from the Myths* helps more advanced remedial students become acquainted with these concepts.

Figurative Language.   Figurative language acquaints remedial students with imaginative language use. Two types of figurative language that may be appropriate for use with remedial students are (1) similes (or comparisons) and (2) figures of speech.

In a simile, a trait is compared with an animal or object. Examples are:

as quiet as a mouse
as fierce as a tiger
as white as snow
as slow as a tortoise
as sour as a lemon

Remedial readers can draw pictures to illustrate these and talk about the reasons behind the development of such phrases. Often, similes will fire students' creativity in art and other areas (List, 1982).

Figures of speech are somewhat more advanced. Examples are:

He flew down the stairs
She brought the house down

I'm in a jam
He was on his last leg
I could eat a horse

These figures of speech lend themselves to imaginative illustrations.

Relating Words to Students' Environment.   Words become interesting when they relate to the lives of students (Richek, 1986, 1989). For example, students can look up the meanings of their names in "How to Name Your Baby" books. Students may also enjoy studying the history of car names. *Chevrolet* was a famous car racer; *Cadillac* was a French explorer; *Seville* and *Granada* are names of cities; *Mustang* and *Pinto* are types of horses. Names of common household products (such as Tide, Wisk, Mr. Clean, Cheer, Vanish) are also chosen for a reason. Common foods, such as *hamburger, frankfurter, tomato, banana,* and *tea* have interesting origins. Students may use them to practice dictionary skills.

Teaching vocabulary is exciting and worthwhile both for you and your students. Share with your students the joy of learning new words and using them in reading and writing. If teachers expose students to a variety of words, welcome questions about words, and foster student comfort, students cannot help but build better vocabularies.

Diagnostic Teaching of Word Meanings

A student's response to instruction in word meaning enables a teacher to evaluate progress. A sure sign of learning is when students actually use the words they have studied in their speech. A willingness to use such words—even if they are not pronounced correctly—shows the ability to incorporate words into everyday life.

In addition, progress with meaning vocabulary can also be seen as students start to become more comfortable listening to or reading material written at a high language level. Or students may show an interest in words by asking the teacher what an unknown word means. If you thank the student for asking, you will encourage further interest in words.

Other student behaviors show a lack of progress in learning word meanings. Students who start to show difficulty in acquiring new word meanings, or who start to feel overwhelmed with words, are showing frustration. Teachers should slow down the pace of teaching word meanings, or perhaps stop altogether for a while. After some rest, students will often be able to absorb more new word meanings.

SUMMARY

Many remedial students have difficulties recognizing words which contain more than one syllable. It is important to learn to apply syllabication strategies while reading text. Words that fit certain patterns should be taught together. Do not overburden students with technical terms. Students may need to learn to recognize syllables in speech.

Structural analysis clues refer to meaningful word parts, such as *-ful* and *re-*. Structural analysis is particularly useful in decoding long words. Five types of structural analysis elements are: (1) compound words, (2) contractions, (3) suffixes, (4) prefixes, and (5) roots. Suffixes are extremely frequent in language. Because roots and prefixes provide clues to word meaning, they are often taught together.

Older readers often need help in reading fluently. Three helpful methods are the neurological impress method, repeated readings, and reading to younger children.

Special problems in word recognition include (1) reversals, (2) finger pointing and lip moving, and (3) difficulty reading silently. Reversals are normal in primary-grade-level remedial readers, regardless of age, but should be corrected when they seriously hamper reading. Finger pointing and lip moving hamper fluent reading, but remedial readers may need them as aids. Teachers should systematically encourage silent reading, which fosters independence and reading for meaning.

It is important for remedial students to learn word meanings. In an incidental approach, students simply learn words by being exposed to them. In direct instruction, words are deliberately taught. Incidental methods for teaching vocabulary include reading to students and modeling difficult words in speech. In direct instruction, words may be taken from student texts, from words students bring in, from a central theme used for instruction, or from word books and lists.

To introduce words found in a text, teachers may use predict-o-rama, knowledge rating, possible sentences, and context clues.

Vocabulary words often need review. Teachers can use conversations with target words, word cards and lists, personal clues, images, semantic maps, and methods for developing automaticity.

It is important to develop student independence through the use of a dictionary. However, the dictionary should not be overused.

Other areas in teaching word meanings include synonyms and antonyms, homonyms, multiple meanings, the history of words, figurative language, and relating words to students' environments.

10

TEACHING READING AND LISTENING COMPREHENSION

This chapter, and the next, focus on comprehension. In this chapter we deal with comprehension of material written in a narrative (or story) form. In the next chapter we present strategies for comprehending textbooks and studying expository (or informational) texts.

INTRODUCTION

Comprehension is the essence of the reading act; indeed, it is the only purpose for reading. Yet, thousands of remedial students lack critical elements of comprehension and are unable to read text in an effective manner. Because remedial readers are often deficient in comprehension, they need to be taught specific strategies that help them become active, competent comprehenders who demand meaning from text.

This chapter first deals with general considerations in reading comprehension. Next, specific strategies are given for fostering the comprehension of narrative text. Finally, strategies for fostering listening comprehension and language growth are presented.

GENERAL FEATURES OF EFFECTIVE
READING COMPREHENSION

Proficient readers share certain attitudes and subconscious knowledge about reading that result in good comprehension. This knowledge may be summarized in the following statements.

1. The purpose of reading is comprehension.
2. Comprehension is an active process.
3. Comprehension employs background knowledge and language skills.
4. Comprehension requires higher-level thinking.

Below we discuss each of these aspects of comprehension as related to the remedial reader.

The Purpose of Reading Is Comprehension

Good readers know that the purpose of reading is to understand, enjoy, and learn from material. In contrast, students with reading problems often think that reading means recognizing words.

We have encountered many remedial students who are baffled by the fact that we expect them to comprehend what they read. Their perception of reading is so distant from comprehension that they think that once they have read all of the words orally, they have finished with the material!

Some easily implemented procedures are effective in helping students understand that reading is comprehension.

1. Always ask students for a comprehension response after they read material. Teachers can ask comprehension questions, ask for a summary, or use some of the more detailed strategies given later in this chapter. By consistently checking for comprehension, teachers help students, even those struggling with word recognition, to realize that the aim of reading is obtaining meaning.
2. Ask for personal responses to the text. Most readers have strong personal responses to stories. Yet teachers rarely ask for their students' reactions (Gambrell, 1986). In asking for these reactions, we show students that their thoughts are valued. Teachers can ask students whether they enjoyed the reading, which parts of a story were the most exciting, or what mental images they formed.
3. Encourage silent reading. When all or most of children's reading is oral, they inevitably come to perceive reading as performance. Teachers should encourage silent reading as an effective way to help students understand that reading is a personal, meaning-focused activity.

Comprehension is an Active Process

When good readers digest a written selection, they are actively engaged. As they read, they construct an entire text in their minds which is parallel to the text that the author has written (Tierney and Pearson, 1983). Good readers predict and judge material as they read. For example, when we read a mystery story or novel, we actively try to construct the clues into a solution for the crime.

In contrast, readers with problems are passive and wait for teacher direction. They often read reluctantly, hesitating to ask questions, and focusing solely on what they think the teacher wants them to remember. In fact, passivity toward learning has been recognized as a key factor in students with reading and learning problems (Jenkins et al., 1986; Johnston, 1984).

One of the hallmarks of passivity is that remedial students do not monitor their comprehension. That is, when remedial students are not sure of the meaning of the material, they do not take action by going back and trying to understand. Instead they continue to read on passively, and, not surprisingly, lose even more meaning. Worse yet, remedial readers are often unaware that something is wrong. The ability to know that you are losing comprehension and to employ "fix-up" strategies is called *metacognitive awareness*. All readers become lost from time to time, but the ability to go back and monitor comprehension is rarely displayed by remedial students.

How can we encourage active reading?

1. Interest students in the material before they begin. Telling students what is good or exciting about a story gives them a purpose for reading. Discussing the author of a story helps students to relate more personally to reading.
2. Make students aware of the need to monitor comprehension as they are reading. Encourage students to use "fix-up" strategies on their own. Teachers can model how to reread material, how to read ahead, and how to check the context to figure out unknown words.

3. Go beyond having students answer questions in their responses to reading. When students predict what will happen next in a story or learn to ask their own questions, they comprehend on a deeper level and have more fun!

4. Encourage group sharing. When adults discuss a book or a movie with a friend, they actively think through the experience, raising new issues. In the same way, group discussion helps remedial readers to comprehend.

Comprehension Employs Background Knowledge and Language Skills

Our ability to comprehend text is highly dependent upon our background knowledge (or schema). Recently in our clinic, Mike, a fifth grade remedial reader, was reading a story in which a boy found a skunk which later turned out to be a mink. Unfortunately, since Mike did not know what minks were, he could not understand how most people felt about these two different animals. In short, Mike did not have the background information to understand the story.

Deficiencies in background knowledge are increased because remedial readers tend to do little reading. Reading itself helps build background information needed in school, since print often presents more sophisticated concepts than does conversation. For example, most of us gained our knowledge of the ancient Greek and Roman civilizations through school reading or free reading, rather than at the dinner table or playing with our friends. Since remedial readers do little free reading and read their school texts ineffectively, they do not learn the many sophisticated concepts needed for success in school (Snider and Tarver, 1987). Hirsch (1987) identified a core of concepts that he feels form the basis of "cultural literacy."

To further compound the problem, researchers find that remedial students do not even use the background knowledge they *do* possess when they read. For example, when reading a story about a party, the good reader subconsciously summons forth the information he or she knows about parties. In contrast, the poor reader often reads the text as if it were not connected to anything previously experienced.

Teachers can easily take steps to help increase students' background information.

1. Help students build background before they read. The first part of a reading lesson is the most crucial and the most neglected (Durkin, 1978–1979). Teachers should ask students what they know about the subject of a text, teach important concepts that students are missing, and relate the subject to the material the students are reading.

2. Impart your own personal knowledge to students. A teacher's rich background knowledge is a repository of extensive cultural information, a valuable resource that should be shared. Further, if remedial students observe their teacher summoning up background knowledge while reading, this serves as a model for their own reading behavior.

3. Discuss, in resource rooms, the knowledge needed for material being read in the regular classroom. For example, if children will read a story about an early airplane flight, discuss the history of aviation.

Comprehension Requires Higher-Level Thinking

Higher-level thinking is important to story comprehension. The ability to identify the organization of a story and to draw inferences helps the reader to connect details, remember the story, and comprehend on a deeper level. When reading a story, effective readers appear to make a representation of organizational features, such as the characters, the problem, and the solution. They also draw inferences from the material.

In contrast, remedial readers have trouble with higher-level comprehension, and often focus merely on unimportant details. Research tells us that all human beings have a very limited memory span, and can only remember about seven unconnected items (Miller, 1956). We increase our memory and our comprehension by linking these items through higher-level comprehension.

How can teachers foster higher-level comprehension?

1. Direct questions skillfully. Too many questions written in teachers' manuals focus on isolated facts. Thus it is not surprising that students come to perceive facts as very important. To redirect comprehension, limit the number of factual questions, and focus on higher comprehension.
2. Emphasize appropriate types of questions. Students improve simply from getting more practice on the type of comprehension that questions probe. Wixon (1983) found that when teachers simply asked more questions requiring students to use their inference skills, students improved markedly in answering inference questions. Wixon notes that "what you ask about is what children learn."
3. Model higher-level thinking skills. Poor readers need to see the thought processes that underlie higher-level comprehension. To show the students an adult comprehender "in action," you might choose a question that many of the students have answered incorrectly and talk through the thinking process needed to get the correct answer.

Table 10.1 summarizes teacher activities which will improve the general reading comprehension of remedial students.

SPECIFIC STRATEGIES FOR COMPREHENSION OF NARRATIVE TEXT

In the previous section, we gave *general* guidelines for helping students to comprehend whenever they read. This section presents several *specific* instructional strategies for fostering comprehension growth in narrative text. (Narrative text refers to stories, rather than informational material.) The strategies we present require remedial students to use consciously reading processes which good readers use intuitively.

Each strategy is directly applied to reading text. Thus students simultaneously learn a comprehension process and apply that process in reading. This direct application eliminates the problem of learning a comprehension process but not being able to apply it in a reading situation.

As noted several times, remedial students do not read enough. The strategies presented in this section are motivating, fun, and encourage students to read more.

Table 10.1

A SUMMARY OF ACTIVITIES FOSTERING STRATEGIC READING

Before Reading

- help students to relate their background information to reading
- build students' background information; gently correct misperceptions
- try to interest students in the text
- to foster a purpose for reading, mention something students might enjoy or learn from the material

During Reading

- encourage silent reading
- encourage students to monitor comprehension while reading

After Reading

- check comprehension
- ask for students' personal responses
- try to focus on high-level (nonliteral) comprehension

Prediction of Story Content: Directed Reading-Thinking Activity

In prediction, students read a portion of a story, predict what will happen next, and then read further to see if their predictions have been confirmed. This simple process is a powerful tool for teaching remedial students to comprehend effectively (Haggard, 1988). Prediction fosters comprehension and sets up an active learning situation, in which students literally create (in their heads) the story along with the author.

DRTA (Directed Reading-Thinking Activity) is a classic prediction strategy. Developed by Stauffer (1975, 1980) some thirty years ago, DRTA is now used with many variations (Richek, 1987; Richek, 1983–9). It is often taught as a group activity, but it is also effective in an individual tutoring setting.

DRTA can add considerable depth to the comprehension of remedial students, for it models, for problem readers, the processes that good readers use to read stories. To obtain maximum benefit, the process should be used on a long-term basis. To use DRTA only once is to deny students the many things they will learn as their reading processes mature.

DRTA should be used with stories that students have not yet read. Before the students see the story, the teacher divides it into sections varying from a few paragraphs to a few pages apiece. Each section should end at a point of suspense in the story. Teachers need not physically divide the text, but just keep the sections in mind.

To introduce the selection, the teacher writes the title on the board before passing out the story. From the title, the teacher then asks students to predict what will happen in the story. For example, in one story, entitled "Nate the Great and the Sticky Case," some fourth grade resource students made the following predictions: "Something will be stolen," "It's about glue," and "Nate will be stuck somewhere."

The students' predictions, or hypotheses, are then written on the board (Richek, 1987). We have found that writing the name of the student who gave each hypothesis next to that hypothesis increases a feeling of ownership. As each prediction is stated, the student is asked the reason for giving that hypothesis. For example, the child who predicted "Something will be stolen" justified his hypothesis by saying "The title says 'case' and that means a crime, and that's stealing."

After each hypothesis is written and explained, the teacher hands out the story, and students silently read the first section. Then the teacher guides the students in reviewing their earlier hypotheses. The students must decide which hypotheses were confirmed, which might still be confirmed (and should be left on the board), which need to be revised or erased, and which new hypotheses they would like to add. They then read the next section to test their predictions and, after reading, they again revise the hypotheses. This sequence continues until they have completed the story. Generally, a story is divided into four to six sections.

We have found DRTA to be an extremely motivating strategy which often stimulates students to read longer selections and to do silent reading. In their predictions, students naturally use their background information and the clues in the story to guess the ending before they actually read it. In doing DRTA, remedial readers also begin to recognize that most stories present a problem and a solution for that problem, and thus they start to learn about story structure.

Teachers will find that reading a story using DRTA is no more time consuming than reading it in a traditional manner. Since almost any narrative story can be used with DRTA, remedial students can work with their basal readers or other texts. A specific set of graded materials, *Thinking About Reading* (see Appendix A), are worktexts which contain stories specifically adapted for DRTA.

Over the years, we have found that children with reading problems will not always feel free to participate in DRTA. Some read so passively that they, at first, have trouble generating predictions. In a group situation, shy students can be encouraged to participate by voting "yes" or "no" on some hypotheses. Including requests for "abstentions" insures that even the most passive students will participate. When using DRTA in an individual situation, a teacher can encourage participation by making hypotheses along with the student.

We are often asked if students ever sneak a look ahead in a story before they make their predictions. Looking ahead is *not* allowed, and teachers should tell students not to do so. In fact, in the many years we have been using DRTA, we have found few students who look ahead. These students should be pulled from a group DRTA, and asked to sit on the side without making comments. The occasional student who looks ahead is giving the teacher a very important piece of diagnostic information. This student is telling the teacher that he or she sees reading as "showing off" the right answer rather than thinking about material. After using DRTA several times, even these students will come to value the role of their own thinking in reading stories.

DRTA without Justification. A variation of DRTA which works well for many remedial readers is DRTA without justification (Richek, 1987). In this method, readers are asked to give predictions about what will happen next in the story, but are not asked to supply the reasons for these predictions. We began to use DRTA without justification when we found that many of our remedial readers were able to give predictions, but could not justify them. In fact, after we asked for justification, several became so uncomfortable that they were unable to continue with the DRTA process. In contrast, when we dropped the justification step, our readers continued to participate in and to learn from DRTA. Thus remedial students first might need to use DRTA without justification. After a few stories, they will be ready to justify their responses.

Silent DRTA. Secondary students are often embarrassed about giving responses in a group DRTA. In addition, as students go through the grades, they should take increased responsibility for their own comprehension processes. The silent DRTA addresses both of these issues (Josel, 1986; Richek 1983–1989; Richek, 1987). In silent DRTA, students are given a story with prearranged stopping points. Each student reads the selection individually and silently until he or she comes to the first stopping point, and is then asked for a prediction. They *write* their predictions at their desks without discussing them. They next read until they come to the next stopping point and write that prediction. In the last part of the story, the ending is, of course, revealed, and each student can see how close he or she has come to predicting the author's ending.

We have been extremely pleased with student responses to silent DRTA. It motivates students to read silently and to make a written response. After they have completed the story, remedial students generally spontaneously go back to inspect their written responses and compare their thinking processes with the clues that have been given in the story. Silent DRTA is an important step forward from standard DRTA, for, by making a written record of their own thinking processes, students begin to monitor their own comprehension.

Using DRTA Diagnostically. DRTA can tell the teacher much about a student's reading process. Student reluctance to give any predictions may indicate passivity and uninvolvement in the material. As DRTA proceeds, reluctant students will become more involved in reading. Other students will not give predictions because they are fearful of being wrong. Teachers can encourage the willingness to take risks by praising students for predictions which, while they did not come true, showed the use of a good thinking process. Teachers should be sure that they are not unwittingly discouraging risk-taking behavior by reacting negatively to remedial readers' predictions or asking them to "think again." When using DRTA, it is important to accept a student's hypothesis, even if an adult would make a far different one.

Students' reactions and hypotheses also reveal whether they are obtaining the literal meaning of the story. If predictions show that students have misread, they should go back and reread the segment more carefully.

The quality of students' predictions provides additional diagnostic information. When remedial readers first start the DRTA process, their predictions are often highly implausible. As they continue using the process through several stories, predictions will improve. In addition, as a group of students approaches the end of any story, their predictions will start to converge and approach a plausible end. These are important signs of progress in reading narrative text.

STRATEGY SNAPSHOT: DRTA IN A LOW-ACHIEVING FIFTH GRADE CLASS

To encourage a group of thirty-one low-achieving fifth graders to read more actively, and to improve their comprehension, we used DRTA on a daily basis with the stories in their fourth-grade basal readers. The first story we used, "Otis's Scientific Experiment," detailed what happened when a misbehaving boy interfered with a class experiment about feeding rats.

We first put the title on the board and asked for hypotheses about the story. The four hypotheses focused on a laboratory with a scientist. Then, we passed out the story and asked children to read the first page, and reformulate hypotheses. After reading the first page, students correctly refocused their hypotheses on a boy named Otis and a classroom. However, the students identified the animal as a *mouse* rather than a *rat*, so they were asked to go back and reread. We finished two more sets of predictions on the first day, for pages 2–3 and 4–5 of the story.

As we proceeded, student excitement mounted. More students made predictions, and the predictions became more plausible. We ended the day by taking a vote on the weights of the rats in the story. At the conclusion of the lesson, one student, Perry, copied the hypotheses from the board for use the next day. (In fact, three other students also copied them, just to ensure accuracy!)

On the second day, Perry recopied the hypotheses onto the board, and the class did two more prediction segments. Students continued to increase their hypotheses. There were so many that we were unable to call on all students who wanted to contribute. As the story progressed, the hypotheses converged. We also began to ask a few students to justify their hypotheses. Thomas, who had been making the others wait because of his very slow silent reading, started spontaneously to speed up his reading rate.

It was clear to the children that, on the third day, the story would end. Keana and Ryan met us in the hall before school, and asked us whether we could reveal the ending, if they wouldn't tell the others. (We declined to do this!). In class, the ending was finally revealed, to the delight of the children. Ending the story was followed by an indepth discussion of the clues the author gave that led toward the conclusion, and of other stories that were similar in plot.

Making Mental Images

Using mental imagery is another strategy that encourages students to read for comprehension and to become more active readers. Imagery strategies are particularly helpful for passive, uninterested readers.

Developing mental imagery has much value for remedial students. (1) Reading becomes more personal and relevant, since each student constructs his or her unique image. When they make mental images, students combine their background information, or information from their own fund of knowledge, with the text that they are reading. Thus, they make a psychological investment in the text. (2) Mental imagery helps students to read better silently, for students focus on their own internal responses to text. (3) Students become more active comprehenders of text, since mental imagery is a creative process. It is both enjoyable and instructive for students to compare their mental images.

Experimental studies show that mental imagery improves comprehension and interest for remedial students (Pressley, 1977; Gambrell and Bales, 1986). One school-based imagery program, *Mind's Eye* (Pressley et al., 1979) had marked long-term effects in improving comprehension.

We recommend mental image strategies for children of eight years and older. Research (Pressley, 1977) and our experience suggest that children younger than eight cannot effectively combine mental imagery with reading. However, young children can effectively *listen* to materials and make images.

Mental imagery is effective in both group and individual situations. To ensure maximum impact, it should be used on a sustained basis.

Building Readiness for Mental Imagery in Reading. Readiness for building mental imagery in reading should first be established by building the ability to form images while listening. Remedial students generally enjoy listening to imagery activities and learn easily to image. The students we have worked with master the skill within one to three class sessions. Some activities that foster imagery are:

1. Ask students to close their eyes, and imagine that they are seeing their mother or father. Then each student, in turn, describes his or her parent.
2. Ask students to imagine that they see a dog. Then each student describes exactly what the dog looks like.
3. Have students imagine everyday situations such as "Two boys were in the car," "I lost my homework," "I didn't like what my mom cooked for dinner," and to describe what they see in their minds.
4. Instruct the children to imagine a hot fudge sundae as you, verbally, build it, giving such clues as "I put in two scoops of vanilla ice cream, I slowly pour hot fudge over the top . . . " Students are then asked to describe the colors that they see. Even though teachers should not describe the container, they can ask the children for the type of container that they imagine. By asking children to imagine something that is not directly described, like the ice cream container, children demonstrate to themselves their ability to build an entire mental picture out of partial clues. This is precisely what we do when we make mental images during reading!
5. Read descriptions or short stories to students and ask them to form mental images. The children should share their descriptions.
6. Have the children listen to music and then tell how the strains made them feel and then analyze why they felt that way (List, 1982).

Mental Imagery in Reading.   After students have practiced mental imagery activities, they will be ready to apply these activities in their reading. When using a mental imagery strategy, the teacher simply asks students to focus on the picture that they see in their minds and to describe this picture. Mental imagery is most effective when combined with silent reading, and will serve to help pupils read effectively in a silent mode. The mental imagery strategy can be used with any type of narrative reading material, including basal reader stories and literature books.

A teacher can ask pupils for an image during several points in instruction. (1) Asking for an image after students read the first one or two paragraphs helps them "put themselves" into the story, and will foster comprehension throughout the rest of the story. (2) Teachers may ask for imagery at points in the story where students would normally be stopped for questions. We advise that if students will both be asked for imagery and for specific comprehension questions, that the students give their image first, while it is still fresh in their minds. (3) Finally, imagery may be used after the reading of a story. This is particularly useful for older students, who may be reading a story as an out-of-class assignment. When they come back to discuss the story, ask them to imagine the most exciting part, and to describe it.

Oral reading can be used effectively to reinforce certain aspects of imagery. After the class reads a few paragraphs silently, one student is chosen to reread the segment orally, while the others listen. The listening students will find that this oral reading reinforces and deepens their images.

Using Imagery Diagnostically.   Despite the value of imagery, remedial students often find it difficult to form images from the material that they are *reading*. Teachers need to be patient with a student who reports seeing " nothing," on the first day of reading with imagery. Within a week of instruction, such readers will often start to image. The following simple techniques can be used to encourage the forming of images. (1) Ask students to reread the material and imagine again. (2) Instruct students to close their eyes immediately after finishing reading, and to try to imagine what they have read. (3) Ask students to use their five senses, imaging what they see, hear, smell, feel, and taste.

Recently, one of the authors used mental imagery to help Bobby, a remedial third grader who showed a lack of interest and poor comprehension in reading. She asked Bobby to read silently the first two paragraphs in a story about a snowstorm. When he completed these, she asked him to report what he saw in his mind. Bobby could not report anything. However, after rereading the paragraphs, Bobby said he saw snow on the lawn, children building a snowman outside, and a car riding shakily up the street. This imagery gave Bobby a basis for interacting with the text and, although imagery was not used further in the story, Bobby's comprehension of the story improved markedly.

Difficulty forming and reporting images is often linked to problems in getting information or enjoyment while reading silently. In addition to working directly on imagery, you may also want to give your students additional practice on silent reading of short but interesting selections.

When asked to give images, some remedial students simply list off the sequence of events that they have read. Special attempts should be made to focus these students on the exciting aspects of material, so that they will become personally involved enough to form an image.

Other students report seeing images that do not correspond with the text. For example, a student might report seeing a cat, while the main character in the story is a dog. These students are misreading and not attending enough to the text. Encourage them to reread the material silently and see if the image changes. If students consistently misread, the teacher should break up stories into shorter segments and follow silent reading with oral reading. This focuses the students' attention on the need to read the text more carefully.

In summary, mental imagery is an effective and enjoyable method for helping readers develop comprehension abilities and interest. Students often report that they enjoy seeing the things that they read "with my mind's eye."

Brad closes his eyes to retain his mental image.

Using Story Structure

The use of story structures can help students to grasp the overview of narrative text. Remedial readers often have not developed a strong concept of a story, and lack organizational comprehension, an important higher level of comprehension.

They tend to identify minor events as major and to miss the central problem presented by stories. When asked what a story is about, they commonly relate only literal details.

A child's ability to grasp the sense of a whole story is, in part, dependent upon maturity. Therefore the strategies on using text structure presented in this section are recommended for students in the intermediate and upper grades. Four strategies which actively engage the reader in reconstructing the text are: (1) using story grammar and story maps, (2) finding the problem and the solution, (3) making telegram summaries and (4) recognizing literary genres.

Story Grammar and Story Maps.   Although we commonly think of grammar as applying to sentences, stories are also written according to grammars. For example, if you think of a story you read recently, it had characters, events, and a conclusion. In addition, the characters probably had a problem that they needed to solve. Good readers implicitly know these story features, and use them as a road map to orient their comprehension. In contrast, readers with problems are often unaware of such maps, and consequently they often become lost while reading. Research shows that students who lack a sense of story structure profit from instruction in story grammar (Fitzgerald and Spiegel, 1983).

Story maps are a useful instructional tool for guiding remedial students. These are visual diagrams which show students elements that all stories contain. As children read a story, they check their comprehension by locating the elements of the story grammar. This procedure teaches them to identify the most important elements in a story.

Remedial teachers need not use complex story maps with students. The following simple map will teach elementary grade level remedial children the most important features of a story:

Characters	*Setting*
Problem	*Solution*

To illustrate this a story map has been filled in for "The Case of the Missing Homework."

Characters	*Setting*
Stuey	Stuey's classroom
Teacher	Stuey's bedroom
Mother	

Problem	*Solution*
Stuey's	Stuey remembers his
homework is	neatly done
not neat	homework was written
	in invisible ink
	and he makes it
	reappear.

A more complex story map, one suitable for older students, is given below. In this map, the problem and the solution are linked by the major episodes.

Characters: Setting:
Problem:
Goal:
Episodes:
   Episode 1
   Episode 2
   Episode 3
   .
   .
   .
Resolution

The more complex map is filled in for "The Case of the Missing Homework:"

Characters: Stuey, teacher, mother
Setting: Stuey's home and classroom
Problem: Stuey's homework is not neat
Goal: Stuey must make his homework neater
Episodes:
1. Stuey learns to use invisible ink which disappears with heat.
2. The teacher complains about his messy homework.
3. At home, he does his homework neatly.
4. Then he loses his homework and only finds it when he puts it on the radiator.
5. The next day, Stuey can't find his homework when the teacher collects it.
Resolution: He realizes that he did it in invisible ink, and makes his neat homework appear by putting it on the radiator.

Story grammar may be taught in several ways. (1) Introduce a story map frame *before* students read the story, and ask students to fill in the frame either during or after reading. (2) Introduce the story map *after* the story is read, then ask the students to fill in the map. (3) Without actually using a formal story map, simply use a story map framework to guide questioning, asking students such questions as: Who was the main character? What was the central problem in the story?

Remedial readers may need teacher modeling before they can successfully deal with story grammar. Patient teacher demonstration, followed by discussion, will lead to remedial students using story grammar independently. Sustained practice with the story mapping strategy helps students recognize the consistent elements that enable them to understand stories as wholes.

Problem-Solution Identification.   The identification of the problem and solution to that problem in a story is a shortened form of story grammar. Optimum problem-solution identification occurs when students practice this strategy over many stories. We often have students make charts of stories that they have read, showing the problem of the story in one column and the solution in another.

Since the ability to identify the problem and solution of a story is a sophisticated skill, it requires careful teacher guidance. At first, students tend to misidentify the main problem of a story, simply recounting it as the first event. When this occurs, teachers should carefully discuss stories with the students. Often, having students retell stories orally improves their ability to understand them. Similarly, readiness for identifying problem-solution in reading can be developed by using listening activities. The teacher reads a story aloud, asking students to identify the problem and the solution.

Telegram Summaries.   The process of writing a story summary helps the reader capture the essence of that story. We have successfully encouraged summarization by asking remedial students to write telegrams encapsulating the stories they have read. Since telegrams are expensive, students must compose their telegrams using thirty words or less. To make their telegram more concise, children will often eliminate the small function words (such as *the, and, a*).

The skill of making a summary is developed through abundant practice. The first few times that students write a summary telegram, they will probably need the teacher's summary as a model. In addition, some students will need to practice summarizing stories they have listened to before they can do this activity with material they have read.

Understanding Different Genres.   To understand story structure, students must be able to recognize the characteristics of different types of narrative genres: fiction, mystery, adventure stories, science fiction, fantasy, folk tales, fables, and so on. Each genre has its own structure, and children must learn these to be effective readers. For example, in a mystery, we expect a crime, clues, and a solution. In a science fiction story, we expect some scientific or technological advance which would be impossible in today's world. In a fantasy, we expect strange events, such as animals that can talk.

Remedial readers typically do not do much reading, and therefore do not have the opportunity to develop an appreciation of genre. If teachers acquaint students with the concept of genres, they have more options for choosing material for free reading.

How can teachers help remedial students develop a sense of genre?

1. Discuss the genres of the stories that students are reading. When reading a fantasy story, for example, note the elements one would expect to find. After reading, the children might report the "fantastic" things that they have found.
2. At a somewhat higher level, ask the students to identify the genre of a story that they have read. Make a chart displaying the different stories that pupils have read, and the genres to which each story belongs. Books and stories read during leisure time should be included in this chart.
3. Systematically provide reading materials of different genres. The following cost-free

program both encourages free reading and acquaints primary and intermediate children with different types of stories. Using discarded basal readers of appropriate levels, cut out the stories that are most interesting. Group the stories into genres (e.g., adventure stories, stories from other lands, animal stories). Cover each story with construction paper in a color that identifies its genre. For example, adventure stories are bound in red; animal stories have blue covers. Assign each child to read at least one story per week, of his or her own choosing, and record its title in a notebook. Over a period of two months, each child must read at least one story from each genre.

Using Story Structure Diagnostically.   How can teachers obtain insights into students' cognitive and reading processes through the teaching of story structure? Teachers may observe that some remedial readers will focus almost entirely on part of a story, usually the first part, or the most exciting part. These students are demonstrating a need for additional help in grasping story structures. To provide aid, the teacher might read a short story to the students while placing a story grammar frame on the board or on an overhead projector. After the teacher has completed reading, the children try to fill in the story grammar. Then the teacher rereads the story, with the children listening again, and has them confirm or revise their story grammars. It is best to use very short stories for this activity, although length can gradually be increased.

Additional help may also be provided when the teacher composes short passages about fictional incidents concerning students and asks them to read these for story grammar. Since the incidents are personalized, the students will be better able to understand them. An example follows:

> Leroy lost his notebook with his homework in it. He couldn't hand it in when the teacher went to collect it. He looked in his locker, but it wasn't there. It wasn't in the lost and found either. He remembered he had taken the school bus that morning. The school office called the bus office and had the bus searched. There was Leroy's notebook.

Children identify with the problem and the solution to this story. Students also enjoy writing their own problem-solution passages.

Working with story grammar also gives insight into the student's current developmental level. As mentioned above, not all children have achieved a developmental level at which they can understand stories as a whole (Appleby, 1978), and only a few story grammar activities are suitable for primary children. Although ability to comprehend is partially dependent on maturity, this maturity will come faster if the child is given broad exposure to stories. If the child is not currently able to deal with story grammar, provide readiness skills that will improve the basis of organizational comprehension. Reading stories to children, followed by a discussion of the organizational features (characters, setting, problem) of the story fosters such readiness. Encouraging students to do their own wide independent reading also helps build a sense of story structure.

Diagnostic insight is also obtained through noting students' enthusiasm for story structure activities. Story grammar should not be allowed to become tedious. If students seem bored, move off of this strategy for a while, returning to it in a few weeks. Remember that people read stories in order to enjoy them.

Conceptually Related Instruction (Themes)

In conceptually connected instruction (or instruction through themes), students concentrate upon one interesting topic and pursue this interest by reading and writing about various aspects of the topic. Centering reading instruction around themes offers a peerless way to use interest to build background knowledge and schema and to develop the ability to read different types of materials (Crafton, 1983).

Studying materials which all relate to a central theme builds background knowledge and schema because students make associations from known to unknown material. For example, a student's interest in football may lead to understanding the business concepts of negotiating contracts, bringing law suits, and judging profit margins.

A theme can also lead students to varied types of reading materials. Students may explore stories, newspaper articles, record covers, encyclopedias, books, and manuals. For example, a student interested in football might be motivated to read an encyclopedia article or a long book about the subject. Students will be better able to grasp the structures of sophisticated types of text if they deal with familiar topics.

The theme approach can be effectively used by students of any age, either for individual or group instruction. It is particularly successful with students who are quite far behind in their reading skills and need a highly motivating activity in order to continue reading. After concentrating on a theme, students can return to a more standard curriculum with renewed enthusiasm.

There are many examples of students who have used themes successfully, Elizabeth, a seventeen-year-old, decided to concentrate on successful women who had, in her words, "made it." Three women were chosen, one each from entertainment, sports, and business. Elizabeth read books about them and collected newspaper articles. She also watched sports events on television and listened to phonograph records and tape recordings. As each woman was studied, the teacher brought in technical vocabulary from the field that was represented. At the end of three months, Elizabeth had considerably improved her fifth grade-reading level.

Edmund, a fifth grader reading on a second grade level, became interested in Hawaii and volcanoes. He collected pictures on these subjects. The teacher gave Edmund an assignment of going to the supermarket to find the many ways in which pineapple could be purchased. This trip was written up into a language experience story. Travel brochures, annotated maps, and social studies textbooks were used for reading material. At the end of instruction, the teacher was given a fresh pineapple as a gift!

Twelve-year-old Eugene, reading on a third grade level, developed an interest in the escape artist, Houdini. After reading some easy books in the clinic, he read through all the other books in the school and local library. Before another hero replaced Houdini, he had made several trips to the central New York City Public Library.

The theme approach allows the reader to pursue an interest and thus motivates remedial readers to read widely and take an active orientation toward their reading. At the same time, the teacher may focus on selected comprehension strategies that are relevant to the student's needs.

Using Conceptually Related Instruction Diagnostically.

Because themed instruction is largely student guided, it provides the teacher with many diagnostic opportunities. For example, themed instruction inevitably involves much research on the part of students, so teachers can observe students trying to find information, and can easily assess their ability to do this. Or a teacher might observe a student who, by repeatedly choosing one type of material (such as stories), demonstrates a narrow concept of reading.

Initially, some students will not be able to think of a theme that interests them. This is a clue to the teacher that these students are uninterested in reading, and perhaps the world around them. The teacher needs to suggest possible themes. After questioning students about their activities and trying to find reading material that would interest them, we always find that students can identify a motivating theme for instruction.

In the case of Oneka, a very passive fourteen-year-old student, the topic of food was chosen for a theme. She explored the history of popcorn, the taste of egg rolls, and how to eat gyros, incidentally gathering much information about the world.

Understanding the Question and Answer Process

School comprehension instruction often requires students to read questions and respond with answers. This type of activity is, in addition, usually included in standardized tests. The two strategies that follow, (1) The Question-Answer Relationship and (2) composing questions, will help remedial readers to understand questions and thus to answer them more effectively.

Question-Answer Relationship (QAR).

This strategy (Raphael, 1982, 1986) demonstrates the different processes that students go through to answer questions. It is particularly valuable for fostering an understanding of inferential questions. It also helps students to prepare for standardized tests.

Raphael identifies four types of relationships between a passage and its questions. These relationships define what the reader must do to answer a question (Pearson and Johnson, 1978). The four types are *right there, think and search, on my own,* and *author and me.* Figure 10.1 gives students an explanation of each type.

To illustrate QARs, a passage with questions follows:

> While we were in the Grand Canyon, several exciting things happened. One day, as we were about to eat lunch, the sky darkened. Suddenly, torrents of rain began

In the Book QARs

Right There
The answer is in the text, usually easy to find. The words used to make up the question and words used to answer the question are **Right There** in the same sentence.

One day there was......

So, Jack rode a horse to school today!

What did Jack ride to school today?
(a horse)

Think and Search (Putting It Together)
The answer is in the story, but you need to put together different story parts to find it. Words for the question and words for the answer are not found in the same sentence. They come from different parts of the text.

First, you get some bread.
Second, you get a knife.
Third, you get the peanut butter.

How do you make a peanut butter sandwich?

In My Head QARs

Author and You
The answer is *not* in the story. You need to think about what you already know, what the author tells you in the text, and how it fits together.

On My Own
The answer is not in the story. You can even answer the question without reading the story. You need to use your own experience.

Figure 10.1 Illustrations to Explain QAR to Students.

From Raphael, 1986, p. 519.

to fall. Next came hail balls, all over our peanut butter and jelly sandwiches! Some of us exercised, running in place just to keep warm. Others pitched a roof over the food large enough to try to keep the food dry. But it was too late. Our lunch had already been ruined.

1. What did some people do to keep warm? (RIGHT THERE)
2. What happened right after the rain began to fall? (THINK AND SEARCH)

3. Do people find it comfortable to eat in the rain? (ON MY OWN)
4. Why did the people not enjoy their lunch? (AUTHOR AND ME)

Instruction in QARs fosters students' comprehension of text. Begin by explaining four types of relationships. Then show passages and questions containing each type. (It may be necessary for the teacher to write some of the questions for passages.) Next, under a teacher's guidance, have the student read the passage, answer questions, and identify the QAR that each question requires. Instruction should proceed from very short passages to longer selections.

The QAR strategy demonstrates to remedial students that they are active participants in the question answering process. This helps them to deal better with the everyday task of answering questions.

Learning to Ask Questions. Part of the skill of answering questions requires an understanding of how questions are formed. Encouraging remedial students to create questions about the material that they are reading can make them into more active readers and help them to comprehend stories on a deeper level. This is a motivating group activity, since students can ask each other questions. It is also an excellent individual activity, for students will enjoy seeing whether teachers can answer their questions. Be sure that students know the answers to their own questions!

At first, students may be asked to formulate questions for which they can point to answers (literal questions). After some of these have been composed, ask for questions in which the answer cannot be directly pointed to, but must be inferred.

The authors worked with a reading resource room of fourth graders. We brought in several cereal boxes, telling the children to read the box and then to ask two questions using information about the box. The children had to be able to point to the answer.

Two questions from a Raisin Bran box were:

> What cereal is this? (Raisin Bran)
> What company makes Raisin Bran? (Post)

These came from a Cheerio's box:

> If you're a winner, who should you send it too? (sic)
> What vitamins are in Cheerios?

Next the children were asked to make up one question on their box for which they could not point to an answer. This was an inferential question.

The Raisin Bran question was:

> Does Raisin Bran have raisins?

The Cheerios question was:

How many prizes are there?

The children enjoyed these activities, and they began to see how different types of questions are related to the reading material. The comment of one child was: "You taught us how to read cereal boxes." This material figures prominently in the environment of many young children.

On a higher level, seventh and eighth graders in a resource room learned to ask each other factual and inference questions using the stories in their reader. The students had previously been formed into small groups of three or four. Groups wrote questions, and then asked other groups to answer them. These question-composing activities gave students a more active part in the reading process and helped them to see that reading is comprehension.

Using Questioning Strategies Diagnostically. The ease with which your remedial readers can identify question types and learn to ask their own questions reveals information about their reading process. Students who are unable to ask questions demonstrate difficulties with the language processes underlying reading and will profit from strategies for fostering language growth (in this chapter). We specifically recommend the sentence-building strategy.

In addition, to help students improve question asking, discuss the words that begin questions: *who, when, where, what, why,* and *how.* These words, commonly known as the 5-W's and H, help students to start framing their questions.

Difficulty in formulating inference questions generally indicates that a child lacks the background needed for understanding inference questions. Remedy this by working with pictures and oral language to foster readiness. For example, bring in a picture of a high building, and ask students whether, based on the picture, the following questions are "right there," or require an inference: "How many stories does the building have?" (The student's can count them); "Does the building have an elevator?" (The student's must infer the answer from the height of the building).

DEVELOPING LISTENING COMPREHENSION AND LANGUAGE

A student's comprehension of oral language provides the foundation for reading comprehension. To prepare students to comprehend the advanced texts and books written for mature readers, we must help them to develop a solid basis of oral language comprehension skills.

Students with reading problems may need specific instruction in advanced language structures and listening comprehension. Written language tends to be more complex than spoken language (Schallert, Kleinman, and Rubin, 1977), and exposure to written language can stimulate language growth. Students who read extensively have many opportunities to build their vocabularies and learn complex sentences from written language. However, since poor readers do little reading and the material that they do read tends to be simple, they are deprived of experiences with the written language as a rich source of language growth (Snider and Tarver, 1987).

In addition, remedial readers often lag in language development. In some cases, high level, expressive oral language is not part of their environmental experiences. In other cases, remedial students have a global language disability which created the reading problem.

Remedial teachers must help the language of their pupils continue to develop and grow. In the following section, we explore methods to nurture language growth. These strategies encourage creative and enjoyable responses to language.

Listening Comprehension

Listening comprehension provides a basis for reading comprehension. Through listening to stories containing sophisticated language and structures, students acquire the readiness to read such stories. We highly recommend reading to remedial children a few times per week.

Listening to a teacher reading stories is beneficial for several reasons. (1) Students absorb higher-level language, build background knowledge, and learn story organization. (2) Students are motivated to learn to read as they become aware of the many interesting things that can be read. (3) Listening to a teacher read is a relaxing, nonthreatening activity.

What kinds of materials should a teacher choose to read to students? Books that are above students' reading level, and on the "cutting edge" of their language will foster language growth. The books should contain language that is challenging for students. To build background knowledge, teachers should try to find books that are set in a different time and place, or contain elements of fantasy. Reading a full-length book to children will expose them to longer materials, helping them to develop the skills to read such books for themselves.

Primary grade teachers might read the following books to their students: *Amos and Boris, Kate and Caleb*, both by W. Steig; *Many Moons* by J. Thurber; *The Wind in the Willows* by K. Grahame; *And to Think that I Saw it on Mulberry Street, McElligot's Pool, Bartholomew and the Oobleck* by T. Geisel (better known as Dr. Seuss). For the intermediate grades, the following are recommended for reading to children: *Mrs. Frisby and the Rats of NIMH*, by R. O'Brien; *Ben and Me*, by R. Lawson; *North to Freedom*, by A. Holm; *Call it Courage* by A. Sperry. Middle school and junior high students, as well as high-school students, will profit from listening to teachers read difficult material. The short stories of Edgar Allen Poe, Jack London, Mark Twain, and Arthur Conan Doyle are highly recommended for their interesting content, sophisticated concepts, and high-level language.

Paired Story Reading

Some teachers feel that their students will not be able to grasp classic tales, yet recognize a need to improve language growth. Paired story reading is a way to present the classics in a fashion which provides a scaffold to higher language (Richek, 1983–1989). It is particularly recommended for students with reading problems in grades one to six. To do this, the teacher needs to obtain an easier and a more difficult version of the same fairy or folk tale. Collections of fairy tales told in easy versions are available, for example, in the *Dolch Book of Fairy Tales*, by E. Dolch, (First Reading Book, Developmental Learning Materials, see Appendix A). More difficult versions of fairy tales can be found in A. Lang's *Green Book of Fairy Tales* (or in the red, yellow, and blue books).

To do paired story tellings, simply read an easy version of one tale to children on one day (say, "Cinderella" from the Dolch book) and discuss the story. This will enable them to learn and enjoy the basic story. On the next day, read the difficult version of the same tale. Having the background of the easier tale, the children will thoroughly enjoy the greater detail and richer language of the harder version.

Directed Listening-Thinking Activity (DLTA)

This activity parallels the Directed Reading-Thinking Activity (DRTA) presented earlier. Like DRTA in reading, DLTA fosters active comprehension, as well as enjoyment. DLTA is recommended for primary children who need to develop a sense of story structure and for students of any age who need to improve their sense of story grammar and language. In DLTA, as in DRTA, students are exposed to one section of a story at a time, and they predict what will happen next. However, in DLTA, they *listen* to a story being read rather than reading the story themselves (Richek, 1987). Freed from the constraints of having to recognize words, students can apply all of their energies to thinking about the story. In this way, they can dramatically extend their language level and their sense of story structure. It is important to formalize the thinking process of DLTA just as we do in DRTA. Thus, when using DLTA, we carefully write down all of the student's predictions, take votes, and so on. Writing down students' hypotheses encourages a reading response, since students will invariably want to read their hypotheses, as written on the board.

The Auding Process

Auding refers to simultaneous listening and reading. In the auding process, students follow along in their texts while listening to a cassette recording of a book or selection. Or the teacher may read aloud while the children simultaneously follow in their texts. When using the auding technique, it is important to choose material that is difficult enough that students cannot read it for themselves. Auding is an effective way to expose older disabled readers to textbooks or literature books that are used in their content area classrooms, but are too difficult for them to read. It may serve as a way to familiarize pupils with good literature. When using auding, however, teachers need to assure that students are paying attention and following the text.

Auding is effective in promoting both language and reading growth. Aulls and Gelbart (1980) found that a group of seventh grade remedial readers improved in comprehension when they listened to audio tapes while simultaneously following the text in a book. Chomsky (1978) reported dramatic improvement in the reading levels of primary remedial readers who listened to tape-recorded versions of books as they followed the text. The auding technique was particularly effective in increasing motivation for reading.

Sentence Building

Students with reading problems often have difficulty with sentence comprehension. The sentence building strategy is a creative way to show how long sentences are created. While best suited to a group situation, it can also be used individually. The teacher writes a simple sentence such as

> The boy walked the dog.

on tag board strips, and mounts it on the board. The teacher then tells the students that they can add to the sentence. The rules are, however, that the student must look at the sentence as it is printed on the board, and read the sentence *plus the addition the student wishes to add*. Only then will the teacher make the addition. The first student might say "The boy walked the dog to the park." Then the teacher will change the sentence on the board from

> The boy walked the dog.
>   to
> The boy walked the dog to the park.

The object is to create a sentence that is as long as possible. Since students will invariably add to the end of a sentence, the teacher should also demand that they make additions to the beginning and the middle. The following sentence was created by fourth grade resource room students:

> Johnny and the big muscle-bound boy who had never seen that kind of dog walked their dog to the park and through the alley and a girl asked them if she could hold the dog.

This one was created by fifth and sixth grade learning-disabled students in a resource room:

> Who was the dumb ugly boy with a holey shirt and holey pants who walked the dog all the way home and gave him a bone and gave him some food with water?

Sentence building is a creative activity which is both fun and will foster growth of sentence comprehension and higher-level language.

SUMMARY

Remedial students often have problems in reading comprehension. They need to acquire four understandings (or attitudes) about reading which will result in comprehension. These are: (1) the purpose of reading is comprehension; (2) comprehension is an active process; (3) comprehension employs background knowledge and language skills; (4) comprehension requires higher-level thinking.

Teachers can foster these attitudes before reading by recalling and supplementing background knowledge and building an interest in the text. During reading, silent reading and comprehension monitoring should be encouraged. After reading, teachers should check for comprehension, encourage personal responses, and increase the number of higher-level questions.

There are many strategies for fostering comprehension of narrative text.

1. The Directed Reading-Thinking Activity (DRTA) and its variations encourage students to predict what will happen next in a story. Variations include DRTA without justification and silent DRTA.
2. Making mental images while reading encourages silent reading and a personal response to reading.
3. Using story structure encourages the development of organizational structure. Students may use story grammar and maps, identify a problem and a solution, make telegram summaries, or work to understand different literary genres.
4. Conceptually related instruction, centered around themes, uses student interest as a springboard to extend background knowledge and move students to many different types of reading materials.
5. Understanding the question and answer process helps students to deal with everyday school tasks. Students may use Question-Answer Relationships or may compose their own questions.

Remedial students often need to extend the language abilities that form the basis for reading comprehension. Effective ways are (1) to listen to the teacher read books; (2) to use paired story readings, in which one easy and one difficult version of a story are read; (3) to do the Directed Listening-Thinking Activity, in which students predict material that they listen to; (4) to aud, or follow along while listening to a text; and (5) to use sentence building, in which students build progressively more complex sentence structures.

11

IMPROVING COMPREHENSION
Reading and Studying Expository Texts

In this chapter, we describe expository text, discuss why it is difficult for remedial students, and suggest methods to aid students. Expository text refers to informational material, such as textbooks used in science, health, and psychology.

INTRODUCTION

The topics in the chapter include (1) a description of expository text; (2) general guidelines for helping students to read all expository text better; (3) specific strategies for helping students to cope with expository text; (4) methods for helping students with the demands of studying; and (5) reading rate.

As children move through the intermediate grades, the tasks that confront them in school change dramatically. The reading of basal texts and literature becomes less important, and work with expository materials, especially school texts, increases. Children spend less time in reading groups, and more time reading in content area subjects. In brief, "learning to read" has been replaced by "reading to learn."

Often students are assigned to read science and social studies books independently, without supervision. No longer is the teacher readily available to help with unknown words. At this stage, teachers usually assign a chapter, obtaining feedback by requiring the students to answer the questions at the back of the chapter or section. It is not surprising that many remedial readers cannot do these assignments. In addition, students whose reading has been limited to basals, which consist largely of narrative stories, lack experience with expository text.

THE NATURE OF EXPOSITORY TEXT

Expository text conveys information, explains ideas, or presents a point of view. Subject area textbooks (including this one) are expository texts.

Types of Expository Text

There are several types of expository text.

1. *Directions* include manuals, income tax forms, cookbooks, and other such "how to do it" materials.
2. *Comparison and contrast* give similarities and differences. For example, a social studies text might compare a congressional system of government with a parliamentary system, contrasting them in terms of elections, party discipline, and so forth.
3. *Listings* give features. For example, a biology textbook could list the characteristics of reptiles, giving their body temperature, reproductive habits, eating habits, etc. Each of these separate topics might take a paragraph, a page, or more.
4. *Time ordered sequence*, often used in history texts, presents events chronologically.
5. *Cause and effect* outlines reasons for events. For example, a seventh grade text in

world history might explain that the world economy changed in the nineteenth century because of industrialization and improved communication.

If remedial students can recognize these types of text organizations when reading, they will be better able to comprehend material. However, expository texts are seldom organized just in one way. For example, it is common for a cause and effect organization to be intertwined with a list organization.

Difficulties of Reading Expository Text

There are several reasons why expository text may present difficulties for remedial students. (1) It is less personal than narrative text. The writer of a story seeks to engage and amuse the reader; however, the writer of a textbook is usually trying to give information, a far less personal task. (2) Expository text usually contains more difficult vocabulary than narrative text. In fact, one of the aims of school textbooks is to teach new technical terms. To understand events such as the U.S. Civil War, one must know the meaning of "abolition," "emancipation," and "Reconstruction." This technical vocabulary contributes considerably to the difficulties remedial readers encounter in expository text. (3) Expository texts tend to be longer than narrative texts. Even in the fourth and fifth grade, it is not uncommon to have twenty-page chapters in a textbook. (4) Finally, expository text is too often "inconsiderate," or poorly organized (Armbruster, 1984), making reading and studying difficult. Inconsiderate text profoundly affects the remedial reader who cannot read disorganized material well enough to get the "hidden message."

Even though expository text presents many hurdles, students with reading problems are usually eager to receive instruction in reading their textbooks. They know that if they are to achieve better in their classes, they must master textbook reading. Recognizing that such help is important to success in school, remedial readers frequently request help in reading textbooks for their content-area classes.

GENERAL GUIDELINES TO HELP STUDENTS READ EXPOSITORY TEXT

The guidelines discussed in this section can be used by resource teachers, clinicians, and classroom teachers to help remedial students better comprehend expository text. The procedures should be used on a continuing basis, and, over time, students will learn to read their textbooks more effectively and efficiently.

Before Reading

Before reading, teachers should try to make the reading meaningful by linking the reading material to other material that students have covered, and to the students' thoughts and feelings. For example, we recently taught a social studies lesson to a group of low-achieving urban fifth graders. The text dealt with farming after the U.S. Civil War, a topic to which these children had no easy way to relate. To make the topic more meaningful, we asked the children to remember the last topic studied, which happened to be the end of the Civil War. They talked about the Civil War, and how it might affect farmers both in the North and the South. Then to relate this discussion to some type of personal experience, we asked what problems they might have faced if they had been farmers during this period.

Encouraging students to preview their material gives them an orientation to the text as a whole. It also helps them to develop expectations from the text. (We will discuss previewing further in the section on study strategies.)

Since technical vocabulary is a stumbling block for many remedial students, key vocabulary should be introduced before reading. This activity sets an expectation for the content of the text, and enables students to read it and understand new concepts.

During Reading

We strongly urge that students read expository material silently rather than orally. Frequent halts for discussion will aid students who have difficulty reading long sections of expository text silently. When students encounter severe difficulty with a particular section, that section can be read orally and discussed. When assignments are read independently, away from supervision, students should be especially alert to the need to monitor their comprehension.

After Reading

After reading a selection, meaningful follow-up helps refocus on textbook material. Asking students what in the text they found most interesting helps them to develop a personal reaction to the material. Asking what they think were the major points of the text triggers a teacher-guided discussion of the author's major ideas. This will help remedial students to focus on the organization of the text, and therefore to remember it more effectively.

SPECIFIC STRATEGIES FOR COMPREHENDING EXPOSITORY TEXT

In this section, we present specific teaching strategies for helping remedial students to read expository text. Our major goals are to help students learn to (1) combine their prior experience with the text; (2) understand the organization and main ideas of the text; (3) actively monitor their comprehension; and (4) follow directions. These strategies may be used either with the materials students are using in their classroom, or with other instructional materials.

Combining Prior Experience with Text Reading: K-W-L

When accomplished readers approach informational material, they usually begin by summoning into consciousness the things that they know about the topic. For example, when picking up a magazine article about the State of Washington, a person might think about Seattle, rain, the explosion of Mt. St. Helens, apples, or lumber. This helps readers to relate personally to the material. Next, readers will develop some expectations of what they would like or expect to find out from the material. For example, a reader might like to know (or expect to learn) more about skiing or water sports in the state. After completing the article, the reader has probably gained some new knowledge. For example, the reader might now know that the capitol of Washington is Olympia, that Washington has much wind surfing, and that the climate of western Washington is moderate. This reader has probably read some other facts that he or she already knew, and some that were judged as not being worth remembering. This illustration, a familiar one to all mature readers, shows that reading is a combination of the text and the reader. The text provides information for the reader, but the reader also contributes to the reading process by bringing certain background knowledge, developing expectations of the text, and absorbing information from the text.

In contrast, remedial readers often do not "put themselves" into reading, but remain passive bystanders, often simply reading material because their teacher told them to do it. This passive orientation is one reason why they have comprehension problems (Jenkins et al., 1986; Johnston, 1984).

The K-W-L technique (Ogle, 1986) teaches remedial students to go through the steps that the mature reader goes through in reading expository text. By summoning their prior knowledge and developing realistic expectations of the text, pupils become more active and involved readers. We also find that K-W-L is a study technique which markedly facilitates retention.

K-W-L may be used with any type of informational text, including children's textbooks. It is suitable for both group and individual instruction. Students from the primary grades through high school will enjoy and profit from the technique.

The initials of K-W-L represent:

K - What I know
W - What I want to find out
L - What I learned

1. (K - What I *Know*) Ask students to read the title of the chapter and selection. Then, have them think of everything that they know about the topic. List their responses on the board or (if working with an individual student) on a sheet of paper. Pupils may present some misinformation. For example, while working with a group of low-achieving fourth graders on the State of Washington, we received such "knowledge" as "The President lives in the State of Washington" and "trees let you breathe." Such misconceptions should be tactfully corrected.

Ask students to examine their pooled information and to classify the items into categories. The fourth grade class described above found this direction quite confusing at first. To begin the classification, we had to suggest the category, "mountains." The children were then able to suggest items to fit under this category. Stimulated by this, the children were now able to add categories such as: "work, weather, visiting." The classification activity was personal and meaningful, since students were working with information they had supplied.

2. (W - What I *Want* to *Find Out*) Ask each student to write down the things that he or she wants (or expects) to learn. The W step is often difficult for remedial readers, as they do not have well-developed expectations of expository text. One fourth grade boy wanted to learn "Do nice people live in Washington?" a question he would be unlikely to answer from the text. As he did K-W-L over a period of several weeks, however, his expectations of text began to mature. Other children wanted to learn things that were *not* answered in the text, but could be answered from other sources. One girl wondered how many people had been injured or killed in the eruption of Mt. St. Helens. Such questions help students realize that learning does not stop with a single textbook. During the course of studying the State of Washington using K-W-L, several children began to bring in other resources.

3. (L - What I *Learned*) Ask students to read the material silently. Then, after reading, have each student write down what he or she learned from reading. After recording their learnings, children are usually eager to share them with others.

We worked with the fourth grade class in social studies for two weeks. Before beginning the text chapter, the children listed all that they knew and wanted to find out about Washington. Then, as they daily read each section of the text, they did a K-W-L sheet for that section. To conclude the unit, the children listed *all* of the things that they learned about Washington, and wrote a composition. Working with K-W-L, the students became more adept at understanding expository text and demonstrated improved retention of the material. In addition, since students felt that we valued their ideas and learnings enough to discuss them, they began to value their own personal responses. This resulted in an improved attitude toward learning.

We have successfully used K-W-L with other groups of students and with individual remedial pupils, and similar successful experiences are reported by Ogle (1986). K-W-L is an exceptionally useful strategy for teaching students with reading problems how to relate to textbook materials. Carr and Ogle (1987) have also described K-W-L Plus, a technique involving writing and expository reading.

Diagnostic Teaching with K-W-L. Teaching with K-W-L is useful for obtaining diagnostic information. By observing students during the K phase, teachers can assess background knowledge on a topic, and correct possible misconceptions. The K phase reveals whether students' schema and language are adequate or need further enrichment. By observing students' ability to classify, teachers can determine whether students require instruction in this technique.

During the W phase, teachers can learn about students' perceptions of expository text. Some students do not have enough experience to know the type of information that expository text provides, and they will need independent reading assignments with short, easy informational books.

The *L* phase allows the teacher to assess the student's ability to learn from text. Is the student able to gather *any* information from text? Can the student distill the major points of the textbook, or only pick up random facts? For students who are not absorbing major points, the teacher should focus on the most important parts of the chapter after the K-W-L procedure is completed

Strategies for Determining Main Ideas

Competent readers try to determine the main ideas in reading expository text. In doing so, they effectively interrelate facts and thereby remember them better. A central core of main ideas allows students to cluster facts.

However, many remedial readers have great difficulty organizing texts into main ideas. Constructing the main idea is a complex ability requiring many component skills (Afflerbach, 1987; Brown and Day, 1983). Since main ideas are often not stated directly in text, learning to identify them requires careful and systematic teaching, often over an extended period of time. Primary-grade students whether disabled or on level, usually have not matured to the point where they can deal effectively with main ideas in extended text.

Four different strategies are presented in this section for teaching main ideas and textual organization: (1) the GIST strategy, (2) visual outlining, (3) direct instruction, and (4) teacher modeling. Each of them is meant to be used with expository text, as narratives do not usually contain main ideas (but rather are organized according to a problem-solution format).

As noted earlier, there are many different types of expository text (directions, comparison and contrast, etc.). When working with students to determine the main ideas, point out how each text is organized. Discuss organization before students work to find the main ideas, and then reconsider it afterward. In this way, students can see how an overall plan affects the main idea of text.

The GIST Strategy. A *gist* refers to the essence of a text. The GIST strategy teaches students to make and evaluate successive hypotheses about a main idea as they read through segments of the text. There are two parts to the hypotheses: (1) What is being talked about (the topic) and (2) what is the main thing being said about it (the comment). For example, a selection might be about noise (the topic) and how it hurts your ears (the comment). Afflerbach (1987) reports that good adult readers construct main idea statements using both parts: topic and comment. The GIST strategy was developed by Schuder, Clewell, and Jackson (1988) for the Montgomery County, Maryland Public Schools. It is useful (and popular) with remedial readers. It can be used with individual students or with groups of students. Classroom texts or other materials can be employed.

To employ the strategy, choose a selection that has one cohesive main idea. The selection may vary from one to several pages.

The GIST strategy consists of seven prompts (or questions). Prompts 1 and 2 are asked during the prereading phase; prompts 3, 4, and 5, are asked, usually several times, during the reading phase; prompts 6 and 7 are asked during the postreading phase. A GIST statement is a summary of the material containing a topic and a comment.

PREREADING PHASE:

Ask the students to scan the selection (or chapter) to see what it is going to be about. Then ask:

Prompt 1: What do you think this text will be about? (the topic)
After students have given answers, ask them why they chose these answers. This helps them to relate their predictions to the material in the text. Next ask:

Prompt 2: What do you think the text is going to tell you about? (the comment)
Once again, after students have given answers, ask them to defend these answers. At this point, the class should reach a consensus on a GIST hypothesis. This is written on the board.

For example, one sixth grade Chapter I class formulated the following GIST about a two-page selection:

What it's about: "The moon"
What it tells about: "The moon affects animals on earth"
In this case, students had focused on a picture of a sleeping animal.

READING PHASE:

Next, the teacher divides the text into three to five meaningful segments. Students silently read each of these segments to see if they must modify their GIST statement.
After reading *each* segment, ask:

Prompt 3: Did you find information that supports your GIST statement? What was it?
Prompt 4: Did you find information that does not support your GIST statement? What was it?
Prompt 5: Do you want to change your GIST statement at this point? (If students say yes) *How do you want to change it?* (If students say no) *Why not?*

The sixth grade students we worked with answered these questions after each of three segments. Since the first segment gave information only about animals, they did not want to change their statement of GIST. In the second segment, however, the text gave information about how the moon affected both people's moods and plant growth. The students then formed the following GIST statement: "The moon affects people, animals, and plants." When we asked them if they could summarize this, they agreed that they might say, "The moon affects living things on earth."

The third segment of the text explained how the moon affected ocean tides. The group agreed that the GIST had to be changed. They suggested it be changed to "The moon affects living things and tides."

POSTREADING PHASE:

After reading the entire selection, ask:

Prompt 6: Do you want to make any changes in your GIST statement? (If yes) *What changes do you suggest? Why?*

After considering their GIST statement, our sixth grade group thought that it was accurate, but sounded a bit funny. We suggested that the reason might be that "living things" was a more general category than "tides." One student suggested that we might say "The moon affects living things and dead things on earth," but another suggested that we should substitute "nonliving" for "dead." Everybody agreed that "The moon affects living and nonliving things on earth" was an excellent GIST statement.

After the final statement of the GIST, students were asked the last prompt.

Prompt 7: What did you learn that you didn't know about before you read?

Students responded with many newly acquired facts about the moon's effect on the earth.

As is evident from this example, the GIST strategy involves students in formulating main idea hypotheses, checking them and changing them as they read, and supporting their hypotheses with evidence. This procedure involves the active reconstruction of main ideas in much the same way that adults reconstruct them (Afflerbach, 1987). In fact, after using the GIST strategy a few times, students often start to internalize it and to ask themselves the prompts spontaneously. The GIST strategy also involves students in classifying information into general categories as they are reading. There is usually much enthusiastic student participation. In addition, teachers should feel free to give support and guidance to students.

Visual Outlining. Teachers have traditionally instructed students to make outlines in order to clarify the structure of their reading and writing. While outlining is a sound way to gain a knowledge of the structure of text, students do not always find it to be a motivating activity. One lively variation of outlining is the visual outline. In visual outlining, students compose a graphic form, using varied shape and colors.

Visual outlining can be done in small groups or individually. A large class can be divided into several small groups.

We generally use visual outlining to show students how to use the headings in their texts to summarize information. Thus we expect them to outline a chapter using headings and to differentiate between the various levels of headings.

When working with younger students, we often *tell* them to use the headings to outline. However, when working with students who are in sixth grade and beyond, we simply direct them to outline the chapter the way that the author outlines it. Often it takes them quite a while to see that the headings can form an outline!

The visual outline displayed in Figure 11.1 was made by a group of three remedial seventh graders. To encourage group participation, each of the small groups in this large classroom chose a name. The name this group chose was composed of their initials; other groups chose the names of rock groups (such as Duran Duran).

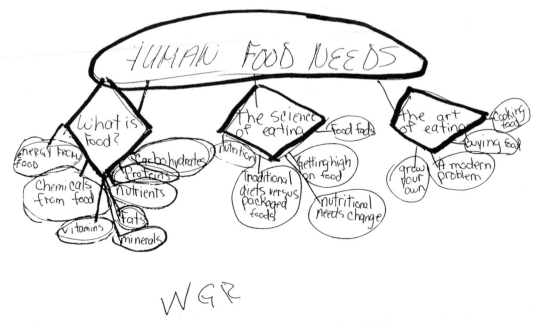

Figure 11.1 Three students' Visual Outline of "Human Food Needs," a Chapter in a Junior-High Health Text (from Richek, 1983–1989)

After making visual outlines with pupils, teachers should discuss how these outlines can be used to recall and summarize information. By concentrating on one category (or heading) on the outline and trying to remember what they know about it, students can review material.

Sometimes students cannot independently construct an entire visual outline. In this case, the teacher can give students a partially filled out outline, and they can fill in the blank spaces.

Direct Instruction in Main Ideas. Often, teachers use exercises containing short paragraphs which require students to find the main ideas. When teachers do this, they are providing direct instruction in main ideas. Research shows that direct instruction in finding main ideas can be effective with middle- and upper-grade students (Baumann, 1984).

How should material be chosen and lessons be sequenced to provide for maximum learning? Baumann suggests that teachers give a few lessons each using the following types of materials:

1. Main ideas and details in paragraphs in which the main idea is specifically stated.
2. Main ideas and details in paragraphs in which the main idea is *not* stated.
3. Main ideas and details in short passages in which the main idea is specifically stated.

4. Main ideas and details in short passages in which the main idea is *not* specifically stated.

To provide for more effective learning, students should write out the main ideas and details, rather than simply choosing from multiple choice alternatives. After students have found main ideas in the passages described above, two more exercise types should be added:

5. Outlining main idea and detail statements in a short passage where the main idea is specifically stated.
6. Outlining main idea and detail statements in a short passage where the main idea is *not* specifically stated.

The use of this sequence is effective in teaching sixth grade students to find main ideas (Baumann, 1984). Commercial materials for finding the main idea can easily be adapted to these activities.

It is important to follow direct instruction with reinforcing strategies for finding the main idea in longer texts. After finishing this instructional sequence, make sure to apply these learnings in the textbooks that the students are using.

Modeling.   Teacher modeling is an effective way to show students how to construct main ideas (Afflerbach, 1987). As noted earlier, in modeling, teachers demonstrate the processes that they use, stating thoughts aloud as they use them. In doing this, teachers bring thought processes that are usually subconscious to students' attention.

Afflerbach finds that adults use these processes: (1) reducing information by realizing when they have read the same thing over in different words; (2) listing the details to see which main idea can be constructed from them; (3) constructing a tentative main idea, and continually revising while reading.

To use teacher modeling, locate an expository paragraph or short passage that is difficult for students. Then read it aloud, talking through the processes you use to construct the main idea. Afterwards, discuss your thought processes with the students. Writing information on the board or an overhead projector is often helpful in clarifying mental processes for the students.

Diagnostic Teaching of Main Ideas.   The ability to categorize (classify objects, words, and ideas) is prerequisite to the ability of finding the main idea. If, in teaching main ideas, you observe that students cannot classify things into categories, have them practice classifying lists of words. They might, for example, separate lists such as: *ham, apple, orange, sirloin, banana, chicken breast* into the categories meat and fruit. To further develop categorization skills, ask students to classify words without giving them categories to use. Thus, the students will have to construct their own categories.

In dealing with main ideas, students will have most trouble when these ideas are *not* stated in a passage. To help students deal with unstated main ideas, work with them to classify facts in the text into groups. Then help them to construct (or infer) the overarching categories for each group. After these activities, students will often be able to construct main ideas.

Even after students have learned how to find a main idea in a short passage, they commonly encounter difficulties transferring this strategy to a longer section of a chapter or a several-page expository text. Strategies such as GIST and visual outlining help students accomplish this transfer.

After focusing for a time on strategies for teaching the main idea, continue to review them, encouraging students to find the main idea in any expository reading that they do.

Monitoring Understanding of Text

Many remedial readers are unable to monitor their reading. When they lose understanding of a text, they continue reading without realizing that they should go back and try to regain comprehension. At times, all readers are unable to make sense of text; however, only good readers monitor their difficulties. Additionally, good readers monitor their reading by anticipating what they are about to read. To do this, they make predictions and ask questions of the text.

The awareness of one's own mental activities is often called *metacognition*, that is, the activities deliberately directing one's cognition (or learning) process. As students learn strategies they can use to comprehend text, they develop metacognition, or an ability to self-monitor comprehension of reading material.

Brown and Palinscar (1982) show that by developing an awareness of monitoring strategies remedial readers increase their learning competency. The strategies given below, the Think Aloud and the ReQuest procedure, help students both to demand and to obtain meaning from text.

The Think-Aloud Strategy. The Think-Aloud process shows students how adults read. In this strategy the teacher models the way in which a competent reader makes sense from text (Davey, 1983). Through displaying their thinking, teachers show students how good readers actually read. The purpose of the Think-Aloud strategy is "to remove the cloak of mystery surrounding the comprehension process" (*New Directions in Reading Instruction,* 1987).

To use the strategy, select a short passage that contains ambiguities, unknown words, and several other points of difficulty. Give the passage to each student, retaining one copy. Next read the passage aloud, interspersing verbalization of all of the thought processes you use in trying to make sense of the passage. Davey (1983) suggests you do these things as you read:

1. Make predictions about topics. Hypothesize what the passage will be about early in the reading, and change the predictions if needed. For example, say "The title makes me think that this will be about . . . " or "Now in this next part, it looks like the topic is changing to . . . "

2. Describe any images you form while reading. For example, say "As I read this, I see a sandy beach by the sea . . . "

3. Give analogies to relate the material to your own experience. Say, "This part about how discipline is important to athletes reminds me of how I used to make a schedule to practice the piano."

4. Note confusing points. Say "I really don't understand what is going on here" or "This doesn't make sense." This is important because it allows students to see that adults, too, have difficulties.

5. Demonstrate fix-up strategies. These show how to correct misunderstandings. Say, "I think I'll read this page again and see if this gets clearer." or "I wonder what that word means. The rest of the sentence makes me think it means_____"

After teachers model the Think-Aloud process several times, students should apply it to their own reading. Have students report on the effect of the activities listed above. Reporting may be done either after they have finished reading or after they have read each paragraph. Davey suggests that, after reading, students can fill out a checklist reporting which strategies they used in reading. The one given below is adapted from her model.

What Did I Do When I Read?

	Yes	No
Made predictions		
Formed pictures		
Used "this is like"		
Found problems in reading		
Used fix ups		

Discuss these checklists with students immediately after they read, while the memories of the reading process are still fresh.

The ReQuest Procedure. The ReQuest procedure (Manzo, 1969) requires students and teachers to alternate asking questions about text. The teacher both answers and asks questions, so the procedure becomes almost a game. The process is particularly useful with very passive students, for it teaches them how to monitor their comprehension, participate in the reading process, and ask questions of text. Developed as an individual activity, the ReQuest procedure can also be used with small groups. The procedure is as follows:

1. The teacher tells the student that the purpose of this lesson is to learn to ask and answer questions about text, and that both the teacher and student will ask and answer questions.

2. The student and teacher read the first sentence of a short selection silently.

3. The student asks the teacher as many questions as he or she can think of about the first sentence. (The teacher tells the student to ask the types of questions that a teacher might ask.) Then the teacher answers as many questions as can be answered, making the answers clear and complete, and verifying responses by, say, pointing to a word. If a question cannot be answered (that is, if the information is not in the

teacher's prior experience or the passage), the teacher tells why it cannot be answered.

4. Next, the teacher takes a turn at asking questions about the sentence. The teacher should model good questioning skills by asking questions that involve comprehension of many different parts of the sentence. The student then answers the questions, and the teacher asks the student to verify answers by saying, for example, "Where does it say that?" If the student cannot answer a question, he or she should state why. (It is sometimes helpful to insert a question that cannot be answered.)

5. The teacher and student read the next text sentence, proceeding in the same manner through several sentences. During this time, teachers should begin to require students to ask inference as well as factual questions.

6. After the teacher thinks that the student has a grasp of the process, they can move to the paragraph level asking each other, say, five questions about a paragraph.

Diagnostic Teaching of Comprehension Monitoring.   Since comprehension monitoring strategies bring one's thought processes about reading to the forefront, it is relatively simple to gather diagnostic information. When implementing strategies, be alert to student comments that indicate a growing awareness of the need to monitor. Students should increase in their ability to identify their own trouble spots in reading and in their awareness of what they can do to correct difficulties. When using the ReQuest procedure, look for growth in the student's ability to ask and answer questions and to recognize how questions are related to text.

In addition, be alert to students' increasing awareness that problems in reading are to be expected. Comments, such as "I didn't realize you didn't understand either," or "I just don't get it here, can you help me?" are diagnostic demonstrations of considerable growth in the use of metacognitive, monitoring processes during reading.

Following Directions

In school, as well as in sports and hobbies, students must often follow exact directions, a procedure that requires precision and care in reading. Following directions is a particularly useful skill to teach remedial students who have very few comprehension skills. By learning to follow steps carefully, students become aware of the meaning-gaining function of reading and general comprehension is likely to improve. Some activities for following directions are given below.

1. Real-life and everyday materials may be used to teach following directions. These include labels from canned food, directions for opening packages, and recipes.

2. In treasure hunts, students have to follow directions. Each student can be given a different set of simple directions that enables him or her to reach a "treasure."

3. Origami, a paper-folding art that originated in Japan, may be used. Precise directions must be followed to make an object. Many books on this art can be found in the library and in bookstores.

4. Individual gamelike activities may be used to transform words if directions are followed carefully. For example,
   (1) *The word is HORSE.*
   (2) *Delete the first two letters.*

(3) *Put the first letter of the alphabet after the R.*
(4) *Put an I in the middle of the word.*
(5) *What word do you have? (RAISE)*

Diagnostic Teaching of Following Directions. The inability to follow directions may provide insight into students' impulsivity and lack of personal organization skills. Students who do not perceive the sequential steps in following directions often cannot organize their thoughts for instruction and systematic learning. For such students, instruction should be broken into carefully sequenced and controlled steps. See Chapter 13 for further suggestions.

STUDY STRATEGIES

In this section, we present an overview of some important study strategies. Students in the upper grades must read and remember material without teacher guidance. Independent studying calls for considerable self-guidance and a systematic approach. While good readers may be able to develop useful study strategies on their own, remedial readers usually need explicit instruction. The strategies discussed earlier for identifying and constructing main ideas will help students learn to study by allowing them to separate important from unimportant information.

In addition, other abilities are important to studying, including locating information, previewing, using teacher-prepared study guides, developing a study system, and using map skills.

Locating Information

To answer questions and to review material, students first need to be able to locate needed information. This ability is useful even in the primary grades, and it assumes more importance as children grow older. Good readers learn to locate information quickly by using a scanning strategy. Scanning refers to the ability to locate specific information such as facts, names, and dates. A reader scans the text quickly until the desired piece of information is located.

Remedial readers should be taught a systematic approach to scanning. First, they should learn how to locate appropriate headings in chapters. For example, to locate information about how a fish breathes, the student should first locate a heading about "Fish" in a chapter, rather than looking under a heading about "Reptiles," or, as many remedial readers do, simply searching from the beginning of the chapter. To develop scanning ability, begin by having students search through headings on one or two pages, gradually working their way up to dealing with an entire chapter.

After learning to scan for appropriate headings, students need to search for a few key words. For example, students who want to locate the date of birth of former U.S. President John Kennedy, need to search for key words such as *Kennedy*, *birth*, and *born*. The teacher needs both to share with students the process of deciding upon key words and to provide practice in this activity.

Remedial readers tend to read material slowly rather than to scan it quickly. To practice scanning, students may enjoy using the telephone book or another directory to locate needed information expeditiously.

Learning how to use an index is another important locational skill. Students need to learn how to decide which entry word(s) to look for, how to quickly locate such words in an alphabetical index, and how to use the index entry to locate a page.

Previewing

Often remedial students simply jump into reading without getting any orientation. They become awash in waves without knowing what sea they are swimming in! Previewing, or getting a general orientation to material before reading, enables remedial students to summon their background knowledge and to understand how the material is organized.

Using Parts of Books.   Understanding the parts of books helps students to preview. To aid students in becoming acquainted with book parts, systematically introduce title page, foreward, table of contents, chapter headings, index, and glossary. Practice activities to aid students follow.

1. *Title pages.* Ask students to find the oldest and newest book (by copyright) they are using.
2. *Table of contents.* Give students five to ten facts and ask them to use the table of contents to locate the chapters in which these facts are found.
3. *Index.* Give the students several words and, using an index, have them locate the pages where these terms first appear.
4. *Glossary and index.* Ask students to define three words using the glossary, and then, using an index, to copy sentences from the book containing the words. This enables students to compare glossary definitions with sentences used in context.
5. *Making a book.* Several book concepts become clear when students make books for themselves. Maurice, an eighth grade student reading on a third grade level, made a book of photography, filling it with pictures he had taken and captioned. In addition to his text, he had a copyright page, a dedication, a table of contents, and a glossary.

When using parts of books to preview, guide students to use book parts systematically. A sample guide is:

1. Look at the book title and jacket.
2. Look at the table of contents.
3. Look for illustrations, figures, and charts throughout the book.
4. Read the first portion of the first chapter.

The Five-Minute Summary.   Teachers can help remedial students by guiding them through a preview of a chapter. When the teacher and the students cooperatively preview a chapter, students develop an orientation toward previewing, and learn to value its use. However, if students are to learn good study habits, they eventually must learn to preview material without teacher guidance.

We have used a technique called the "five-minute summary" to check and further develop students' independent previewing strategies. The procedure is: (1) Students take a book chapter that they are about to read, and preview it for five minutes. To make this more dramatic, you can time the five minutes with a stopwatch. (2) Students summarize the chapter orally or in writing, using the information they have obtained. Students who have previewed properly will be able to give some main ideas, and will produce summaries containing information from all parts of the chapter. Students who have simply read from the beginning of the chapter will not be able to give a good summary.

The Five-Minute Summary is a worthwhile group activity because students can compare their summaries. As they relate the information that they obtained to the processes they used to obtain it, students begin to understand the process of previewing and its value. The teacher can also preview the material and compare his or her own processes with those of the students.

Teacher-Made Study Guides

Teacher-made study guides can help students who have difficulty studying in their content areas (Herber, 1978). Resource teachers and clinicians may make study guides to help students deal with difficult texts in history, biology, health, or other content areas. Classroom teachers may want to provide them to all students.

A sample summary might contain:

1. The title of the chapter
2. The major topic of the chapter
3. New terms. Depending upon the maturity of the students, new words might be simply listed, listed with the page on which they first appear, or listed and defined.
4. The major ideas in the chapter
5. The purpose for reading the chapter. That is, what the students should learn from the chapter

When using study guides, remember that the goal is eventual student independence. At first, the teacher fills out the study guide completely, then students partially develop study guides. For example, after using a study guide several times, the "new terms" section can be left blank, and students can be encouraged to locate their own technical terms and definitions while reading the material. This procedure can also be used with the "major ideas" section of the text. Teachers should discuss student-completed study guides. Have students compare their completions with those of other students.

Using a Study System

Learning to study systematically for tests in the content areas will dramatically help remedial readers. Problem readers need direct help to learn how to approach and remember material. One useful system for study, suggested by Pauk (1984), is the OK5R (see Table 11.1). It combines many of the concepts we have mentioned in this chapter: previewing, locating key ideas, and supporting details. While students find this method useful in coping with the demands of school, they need teacher guidance using the system through a few chapters before they can use it independently.

Table 11.1   The OK5R Study System.

O	OVERVIEW	Sample the chapter to find out what it is all about. Glance at the headings and subheadings to determine what ideas are being explained, what problems raised, and what questions posed. Get the big picture. Don't burrow into paragraphs. Headings and subheadings will be future categories (advance organizers). Overview to overcome inertia and gain momentum for studying.
K	KEY IDEAS	All textbook writing is made up of just three literary elements: main ideas, supporting material, and transitions. Your main job is to separate the main idea from the mass of supporting material.
R_1	READ	Read only a paragraph or short section. Then stop to ask: What is the main idea? How do the supporting materials support it? Which transitional words point to the main idea and organize the supporting material? Finally, what is it in this paragraph that I need to know, to describe what I have read?
R_2	RECORD	Make marginal notes, and underline only key words and phrases. Better still, summarize main ideas and supporting materials in your notebook. Don't summarize each sentence. Summarize ideas, not words.
R_3	RECITE	To counteract forgetting, recite! Cover your textbook or notebook page, exposing only your notes in the margin. Then, using your own words, recite the ideas and supporting material aloud. After reciting, check on how accurate you were. Read, record, and recite paragraph by paragraph, until you complete the chapter.
R_4	REVIEW	Immediately after reciting, take a fresh look at your notes to fit them into the overall picture. It is easier to remember one complete jigsaw picture than a multitude of separate, seemingly unrelated puzzle pieces. A review now will give you the total picture. And review occasionally to keep you retention at a high level.
R_5	REFLECT	Now, mentally manipulate these ideas, turn them over, speculate on them, compare one with the other, notice where they agree and differ. Organize and reorganize them into larger categories, or compress them into smaller units. Finally, free these ideas from the chapter and the book by weaving them into your existing knowledge.

(From Pauk, 1984, p. 169)

Pauk emphasizes that the OK5R system should be used flexibly. He warns that the student should not become like a knight who is overburdened with armor. When guiding students to using this system, remember to help them to adapt it to their individual needs.

Map Skills

Maps and globes are indispensible to the study of social studies and to an intelligent reading of current events. Many students with reading problems have particular trouble with these areas of "visual literacy." Teaching these concepts also serves to enlarge students' experiential backgrounds and schema. Students need to know several concepts, including geographical terms (city, state, lake, country) and direction terms (north, south). Map skill instruction for remedial readers may begin with maps of familiar territory such as maps of rooms, buildings, and the neighborhood.

Several activities may help students understand map concepts:

1. Students may make maps of their classrooms. This activity helps to clarify the concepts of direction and map scale.
2. Using road maps, students may plan a trip from one place to another, finding alternate routes.
3. Students may use the map of a country, or continent, to answer questions such as "If you were planning a trip from Mexico to Chile, what countries would you pass?"

Diagnostic Teaching of Study Strategies

When teaching study strategies, teachers gain insight into students' abilities to generalize and to organize information into categories. Teachers can also determine if students can review systematically enough to remember material.

Teachers can learn much by observing students trying to implement study strategies. For example, it is diagnostically valuable to watch students trying to preview. Teachers should note the processes that they use. This type of observation provides an overview of a student's ability to put strategies into practice.

Remember that the purpose of teaching study strategies is to improve students' comfort in their content area classrooms. If they cannot transfer their newly learned study habits to other classrooms, remedial teachers may need to change the instruction they are giving in studying.

READING RATE

Increasing reading rate can be an instructional goal for advanced remedial readers. However, students should be comfortable with other aspects of reading before striving to improve rate. Unfortunately, we find that many older remedial readers are motivated to improve their rate simply because of the publicity given to this topic.

Assessing Reading Rate

Rate of reading may be assessed using informal measures. Students read a passage in a book silently. The teacher times the reading with a stopwatch. At the end of five minutes, the teacher says the word "mark" and students put a slash by the line they are reading. The words per minute (WPM) are determined by counting the total number of words read and dividing by five (for the number of minutes of reading).

Factors in Reading Rate

Although no one figure can be given as a "normal" reading rate, adult readers average about 250 words per minute. This rate is reached at about the ninth grade reading level. The norms given in Table 11.2 (adapted from Harris and Sipay, 1985) give estimates of reading rates for standardized tests. However, readers should have a variety of different rates. A relatively fast rate might be used for reading easy fiction material; a moderate rate for reading in school; and a slow rate for reading detailed directions. In short, reading rate should be flexible.

When reading material, the eye does not move at a smooth pace across the page. Instead, it uses *saccadic movements*, jumping from place to place. When the eye stops, it absorbs information, and this pause is called a *fixation*. A mature normal reader will make about three or four fixations in a line of print the size of this book. Sometimes readers retrace information. Eye movements that look back over previously read material are called *regressions*.

Slow reading is often simply the result of inefficient reading habits. Other causes of slow reading are (1) problems with reading fluency, (2) subvocalization or lip movement, and (3) a slow personal tempo.

1. Problems with reading fluency. Students who are having trouble recognizing words quickly will read slowly. These students need help in reading fluently. Many suggestions are given in Chapters 8 and 9.

Table 11.2 Median Rates of Reading for Different Grades as Determined by Several Standardized Reading Tests

	GRADE								
	2	3	4	5	6	7	8	9	12
Highest test	118	138	170	195	230	246	267	260	295
Median test	86	116	155	177	206	215	237	252	251
Lowest test	35	75	120	145	171	176	188	199	216

Note: The number of tests included in the table is 7 for Grades 2, 3; 8 for Grades 4, 5, 6, 7; 6 for Grades 8, 9; and 3 for Grade 12.

From Harris and Sipay, 1985, p. 533.

2. Some readers "whisper" or *vocalize* during silent reading; others reproduce words inaudibly, or *subvocalize*. Students with low reading levels may still require the supports that these habits provide, and teachers should not attempt to eliminate them. On the other hand, if vocalization has become a crutch that is no longer needed, the teacher may try to discourage these habits by presenting material rapidly so that students cannot vocalize. Reading pacers are useful for this purpose.

3. *Slow personal tempo.* People think and react at different rates. This difference, which may depend on metabolic rate or other physical factors, affects the reading process. Buswell (1951) found that the rate of reading was related to the rate of thinking. However even slow-tempoed individuals may profit by learning more efficient reading habits.

Increasing Reading Rate

Much improvement in reading rate may be gained by simply making students aware of their problems and motivating them to improve. Some commercial programs promise wonders in rate improvement; however, reading rates of thousands of words per minute have yet to be substantiated by carefully conducted research.

Often, simply practicing a faster reading rate for an extended period of time improves rate markedly. The teacher selects a ten- to twenty-minute period for such practice. It is best to use one source of materials consistently, and this source should contain several fairly short selections (from one to three pages) that are at the student's independent level. Students should time their readings and keep a record of their progressive improvement. Students should not neglect to read for meaning as they improve their rate. Comprehension questions should accompany all rate training.

By emphasizing the importance of reading in meaningful phrases, students learn to read faster by absorbing material in meaningful language units. Fast readers tend to group their fixations in meaningful phrases such as

The boy / saw the dog / in the yard.

A slow reader will either read word by word,

The / boy / saw / the / dog / in / the / yard.

or group in meaningless phrases,

The / boy saw the / dog in / the yard.

To facilitate the perception of words in phrases, students may be given duplicated copies of text and asked to group words into phrases. The teacher should limit these selections to about one hundred words. After students mark these, they may compare their answers. To encourage phrase awareness, the student may be asked to read orally the text divided into such phrases.

The reading accelerator, a mechanical device (see Appendix A), can be placed over a book and set at a given pace (say 180 words per minute). It then covers the page, from top to bottom, at this rate. To read, the student must stay ahead of the pacer. The accelerator, if used judiciously, helps students to read in meaningful phrases and to avoid subvocalization.

SUMMARY

Expository texts are subject matter texts that give information. Types of expository text include directions, comparison and contrast, listing, time-ordered sequence, and cause and effect.

Features that make expository text difficult are (1) it is less personal than narrative text, (2) it contains much difficult vocabulary, (3) students are generally required to read longer selections than in narrative texts, and (4) expository text is often inconsiderate, or poorly organized.

General guidelines that teachers can implement on a daily basis before, during, and after the time students read will help them to cope with expository text.

There are many specific strategies for comprehending expository text. In K-W-L, students list what they know before reading, what they want to learn, and what they have learned from reading. To help students determine main ideas, four options are presented: the GIST strategy, visual outlining, direct instruction, and teacher modeling. To help students monitor their understanding of text, teachers may employ Think Aloud or the ReQuest technique. Finally, teachers should help students to learn to follow directions.

Remedial students need to learn study strategies. They can learn to locate information quickly by scanning, to preview, to use teacher-made study guides, to use a study system, and to understand maps.

Increasing reading rate may be an instructional goal, but students should only aspire to this if other areas of reading are well developed.

12

FOSTERING THE READING-WRITING CONNECTION

The strong link among the various areas of language is becoming increasingly evident. The ability to read and the ability to write are closely connected. Like reading, good writing requires many years of practice. Teachers must provide effective and motivating ways to encourage that practice.

INTRODUCTION

In this chapter, we discuss areas related to becoming a writer, including the writing process, spelling, and the development of handwriting.

School systems throughout North America have come to realize that the content and mechanics of written expression need more attention in the curriculum. All students, but particularly those with difficulties in reading, need careful teaching and practice in learning to write.

THE NATURE OF THE READING-WRITING CONNECTION

Research shows the processes of reading and writing are intimately connected. Moreover, experiences with writing and composing facilitate the acquisition of reading. For example, Stotsky (1983) found that the relationship between reading and writing was so strong that instruction in one area improved performance in the other.

In what ways do reading and writing interrelate? There are at least four connections: (1) Writing and reading require similar processes. (2) Writing demands active involvement in literacy. (3) Writing fosters phonological awareness. (4) Writing requires reading.

Writing and Reading Require Similar Processes

Tierney and Pearson (1983) explain the similarity of the reading and writing processes. When we read, we construct, in our own minds, a text parallel to the one we are reading. Thus, they conclude, the process of reading is actually the process of constructing, or writing. For example, while working through either reading or writing, we set and revise goals, refine and reconstruct meaning as we go through material, develop expectations about what we will read or write next, develop attitudes toward the text, and monitor the information we wish to convey or remember.

In addition, writing helps to give insight into reading. When students write, they go through the process of creatively composing original text. After many composing experiences, students come to realize how written material, including the text in their reading books, is developed. By understanding the composing process, students begin to comprehend reading material at a deeper level (Goodman and Goodman, 1983). Both Newkirk (1982) and Hansen (1983) found that students who authored gained enthusiasm and competence in reading.

Writing Demands Active Involvement in Literacy

By its nature, writing is an active process. Writers perform the actions of picking up a pen or pencil and recording their thoughts. They work at producing something that did not exist before, using their own background knowledge, reading skills, and critical facilities.

Writing, as an activity, is more self-involving than reading, since the meaning of a writer's message originates from within the writer. Chomsky (1971, 1979) suggests that writing may be easier than reading, and it may actually develop earlier. Reading requires the ability to penetrate someone else's use of language and meaning, a more abstract and difficult task than expressing one's own meaning.

Writing Fosters Phonological Awareness

Phonological awareness, the realization that words can be segmented into sounds, greatly aids the early stages of reading (see Chapters 8 and 13). Writing increases phonological awareness. As beginning writers attempt to put their ideas into print, they explore and refine the alphabetic nature of written English (Dyson, 1984).

Nine-year-old Joy, a student in our clinic, was at the beginning stage of reading acquisition. Joy kept a journal, in which she recorded her thoughts in writing. Her teacher wrote responses to Joy's journal writings. At first, Joy's spellings showed only a low developmental awareness of the English sound system. For example, she often represented a word by one letter (see Figure 12.1). However, as Joy and her

Figure 12.1 Journal Writing of Joy, a Beginning Reader.

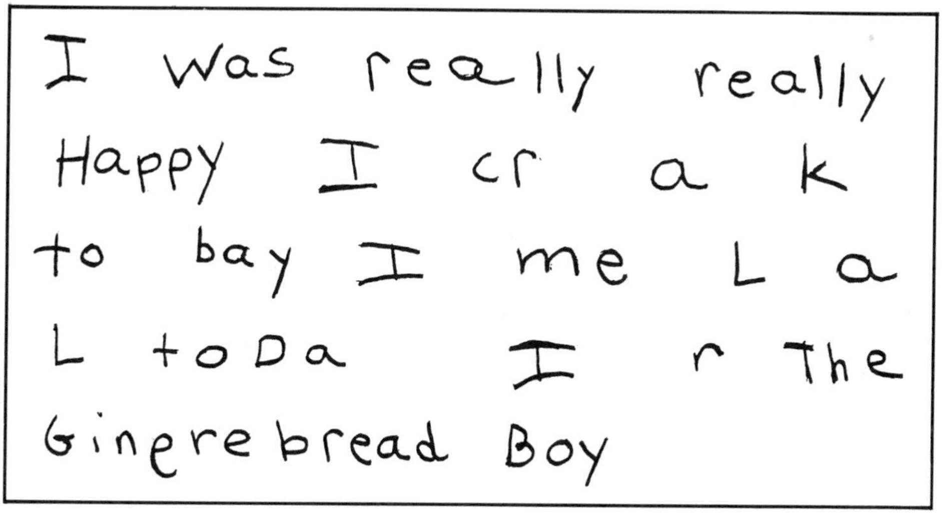
I was really really Happy I cr a k to bay I me L a L toDa I r The Ginerebread Boy

teacher continued to exchange communications, Joy began to display active interest in spelling. Soon, her writings began to represent many of the sounds in the words. Spontaneously, by practicing writing, Joy began to improve her spelling and reading.

Writing Requires Reading

Reading is needed during the process of writing. Stephens (1986) studied adults engaged in composing. She found that over half of the "writing" time was actually devoted to reading activities. For example, as soon as people completed writing a section of text, they often reread it. They also reread to see how to connect a previously written section to a section they were about to write. When people finished an entire text, they normally reread it both at that time and a few days later. The reading involved in writing was quite intensive, involving much self-evaluation.

THE WRITING PROCESS

Good writing requires many years of practice. The use of the writing process will enable your students to practice in a motivating manner. This process is described below.

Steps in the Writing Process

Effective writing actually involves several stages (Humes, 1983; Graves, 1983). Because of the sequential nature of writing, we often speak of "the writing process." Good writers do not simply sit down and produce a text. Rather, a writer composing a text goes through several steps.

1. *Prewriting.* The author gathers ideas and refines them *before* formal writing begins. The author may jot a few notes in a margin to record the idea. During this time, the author also identifies an audience.
2. *Drafting.* The author records thoughts on paper. This is the stage which many people erroneously identify as all of "writing."
3. *Revising.* The author refines the written work. Sometimes authors use input from other people to make revisions. Changes are usually made in the content and expression of text. However, a last step is editing, checking for grammatical, punctuation, and spelling errors.
4. *Publication/sharing.* Some favorite texts or productions may be shared with others. Many times a student will simply show a piece to the teacher once it is completed. However, in some cases, the student may choose to illustrate and perhaps bind a story for public display.

Adults who write fluently use this process unconsciously. If you think about a recent report or essay you wrote, you probably used these steps. The writing process can be facilitated by using a computer for wordprocessing (see Chapter 14).

The Importance of the Writing Process
for Instruction

The realization that writing is a process has several important instructional implications for teachers.

1. *The writing process frees students from overconcentration on the mechanics of writing.* All writers, children and adults, make grammatical and spelling errors on first drafts. These mistakes should certainly be corrected if a formal product is to be produced. However, they need not be corrected immediately. Rather, students should be able to go through the drafting and much of the revising stage simply focusing on the content and expressiveness of the writing. Then, after this is set, students should "clean up" their work through editing.

Doing editing as a last step enables students to do it more thoroughly. In addition, it avoids the inevitable demoralization that results when teachers *constantly* focus on spelling and other mechanical errors. In fact, when writing is used only for private expression, the teacher might choose to encourage free composing by simply ignoring errors in mechanics. Some remedial students react very negatively to "teacher improvements" and the work of these students should be left alone until they are experienced enough in writing to accept criticism.

2. *The writing process helps students to revise their work.* Too often, inept writers imagine that writing is done when they complete their first draft. They interpret requests for revision as criticism. However, the author who does not learn to revise will never produce a polished product. To encourage revision, teachers can bring in some of their own first drafts, complete with the "red marks" and edits that we all use. Or, teachers can bring in their first drafts and ask children to help them revise. As students become more sophisticated, they may be able to form small groups for reviewing each other's work.

Teacher-made checklists can help pupils revise and edit their work. A sample checklist is given below.

CHECKING MY WORK

1. Does my story have a beginning and an end?
2. Did I read my story over to myself to check if it makes sense?
3. Are any sentences too long?
4. Does my story have enough paragraphs?
5. Do all the sentences begin with a capital letter?
6. Do all the names begin with a capital letter?
7. Do all the sentences end with a period, a question mark, or an exclamation point?
8. Does my spelling look right?
9. Did I indent all my paragraphs?

3. *The writing process underscores the importance of prewriting.* Most writing work is done before drafting. The good writer needs to explore and develop ideas.

How do ideas come to the writer? Reading can bring many inspirations (a process which, at the same time, provides a purpose for reading). The Fairfax County, Virginia Public Schools have developed a reading-writing program in which writing activities are often stimulated by reading. They suggest that ideas for writing may be taken from (1) children's experiences; (2) diaries and journals; (3) stories from readers, trade books, and magazines; (4) art work; (5) the content areas (music, social studies, health, math); (6) dramatization and role playing; (7) films, filmstrips, television, records. The Fairfax County program also identifies several prewriting activities, including discussion, brainstorming (thinking of everything one knows), semantic mapping or webbing (see Chapter 9), classifying ideas, sequencing, using story structure (see Chapter 10), and using data retrieval charts, which summarize knowledge on a topic (*Elementary Writing Guide*, 1983).

Like reading, writing is learned through practice. The more students write, the more proficient they become. It is important to encourage all forms of writing—lists, notes, journal, stories, reports. As you encourage writing, remember not to be too critical of students' products. If students perceive that they have produced an unacceptable piece, they will often refuse to continue to write.

Judicious use of the steps in the writing process will help students to maintain motivation as they learn to improve their writing in a gradual way. As teachers explore writing with children, they should be aware that there are many different types of compositions. Just as we distinguished the reading of narrative texts from the reading of expository texts (in Chapters 10 and 11), children should also be taught to write both types of text (Boss, 1988).

WRITING AND COMPOSING PROGRAMS AND ACTIVITIES

In this section, we discuss different writing and composing programs for students with reading difficulties. These include journals, written conversations and correspondence, the LEARN composing program, and themed writing in secondary school.

Journals

A journal can be used to express one's most private thoughts and feelings. It is a notebook or binder in which each student writes privately. The teacher is allowed to read these journals only with the student's permission (they are not to be shared with other students or parents), and the teacher may choose to respond to the student's thoughts by keeping a "dialogue journal."

To prepare a journal, each student must have a private notebook or binder. Students need to do a minimum of writing, for example, two lines once a week. However, the more often students write in a journal, the more personal and expressive they become. The journal presents an unparalleled opportunity for expressing doubts and discomforts, as well as personal triumphs.

Some severely disabled readers, or young children, need to *dictate* their journal to a teacher. One first grade teacher kept a "Secrets Book" in which each child dictated thoughts to the teacher. As students progressed, the children were gently moved from dictation to direct writing.

Since journals are private places, they should not be subject to the revision and sharing stages of the writing process. Do *not* correct spelling and other mechanical errors. If you cannot read a journal, simply ask the student to read it to you. Teachers can, however, model correct spelling and mechanics in their responses. The following delightful sequence was recorded in the dialogue journal of a remedial second grader:

> Child's Writing: I had fun. I went to the zoo. I had too cupcakes.
> Teacher's Response: *Two* cupcakes, wow!

Written Conversations and Correspondence

In written conversations, a technique developed by Carolyn Burke (S. Anderson, 1984), two students, or a student and a teacher, sit beside each other and communicate using the same piece of paper. They are allowed to communicate *only* in writing, and cannot speak. If one person records something unclearly, the partner must ask for clarification in writing. Written conversations stress the role of *communication* in writing. When students do this activity once or twice a week, perhaps for fifteen minutes at a time, they learn to record their thoughts in written form.

A variation of written conversations that has proven particularly effective for remedial students is "conversations from afar" (Richek, 1983–1989). In this method, students are randomly assigned a partner, with whom they communicate for a long period of time. Class time is set aside, perhaps twice a week, where students write "notes" to their partners. They communicate back and forth, continuously filling several sheets of paper. The teacher (or other helper) acts as the "mail carrier," delivering the communications. We find that remedial readers respond well to forming a writing relationship with a peer, and they often use this opportunity to express their innermost thoughts. Students can communicate with others in the same classroom or resource room. Alternately, students can be assigned a partner from another class, or one who comes to the resource room at another time.

To further encourage correspondence, many schools have class mailboxes where pupils receive letters from their classmates and students in other rooms.

The LEARN Composing Program

LEARN is a composing program that fosters the reading-writing connection and has improved performance in reading. In the LEARN program (Rauscher-Davoust 1986, 1987) students compose, dictate, and edit group stories in both narrative and expository modes. LEARN originated in DuPage County, Illinois District 45. Implemented with small groups (five to twelve students) in grades 2 through 6 as an after-school program, students, on average, gained two months in achievement for each of the four months they were enrolled in the program. The program focused on students who functioned inconsistently in their classrooms. Often, such children were in a "low average" reading group. Instruction was given for fifty minutes, three times per week.

Instruction was organized into units. Each unit, whether narrative or expository, took one to two weeks to complete. When focusing on composing *narrative* stories, the teacher presented an exciting stimulus, such as a picture or story. *The Mysteries of Harris Burdick* (by C. Van Allsburg) was often used. This book contains stimulating pictures, each with a provocative caption. Students reacted to the pictures in the book. Then, to prepare for writing, they considered the characters, setting, problem, and solution to the story (see Chapter 10). Finally, they reached a consensus and dictated the story, which the teacher wrote on the board or on an overhead projector. The next day, students reviewed and revised their class story with the teacher's help, checking for a beginning, middle, and end. The story was then used for many follow-up activities. These included completing cloze activities (see Chapters 5 and 8), composing questions, making a word bank, focusing on skills being currently taught in the basal reader, composing related poetry, and illustrating. Completed stories were displayed in the school halls or printed in the weekly district newsletter.

When focusing on an *expository* unit, the teacher first selected a subject, often using something that children had recently studied in a content area. Then, children gave all of the words that they could think of about that topic. For example, in response to "weather," third and fourth grade children generated *storm, spring, tornado, breeze, snow,* and many other words. The words were next classified into topics by the use of a semantic map (see Chapter 9). That is, similar words were grouped together (say *winter, fall, spring, summer*) and assigned a topic (say *seasons*). When a complete semantic map had been produced, it served as an outline for an expository composition. Each topic was a main idea, and the words within this topic then served as details with which to compose individual sentences. Each topic was written out as a paragraph, and the final composition contained several paragraphs (see Figure 12.2). Using this framework, the children dictated a story and the teacher wrote it on the board or an overhead projector. The next day was reserved for joint revision. Then follow-up activities were done, as described in the section on narrative text.

In the LEARN program, students collaborated with a teacher to compose text. All steps of the writing process were done, including prewriting, revision, and sharing. However, the drafting process became a composing process, in which students dictated text. As students became more proficient with composing, they were better able to draft their own stories. As a result of the LEARN program, children gained competence and confidence in coping with their classroom situations.

Themed Writing in a Secondary School

Writing can help severely disabled students to create new-found enthusiasm for reading. The students in one self-contained high-school learning disabilities room discovered the power to create through writing and developed reading skills that they

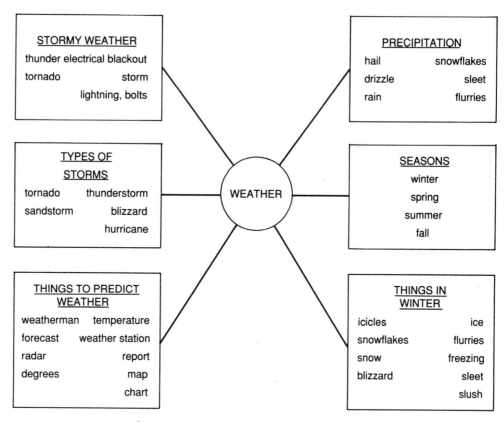

Stormy weather can be very frightening. Thunder can make a loud noise and scare people. Lightning might strike a tree and it could fall on a house. Lightning could cause electrical blackouts and the dark could be creepy. Storms can be frightening to people all around the world.

Figure 12.2   Expository Semantic Map and First Paragraph of Story of LEARN Program.
(from Rauscher-Davoust, 1986, p. 26, 28).

had unsuccessfully tried to build for years. The ten teenage boys decided to create disaster stories. They wrote stories entitled *The Roach*, *The Big Flood*, *The Crash*, *The Day the World Ended*, and *The Tidal Wave*. Then the boys edited them as a group to make them even more frightening. Final copies, some several pages long, were typed and duplicated. The typed copies were then used as scripts for tape-recorded stories, which were made complete with sound effects and musical backgrounds (Beethoven's Ninth Symphony was used). After composing and editing these stories for several months, the boys improved their reading skills considerably. A portion of one story follows.

The Tidal Wave

Tom saw a tidal wave in his mind. He saw it about four or five times a week. He didn't tell anyone. The last time he saw the tidal wave he also saw the date that the tidal wave would happen. He told his Mother and Father and they sent him up to his room. The next day he told everyone about his vision. They all just laughed. He went back home and took his family away.

About three hours later, strange things began to happen. Things started to blow. On the news they said that the rain was coming from unknown sources. The wind will be going about one-hundred-seventy-five miles an hour. The tidal wave will hit in about one hour. The news told everyone to leave the area.

So it hit. The wind started to blow harder and harder. . . .

TEACHING SPELLING

Called "the invention of the devil," spelling is not an easy task, even for those who are *not* remedial readers. Spelling a word is a more difficult task than reading it. In reading, several clues aid the reader in recognizing a word in print: context, phonics, structural analysis, and configuration. In spelling, however, there is no opportunity to draw upon peripheral clues in reproducing a word. Only one pattern or arrangement of letters can be accepted as correct; there is no compromise or leeway. Many students who are poor in the ability to reproduce words in spelling are skilled in the ability to recognize them in reading. However, the student who is poor in decoding words in reading is almost always poor in spelling as well.

To make spelling even more difficult, in the English language there is not always a dependable correspondence between the spoken sounds and written form of the English. To illustrate the inconsistencies in spelling, George Bernard Shaw, an advocate of spelling reform, is credited with the suggestion that, using the spelling rules in English, the word "fish" be spelled *ghoti*; *gh* as in "cough"; *o* as in "women"; *ti* as in "nation." One teacher found that pupils' spelling of the word "awful" varied greatly, including: *offul, awful, offel,* and *offle.* Each is an accurate phonetic transcription of the sounds of the word.

Reading and Spelling

Reading and spelling are closely related. Despite the irregularities in English spelling, learning letter-sound associations in reading facilitates learning to spell. In the course of learning to read, children see words repeatedly. Through reading practice they come to know that words are sequences of letters bearing some relationship to sounds. As they gain proficiency in reading words, students learn to abstract such regularities and use that knowledge in reading new words and in spelling (Wong, 1986; Henderson, 1985).

Developmental Stages of Learning to Spell

There appears to be a developmental sequence in learning to spell. An analysis of spelling errors suggests that children go through four stages (Henderson, 1985; Gerber, 1986).

1. *Prephonetic stage*, in which children's writing reveals that important sound features of the word are omitted, though the child might have rudimentary beginnings of an awareness of spelling. For example, SM for "swimming."
2. *Phonetic stage*, in which spelling attempts use some representation for sounds, but exhibit limited knowledge about conventions in English. For example, HIKT for "hiked" or PEKT for "peaked."
3. *Transitional stage*, in which the spelling attempts are readable, pronounceable, and recognizable to adults as approximates to conventional spelling, even though the spelling is not precise. For example, MONSTOR for "monster" or ELAVATER for "elevator."
4. *Correct spelling stage*, in which the word is spelled correctly.

Gerber (1986) suggests that all spellers go through these stages and that poor spellers have a delay in spelling skill acquisition rather than a deficit in cognitive functioning. It is also important to analyze a student's spelling attempts to determine the student's stage of spelling development. In discussing reading miscues, we noted that these provide an opportunity to analyze how the student is processing the reading. Similarly, in spelling, rather than merely deciding if the student spelled the word correctly or incorrectly, it is important to look at qualitative changes in the student's errors. Even though the word is spelled incorrectly, the student's attempt can indicate a progression to a higher level in the developmental spelling sequence.

Inventive Spelling

Invented spelling reflects a beginning writer's attempt to write words by attending to their sound units and associating letters with them in a systematic, though unconventional, way (Richgels, 1987). Examples of inventive spellings used by young children are *nabor* (neighbor), *ez* (easy), *trke* (turkey), and *10001LND* (thousand island). A substantial body of research shows that children who are allowed to invent their own spelling at an early age become either better spellers or as good as those who are not given this instruction (Ehri and Wilce, 1985). More important, children who are encouraged to use inventive spelling are much more willing to write. Children who are allowed to compose freely, using their own spellings, become fluent writers. They learn to take risks in a failure-free environment and come to understand that writing is pleasurable and is communication in which thoughts are translated into symbols that mean something to other people. Chomsky's (1971) research supports the concepts, "Write first, read later."

When encouraging children to use inventive spelling, it is important to communicate with parents so they understand the purpose behind this procedure. It is important that parents understand the purposes and goals of inventive spelling.

Assessment of Spelling

Some tests of spelling are part of a comprehensive academic achievement battery. Other tests are individual spelling tests. Some commonly used spelling tests are:

> *Test of Written Spelling* (Pro-Ed)
> *Test of Written Language* (Pro-Ed)
> *Peabody Individual Achievement Test* (American Guidance Co.)
> *Wide Range Achievement Test-Revised* (Jastak)

Informal spelling tests are very useful. Teachers can give students ten words or so at each grade level. A short informal spelling test was developed by selecting ten words from a frequency-of-use word list (Durrell, 1956), as shown in Table 12.1. The student is asked to spell (on paper) words from the lists. The student's spelling level can be estimated as that at which two words are missed (Lerner, 1989).

Spelling demands many abilities. Students with spelling difficulties may be unable to read the words they are trying to spell; they may have difficulty using the needed phonics and structural analysis to spell the word correctly; they may be unable to apply appropriate phonic generalizations; they may be unable to visualize the appearance of the word; or they may not have the motor facility to write the word. A difficulty in spelling may reflect any or several of these problems.

Methods of Teaching Spelling

Several approaches to teaching spelling are described in this section: cognitive learning strategies, the multisensory approach, and the "test-study-test" and "study-test" methods.

Table 12.1   Informal Spelling Test

GRADE 1	GRADE 2	GRADE 3	GRADE 4	GRADE 5	GRADE 6	GRADE 7
all	be	after	because	bread	build	although
at	come	before	dinner	don't	hair	amount
for	give	brown	few	floor	music	business
his	house	dog	light	beautiful	eight	excuse
it	long	never	place	money	brought	receive
not	must	find	sent	minute	except	measure
see	ran	gray	table	ready	suit	telephone
up	some	hope	town	snow	whose	station
me	want	live	only	through	yesterday	possible
go	your	mother	farm	bright	instead	straight

Using Cognitive Learning Strategies. Wong (1986) argues that effective spelling instruction contains two components: (1) domain-specific knowledge (knowledge of phonics and the linguistic structure of words), and (2) strategies (knowing how to think about spelling). For *domain-specific knowledge* teach students specific word knowledge, such as letter-sound associations and spelling patterns, phonics, structural analysis, word parts, and similar word skills required for word recognition (Chapter 8 addresses this area of knowledge). For *strategies* teach students to use cognitive learning strategies during spelling, such as self-questioning strategies and monitoring strategies. To encourage the self-questioning strategy, Wong (1986, p. 172) taught children to ask themselves the following seven prompts, listing them on a prompt card:

1. Do I know this word?
2. How many syllables do I hear in this word? (Write down the number.)
3. I'll spell out the word.
4. Do I have the right number of syllables down?
5. If yes, is there any part of the word I'm not sure of the spelling? I'll underline that part and try spelling the word again.
6. Now, does it look right to me? If it does, I'll leave it alone. If it still doesn't look right, I'll underline the part I'm not sure of the spelling and try again. (If the word I spelled does not have the right number of syllables, let me hear the word in my head again, and find the missing syllable. Then I'll go back to steps 5 and 6.)
7. When I finish spelling I tell myself I'm a good worker. I've tried hard at spelling.

Multisensory Approaches in Spelling. Multisensory approaches are useful for teaching spelling. When students are asked to study spelling words, they are frequently at a loss as to what to do. The multisensory approach utilizes the visual, auditory, kinesthetic, and tactile senses (Lerner, 1989; Fernald, 1943, 1988).

1. *Meaning and pronunciation.* First, have students look at the word, pronounce it correctly, and use it in a sentence.
2. *Imagery.* Ask students to "see" the word and say the word. Have them say each syllable of the word, say the word syllable by syllable, spell the word orally, and then trace the word in the air or trace over the word itself with a finger.
3. *Recall.* Ask students to look at the word and then close their eyes and see the word in their "mind's eye." Have them spell the word orally. Ask them to open their eyes to see if they were correct. (If they make an error, they should repeat the process.)
4. *Writing the word.* Ask students to write the word from memory, check the spelling against the original, and then check the writing to make sure every letter is legible.
5. *Mastery.* Ask students to cover the word and write it. If they are incorrect, they should cover and write it two more times.

"Test-Study-Test" Method and the "Study-Test" Method. In teaching spelling, there are two common study approaches, the "test-study-test" and the "study-test" procedures. The "test-study-test" method uses a pretest, which is usually given at the beginning of the week. The student then studies only those words that were

missed on the pretest. This method is well suited to older students who have fairly good spelling abilities, since there is no need to study words they already know. The "study-test" method, which omits a pretest, is better suited to young pupils and those with poor spelling abilities. Since too many words would be missed on a pretest, this method permits the study of a few well-selected words that the teacher feels need particular concentration.

DEVELOPING HANDWRITING

Handwriting is the most concrete of the communication skills. It can be directly observed, evaluated, and preserved. Some remedial students have severe difficulties with handwriting. These difficulties may reflect the underlying presence of many other deficits. For example, students with poor handwriting may have difficulty with the motor movements required to write. They may be unable to transfer visual information to fine motor movement, or they may be poor in other visual-motor functions and in activities requiring motor and spatial judgments (Lerner, 1989).

Left-handed students often encounter special problems since their natural tendency is to write from right to left on the page. In writing from left to right, left-handers have difficulty seeing what they have written because the hand covers it up, and there is a tendency to smudge the writing as the left hand moves. To avoid the smudging, some left-handed students begin "hooking" the hand in writing when they start using ball-point pens. They need careful instruction.

Manuscript and Cursive Writing

Usually children use manuscript writing (sometimes called printing) in the primary grades, and they shift to cursive writing (sometimes called script) at about third grade. Often remedial students find it difficult to make this shift. They need additional time, instruction, and practice to change to cursive writing. Manuscript writing is easier to learn since it consists only of circles and straight lines, and the manuscript letter form is closer to the printed letter used in reading. Some educators feel it is not important to transfer to cursive writing since the manuscript style is legal for official signatures, legible, and can be just as rapid.

Methods of Teaching Writing

For students who are very poor in handwriting, the microcomputer has been a real boon. These students should be strongly encouraged to learn typing skills and to use a word processing program (See Chapter 14).

It is often beneficial to practice handwriting on a chalkboard before using paper. Have children make large circles, lines, geometric shapes, letters, and numbers with large free movements using the muscles of the shoulders, arms, hands, and fingers.

Some children need to practice tracing print. Make heavy black letters on white paper and clip a sheet of onionskin paper over the letters. Have the student trace the forms and letters using a crayon or felt-tip pen. Start with diagonal lines and circles, then use horizontal and vertical lines, geometric shapes, and finally letters and numbers. Another idea is to put letters on transparencies and project the image with an overhead projector onto a chalkboard or a large sheet of paper. The student can then trace over the image.

Some students are helped in the motor act of writing by hearing directions. For example, say "down-up-and-around" as children form letters.

SUMMARY

Writing and reading are intimately connected, and acquiring skill in one increases skill in the other. Four connections between reading and writing are (1) writing and reading require similar processes; (2) writing demands active involvement in literacy; (3) writing fosters phonological awareness; and (4) writing requires reading.

The writing process includes the steps of (1) prewriting; (2) drafting; (3) revising; and (4) publication/sharing. Good writing requires years of practice.

Programs to help remedial readers write include journals, written conversations and correspondence, the LEARN composing program, and themed writing.

Learning to spell a word is more difficult than learning to read it. Young students go through four stages of spelling: prephonetic, phonetic, transitional, and correct spelling. Allowing students to use their own, inventive spelling while writing helps to foster a love of writing and will not detract from subsequent spelling achievement.

In teaching spelling through cognitive learning strategies, two components are used: (1) domain-specific knowledge (knowledge of phonics and the linguistic structure of words) and (2) strategies for monitoring spelling. In multisensory approaches to teaching spelling, students use visual, auditory, kinesthetic, and tactile modes. In the "test-study-test" method, students restudy words they have missed; in "study-test" they study words and are then tested.

Handwriting, particularly cursive writing, is often difficult for remedial students. The computer can aid students with handwriting problems. Chalkboard activities, tracing, and verbal clues provide practice with handwriting.

TEACHING
THE SEVERELY
DISABLED READER

In this chapter, we consider individuals who have extreme difficulty with reading. The characteristics of severely disabled readers are examined in the first part of the chapter. Methods for teaching severely disabled readers are presented in the second part.

INTRODUCTION

Most students who are referred for special reading instruction respond well and make considerable gains in a short period of time. But for a small percentage, progress is extremely slow and problematic, even with well-taught lessons and sensitive teachers. Many of these individuals remain virtual nonreaders, in spite of repeated attempts at reading instruction. These "severely disabled readers" are the concern of this chapter.

CHARACTERISTICS OF SEVERELY DISABLED READERS

Professionals from several fields recognize a "core" of extreme reading disability, individuals who can only learn to read with extreme difficulty. In the field of neurology, Critchley (1970) refers to a core of cases where the origins of the learning defect are inborn and independent of any intellectual shortcomings,.

The condition of severe reading disabilities has been described in professional literature for over seventy years under various terms, including *word-blindness* (Hinshelwood, 1917), *primary reading disability* (Rabinovich, 1969), and *dyslexia* (Critchley, 1970). The most persistent term is "dyslexia," which is derived from the Greek root *dys* ("bad, difficult") and *lexia* ("read"). Although used in a variety of ways, all of the definitions of dyslexia focus on extremely poor reading ability (Lerner, 1989). As defined by Vellutino (1987, p. 34)

> Dyslexia is a generic term that has come to refer to an extraordinary difficulty experienced by otherwise normal children in learning to identify printed words, presumably as the result of constitutional deficiencies.

As discussed in Chapter 3, there is growing evidence that the condition of dyslexia is caused by a neurophysical dysfunction which interferes with the ability to learn to read (Cruickshank, 1986). Specialists in the medical professions (pediatricians, neurologists, and psychiatrists) often use dyslexia as a diagnostic classification.

Whatever term is used to refer to severely disabled readers, teachers of reading need to understand the learning characteristics of these students and to be familiar with the special methods that are used to teach them.

Variations in Characteristics

For many years, educational researchers have tried to ascertain the traits that characterize severely reading disabled students (who are frequently identified as learning disabled) have in common. However, attempts to document a single set of characteristics to describe these students have been unsuccessful. It appears that such students are characterized as much by their differences as by their similarities (Keogh, 1986). Individuals manifest problems in different ways. Moreover, symptoms change at various developmental stages. Young children with learning disabilities have different characteristics from adolescent or adult disabled learners. In trying to bring order to the diverse traits of severely disabled students, researchers are attempting to establish subgroups of learning disabilities through subtyping (McKinney, 1986; Lyon, 1983), and identifying common marker variables (Keogh et al., 1981).

The characteristics of severe reading disabilities encompass multiple problems, and each learner is unique. Although one set of characteristics is not descriptive of all severely disabled readers, the characteristics discussed in this section do describe many students with severe reading and learning problems.

Deficiencies in Auditory Processing

Auditory processing skills include a cluster of abilities in which information is received through the sense of hearing. Auditory processing skills identified as prerequisites for reading include: phonological awareness, auditory discrimination, rhyming, blending, and auditory memory. (These skills are described later in this chapter.)

Accumulating evidence shows that children who encounter severe difficulty learning to read lack phonological awareness. These children differ from children with normal reading skills in their ability to recognize that words spoken orally can be divided (or segmented) into smaller units or sounds, a skill that is essential for acquiring reading skills (see Chapter 8). In other words, these children cannot represent and access the sounds of a word in order to help remember the word (Stanovich, 1985, 1986a,b; Liberman and Shankweiler, 1985; Vellutino, 1987; Bradley and Bryant, 1985; Williams, 1984).

One way to test a child's phonological awareness is to ask the child to count or tap out the number of sounds in a word. For example, the word *pack* has three sounds. Such tasks assess the child's ability to segment words into phonemes. A series of studies conducted by Liberman and her colleagues over a number of years suggests that the ability of kindergarten children to segment words into phonemes is the single most powerful predictor of future reading and spelling skills. Children who were destined to have severe reading disabilities could not perform this task, and they were also less proficient than peers in counting the number of syllables in a word (Liberman and Shankweiler, 1985; Liberman, 1984; Liberman et al., 1983).

Another series of longitudinal studies on phonological processing and reading failure, conducted by Bradley and Bryant (1985), showed that the inability to recognize rhyming words was a powerful predictor of reading failure. Students who became disabled readers did poorly, as young children, on rhyming tasks.

In a summary of studies on phonological and auditory processing, Vellutino (1987) concluded that deficiencies in sound segmentation are a major factor in reading difficulties. Further, severely disabled readers are much less proficient than normal readers in learning to use letter sounds to decode nonsense words. Stanovich (1985) concluded that the locus of the problem for severely disabled readers is likely to be at the basic phonological awareness level.

Suggestions for teaching phonological awareness and auditory processing are presented later in this chapter and also in Chapter 8.

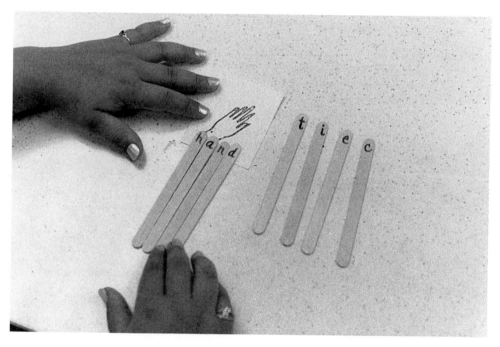

The use of the "phonematic hearing" program, described in Chapter 8, develops phonological awareness.

Deficiencies in Visual Processing

Visual skills for reading include various cluster abilities in which information is taken in through the eyes and interpreted. Visual skills include visual discrimination, visual sequencing, and visual memory. These skills and activities are presented later in this chapter. Research of the last ten years suggests that the cause of a severe reading problem is more than a deficiency in visual perception. In recent reviews of the characteristics of severe reading problems, Stanovich (1985) and Vellutino (1987) conclude that deficiencies in visual processing account for only a small proportion of the variance in reading ability. Many of the problems that appear to be visual problems are linked to other dificiencies such as memory, attention problems, and auditory/linguistic deficiencies.

Further, research shows that the remediation of visual perception is most effective when linked directly to reading tasks. Training visual processing skills in isolation was not as effective as visual training that was directly linked to reading (Swanson, 1987).

Methods for improving visual processing in reading are presented later in this chapter. Word recognition strategies presented in Chapter 8 are also useful.

Memory Problems

There is considerable evidence showing that severely disabled readers perform poorly on a wide variety of memory tasks. Moreover, there appears to be a causal connection between short-term memory deficits and reading disorders (Stanovich, 1986a). Severely reading disabled students are slower than normal students in tasks requiring rapid naming of symbols and objects, such as letters, numbers, pictures, etc. (Denckla and Rudel, 1976).

Samuels (1987) notes three areas in which memory deficits impede the severely disabled reader: visual memory, phonological memory, and semantic memory. The reader needs *visual memory* to recognize word units. Poor readers spend too much time trying to recognize words because they have poor visual memories; consequently, they have little energy left to concentrate on comprehension of text. They need abundant practice in reading to build automaticity in word recognition. Several suggestions are given in Chapter 8.

Phonological memory refers to the memory for sounds. The reader must learn to remember both letter sounds and how to map sounds onto visual units. The print-to-sound decoding must be done quickly, accurately, and automatically. Poor readers have severe problems with this aspect of learning to read. *Semantic memory* pertains to memory for word meaning. Poor readers have difficulty accessing lexical word information; they cannot recall the meaning of words.

Samuels (1987) concludes that multiple memory problems require poor readers to spend much more effort in remembering than normal readers do. Their behaviors in these tasks do not become automatic, as they do for normal readers. A lack of automaticity means that poor readers spend so much effort and time trying to remember and recall, that they cannot concentrate on meaning and comprehension.

Inefficient Learning Strategies

There is a growing conviction that a primary characteristic of severely disabled readers is that they are inefficient learners. That is, they do not know how to go about the business of learning.

Studies of successful readers show that efficient learners know how to use and direct their own cognitive and thinking processes to facilitate learning and to deal with the abstract concepts needed for academic work. As they read, efficient learners ask themselves questions and organize their thoughts; they connect and integrate the new materials they are trying to learn with the experience and knowledge they already possess; they try to predict what is to come and to monitor the relevance of new information. In short, efficient readers have at their disposal a repertoire of cognitive strategies that work for them. Their behavior reflects an active interest in learning and solving problems (Schumaker, Deschler, and Ellis, 1986).

In contrast, learning disabled students lack such cognitive learning strategies. They do not know how to control and direct their thinking, how to gain more knowledge, or how to remember what they have learned. They approach learning in a dependent, passive manner, waiting for the teacher to do the work, a style that has been referred to as "learned helplessness."

Fortunately, research shows that cognitive learning strategies can be taught and that reading disabled students do improve after instruction in specific strategies for learning (Schumaker, Deschler, and Ellis, 1986). Some of the instructional strategies for teaching reading comprehension from this perspective are:

Self-Questioning. In this strategy (also referred to as verbal mediation), students quietly ask themselves questions about their learning tasks. Their internal language, or covert speech, helps them to organize material and behavior. Students ask themselves questions such as:

> What am I supposed to do? What is the problem?
> What is my plan? How can I go about doing it?
> Am I using my plan? How did I do?

Predicting and Monitoring. In *predicting*, students hypothesize about what they will learn in the lesson or what will come next in the story. In *monitoring*, they check on whether their hypotheses were correct and monitor whether what they have learned is reasonable and fits in with previous learnings (see Chapters 10 and 11.)

Self-Rehearsal. Students practice and review what they have learned. This self-initiated verbal rehearsal helps them remember. People easily forget when the brain trace fades away. Recitation and verbal review helps the student understand and remember material.

Cognitive Behavior Modification. This strategy requires self-instruction, self-monitoring, and self-evaluation. The steps are: (1) the teacher models the desired behavior while providing an explanation; (2) the student performs the task while the teacher describes it; (3) the student talks the task through out loud; (4) the student whispers the task to himself or herself; and (5) the student performs the task with nonverbal self-cues.

Attention-Deficit Hyperactivity Disorder (ADHD)

Students differ in their abilities to attend to a learning task. Some students lack "selective attention," the ability to attend to relevant stimuli while screening out irrelevant stimuli. If the pupil is not attending while the lesson is being taught, learning cannot occur, since information is never received. Selective attention is a critical problem for many students with reading disabilities.

Selective attention helps to limit the number of stimuli being processed at any one time. Students are bombarded constantly by many stimuli, both external and internal. While the teacher is trying to teach a word in reading, there are many distracting stimuli in the pupil's world. Among the distractions are sounds in the room, noises outside, movement about the room, the temperature, the lights, the pupil's digestive system, and thoughts in the pupil's mind. However, the student must concentrate only on the reading task. Without selective attention, the student is overwhelmed with other stimulation. Unable to receive the desired information, the student fails to learn reading skills.

Three attributes of attention have been identified by Keogh and Margolis (1976): (1) The "set," or coming to attention, (2) actually attending to the task, and (3) concentrating over a long period. The first attribute refers to the set for learning. This is a very important phase and the severely disabled reader may not know how to come to attention. The second attribute refers to the actual learning and solving of problems. The third attribute, maintaining attention, means that the student must concentrate for a long period of time. Severely disabled readers, however, may be distracted easily and lose their powers of concentration. The assessment of problems in attention may provide valuable clues to understanding a student's reading problem.

The medical profession is also very much aware of the relationship of attention deficits to learning problems. A recent recommendation of the medical profession was that the term *attention-deficit hyperactivity disorder* (ADHD) be used to identify such students (*Diagnostic and Statistical Manual of Mental Disorders*, 1987). The characteristics of ADHD are shown in Table 13.1.

In addition, *the Diagnostic and Statistical Manual III-R* (1987) notes that there is an attention deficit disorder without hyperactivity, referring to it as *Undifferentiated Attention-deficit Disorder*. It is defined as (p. 95):

> A residual category for disturbances in which the predominant feature is the persistence of developmentally inappropriate and marked inattention that is not a symptom of another disorder, such as Mental Retardation or Attention-deficit Hyperactivity Disorder, or a disorganized and chaotic environment.

INSTRUCTIONAL OPTIONS FOR SEVERE READING DISABILITIES

The following sections present instructional methods and techniques that have proven useful for severely disabled students. The methods are grouped into three sections; each presents an option for instruction.

1. *Building auditory and visual prerequisite skills.* These include activities to help prepare children for successful reading by building a foundation to overcome the deficiencies that are impeding the child's learning to read.
2. *Adaptations of standard reading methods.* Many of the reading methods that are used

Table 13.1   Diagnostic Criteria for Attention-deficit Hyperactivity Disorder (ADHD)

Note: Consider a criterion met only if the behavior is considerably more frequent than that of most people of the same mental age.

A. A disturbance of at least six months during which at least eight of the following are present:

1. often fidgets with hands or feet or squirms in seat (in adolescents, may be limited to subjective feelings of restlessness)
2. has difficulty remaining seated when required to do so
3. is easily distracted by extraneous stimuli
4. has difficulty awaiting turn in games or group situations
5. often blurts out answers to questions before they have been completed
6. has difficulty following through on instructions from others (not due to oppositional behavior or failure of comprehension), e.g., fails to finish chores
7. has difficulty sustaining attention in tasks or play activities
8. often shifts from one uncompleted activity to another
9. has difficulty playing quietly
10. often talks excessively
11. often interrupts or intrudes on others, e.g., butts into other children's games
12. often does not seem to listen to what is being said to him or her
13. often loses things necessary for tasks or activities at school or at home (e.g., toys, pencils, books, assignments)
14. often engages in physically dangerous activities without considering possible consequences (not for the purpose of thrill-seeking), e.g., runs into street without looking

Note: The above items are listed in descending order of discriminating power based on data from a national field trial of the DSM-III-R criteria for Disruptive Behavior Disorders.

B. Onset before the age of seven.
C. Does not meet the criteria for a Pervasive Developmental Disorder.

Criteria for severity of Attention-deficit-Hyperactivity Disorder:

Mild: Few, if any, symptoms in excess of those required to make the diagnosis and only minimal or no impairment in school and social functioning.

Moderate: Symptoms or functional impairment intermediate between "mild" and "severe."

Severe: Many symptoms in excess of those required to make the diagnosis and significant and pervasive impairment in functioning at home and school and with peers.

Source: American Psychiatric Association. *Diagnostic and Statistical Manual of Mental Disorders*, III-R. Washington, D.C.: APA, 1987, p. 52–53.

with normal readers are also useful with severely disabled readers, if appropriate adaptations are made in the way the methods are used.

3. *Special remedial methods for severely disabled readers.* These are special methods that are not usually used in the developmental reading classroom but are intended specifically for students with serious reading problems.

BUILDING AUDITORY AND VISUAL PREREQUISITE ABILITIES

This section details techniques for teaching prerequisite skills to remedial students.

Issues in Building Prerequisite Abilities

Building auditory and visual prerequisite skills can help to prepare severely disabled learners for reading. Teachers should, however, think carefully before deciding to provide instruction in these prerequisite skills. Some guidelines are given below.

1. Instruction in prerequisite abilities is more likely to be needed by severely disabled readers than by students with mild reading problems. Using the analogy of swimming instruction, why teach a student to jump into a pool if that student is already proficient in diving?
2. Not every severely disabled reader need be taught prerequisite skills. Such instruction is needed only if (a) there are specific deficits and (b) if it appears that these deficits are interfering with reading acquisition. Prerequisite skills are more often needed by young children than by older students.
3. Teachers should teach skills in relation to reading tasks. The closer the prerequisite instruction is to the actual reading situation, the more effective it will be. If the student cannot learn phonics because that student cannot blend component sounds, then the prerequisite skill of blending should be taught. Similarly, using reading-related materials, such as letters and words, to teach auditory and visual discrimination is more effective than using environmental sounds or geometric shapes (Barrett, 1967).
4. Teaching prerequisite abilities is not a substitute for the teaching of reading. These skills are prerequisites for learning to read, and training in these skills can help the severely disabled reader eventually to learn to read. However, teaching prerequisite abilities is not, by itself, a method for teaching reading.

With these cautions in mind, this instruction is an important and useful part of the remediation of some severely disabled readers. Tests of processing or prerequisite skills are given in Test Inventory 13.1. Some activities for processing skills are given below.

Visual Prerequisites

Visual skills include a cluster of abilities in which information about the world is taken in through the eyes and interpreted. These skills include visual discrimination, visual sequencing, visual memory, and recognizing letters of the alphabet.

Visual Discrimination. Visual discrimination is the ability to see likenesses and differences in visual stimuli. For example, can the student pick out two letters or words that look the same? Reading requires the reader to discriminate between visually similar letters and words (*on, no; dog, boy; b, d*). With practice and training, students can learn this skill. Visual discrimination can be taught using many types of objects such as geometric shapes. We recommend, however, that letters and words be used for visual discrimination exercises since these are most closely related to reading. Pupils who have problems acquiring reading skills because they confuse letters and words can be helped with the following exercises:

1. The student matches words that are the same in a row. For example,
   today: dobay tobay today todab
2. The student is given a sheet of paper containing many words and is asked to circle all the examples of one word.
3. The student lists all the words that begin or end with a given letter. A clear example of the letter should be in front of the student.

Visual Sequencing. Visual sequencing involves the ability to perceive objects and letters in an appropriate order. Words in the English language owe their unique identity to the order of their letters. Thus "on" is one word, and "no" is another. Therefore, sensitivity to sequence is important for reading. The following exercises can be used to help the student develop visual sequencing abilities:

1. Students can arrange alphabet letters to match model words.
2. Students can look for words that contain a certain sequence of letters, such as "igh."
3. One visual sequencing problem common to many remedial readers is reversals of letters. For example, the student reads "was" for "saw." Methods of overcoming reversals are discussed in Chapter 9.

Visual Memory. This refers to the ability to remember stimuli (letters and words) that are presented visually. Many students, particularly those who have trouble learning sight words, appear to have problems in this area. However, research does not provide evidence that visual memory itself can be substantially improved (Samuels, 1987). What students can learn, with training, is how to combine several types of clues to enhance their memory for words. Therefore, activities in this area should be related closely to reading tasks, utilizing words and letters.

1. The teacher holds up a word for five seconds and then puts it down. The student then tries to identify it from choices printed on a card.
2. The teacher holds up a word for five or ten seconds and then puts it face down. The student tries to write it from memory. Several exposures may be given. This "overlearning" method is also useful for learning troublesome sight words.

Recognizing Alphabet Letters. The ability to name letters has been found to be an excellent predictor of reading achievement (Richek, 1977–1978). Despite this finding, it should be noted that (1) letter-naming ability is not an essential prerequisite skill for learning to read and (2) that training students to name letters does not automatically increase reading abilities (Samuels, 1972; Venezky, 1975). Nevertheless, students often feel more comfortable if they can identify letters, which are the building blocks of reading. Automaticity in letter naming appears to be important in the early stages of reading (Walsh, Price, and Gillingham, 1988).

Several cautions should be observed when teaching letter names. First, instruction in alphabet recognition should be done with the letters out of order. It should not be assumed that students who can recite the alphabet in order (i.e., "a, b, c, d, e, . . . ") can recognize letters when they are out of order. Second, many remedial readers need practice in matching uppercase letters to lowercase letters. Other remedial students recognize uppercase letters but are unsure of lowercase letters, which are visually more confusing. The following activities are suggested for helping students to recognize and match letters:

1. Have students look for and collect letters from magazines, putting all the "a's" on one page, all the "b's" on another page, and so on.
2. Give students a page filled with letters and ask them to find all the examples they can in one minute.
3. Use poems and children's books, based on the alphabet. These books and poems appeal to many age ranges and interests.

Many commercial programs contain activities for training visual prerequisite skills. In most of these programs, however, visual skills training is combined with motor skills training. Among the activities found in these programs are cutting, coloring, and tracing (See Appendix A).

Auditory Prerequisites

Auditory skills include a cluster of abilities in which information taken is perceived through the sense of hearing. Many auditory processing skills have been identified as prerequisites for reading (Samuels, 1988). Skills related to auditory perception include auditory discrimination, rhyming, blending, auditory memory, sound segmentation, and knowledge of letter sounds.

Auditory Discrimination.   Auditory discrimination refers to the ability to hear differences in sounds. In relation to reading, auditory discrimination is the ability to distinguish differences in phonic elements or phonemes. Can the student tell if two spoken words are the same or different? Teachers should make sure that what appears to be an auditory discrimination problem does not stem from another cause. Some problems appear to be auditory discrimination problems but are actually due to a loss of hearing acuity or to differences of the student's language from standard

English (Knafle and Geissal, 1977). Such students need other therapies. Some exercises for those students who do need to improve auditory discrimination are given below:

1. Say a list of words and ask the students to raise their hands whenever a word beginning or ending with a certain sound is said. It is helpful for the teacher to stand behind the student so that visual clues are avoided.
2. Show two or three pictures with verbal representations that are close in sound (e.g., ride, red, rod). Then say a word representing one of the pictures. The student selects the correct picture.

Rhyming. The ability to rhyme is essential to learning to read with many phonics approaches. Phonics instruction often requires that the student recognize words that are a part of a rhyming "word family." Teachers should realize that dialect-different and foreign-language-speaking students may have learned other rhyming systems. For example, both the French and Persian (Iranian) rhyming systems are different from that used in English.

It is sometimes difficult to accurately assess rhyming abilities. For example, the student may not be able to answer the question, "What word rhymes with 'at'?" Instead, the teacher might ask (especially with younger students), "What word does 'at' make you think of?" Or the teacher might start a sequence, such as: "at, bat, ... " If the teacher is flexible in the assessment of rhyming, students often demonstrate unexpected rhyming abilities.

Rhyming can be taught using a variety of interesting and motivating activities. Some suggestions for teaching follow.

1. Say two words and ask the student if they rhyme.
2. Have students complete rhyming couplets, such as
   It is a nice day
   I would like to. . . .
   At first provide two or three choices, only one of which rhymes. Then ask students to think of a rhyming word. Some students get so involved in this exercise that they begin to create their own rhyming couplets!
3. Songs and poems can be used to teach rhyming. The *Mother Goose* rhymes are a particularly good source. Pupils can fill in missing rhyming words or memorize these lovely poems.

Blending. Blending refers to the ability to combine isolated letter sounds into words. This ability is very important if a student is to learn to read through a phonics method, where letter sounds are blended together to form words. Some students can produce individual letter sounds but can get no farther than helplessly repeating these isolated sounds, such as "p"-"e"-"t." To use phonics effectively, students must be able to form words from isolated sounds. It should be noted that blending is a somewhat artificial skill, since sounds produced in isolation are different from sounds in words.

Teachers can use a sequence of activities (from easy to hard) to help children learn this vital skill. A suggested sequence for teaching blending skills follows. Not all students will need to start at the very first stage.

1. Pronounce a two-syllable word with the syllables disconnected. Ask, "What word is this?" (for example, "bas-ket").
2. Next, select a one-syllable word with three sounds (e.g., "rat"). Say the word with the last sound separated: "ra-t." The student is asked to blend the sounds and identify the word.
3. Then say the word with the first sound separated from the middle and ending sounds: "r-at." The student blends the sounds and says the word.
4. Finally, the word is divided into three distinct sounds: "r-a-t." The student blends the sounds and says the word.

Words with four and five sounds may then be presented for the student to blend and identify. Words need not exceed five sounds.

Auditory Memory. Human beings use their auditory channel to remember most types of information. For example, to remember phone numbers, people "rehearse" them orally. Auditory memory is important in learning phonics. When students are using a decoding process, they must store separate sounds in their memory long enough to blend them together into words. There is also evidence that auditory memory plays a part in learning sight words (Richek, 1977–1978). To develop auditory memory while maximizing reading skill, exercises should concentrate upon words and sounds. Some suggestions follow:

1. Present sentences orally and have students repeat the sentences. The sentences should become longer as the students progress.
2. Present groups of syllables or unrelated words for repetition.
3. Have students memorize songs and poems.

Phonological Awareness. Phonological awareness refers to the ability to recognize that words spoken orally can be divided into smaller segments of sounds. As discussed earlier in this chapter and in Chapter 8, this ability greatly facilitates learning to read at beginning levels. It is particularly useful for students learning phonics (Liberman and Shankweiler, 1985). Phonological awareness appears to be a learned skill rather than a natural one. There are no natural acoustic divisions between the segments in spoken words. That is, the phonemes that comprise spoken sounds are not clearly isolated, nor do they maintain their constancy in different syllables or words. The acoustical properties of phonemes overlap in time rather than follow neatly after one another in the sound stream, and they also vary acoustically in different speech contexts (Liberman, 1984; Wallach and Wallach, 1982).

Because of these facts, students must often be specifically taught phonological awareness. Although exercises in auditory discrimination, blending, and letter sounds will reinforce this ability, direct instruction may also be needed. For one suggested method, see "sound counting" in Chapter 8. In addition, Wallach and Wallach (1982) found that the following two methods in segmentation dramatically increased the reading ability of remedial readers.

1. Separate the beginning phoneme of a word from the rest of the words by a pause. The teacher can say "*m—an*" and have students identify the first phoneme. Students can also pronounce these separated words.
2. Use a "stuttering" pronunciation such as *p-p-p-an*. The student first imitates the teacher and then proceeds alone.

Wallach and Wallach feel that the vowel sound attached to stopped consonants (*p, b*) when they are pronounced alone (e.g., *puh, buh*) does not hamper students' learning. Teachers can feel free to use the above strategies even though they must pronounce stopped consonants in isolation.

Teachers can also help young children become aware of the segmentation of speech sounds through the use of nursery rhymes, word play, and word games. Instruction should go from large to small units, first words, then syllables, finally sounds. Effective commercial programs for teaching segmentation include Auditory Discrimination in Depth (see Appendix A).

TEACHING READING TO SEVERELY DISABLED STUDENTS: ADAPTATIONS OF STANDARD READING METHODS

Often a technique designed for teaching reading in the developmental (or regular) classroom can be modified for use with severely disabled readers. When using standard methods, some cautions should be observed. A student may be confused if several approaches are used simultaneously. Therefore, avoid exposing the student to one method in the classroom, another method in a special class, and yet a third in instruction after school. Severely disabled readers need to have a consistent method for acquiring reading skills. Thus, the teacher should select a method which is consistent with both the student's aptitudes for learning and classroom demands. This method should be used consistently for a period of time.

It is also important to anticipate the slow pace with which severely disabled readers may acquire reading skills. This is particularly true for the beginning phases of instruction. One boy in our reading clinic spent ten weeks acquiring eight sight words. Although this seems very slow, even by remedial standards, the acquisition of these words was a remarkable achievement for him. They were the first words that he was able to learn and retain consistently. Because progress is often very slow, it is important to chart each step in the road toward reading acquisition and accentuate successes.

Standard reading methods can be readily adapted for use with severely disabled readers. This section describes useful adaptations in (1) the sight word approach, (2) the language experience approach, (3) the synthetic phonics approach, and (4) the analytic phonics or linguistic approach. Adaptations of standard methods are relatively easy to use; they require few specialized materials and allow much flexibility in teacher presentation. Since these methods often produce rapid reading gains, it is recommended that instruction for severely disabled readers begin with one of these methods. If, after a trial period, these approaches prove not to be effective, the teacher should consider using one of the special remedial methods described later in this chapter.

Selecting a Method

There are three ways to determine the best method for an individual student: (1) determining learning strengths; (2) determining learning preferences; and (3) considering other instructional programs.

See if the student exhibits distinct strengths in learning through either a whole-word approach or a phonics approach. A whole-word approach, such as sight words or language experience, initially favors visual skills. A phonics approach, such as synthetic or analytic phonics, initially favors auditory skills. The teacher might try matching the initial instruction method to the student's strengths. Eventually, of course, the student would need to learn both approaches.

If a method utilizing a stronger learning area is chosen, the student may also be given activities to build the weaker one.

A diagnostic word learning task can be given to determine the student's comparative abilities in learning through (1) a sight word or language experience method and (2) a phonics method. The student is given the task of learning two sets of words: six words are presented as sight words and six words are presented as phonics words. By comparing performance on these two tasks, the teacher can make a judgment about the student's learning strengths. Detailed directions for a word learning task are presented in Table 13.2.

Another important factor in choosing a reading method is the student's personal preferences for learning. Some students prefer to "sound out" words, while others simply have an aversion to this activity. Sometimes disabled readers associate certain activities with "unpleasant," previous programs, and so they want to avoid that particular approach.

A third factor to consider in choosing a method for instruction is the student's other current instructional programs. The teacher should try to harmonize the remedial program with the student's existing classroom program or other reading programs. For example, if a student is using materials with a special alphabet (e.g., *Reading Mastery: DISTAR*) in the classroom, and books with a regular alphabet in the reading clinic, the student could well be confused, and learning would be impeded.

The Sight Word Method

The sight word method involves teaching students to recognize the visual form of words instantly, without further analysis. Although the teaching of sight

Table 13.2   Diagnostic Word Learning Task

1. *Sight word task:* Words are "house," "children," "boy," "farm," "wagon."
   a.   Print the words carefully on cards.
   b . Go through each word. Read it to the student, use it in a sentence, point out visual features of the word ("children" is long; "boy" is short, etc.).
   c.   Mix up cards. Present five trials of the word, with the words mixed after each trial.
      (1)   for the first three trials, pronounce incorrect words for the student and use them in a sentence.
      (2)   For the last two trials, do not correct incorrect responses.
   d.   Mark results of all trials on the form below.
2. *Phonics word task:* Words are "at," "bat," "cat," "rat," "fat."
   a.   Print the words carefully on cards.
   b.   Present the "at" card first; pronounce this word for the student. Present the other words by showing the "at" within the words and then blending the first letter ("at," "f-at," "fat"). Use each word in a sentence
   c.   Mix up cards. Present five trials of the word, with words mixed after each trial.
      (1)   For the first three trials, pronounce incorrect words by blending parts together.
      (2)   For the last two trials, do not correct incorrect responses.
   d.   Mark all results on the form below.
3. *Response form:* Mark correct or incorrect.

Sight Word Task
Trial

	1	2	3	4	5
house					
children					
boy					
farm					
wagon					

Phonics Task
Trial

	1	2	3	4	5
at					
bat					
cat					
rat					
fat					

Adapted from Barr, 1970.

words is explored fully in Chapter 8, special adaptations for very disabled readers are presented here.

The words to be taught should be selected very carefully. In general, long words are harder to·learn than short words, although an occasional long word serves to add interest. Concrete words are easier to learn than abstract words. For example, the student's name, parts of the body, the name of the school, and so on are far easier to learn than are function words such as "the," "when," or "to." The words selected for instruction should be also varied in configuration and number of letters to avoid visual confusion.

Words should be reviewed as often as possible so that they may be established firmly in memory. The teacher should be careful to use standard manuscript writing for all hand-made materials. Severely disabled readers tend to focus on very small differences and may be confused by a "d" with a tail attached.

The Language Experience Method

Severely disabled readers often find the language experience method, in which students read stories they have created by themselves, to be highly motivating. Generally, students dictate stories to the teacher, who writes them carefully in manuscript handwriting. Students then learn to read these stories and to recognize words from them. Disabled readers tend to feel a sense of ownership and excitement about having created stories. As detailed in Chapter 8, the language experience approach enables readers to become familiar with necessary concepts about reading, such as the concepts of word and sentence.

A disadvantage of using language experience stories with severely disabled readers is that experience stories are not controlled for reading difficulty. Since the stories come from oral language, the sight word load may soon outstrip the student's reading ability.

Phonics Methods

The term "phonics" refers to teaching methods that concentrate on printed letters and their sound equivalents (sound/symbol relationships). Although there are several phonics approaches, they can be classified into two groups: the synthetic phonics approach and the analytic (or linguistic) phonics approach. Special adaptations for using these two methods with very severely disabled readers are given in this chapter. Phonics methods for use with other remedial readers are described fully in Chapter 8.

The Synthetic Phonics Approach. In the synthetic method, the student learns to blend letter sounds, or groups of letter sounds, into a whole word. For example, to read the word *rat*, the sounds for the letters *r*, *a*, and *t* are pronounced individually and then blended together. The synthetic approach often requires that the student learn certain phonics rules. A phonics rule, for example, would guide the reader to pronounce "rat" and "rate" differently.

If the synthetic phonics approach is chosen for severely disabled readers, teachers should make sure that students possess appropriate readiness skills. Skill in auditory blending and knowledge of letter sounds are important prerequisites for this method. Because some severely disabled students confuse letter names with letter sounds, we suggest referring to letters by using their sounds.

The synthetic phonics method is often very difficult for the disabled reader when it is first presented. Many readiness skills are needed and many task demands are made. However, once basic phonics concepts are mastered, the student often gains rapidly in reading performance.

Betty is an example of a student who learned through the synthetic phonics approach. As an intelligent thirteen-year-old, with a long history of instructional failure, Betty was anxious to learn to read and was willing and able to memorize letter sounds and rules. Her teacher taught her the sounds of consonants and the long and short vowels. Although this was a tedious process consuming many months, Betty learned to sound out words rapidly once these initial steps had been mastered. In her second six months of instruction, Betty made over two years of progress and was able to read independently.

The Analytic (or Linguistic) Phonics Approach. In the analytic method, the student looks at whole words that contain regular phonics patterns. Words are never broken apart, but by presenting the words over and over again in patterns (or word families), such as "at," "bat," "cat" or "run," "sun," "fun," the student learns their sound regularities. Books using the linguistic approach are based upon patterns of word families, resulting in text such as

- Dan ran the fan.
- Can Dan fan Nan?
- The pet is wet.
- Is the pet wet?

The analytic phonics method often proves to be highly effective for teaching students who can recognize phonics correspondences but are not ready for a synthetic phonics approach. One important prerequisite skill for learning the analytic or linguistic phonics method is the skill of rhyming.

Ten-year-old Billy was a nonreader who was instructed by the analytic phonics approach for several months. His initial learning rate was about one word family per week. After four weeks of instruction, his rate of learning increased to about two word families per week. Billy's teacher controlled the word families carefully so that they would not be too similar. After each word family was learned, it was presented in a story. The words from the word family were at first color coded (with, for example, one family being yellow and another red). Billy's independent reading was done with books containing rhyming words such as Dr. Seuss's (T. Geisel) *Hop on Pop* and *Green Eggs and Ham*.

Many older severely disabled readers prefer the analytic approach, as it allows them considerable independence. One thirteen-year-old boy learning by this approach decided to create his own book of word families. Under each word family ("ight," "ag"), he entered all the words he could find.

TEACHING READING TO SEVERELY DISABLED STUDENTS: SPECIALIZED REMEDIAL METHODS

When adaptations of standard or classroom reading methods are not successful with the severely disabled reader, special remedial methods can be used. These specialized methods are not normally used in the regular classroom since they may require special training, individual instruction, and more time than a classroom teacher can afford.

We have classified the special remedial methods into two categories: (1) methods that use the kinesthetic approach (or sense of movement) and (2) methods that use phonics instruction. Materials for these methods are listed in Appendix A.

Kinesthetic Approaches

A variety of approaches, known as "kinesthetic" approaches, use the sense of movement to reinforce word learning. They include the VAK method, the VAKT method, and the Fernald method.

The VAK Method.   The VAK method combines visual and auditory association with writing. The student sees and says the word while writing it from memory. VAK uses the following procedure: The student (1) sees the word to be learned, (2) says the word, (3) tries to write it from memory, and (4) compares the results with the original word. This procedure is repeated until the word is reproduced correctly.

The VAKT Method.   The VAKT method utilizes visual, auditory, kinesthetic, and tactile senses to reinforce learning. It is reserved, generally, for the most severe cases of reading disability. The method emphasizes tracing and tactile stimulation to promote learning, and it is sometimes referred to as a "multisensory" approach. The student sees the word to be learned and listens to the teacher pronounce it. Then the word is traced as the student says it. For the tracing stage, words may be printed in crayon or another medium that raises the surface of the word from the paper. Finally, the student writes the word from memory.

There are many variations of the VAKT approach. Since some students learn best through physical movement, they require a more forceful kinesthetic and tactile stimulus than tracing and finger contact offer. For a stronger stimulus, students may trace over sandpaper letters or words or they may form the letters in sand or cornmeal poured into a tray to a depth of about one inch. Some students may benefit from tracing letters from different materials (raised letters of hardened starch, wire, pipe cleaners, or yarn), or from tracing letters in the air, or from tracing letters while blindfolded. These variations, however, are even more time consuming than the regular VAKT approaches and should be used only when needed.

The Fernald Method.   Grace M. Fernald and Helen B. Keller (Fernald, 1943, 1988) developed a method for use with severe reading disorders that combines the language-experience approach and the VAKT modes of learning. The approach is designed to be used on an individual basis. The Fernald method emphasizes the wholeness of words and does not require the student to learn separate phonic elements. Because progress may be very slow, the method generally is used only when other methods have failed. Fernald outlines some very specific procedures. There are four stages in the Fernald approach. Each stage is a complete way of learning words. Students start learning words by stage 1; after this has been mastered they move to stage 2; and so on. The four stages of the approach are:

1. Tracing and writing from memory individually presented words.
2. Writing from memory individually presented words.
3. Writing from memory words found in text.
4. Learning by sight words presented in text.

Stage 1. At the beginning of stage 1, the student selects a word that he or she would like to learn to read. Then the following procedure is undertaken.

1. The word is written on large cards or paper (in manuscript or cursive script) in chalk-board size using crayon. While writing, the teacher says the word.
2. Using one or two fingers, the student traces over the word while saying each part of the word as it is traced.
3. The tracing is repeated until the student feels that the word can be written (or printed) from memory.
4. The student tries to reproduce the word from memory without looking at the word. As the word is written, it is, again, pronounced in parts.
5. If the student cannot write the word correctly, the tracing procedure is repeated until the student is able to successfully write the word.
6. After the word is written correctly from memory, it is filed in an alphabetical word file box.

No errors are permitted during this procedure. If the student makes a mistake during the tracing process, or if the word is written incorrectly, the student is stopped and told to begin the process again. Any activities that break up word learning are discouraged.

After several words are learned, students begin to appreciate their powers to read and write words. At this time, students start to write their own stories. Words to be learned are now identified as additional words that the student needs to write these stories. Again, new words are filed in the word file bank.

Stage 2. When the teacher feels that students no longer have to trace words for learning, they are ready for stage 2. In this stage, words may continue to be taken from the student's stories. The method for word learning differs from stage 1 in two ways: (1) the words may be presented on smaller cards (say, index-sized cards) and (2) the tracing stage is eliminated. In stage 2, the word is printed (or written) on a file card. The student looks at it, says it (emphasizing its parts), and then attempts to write it while saying it without looking back at the original.

Stage 3. In this stage, students begin to read from actual texts, and the words to be learned are drawn from these texts. Index cards are no longer used for introducing words; rather, students learn words directly from text. Students are permitted to read whatever they desire to read. When new words are encountered, the student looks at the word on the printed page and tries to write it from memory. Words learned are again filed into the word bank.

Stage 4. In this stage, the student is able to read a word in text, say it, and remember it without the crutch of writing from memory. Students are encouraged to figure out unknown words by associating them with known words or by using context (or meaning) clues rather than by recognizing them by sight. Only words that the student cannot "figure out" are written down for further review. Identification of unknown words should precede reading. Fernald suggests that students survey material before they read it to locate unknown words and try to figure them out. If unknown words are subsequently encountered during reading, teachers are advised to supply them for students rather than to interrupt the meaning-gaining function of reading by letting students sound out words.

Phonics Approaches

Some special remedial reading techniques emphasize the learning of phonics and phonics generalizations. These include the Gillingham method, the *Reading Mastery: DISTAR*, the *Phonics Remedial Reading Lessons*, and the *Glass Analysis* method.

The Gillingham Method. The Gillingham method is a synthetic phonics approach employing a tracing technique for teaching single letters and their sound equivalents. The method is an outgrowth of the early work of Samuel T. Orton (1937), who studied the relationship of cerebral dominance to reading and language disorders. The Gillingham method requires specific instruction five times a week for a minimum of two years. Initial instruction may be divided into three parts: learning letter sounds, learning words, and using words in sentences (Gillingham and Stillman, 1970).

The Gillingham method emphasizes a multisensory approach. There are six sensory associations. These associations are particularly important at the initial stage, which is the teaching of letters. The six fundamental associations are:

- *V-A (Visual-Auditory).* Written words and letters are associated with their sounds. The student does not have to vocalize these sounds.
- *A-V (Auditory-Visual).* The sounds of letters and words are associated with the visual image. This is a spelling-like task.
- *A-K (Auditory-Kinesthetic).* The sounds of letters and words are associated with muscle action through speech and writing.
- *K-A (Kinesthetic-Auditory).* The student's hand is guided to trace or to write a letter form while associating it with the name or sound of the letter.
- *V-K (Visual-Kinesthetic).* Printed letters and words are associated with the muscular actions of speech and writing.
- *K-V (Kinesthetic-Visual).* The muscular act of speech or writing is associated with the visual appearance of the letters.

Learning letters and their sounds. This consists of three phases:

Phase I

1. A visual and auditory (V-A) association with the letter name is established. The teacher shows a card with a letter on it and says the letter name, which the student

repeats. In saying the letter, an A-K association is made. This step is the foundation for oral reading.

2. When mastery of the letter name has occurred, a visual and auditory association with the sound is developed. The teacher says the sound, while exposing the card, and the pupil repeats it. This also involves V-A and A-K associations.

Phase II

The student develops the ability to relate the sound to the letter name. The teacher, without showing the card, makes the letter sound, and the pupil tells the name of the letter. This is the basis for oral spelling.

Phase III

1. The letter is printed by the teacher and its construction is explained. The student then traces over the original, copies it, and, finally, writes the letter from memory while averting his or her eyes from the paper. This association is V-K and K-V.
2. The teacher says the sound and the pupil must write the letter that has that sound, thereby developing the A-K association.

Reading Words. Learning to read words starts by blending letter sounds and spelling the words. The initial words taught contain two vowels, "a" and "i," and eight consonants, "b," "g," "h," "j," "k," "m," "p," and "t." The blended words follow a consonant-vowel-consonant pattern (CVC), and blending occurs by pronouncing the first consonant and vowel together ("ra") and then adding the final consonant ("rat"). At first, the words are limited to the vowels and consonants given above. Such words, commercially distributed on colored cards, are known as the student's "jewel case." Sample jewel case words are "hat," "hip," "bib," "jab." After these words are mastered, words containing other letters are added.

Combining Words Learned Into Simple Sentences. After a basic set of words has been learned, the words are combined into sentences and stories, and the student learns to read these. Reading continues to be taught by a phonics method and combines spelling and dictation exercises.

The Gillingham method has been modified by Slingerland (1974), who has provided an extensive set of supplementary materials. Another set of materials based on the Gillingham approach has been developed by Traub and Bloom (1970). Their *Recipe for Reading* is accompanied by twenty-one supplementary readers.

Reading Mastery: DISTAR Program. This program is a highly structured decoding message that requires following a very specific step-by-step procedure. The emphasis is on programmed learning, drill, and repetition. It has proven to be successful for students with learning disabilities, mental retardation, and disadvantaged backgrounds (Guinet, 1971). In a review of research, Haring and Bateman (1977) found that DISTAR was successful with students who had experienced school failure previously. There are three types of DISTAR programs: one for language, one for arithmetic, and one for reading. Because we are concerned with remedial reading, only the reading program is discussed in this section.

In Reading Mastery: DISTAR, the teacher is given specific procedures and oral instructions to say throughout each step of the program. Pupil instruction is given in small groups for thirty-minute periods, five times per week. Skill mastery in the program is measured by criterion-referenced tests. If a student has not mastered skills, special additional lessons are provided.

The program is based largely upon a synthetic phonics approach, with students being taught specifically the prerequisite skill of auditory blending, which is needed to form isolated sounds into words. Another distinctive feature of the program is that, in beginning stages, the shape of some alphabet letters is modified so that they reflect letter sounds. Thus the letters "th" are written in a connected fashion so that it is apparent to the student that they represent one sound. Or a silent "e" at the end of a word is written smaller than the rest of the letters. (See Figure 13.1.) While this alphabet gives students clues to sounding out words, the teacher must be cautioned that exposure to both the DISTAR alphabet and the ordinary alphabet may be confusing. The special alphabet of DISTAR is gradually phased out as instruction in DISTAR continues.

The Reading Mastery: DISTAR program is a complete reading program, containing both isolated drills and instructional reading. It uses a behavioral management approach, building in small progressive steps and using specified praise as reinforcement. Criterion-referenced tests are used to monitor progress. The teacher is guided in specific procedures and oral instructions through each step of the program.

The SRA Corrective Reading Program, Decoding A, B, and C (Englemann et al., 1978), is based upon the DISTAR concepts but is geared toward the older student (grades four through twelve). This program develops primary and intermediate reading skills using materials of interest to older students. As with the DISTAR program, instruction is constructed and guided very carefully. Materials include a teacher's management and skill manual, presentation books, and assessment materials. Students use stories, student contracts, and progress charts. There is also an SRA *Corrective Reading Program* which concentrates on comprehension.

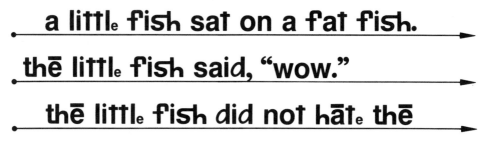

Figure 13.1 The DISTAR Reading Alphabet

Phonic Remedial Reading Lessons. These exercises are designed to give students drill and practice in recognizing phonic elements and in blending letter sounds. Each page of the workbook has lines of regularly-spelled words. Students practice by going across the page saying each word in a line. The method uses the principle of minimal change in component words; words such as "rat" and "ran" are presented side by side. Repetition and practice are also important. The method has proven successful with students who have failed to profit from conventional reading methods yet can be educated in phonics principles. The drills provide practice in isolated words, and they must be supplemented by reading contextual materials.

Glass Analysis. The Glass Analysis method approaches words through clusters of word elements ("pl"-"ay") rather than individual sounds. It emphasizes "perceptual conditioning" to develop the ability to identify visual clusterings of letters in known words. The Glass Analysis system is designed to teach "decoding" rather than "reading." Reading is considered to be a response to meaning, whereas decoding, which precedes reading, involves knowing the sounds of a word and should be taught apart from reading. According to Glass (1973), words are recognized first by viewing them as a whole and then by identifying structural sound elements and the letter clusters within them.

The Glass Analysis teaching procedure involves (1) presenting a whole word that is known to the student; (2) directing the student to note what clusters make specific sounds (e.g., for the word "track," the student notes which letters make the sound "tr" and which letters make the sound of "ack"); and (3) having the student look at letters and give the sounds that they make (e.g. the student is shown the whole word "track" and is asked to give the sounds of the letters "ack" and "tr"). It is recommended that the Glass Analysis procedure be followed for about two ten-minute periods per day, five times a week.

The Glass Analysis materials are written on three levels. In addition to exercises using isolated words, paperback books are available that contain these words used in sentence contexts. These books provide some contextual reading.

Teachers can easily make their own word cards to teach this method. If they wish, Glass Analysis materials can be purchased commercially.

SUMMARY

Severely disabled readers are students with extreme difficulties in learning to read. Only a small percentage of students with reading problems fall into this category. "Dyslexia" is a term that is often used to describe severely disabled readers. The term "dyslexia" implies that the condition is associated with a neurological anomaly.

There are many variations among individuals with severe reading disabilities. No one trait will be characteristic of all individuals with this condition.

Common characteristics of severe reading disabilities are deficiencies in auditory processing and phonological awareness. Phonological awareness refers to the ability to hear and segment the sounds in words.

Deficiencies in visual processing refers to the ability to take in information visually and interpret that information. Recent research suggests that auditory and phonological processing deficiencies are more related to reading disability than visual processing deficits.

Many disabled readers manifest various kinds of memory problems that appear to interfere with reading.

Severely disabled readers are inefficient learners. They must be taught cognitive learning strategies so that they can learn how to take control of their own learning. Among the strategies are self-questioning, predicting and monitoring, self-rehearsal, and cognitive behavior modification.

Attentional deficit disorders is another characteristic of severely disabled readers. These students cannot concentrate selectively on tasks and consequently do not learn to read.

Instructional methods for severe reading disabilities are grouped into building prerequisite skills, adaptations of standard reading methods, and special remedial methods.

Activities for auditory and visual prerequisite skills may build a foundation for the student to overcome deficiencies if these activities are closely related to reading.

In teaching reading to severely disabled readers, teachers should first try an adaptation of a standard method of teaching beginning reading, for this permits the most rapid progress. The choice of this method should be based on student aptitude, student preference, and the other instructional programs that the student is receiving.

Four standard methods that may be modified for remedial use are (1) the sight word method (learning to recognize words instantly), (2) the language experience method (reading stories that students have written), (3) the synthetic phonics method (learning letter sounds and blending them together), and (4) the analytic phonics method (learning by the repetition of whole words in phonically regular patterns). The teaching of prerequisite skills may be combined with these methods.

If adaptations of standard methods do not succeed, special remedial methods may be used. These may be divided into two types: (1) kinesthetic approaches and (2) phonics approaches.

Test Inventory 13.1   Tests of Prerequisite Skills

Bender Visual-Motor Gestalt Test

American Orthopsychiatric Association   *Ages: 4 years-adult*

Subject copies nine designs that are interpreted for perception and organization. One interpretation system for children was done by Koppitz (1964).

Individual test: 10–15 minutes. May also be used for personality interpretation. Examiner should be specifically trained in administration.

Detroit Tests of Learning Aptitude (DTLA–2)

Pro Ed   *Ages: 3–19 years*

Tests visual, auditory, and motor processing abilities through nineteen subtests including verbal absurdities, free association, number ability, and social adjustment. Yields MA and IQ and may be used diagnostically. Primary battery-ages 3–5.9; DLTA–2 ages 6–17.

Individual test: 1 hour.

Developmental Test of Visual Motor Integration (VMI)

Modern Curriculum Press   *Ages: 2–15 years*

Student required to copy geometric forms arranged in increasing order of difficulty. No erasures or second trials allowed. Short form ages 2–8; long form ages 2–15.

Individual or group test: about 20 minutes.

Frostig Developmental Test of Visual Perception (DTVP)

Consulting Psychologists Press   *Ages: 4–8 years*

Consists of five visual perceptual subtests including, (1) eye-hand coordination, (2) figure-ground separation, (3) constancy of shape, (4) position in space, and (5) spatial relationships. Yields scaled score, age equivalent, and perceptual quotient.

Group or individual test: 45 minutes.

Goldman-Fristoe-Woodcock Auditory Skills Test Battery

American Guidance Services   *Ages: 3 years–adult*

Assesses auditory perception through twelve tests that include auditory discrimination, memory for content, sound recognition, sound blending, and spelling of sounds. Yields percentile ranks.

Individual test: 2–3 hours for total test.

Illinois Test of Psycholinguistic Abilities (ITPA)

University of Illinois Press   *Ages: 2-4 to 10-3 years*

Assesses abilities to process cognitive information. Tests are divided into auditory-visual, receptive-expressive, and association-integration behaviors. There are twelve subtests, two of which are supplementary: (1) Auditory Reception; (2) Visual Reception; (3) Visual Sequential Memory; (4) Auditory Association; (5) Auditory Sequential Memory; (6) Visual Association; (7) Visual Closure; (8) Verbal Expression; (9) Grammatic Closure; (10) Manual Expression; (11) Auditory Closure (supplementary); and (12) Sound Blending (supplementary). Yields scaled scores and age scores for each of the subtests and an overall psycholinguistic age.

Individual test: 1 hour. Examiner should be trained in administration.

Monroe Reading Aptitude Tests
C. H. Nevins   *Ages: 6–12*

Identifies those needing remediation and those ready to read. Basic visual tests assess discrimination of reversals, eye movements, and visual memory. Motor tests assess speed of movement and ability to stay on the lines. Auditory tests measure discrimination and blending. Language tests measure vocabulary. Additional subtests measure auditory story retention, speech defects and facility, vocabulary command, sentence ability, and motor control-visual memory. Percentiles given. Also: Monroe Reading Diagnostic Test.

Group test: 30–55 minutes.

Motor-Free Visual Perception Test (MVPT)
Academic Therapy   *Ages: 4–8 years*

Assesses visual perception through pointing. Five categories involved: (1) spatial relationships, (2) visual discrimination, (3) figure-ground, (4) visual closure, and (5) visual memory. Yields a perceptual quotient and perceptual age.

Individual test: 10 minutes.

Roswell-Chall Auditory Blending Test (RCABT)
Essay Press   *Grades: 1–4*

Three subtests require students to blend individual sounds, pronounced by teacher, into words. Yields ratings of inferior or adequate blending ability. Two forms available.

Individual test: 15–20 minutes.

Slingerland Screening Tests
for Identifying Children
with Specific Language Disability
Educators Publishing Services   *Grades: 1–6*

Assesses visual, auditory, kinesthetic, and perceptual-motor areas. Nine tests include copying, matching, remembering, writing, dictation, sound discrimination, and story retelling. Test uses words and letters rather than forms. No standardized scores.

Group test, except for test 9: 40 minutes.

Southern California Sensory Integration Tests
Western Psychological Services   *Ages: 4–10 years*

Detects and determines the nature of sensory integrative dysfunction through seventeen tests including figure-ground perception, position in space, finger identification, crossing midline of body, and right-left discrimination. Yields standard scores.

Individual administration: 1½ hours. Requires administration by individual with specialized training on the test.

Test of Auditory Discrimination (Wepman)

Western Psychological Services   *Ages: 5–8 years*

Assesses student's ability to discriminate the fine differences between English phonemes. Word pairs (man-pan) are read aloud, and the student notes whether they are the same or different. The student faces away from the administrator. Two forms available.

Individual administration: 5 minutes.

14

USING MICROCOMPUTERS IN READING INSTRUCTION

Many machines have invaded the reading classroom over the years: the tachistoscope, teaching machines, and machines to control eye movement. After a brief encounter, most have faded from use. Is the microcomputer just another technological fad being thrust upon us which will soon be put into the closet to gather dust?

INTRODUCTION

In contrast to other machines, the microcomputer is here to stay. Stimulating an unprecedented curriculum reform movement in all areas of schooling, the computer holds great promise for the teaching of reading. With over one million computers now owned by the schools (Gerber, 1986), microcomputers are already in many classrooms. The prediction that the microcomputer will soon become as handy and useful as a pencil is fast becoming a reality. Employability in the 1990's will require the ability to "read" a computer screen and to use a computer keyboard. Even for many toddlers the microcomputer is becoming an integral part of their overall development. The first words of young children who have access to computers include functional computer concepts and vocabulary, such as, "puter," "all gone," and "boot me." To help students make effective use of this exploding technology, teachers must learn to apply these electronic tools to their curriculum.

THE MICROCOMPUTER REVOLUTION

The microcomputer has enormous potential for altering the educational experience of pupils with special learning needs. In fact, the value of the computer may be greater for students with special needs than for any other population. We often hear that the technology of the microcomputer enables ordinary people to do extraordinary things. For the student who has special learning needs, however, the microcomputer has the power to enable an extraordinary individual to do ordinary things.

The computer helps children with special learning needs "close the gap;" it helps to remove overwhelming hurdles, thereby allowing them access to learning. A computer can bring voice and communication to nonvocal children, overcome vision handicaps for visually impaired children, bring language and communication to language disordered and hearing impaired children, provide new learning opportunities for mentally retarded pupils, overcome attention deficits for children with learning disabilities, extend movement and motor control through adaptive devices for children with physical handicaps, and offer new creative challenges for gifted children.

For children with reading problems, the microcomputer provides privacy, patience, and practice. It allows students to learn new reading skills without displaying failure in front of peers and teachers, to practice recently acquired reading skills as often as they need or desire, and to spend more "engaged" time in reading tasks. The computer can also integrate the various components of language—listening, speaking, reading, writing—and offer opportunities to integrate thinking skills with the reading process.

The computer helps students in all language arts areas.

INSTRUCTIONAL APPLICATIONS

The use of the microcomputer as a pedagogical tool in the reading class is based upon familiar and sound principles of learning. For example, it offers individualization of instruction, sufficient review and repetition, sequential steps of presentation, opportunities to learn through experimentation, integration of reading and writing, and time to think. The major types of instructional applications include drill-and-practice, tutorials, wordprocessing, simulations and creative problem-solving, and authoring systems.

Drill and Practice

The most common and familiar uses of microcomputers are drill and practice programs. About 60 to 85 percent of computer-use time falls in this category (Cosden et al., 1987). Designed to provide motivating opportunities for pupils to increase mastery of already introduced concepts and skills, drill and practice programs allow the student to practice and review skills in an interesting context and in privacy. Research shows that pupils improve in reading fluency skills through drill-and-practice types of computer reading programs (Torgeson, 1986).

Tutorial Instruction

Tutorial programs are designed to teach a new skill to the pupil. The quality of tutorial software programs is rapidly improving and beginning to take advantage of the many unique instructional features of the microcomputer, such as graphics, animation, enlarged print, use of color in both graphics and print, music, sound, speech, and branching to adjust the presentation to meet specific learner needs.

Wordprocessing

Reading teachers increasingly report the successful use of word processing programs to help children develop a variety of language skills, including reading, writing, spelling, and grammar. Wordprocessing is proving to be an innovative and motivating way to learn a variety of written language skills. By using a speech synthesizer with the wordprocessing program, the various elements of language (speech, reading, writing), are integrated.

Simulations and Creative Problem Solving

Simulations are teaching games which offer pupils a realistic context for problem solving. Students can make decisions about real-life situations and see what the outcome is and how it affects the environment. By presenting information graphically and using speech synthesis, the need for reading material can be reduced. Creative problem solving applications often use the flexible and versatile computer language, LOGO. LOGO, designed for use by young children, is a simple but powerful language that encourages exploration, manipulation, discovery, and serendipitous learning (Papert, 1980).

Authoring Systems

Authoring language software are programs that allow teachers to create fairly easily a set of lessons using a computer. The authoring software falls between a set commercial instructional program and full computer programming. Authoring systems and authoring languages range from very simple "shell" programs, which require no programming but are not very flexible in format, to more sophisticated and difficult systems requiring some programming but providing a great deal of flexibility in lesson options. Both types allow teachers to create lessons to fit individual or class needs (Pattison, 1985). One of the most useful simple authoring languages is contained in *Create Lessons* (primary) and *Create Intermediate* (intermediate grades), both published by Hartley. Many of the more sophisticated authoring languages are based on *PILOT* (Claris)*. Among them are *SuperPILOT* (Claris), and *EZ Pilot* (Hartley).

---

*In this chapter, when we discuss a computer software package the publisher is noted, after the name, in parentheses.

Important features in choosing an authoring package are answer matching (several answers can be counted as correct), feedback (the program gives the student several types of feedback), flexible branching (the system provides branching depending upon the response), record keeping (records of the student's progress are kept), screen display features (the developer can add graphics), timing (the teacher can change the lengths of exposure time), copy protection (the teacher can make copies of the program), and sound capabilities (sound effects and voice can be added to the program). A good authoring program enables the user to spend time concentrating on the task and not on operating the program.

How would a teacher use an authoring system? He or she could design a system to teach, practice, or review the specific spelling words of the week. For example, one junior high school teacher designed a series of lessons which allowed remedial reading students to practice the basic concepts of the Illinois and U.S. Constitution needed to pass a mandatory competency examination. In another case, the students in a junior high school wrote a program game on trivia questions.

MICROCOMPUTERS AND READING

Computers have significant limitations in the teaching of reading. They cannot and should not take the place of books. Nor can they supplant the teacher's role in the teaching of reading. The technology of the computer, however, can expand instructional possibilities and school experiences. It can link the learner, the teacher, and the instruction. For teaching reading, the computer appears to be more practical as a supplemental practice activity rather than as tutorial or introductory instruction (Torgeson, 1986).

Studies of computer usage show that remedial students use the computer more frequently for math programs than for reading programs. Spelling programs rank next in computer usage. Less computer time is spent on reading and wordprocessing. Overall computer usage by areas of the curriculum is shown in Table 14.1 (Cosden et al. 1987).

Table 14.1   Percent of Computer Time in Different Subject Areas

SUBJECT	RANGE	AVERAGE
Math	33–55	39
Spelling	1–21	12
Reading	1–8	5
Programming	5–15	11
Wordprocessing	3–11	4

What can the computer offer students who have reading problems?

1. *Computer instruction offers the poor reader more time for learning on a one-to-one basis.* Studies of reading instruction in regular classes show that poor readers are not given as much opportunity to read as average and good readers (see Chapter 7). These students have less "engaged" time in reading, and less opportunity to practice their skills. Ysseldyke et al. (1984) found that special education students are only engaged in academic tasks 16 to 53 percent of the time in school. Thus, an advantage of using computers is that poor readers are given the valuable time they need to strengthen and practice reading. Cosden, et al., (1987) observed 305 learning handicapped students and found that "engaged time" increased dramatically when using a microcomputer.

2. *Microcomputers can help poor readers develop automaticity in basic reading skills.* Fluent reading requires automaticity in recognizing words (see Chapters 8 and 9). Some disabled readers exhibit exceptionally slow rates of learning, first in acquiring new information and then in developing facility with newly acquired cognitive skills (Idol, 1987). Extended practice with the microcomputer helps the poor reader reach a level of proficiency in which word recognition becomes rapid and accurate and requires little or no conscious monitoring (Torgeson, 1986).

3. *The microcomputer offers the student private instruction.* Adults with reading problems often relate vivid memories of the embarrassment they suffered when they had to read in front of their classmates. The microcomputer avoids potential problems with peer criticism, poor self-concept, and embarrassment. Since computer instruction is one-on-one, the student is the only one who has to know about the quality of his or her performance.

4. *The microcomputer offers poor readers the opportunity and time to think about the reading passage.* If the program provides interactive feedback, the computer actually guides the student in problem solving and metacognitive skills (Idol, 1987; Goldman and Pellegrino, 1987). Further, since the microcomputer provides immediate feedback, the pupil does not practice an incorrect answer for a long period of time.

5. *The computer enhances the instructional connection between writing and reading.* Many of the strategies that are useful for teaching reading as a total language process can be adopted to computer use.

TYPES OF COMPUTER READING PROGRAMS

The use of the microcomputer in the reading curriculum will be shaped in part by the teacher's perspectives of the reading process and how children learn to read. Computer programs are available to teach reading in the areas of (1) word recognition; (2) comprehension and word meaning; (3) language experience; (4) interactive computer stories; and (5) programs that calculate the readability of a passage.

Computer Programs Stressing Word Recognition

Computers have unique capabilities to meet some of the most basic word recognition needs of children with reading problems. Drill-and-practice programs can help children acquire better reading skills through practice phonological processing and decoding skills. Frey and Reigeluth (1986) reported that using peer tutoring (children teaching each other) with a well-structured computer program was an effective way to help students acquire word recognition skills.

Torgeson (1986) found drill and practice programs were effective with disabled readers. He used *Hint and Hunt I* (DLM/Teaching Resources). This program provides extensive practice recognizing and analyzing words varying in medial vowels and vowel combinations. This program was successful in increasing generalized decoding fluency for words containing medial vowels and vowel combinations. Torgeson (1986) also used the program *Construct-A-Word I* (DLM/Teaching Resources). This program provides practice in recognizing common word elements to increase decoding speed and accuracy. The research showed that children improved significantly in general decoding efficiency.

For computer programs that teach sight word recognition, Shepard (1986) reports that teachers liked the programs *Wizard of Words* (Advanced Ideas) and *Magic Spells* (The Learning Co.). *Repeated Reading* is a shell program from *Lesson Master Authoring System* (Simpac Systems, Inc.) designed to increase the fluency of oral reading by providing practice reading the same passage over several times. The IBM system *Write to Read* stresses mastering sound-symbol phonics correspondences in writing as a key to effective word recognition.

Computer Programs Stressing Comprehension and Word Meaning

There are several microcomputer programs that stress reading comprehension. They utilize the computer's unique capacity to integrate the components of language, to focus on reading as communication, and to capture the cognitive processes of reading. Perhaps the greatest promise of the microcomputer for teaching reading lies in its potential as a tool for students to use to solve problems and to explore new ideas and concepts. Dudley-Marling (1985) suggests the following computer programs invite this kind of reading: *Snooper Troops* (Spinnaker), *Dragon's Keep* (Sierra on Line), and *Gertrude's Secrets* (Learning Company).

A program that builds on a semantic approach to vocabulary instruction is *Semantic Mapper* (Teacher Support Software). It is based on the view that learning occurs through association to what is already known. It teaches meaning vocabulary in a natural manner by associating topics with words. (See Chapter 9).

Using the Computer in the Language Experience Approach

The Language Experience Approach to teaching reading is a classic, time-tested and effective strategy for teaching reading (see Chapter 8). In brief, pupils dictate stories built on their own experiences and natural language patterns. The child then is able to easily read this experience story because it consists of the child's own language. The microcomputer has the capacity to use and enhance the language experience method. There is evidence that using computers results in longer language experience stories and more revisions (Dudley-Marling, 1985). Grabe and Grabe (1985) found that the microcomputer is well suited to the language experience approach. They used the wordprocessor to generate stories and to teach story sequencing and structure. After surveying the literature on the language experience approach and the wordprocessing capabilities of the computer, Smith (1985) concluded that the computer makes language experience instruction easier for the teacher and student and enhances the value of the approach as well.

Advantages of using the computer in language-experience stories rather than using over the chalkboard or chart paper include (Anderson-Inman, 1986):

1. The language experience story can be quickly and efficiently recorded and printed using a computer and a printer. It is faster than a printed story, and it does not have to be recopied from the board.
2. The stories can be easily revised. Adding or deleting words, corrections, and minor improvements become easy. Further, students learn very early that stories are not static entities, but can be molded to achieve better communication.
3. The computer creates opportunities for individualization. The group story can be individualized for each student by adding the student's name. The student can change the beginning or ending, or change details in the story. For example, a group of students can jointly write the beginning of the story and each student can create a different ending.
4. Using synthesized speech, the computer recites the story that the students have written. The child can hear the story repeatedly and learn as he or she looks and listens. The teacher or pupil can also print the story (Vernot, 1987).

Two popular speech synthesizers for the Apple II series are the *Echo+* (Street Electronics) and *Slotbuster* (R.C. Systems). However, teachers can use the language experience approach (see Chapter 8) with any wordprocessing software. There are several commercial software programs that use this approach and many of them add other features to the software. For example, the *Language Experience Primary Series* (Teacher Support Software) allows the student to write an experience story and read it or have it read by a speech synthesizer. In addition, the program analyzes the words used and completes a readability level score of the story. With this software, the user can use either the Echo II or the slotbuster speech synthesizer. Another language experience commercial software program is *My Words* (Hartley) which includes a talking word processor. The programs *Writing to Read* (IBM), designed for the IBM Computer; *Talking Text Writer* (Scholastic Software) for the Apple II series; and *Kidtalk* (First Byte) for Macintosh are talking word processors, which can be used with the language experience approach.

Interactive Computer Stories

Interactive computer software prompts and responds to user input. The value of interactive reading and writing experiences is that they help to break down the distinctions between the reader and the writer. *Windham Classics* (Tom Snyder Productions) are a series of adaptions of classic children's literature. In each, the reader takes on the role of a main character in the story and proceeds through the adventures. In *The Story Teller* (Educational Activities) the reader makes choices to guide the story's actions. In *Story Tree* (Scholastic Software), users can create and read their own branching stories. In *The Writing Adventure* (DLM/Teaching Resources), the program provides an idea generator and the user goes through a series of adventures guided by his or her own choices. As they continue through the adventure, users take notes which later guide them in writing a story.

Readability Software

Computer software programs can easily and quickly calculate the readability (difficulty) of reading selections using various readability formulas. Among available programs are *Language Experience Primary Series* (Teacher Support Software), *Readability Calculations* (Micropower and Light Co.), *Readability Machine* (Prentice Hall) and *School Utilities* (MECC).

READING AND WORDPROCESSING

Wordprocessing, the use of the computer in writing, is proving to be one of the most widely used applications of the microcomputer. It is a very effective tool for teaching reading.

The Reading-Writing Connection

In Chapter 12 we noted that, like reading, writing is a productive and active task which involves children in their own learning. They work at producing something that did not exist before, using their own background knowledge and integrating reading skills as they revise their writing. Instruction in writing can improve performance in reading, and instruction in reading can improve performance in writing (Stotsky, 1983).

However, writing is an arduous task for many remedial readers. The opportunity to work at a computer allows students to write without worrying about penmanship and to revise without making a mess (MacArthur, 1988).

In one study on wordprocessing and reading, Rust (1986) compared two groups who received instruction and conferences in conjunction with their writing. One group used computers; the second wrote by hand. Rust found significant differences in writing and reading between the two groups, and he concluded that improved writing leads to improved reading. Rust found that for the group using the computer: (1) the physical act of composing was easier; (2) students whose handwriting could never be deciphered before were given a fair chance for the first time; (3) revision was easier since sentences could be rearranged, expanded, or combined, and entire paragraphs moved by a few keystrokes; and (4) publishing was facilitated.

Since the students used triple spacing and wide margins, drafts were easier to read and revise. Children were able to change their drafts without producing messy copies; thus students did not consider their drafts sacred. In short, quantity as well as quality of writing increased.

Wordprocessing Programs

There are many excellent wordprocessing programs available for children. The choice depends upon the age and academic level of the child and the type of computer. *Magic Slate* (Sunburst) is a good choice for young children. The user can choose large print (20 or 40 characters per line). These letters are large enough to be read by a small group on a monitor. Other popular wordprocessing programs are *Bankstreet Writer III* (Scholastic Software), *Quill* (D.C. Heath), *Kidwriter* (Gessler Educational Software), *Applewriter* (Claris) and *Appleworks* (Claris).

Another excellent wordprocessing program is FrEdWriter for use with the Apple II series. This is a public domain program, which is available at a very low cost from CUE Softswap or most Apple Computer User Groups. The advantage of this program is that teachers can make copies available for every student. It can be used with one or two disk drives and students can put their story on the program disk or on a separate data disk. In addition, there is a "PROMPT" feature on this program. Teachers can read the child's disk and make comments directly on it without affecting the child's story. The user has a choice between 40 (large letters) or 80 (small letters) characters per line.

Combining Pictures (Graphics) and Text

Several software programs allow students to combine text and graphics in the creation of electronic books. The computer screen becomes equivalent to the printed page and students are provided with electronic tools for writing and illustrating their stores. *Story Maker* (Scholastic Software) allows students to draw their own illustration or select from a pool of prepared graphics. Large-sized types are available, making it a good selection for primary grades. *Bank Street Storybook* (Mindscape) provides a sophisticated yet easy to use graphics programs to illustrate stories. *Kidwriter* has a choice of pictures for writers to use. It is easy to operate and a good choice for primary children. However, it limits topics and story length.

Developing Keyboarding Skills

An important issue in using wordprocessing programs is that of keyboarding skills. If children are to use the computer efficiently for wordprocessing, they will have to learn keyboarding or "typing" skills. There are a number of easy and enjoyable computer programs for learning typing skills, such as *Typing Tutor III* (Scholastic Software), *HypeType* (Comp-Unique), *PAWS* (MECC), *Master Type* (Mindscape), *Alphabetic Keyboarding* (Scholastic Software). It is better to learn the correct finger positions than to get into bad habits using a "hunt-and-peck" method. In general, the earlier keyboarding skills can be taught the better. Teachers have found that third or fourth graders are able to learn these skills effectively.

Reading Activities Using the Wordprocessor

Below are some suggested activities for using the microcomputer to teach reading.

1. *Practicing vocabulary words.* Write a series of sentences with a blank line for the vocabulary word the student is studying. At the bottom of the page, put the vocabulary word. Using the MOVE function, zap out the correct vocabulary word and move it to each sentence.
2. *Learning story sequence.* Children will learn to put a series of sentences in the correct order. Place several sentences of a series of events in mixed up order. Have the student use the MOVE function to put sentences in the correct sequence.
3. *Building vocabulary.* Have students use the FIND and REPLACE function to find overused words (e.g., *very*, *nice*). Students replace the overused word with another appropriate word. They may wish to use a thesaurus.
4. *Story beginners.* Put the beginning of a story on a disk and have the students continue the story. Children can compare their individual versions. Alternatively, use a story starter on a disk. One student continues a segment of this story. Then another student writes the next segment.
5. *Disk diary or journal.* Journal writing of daily events has proven an effective technique for improving reading and writing. Instead of writing on paper, students use a wordprocessor and write on a disk, adding to their journal periodically.
6. *Electronic Mail.* In this activity students send messages with the computer. There are public messages (such as announcements and assignments) and personal messages. Communications can be student to student messages, teacher to student messages, class announcements, and class assignments on the electronic mail.
7. *Bulletin Boards.* News events on bulletin boards can be kept for special interest groups, for example, sports teams, music events, upcoming school programs, club events, and meetings. Students can be responsible for keeping up the bulletin board.
8. *Book Reports.* Book reports can be written on the computer. Use a short format with

student fill-ins or use longer types of reports. To make the reports easier, use a standard format. These can be put on a wordprocessor or a database. The key topics could be: Title of Book, Author, Type of Book, Summary, Rating, Student Name.

Use the COPY function of the word processor to copy the format for each student. Students can then fill in the blanks on short format reports. They can also use a FIND function to see who read the book and what they thought of it.

9. *Pen Pals.* This activity can encourage writing to others—in class, with other classes, schools, special interest groups, etc.

10. *Class Newsletter.* A newspaper can be written using any wordprocessing program. A commercial software program that specifically supports newspaper production is *The Newsroom* (Springboard Software). This popular program allows writers to write, illustrate, pasteup, and print pages that resemble a newspaper or newsletter. Stories can also be sent via a telecommunication modem so that a newspaper can be developed with material contributed by many schools in a district.

11. *Making Predictions.* Provide story starters and ask the students to predict what will happen. They can check their predictions later in the story.

12. *Using Graphics.* Graphics can be easily added to any of the above activities. Provide banks of graphics on disk or have students create their own graphics. The Koala pad (PTI Koala), a touch-sensitive graphics tablet, is useful for making graphics.

SUMMARY

The microcomputer revolution is making microcomputers available in every school and in many classrooms. The computer is proving to be particularly useful for children with learning problems. It provides privacy, patience, and much opportunity to practice. For poor readers, it may provide more reading time.

Instructional applications of the microcomputer include drill and practice to review learned skills, tutorial programs to learn new concepts, wordprocessing to use in writing and simulations, and problem solving programs.

Microcomputers have limitations in the teaching of reading and should not replace reading in books. For children with reading problems, the computer can offer more time for learning on an individual basis, and it can help develop automaticity in basic reading skills. The computer can also offer students private instruction, time to think about reading passages, and a chance to see the connection between writing and reading.

There are many types of reading programs available. Some stress word recognition, providing practice in phonics and sight word recognition. Some programs stress reading comprehension and vocabulary instruction. Others stress language experience stories. Still others focus on interactive computer stories. Finally, computer programs can calculate readability levels.

One of the most popular applications of the microcomputer is in wordprocessing. Many reading disabled students do well with wordprocessing and use the computer for writing.

Reading activities that use the microcomputer offer a new and challenging way to teach reading.

15

ORGANIZING AND DELIVERING REMEDIAL READING SERVICES

Many decisions must be made in order to effectively teach remedial readers. Organizational decisions impact the total program.

INTRODUCTION

This chapter examines topics related to organizing programs for remedial reading instruction. We examine alternative settings for delivering services to remedial readers, some laws that affect remedial reading programs, the organization of the remedial reading sessions, and reports and records.

SETTINGS FOR REMEDIAL READING INSTRUCTION

Several types of placements and instructional settings are used for helping remedial readers. Decisions about placement depend upon many factors: (1) the availability of facilities and reading personnel within the school; (2) the perspectives of decision makers about the optimum settings for delivering remedial services; (3) student or school eligibility for funded programs, such as Chapter I programs, special education, or bilingual programs; (4) the severity of the student's problem; and (5) the age of the remedial student. The major placement options for remedial reading instruction are reviewed in this section.

The Resource Room

The resource room is one of the most popular settings for both remedial reading and special education students. Students are "pulled out" from their classrooms for supplementary instruction.

The Remedial Reading Resource Room.   For the remedial reading class, a special room in the school is set aside in which the reading teacher works with a small group of children. The teacher may be assigned to one or several schools. Pupils typically leave their regular classroom and come to the remedial reading room for a period of about 30 minutes, several days a week. As pupils improve and become able to function in their home classroom, they are discharged from the remedial reading class and replaced by other reading disabled pupils. During the course of a day, the remedial teacher may work with four or five small groups of children, each consisting of two to ten pupils. The remedial reading class should be attractive and inviting and have a rich supply of instructional materials.

In some cases the remedial reading resource room has financial support from the school district. In other cases the remedial classes in the United States receive funding support through Chapter I legislation. Chapter I is a U.S. Department of Education law that offers compensatory education for pupils enrolled in schools that meet certain low-income eligibility criteria. Chapter I focuses upon the basic skills of reading and mathematics. (Chapter I is discussed again later in this chapter.)

The Special Education Resource Room.   The resource room is often the setting for teaching special education, particularly for students with learning disabilities. Learning disabilities is one of the categories of special education specified in the federal law, PL 94-142, the *Education of the Handicapped Act.* Most children with learning disabilities (about 80 percent) have problems in some area of reading (Norman and Zigmond, 1980; Kirk and Elkins, 1975). As the most prevalent type of placement for learning-disabled students, the resource room provides small group instruction in all academic areas, including reading, on a regularly scheduled basis for a portion of the school day. For most of the day, however, students are in their regular classroom.

Advantages and Disadvantages of the Resource Room.   The advantages of the resource room are that it is flexible in terms of the curriculum offered, the time the student spends in the program, and the number of students served (Lerner, 1989). In addition, resource room teachers often develop a close relationship with the children through small-group instruction. Finally, resource teachers are likely to have advanced training in reading.

Disadvantages include scheduling difficulties, lack of coordination with the regular classroom curriculum (Allington and Shake, 1986; Allington and Broikou, 1988), and the stigmatizing effect of being in a special room for instruction.

Regular Classroom Instruction

Within the regular classroom, the reading instruction is usually provided by the classroom teacher. Other models are, however, available. In these models (1) the reading teacher works with disabled readers in the regular classroom setting; (2) the reading teacher provides consultation to help the classroom teacher plan and guide classroom teaching for remedial students; and (3) older students work individually with remedial readers in a peer tutoring program.

As noted earlier, when remedial services are provided in a separate remedial reading class, there may be a lack of coordination between the core reading curriculum of the regular classroom and the instruction of the remedial class. Noting this, some authorities have advocated "push-in" programs, in which remedial teachers go into the child's classroom.

However, for some disabled readers, the regular classroom is not the optimum setting for supplementary instruction. Students who have already failed in the regular curriculum may need individualized goals, methods, and materials, as well as a change of physical setting. The embarrassment of receiving remedial help in front of one's peers may also be a problem.

Some reading teachers report that when they conducted remedial reading instruction in the regular classroom, the children complained of distractions and intolerable noise levels. To help children concentrate, the reading teacher began working with them in the hall outside the classroom. The unintended consequence of this system was that a new "pull-out" remedial reading class, located in the hall, was created.

We recommend that whether a program is "pull-out" or "push-in," remedial and classroom teachers consult with each other to plan a coordinated learning program (Allington and Shake, 1986).

Mainstreaming

In special education, the term *mainstreaming* is commonly used in reference to providing services for handicapped children in the regular classroom. A key provision of the special education law (PL 94-142) is that handicapped children are to be taught in the "least restrictive environment," that is, that they be taught with nonhandicapped children to the greatest extent possible.

The goal of mainstreaming is the social and instructional integration of handicapped children into the regular class. To this end, many special education students who were once placed in "self-contained" classes for the entire day now spend a large portion of their day in a regular classroom.

A more recent mainstreaming proposal known as the "regular education initiative" has been advanced by the Office of Special Education and Rehabilitation Services. This proposal urges fundamental changes in the way that learning-disabled students are identified, assessed, and educated (Will, 1986). It recommends that *all* students with learning problems, as well as low achievers, can be served more effectively through the regular classroom than through the special education system (Lerner, 1987).

The premise of the regular education initiative is that the current special education system contains several shortcomings: (1) many youngsters with various learning problems are not eligible for special education services; (2) there is a tendency to equate poor performance with a handicap, and students in special programs are stigmatized as they are segregated from their peers; (3) instead of placing emphasis on early prevention, special education students are usually identified after serious learning deficiencies have developed; and (4) the special education system does not lead to cooperative school-parent relationships.

To overcome these shortcomings, the regular education initiative recommends the following: (1) a new delivery service system in the regular classroom based on individualized educational needs and experimental trials to test out such a system; (2) identification and intervention of learning problems at the early elementary grades; (3) curriculum-based assessment procedures that identify each student's strengths and weaknesses for instructional planning purposes; and (4) utilization of "effective schools" programs and techniques.

It is critical for parents and professionals to carefully review the key issues of these proposals and to consider the implications of these policies for serving their children. For example, placement in a regular class instead of a resource room may not necessarily eliminate a stigma. What is the real stigma—a label or school failure? We need more careful analysis to investigate the degree to which stigma may be school failure itself.

A basic premise of special education is that even with an excellent education system, special education services are needed for certain children. These are services beyond those that can be provided effectively in normal classroom settings. In fact, most learning-disabled students (77 percent) are in a regular class with support from a consulting or resource room teacher (U.S. Department of Education, 1987). Many of these teachers work closely with the classroom teacher in planning and implementing an instructional program. This kind of cooperative planning and teaching should be continued and encouraged. However, the resource room still may be needed for many students with reading problems and learning disabilities (Lerner, 1987).

The Reading Clinic

Children with reading disabilities who fail to respond to remedial efforts in their schools can be referred to special clinics and schools that offer more intensive services. These may be run by a college or university, by private individuals, or by the school district. The clinics often have multidisciplinary specialists on staff and can concentrate on the unique needs of severely disabled readers. Often, clinics offer individual instruction designed for severely disabled individuals.

LEGISLATION AND READING INSTRUCTION

Educational services that are offered in our schools are shaped to some extent by federal and state laws that mandate services, regulate programs, and provide funds for targeted groups of students. Many children with reading problems are served through special programs that have been created through federal or state legislation.

Federal and state laws play a vital role in many phases of these programs. They help in determining the eligibility of students for services, in structuring the diagnostic and instructional plans, in training and certifying personnel, in guiding assessment and evaluation procedures, and in providing financial resources to support the program.

In this section, we discuss laws that affect special education instruction, Chapter I, bilingual programs, confidentiality, and minimum competency testing.

Special Education—PL 94-142

Classroom and reading teachers play an increasingly active role in the evaluation and instruction of special education students. They are often required to contribute to a student's individualized instruction program (IEP), and many special education students are placed in the regular classroom for instruction. Thus, all teachers should be familiar with special education legislation.

The U.S. Department of Education (1987) reports that about 11 percent of the school population is identified as handicapped and requiring special education services. Of these, 1.8 million children are learning disabled. This is approximately 4.8 percent of the school population. Moreover, learning disabilities account for 44 percent of all handicapped children served in schools (U.S. Department of Education, 1988).

Landmark special education legislation was enacted in 1975 with the passage of Public Law 94-142, entitled the *Education for All Handicapped Children Act*. This law was reauthorized in 1986, and the reauthorization continues federal assistance to state and local education agencies to meet the special education and related services needs of handicapped children and youth. In addition, PL 94-142 was expanded and extended through Public Law 99-457, *Education of the Handicapped Act Amendments of 1986*. The amendments expand services for additional students and for certain areas of special education, including programs for early childhood, technology, transition for handicapped teenagers to the world of work, and blind-deaf children.

Under PL 94-142, all handicapped children and youth, ages three through twenty-one, have the right to a "free appropriate public education." Further, each state must develop a plan that is in compliance with the federal law. As a result, schools in every part of the nation are affected by this far-reaching legislation. Under the law, handicapped children include the categories of: deaf, deaf-blind, hard of hearing, mentally retarded, multihandicapped, orthopedically impaired, other health impaired, seriously emotionally disturbed, specific learning disabled, speech impaired, and visually handicapped. The children and youth in many of these categories will have serious reading problems.

Nondiscriminatory Testing.   Public Law 94-142 specifies that testing must be nondiscriminatory. Tests and procedures must be free of racial or cultural bias. The tests are to be provided and administered in the student's native language, and students cannot be evaluated or placed on the basis of a single test.

Least Restrictive Environment.   The law also specifies that, to the maximum extent possible, handicapped students are to be educated with nonhandicapped children. Schools must develop a "continuum of alternative placements," or an array of placement possibilities to meet the various needs of special education students. Alternative placements for handicapped students are shown in Table 15.1.

Procedural Safeguards.   PL 94-142 is designed to protect the rights of handicapped students and their parents in several ways.

1. Parents must consent in writing to having an evaluation for their child. The parents must also sign approval of the written IEP, the decisions and plans for instructing their child.
2. The assessment must be conducted in the student's native language and the findings reported to the parents in their native language.

Table 15.1 Continuum of Alternative Placements

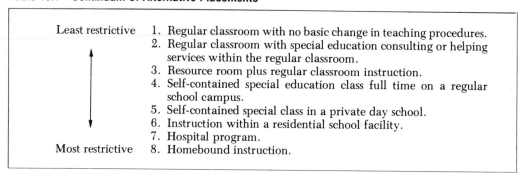

Least restrictive
1. Regular classroom with no basic change in teaching procedures.
2. Regular classroom with special education consulting or helping services within the regular classroom.
3. Resource room plus regular classroom instruction.
4. Self-contained special education class full time on a regular school campus.
5. Self-contained special class in a private day school.
6. Instruction within a residential school facility.
7. Hospital program.

Most restrictive
8. Homebound instruction.

3. The parents have the right of access to all educational information collected and used in decision making regarding their child.
4. Parents and students have the right to an impartial due process hearing if they are dissatisfied with program decisions. The hearing is conducted by an impartial hearing officer appointed by the state. The parent can be accompanied and advised by an attorney or by individuals with special knowledge or training with respect to the problems of handicapped children. Further, the parent can appeal decisions made at this hearing to a higher hearing level. Action beyond this hearing would be a civil action lawsuit.

The Individualized Education Program (IEP). The individualized education program (IEP) developed for each handicapped student is central to the implementation of PL 94-142. The IEP is actually a process involving several stages (Lerner, Dawson, and Horvath, 1980; Lerner, 1989):

1. *Prereferral.* The teacher discusses the child's problem with an in-school team who develop suggestions for regular classroom instruction.
2. *Referral and initial planning.* The teacher refers a student for evaluation and the multidisciplinary evaluation team is selected.
3. *Multidisciplinary evaluation.* The multidisciplinary team members conduct an assessment of the student.
4. *Case conference team meeting and writing the IEP.* A meeting is held to analyze the assessment information, to develop a diagnosis, to make decisions about placement and instruction, and to write the individualized education program (IEP).
5. *Implementating the IEP through placement and teaching.* The written plan is carried out.
6. *Monitoring student progress.* Plans are made for reviewing and reevaluating the student's progress.

The individualized education program does not plan the total instruction of the handicapped student. It merely sets forth in writing a commitment of resources to meet the student's needs. It is also a management tool to allow parents, teachers, and administrators to know what educational services have been allocated. Teachers must develop instructional plans (such as lesson plans) beyond what is included in the IEP.

COMPONENTS OF THE IEP   The following components must be included in each individualized education program:

1. *A statement of the child's present levels of educational performance.* This component of the individualized education program refers to the student's level of functioning. In addition to reading, these levels might refer to other academic areas, vocational or prevocational skills, or self-help skills.

2. *A statement of annual goals, including short-term instructional objectives.* This component provides for both an annual goal and measurable intermediate steps to meet this annual goal.

3. *A statement of the specific education and related services to be provided to the child, and the extent to which the child will be able to participate in regular educational programs.* This component refers to the system of educational services and placement. The plan must designate how much time the student will spend with nonhandicapped students. It also indicates what related services are needed by the student (e.g., speech therapy, adaptive physical education). It is designed to assure that the "least restrictive environment" feature of the law is considered.

4. *The projected date for initiation of services and the anticipated duration of the services.* The purpose of this component is to assure that treatment begins promptly.

5. *Appropriate objective criteria and evaluation procedures and schedules for determining, on at least an annual basis, whether the short-term instructional objectives are being achieved.* This component of the law provides for follow-up and assures that the IEP and the student's progress will be reviewed at least annually. Thus, this component of the law mandates progress reports.

PARTICIPANTS AT IEP MEETINGS   Public Law 94-142 is very clear both in stating that there must be a team meeting to develop the individualized education program and in designating who should participate in that IEP meeting. The team should include

1. *A representative of the school* (someone other than the child's teacher, who is qualified to provide or supervise the provision of special education). This representative could be the principal, the special education director, the director of the learning disabilities program, director of the reading program, or others with supervisory authority.

2. *The child's teacher.* This could be the classroom teacher or the special education teacher of a self-contained room. It refers to the teacher of the child's current placement.

3. *One or both of the child's parents.* Every effort must be made to have the parents in attendance. If the student has no parents, a surrogate parent must be appointed by the legal authority of the courts.

4. *The child, where appropriate.* If the student is an adolescent, it might be appropriate to include the student in the planning meeting.
5. *Other individuals, at the discretion of the parent or the school.* Other persons can be brought into the meeting by either the parent or the school. This could include individuals such as reading teachers, psychologists, speech-language pathologists, special education teachers, physical education teachers, nurses, physicians, child advocates, attorneys, private diagnosticians, and therapists.

In summary, the written statement which is developed during the IEP process becomes the critical link between the handicapped student and the special education that the student requires. The teacher plays a critical role in both the development and the implementation of the IEP.

Chapter I Programs

Many of the reading programs in United States schools are supported through legislation known as Chapter I, *Educational Services for Disadvantaged Students.* Designed to supply compensatory education for disadvantaged students, Chapter I is one of the largest federal education programs. Through Chapter I, supplementary funds are supplied to schools that enroll low-income students. Compensatory education in reading and mathematics is offered to low-achievement students in these schools.

A school's eligibility for Chapter I funds is based on the enrollment of disadvantaged, low-income students. Remedial reading programs in many schools are supported through Chapter I funds. Recent revisions of Chapter I rules require that Chapter I programs develop written policies for including parents in the school's planning and implementation of the remedial services.

Bilingual Education

Many disabled readers receive instruction in bilingual programs, in which they are taught both in their native language and in English. The Bilingual Education Act is a part of legislation known as Chapter II of the Elementary and Secondary Education Act. Bilingual education is designed for students whose first language is not English, which is a characteristic of many of the children in our schools today (Waggoner, 1984). Bilingual Education programs are intended to provide special reading instruction for these Limited English Proficiency students (Long, 1987). Bilingual programs are discussed in Chapter 4.

Confidentiality

The confidentiality of all reports and records of students is protected under the law by the Buckley Amendment, passed in 1974. Students' records cannot be released without the consent of parents or legal guardian. Moreover, parents and students have the right of access to all records concerning their own case, or that of their child. This has important implications for how schools, teachers, and clinics collect, record, and store information on students with reading disabilities. Privacy of audiotapes and videotapes, as well as written records, is guaranteed under the law.

Minimum Competency Testing

Many states have passed legislation requiring schools to give students minimum competency tests. Minimum competency refers to skills thought to be necessary for independent functioning in life, and usually include reading. Students must pass the minimum competency tests to qualify for high school graduation. In some school systems the tests are also used as promotion criteria at certain grade levels. The minimum competency test movement has come about because of a demand for accountability by state legislatures. The hope is that, by setting minimum standards, schools will ensure that students function at higher academic levels.

The minimum competency test movement has created a number of serious questions for teachers of reading and very special concerns for the severely disabled reader. Will teachers "teach to the test," thereby invalidating the intent of the legislation? Will the test prevent poor readers from completing high school and receiving a diploma? Are there alternative ways in which to test the very poor reader? The answers to these and other minimum competency issues are not clear as yet, but the issues provide a challenging subject for the reading teacher.

REPORTS AND RECORDS

Reports and records enable teachers to keep track of a student's progress in an organized manner.

Purposes

Reports and records are needed to clarify information, to assist teachers, and to inform and help others working with the student. Specific purposes include the following.

1. *To measure progress.* When written records and reports are kept of the student's performance, they can be used to measure progress. A review of the record allows the teacher to specify (a) a baseline, or entry, level for the student's skills and (b) the progress that has been made during the time of instruction. In this way, instructional gains can be monitored easily.

2. *To record behavior and events.* Memory cannot supplant a written account. A specific incident and all its details may be clear in the mind of the teacher at the time of an episode, but without written notes, many of the important details are forgotten or overlooked a week or two later. Recording the information in a record book or report enables complex events to be recalled accurately.

3. *To communicate information.* When several professionals (reading teacher, social worker, classroom teacher) are working with the same student, it is necessary for all to have access to records and reports in order to share information. These

written records help professionals to coordinate efforts in meeting instructional goals. Reports also serve to communicate information to parents or legal guardians.

4. *To assure continuous and consistent teaching.* Changes in the school staff and in their instructional responsibilities often occur without opportunities for personal communication. Accurate records can help to maintain a consistent instructional environment.

5. *To meet legal requirements.* Federal and state special education legislation requires that certain records and reports be initiated and kept. Of special concern are the requirements mandated for the IEP, as specified in Public Law 94-142.

The Diagnostic Report and Summary

In a diagnostic report information from tests, the case history, cumulative records, observations, interviews and other sources are integrated into a coherent whole. The key function of the diagnostic report is to provide information to help plan the instructional program. The diagnostic report should suggest goals for the student's reading instruction and methods and materials for accomplishing these goals. In addition, the diagnostic report clarifies the patterns (such as correlated factors) associated with the student's problem. Finally, the report may recommend appropriate referrals outside of reading instruction (e.g., a physical examination).

To facilitate accurate record keeping, a diagnostic summary form is often used, as shown in Table 15.2. This summary is meant for the teacher's personal use and is used to gather information from different sources and placed in a central file. The summarized information can then be used to construct the report.

Although the diagnostic report is prepared for the use of the parents and school, it is also likely to be used by noneducational professionals such as physicians and social workers. Therefore, accurate and professional presentation of data is extremely important.

The complete diagnostic report usually contains several sections. However, depending on the case, not all sections need be included for all students. Sections include:

1. *Identifying data.* This includes the student's name, birthdate, parents' names, address and telephone number, grade placement, classroom, and teacher.
2. *Assessment instruments used.* Because the diagnostic report may involve several tests, it is useful to list these in one section. Test levels, forms, and dates of administration should be included. Often report writers include the scores attained in this section. For certain tests (such as intelligence tests), broad ranges rather than specific scores are generally reported.
3. *Current expected reading level.* The purpose of this section is to assess whether or not a student is reading below the level expected. When intelligence tests are used to determine current reading capacity or potential, results are given (usually reported in ranges), and the results of reading expectancy formulas are given. When practical considerations of reading expectancy are used, they are also included in this section.
4. *Present reading achievement level.* The student's reading achievement level is given in this section. Most achievement tests are divided into subtests that allow some com-

Table 15.2   Sample Diagnostic Summary

Diagnostician: _____ Date of Report: _____

Name: _____ Birthdate: _____ Age: _____

School: _____ Grade: _____ Sex: _____

Parents' Names: _____

Address: _____ Telephone Number: _____

Period of testing: _____

I. Factors Associated with Disability
   A. Enviromental and emotional
      1. Summary of parent interview and home factors: _____
      _____
      _____

      2. School history and behavior: _____
      _____

      3. Social and emotional history and behavior: _____
      _____

      4. Interest inventory: _____
      _____

      5. Sentence completion: _____
      _____

      6. Test and observations
         Date: _____ Test/Observation: _____
         Result: _____
         _____
         _____

   B. Physical Factors
      1. General health history: _____
      _____

      2. Visual acuity
         a. Wears glasses: _____ _____ _____ _____
                           yes   no   how long?   problem
         b. Last eye examination: _____
                                                                      date
         c. Visual Screening test results: _____
         _____

      3. Auditory acuity
         a. Last hearing test: _____ _____
                               date   results
         b. Audiometer results: _____
         _____

   C. Language factors
      1. Language history: _____
      _____

2. Tests and observations

   Date: _____ Test/Observation: _____ Result: _____

D. Previous diagnostic consultations

   Name and title of professional: _____

   Date: _____ Address: _____

   Results: _____

   _____

   Name and title of professional: _____

   Date: _____ Address: _____

   Results: _____

   _____

II. Reading Achievement

A. Informal Reading Inventory

   Name of inventory: _____ Date: _____

   Independent level: _____

   Instructional level: _____

   Frustration level: _____

   Listening level: _____

   Comments and analysis of reading patterns: _____

B. Reading achievement tests

Test	Level	Form	Date	Results

(Comments)

_____

C. Diagnostic batteries and tests of specific areas:

Test	Level	Form	Date	Results

D. Informal assessment tasks:

_____

_____

(Comments)

_____

_____

III. Learning Potential
   A. IQ and other formal measures

   Name of Test   *Date*   *Results*

   _____

   _____

   B. Informal observations: _____

   _____

   C. Reading potential:
   CA _____ MA _____ Reading expectancy age: _____
   Reading achievement level: _____
   Difference of expectancy and achievement: _____
   Practical considerations: _____

   _____

   Is student a disabled reader? _____

   _____

IV. Prerequisite areas
   A. Visual and visual-motor
      Test   *Level*   *Form*   *Date*   *Results*

      _____

      _____

      Informal observations: _____
   B. Auditory
      Test   *Level*   *Form*   *Date*   *Results*

      _____

      _____

      Informal observations: _____
   C. Other
      Test   *Level*   *Form*   *Date*   *Results*

      _____

      _____

      Informal observations: _____
   V. Observations of Behavior During Testing: _____

   _____

parison of reading ability. For example, performance on word recognition and comprehension subtests can be compared. Information given in this section may also include the results of the informal reading inventory and the grade placement of the classroom work that the student is doing.

5. *Analysis of reading strengths and weaknesses.* In this section, the reading performance is described in detail. Test scores and an analysis of their meaning are included, as well as information gained through observation. Since several tests may be used

to assess one type of skill, it is helpful to organize this section around different areas of reading.

a. Informally observed reading abilities

b. Word recognition (sight words, phonics, context clues, structural analysis)

c. Reading comprehension

d. Meaning vocabulary

e. Study strategies

f. Reading rate

g. Class performance

Not all of these areas would be applicable to any single student.

6. *Analysis of prerequisite abilities underlying reading.* The teacher may choose to assess prerequisite abilities, auditory abilities, learning styles, or ability to pay attention. Interpretations of such tests should be included in this section.

7. *Factors associated with reading performance.* In this section, factors that may have contributed to reading problems are summarized. These include environmental, emotional, physical, intellectual, and language factors as well as others. Evidence is collected from the interview, reports of classroom behavior, observation of the student, school records, and the reports of other professionals. Although the weight of evidence may suggest that one particular factor has caused a reading disability, the report writer should avoid absolute statements. Rather than saying "The visual problem is the cause of the reading disability," a more appropriate statement would be "The low score on the nearpoint visual acuity screening test suggests that visual problems may be a factor contributing to reading disability."

8. *Recommendatons for referral.* These should include all nonreading recommendations, such as referral to a pediatric neurologist, a social worker, or a speech-language pathologist.

9. *Recommendations for instruction.* This section states whether, in the report writer's judgment, the student should receive further help in reading and suggests the setting for the instruction. In addition, the examiner recommends initial instructional goals for the student and suggests methods and materials for accomplishing these goals.

10. *Recommendations for parents and classroom teachers.* This section includes ways in which the student's instruction in the classroom can be adjusted. In addition, suggestions for the parents to help their child progress in reading are made.

A partial outline for a diagnostic report is given in Appendix C.

SUMMARY

There are several types of placements and instructional settings for helping remedial readers. They include the resource room, the regular classroom, mainstreaming, and the reading clinic.

Federal and state laws impact the remedial reading program in a number of ways. Legislation has been passed in the areas of special education (PL 94-142), Chapter I, and bilingual education. Other laws that affect teachers are those concerning confidentiality of records (the Buckley amendment) and minimum competency testing.

Reports and records serve many functions in the diagnosis and treatment of students with reading problems.

Appendix: REMEDIAL INSTRUCTIONAL MATERIALS

Basal Readers for Special Needs
Nonbasal Remedial Reading Series Books
Easy Reading Books
   High Interest Books
   Predictable Books
Language Development and Enrichment
Material for Focused Instruction
   Multi-area Development
   Word Recognition
   Comprehension
   Meaning Vocabulary
   Study Strategies/Content Areas
   Rate
Materials for Severely Disabled Readers
   Developing Prerequisite Abilities
   Special Remedial Reading Approaches
   Real-Life Materials/Functional Reading

ABBREVIATIONS USED IN THIS APPENDIX

RL denotes *Reading Level*
IL denotes *Interest Level*

Both interest and reading levels are given in *grades* throughout this table. Interest Levels are only listed when they differ from Reading Levels.

I. BASAL READERS FOR SPECIAL NEEDS

These sets are intended to be used as a core reading program for those who cannot succeed in grade-level basals.

Focus: Reading for Success (Scott Foresman)   **RL** K–7 **IL** 1–8

Series emphasizes oral language development and vocabulary. Uses remedial techniques of proven effectiveness. Contains workbooks and other supplements. Spanish series available entitled *Leer Para Triunfar.*

Key-Text (Economy)   **RL** K–7 **IL** K–8

Series uses phonics approach to reading on lower levels. Workbooks and other supplements available.

New Directions in Reading (Houghton Mifflin)   **RL** 2–7; **IL** 5–10

Series for older remedial students contains high-interest selections, accompanying workbook, and other supplements.

The New Open Highways Program (Scott Foresman)   **RL** 1–8 **IL** 1–8

Stresses literature and skills. Readability at beginning of books is below grade level, but by end is at grade level. Contains workbooks and supplements.

Quest (Scholastic)   **RL** 2–8 **IL** 4–8

Two paperback books at each grade level stress literature. Each book organized into six thematic units. Activity sheets and other supplements available.

The Reading Connection (Open Court)   **RL** 2–11 **IL** 7–adult

Stories and articles appeal to older readers. Newspaper format used at lower levels. Stresses vocabulary, comprehension, writing, study, content areas. Activity masters available.

Programa de Lectura en Espanol (Houghton Mifflin)   **RL** K–6
Spanish Reading Program (Scott Foresman)   **RL** 1–5
Spanish Reading Series (Economy)   **RL** 1–5

Three Spanish language series reflect Hispanic literature and culture. Intended for children reading on grade level.

II. NONBASAL REMEDIAL READING SERIES BOOKS

These books build reading ability systematically through graded selections accompanied by comprehension and vocabulary development.

Challenger (New Readers Press)   **RL** 1–6 **IL** 4–adult

Each of five books contains 20 selections on literature and adult life. Includes writing and reasoning development.

Fact Reading Program (Raintree)   **RL** 3–6.6 **IL** 5–adult

Two packets, each containing eight books, read-along cassettes, skill cards. Builds comprehension, fluency, attitude.

High Action Reading (Modern Curriculum Press)   **RL** 2–6

Comprehension, vocabulary, and study skills developed in separate workbooks at each of five levels. Reading selections are followed by exercises.

Hip Reader Program (Opportunities for Learning)   **RL** 1–4 **IL** 7–adult

Two readers use regular phonics patterns. Realistic photos and "hip" language used. Accompanying workbooks.

In the Know (New Readers Press)   RL 1–4   IL 4–adult

Four-book series contains informational passages on topics found in popular magazines. Includes word study and writing.

Mini Units in Reading (Globe)   RL 4–6   IL 7–12

Paperbacks with 1–2 page contemporary selections grouped around themes like "finding yourself." Skills development.

New Practice Readers, 2nd ed. (McGraw Hill/Webster)   RL 2–7   IL 5–12

Each of seven books contains one page selections followed by questions and vocabulary. Cassettes for levels A–D.

Rally (Harcourt Brace Jovanovich)   IL 7–12

Readers focus on sports, popular music, science fiction. Skills books integrate life functions. Cassettes available.

RD2000 (Reader's Digest)   RL 1–6.9   IL 5–12

Adult-looking magazine series includes sports, mystery, science stories. Vocabulary study; audiocassettes available.

Reading for Concepts (McGraw-Hill/Webster)   RL 1.6–6.7

Eight books contain 1–2 page stories followed by questions keyed to specific skills. Audiocassettes available.

Reading for Today (Steck-Vaughn)   RL 1–5   IL adult

Five books in magazine format stress adult themes. Controlled vocabulary; includes life-coping skills.

Skill Builders, Revised (Readers Digest)   RL 1–6   IL 4–12

Four paperbacks at each level contain passages (about six pages) from *Reader's Digest* issues. Includes skill work.

Sprint Reading Skills Program (Scholastic)   RL 1–5   IL 4–6

Starter level for nonreaders. Levels 1–3 feature stories and plays. Includes skills books and story books for independent reading. *Sprint Starter Library* includes books for each level.

SRA Reading Laboratories–Developmental 1 & 2
(Science Research Associates)   RL 1.2–5   IL 1–8

Each kit contains cards color-coded for graded difficulty, with selection and questions. Self-scoring answer keys.

Triple Takes (Reader's Digest)   RL 1–8   IL 3–12

Each of eight levels contains two books. One page reading lessons followed by questions; life skills included.

III.   EASY READING BOOKS

These provide enjoyable reading experiences for students. Both high interest and predictable books are included.

III.A. High Interest Books

Action, Double Action, Triple Action Unit Kits (Scholastic) **RL** 2-6 **IL** 7-12

Each kit has 2–3 unit books and a reading anthology. Skills book included. Supplemental *Action Library* available.

Adult Learner Series (Jamestown) **RL** 2-3 **IL** 10-adult

Nine novels of mystery and suspense for adults. Questions and two life-skills sections follow each section.

Attention Span Stories (Jamestown) **RL** 2-3 **IL** 6-9

Five paperbacks each contain an exciting story in one page episodes. Students determine plot of stories from choices. Comprehension checks.

Be an Interplanetary Spy (Bantam) **RL** 3-5 **IL** 3-9

Several liberally illustrated paperbacks allow readers to choose how the story will develop.

Beginner Books (Random House) **RL** 1.5-2.5 **IL** K-3

Series of 55 books including *Cat in the Hat, One Fish, Two Fish.* Many use linguistic phonics approach. Fourteen cassettes available.

Bestsellers (Opportunities for Learning) **RL** 1.8-4 **IL** 6-12

Thirty award-winning books covering science fiction, mystery, adventure, romance.

Caught Reading Program (Opportunities for Learning) **RL** 1.4 **IL** 7-12

Seven novels and accompanying worktexts focus on teenage issues.

Choose Your Own Adventure (Bantam) **RL** 3-5 **IL** 3-9

Several liberally illustrated paperbacks allow readers to choose how the story will develop.

Codebusters (Opportunities for Learning) **RL** 2-4 **IL** 4-9

Mystery and adventure stories. Students check comprehension on hand-held "decoder" and mark according to "secret code"

Double Fastback Books; Fastback Books (Fearon) **RL** 4.5-5 **IL** 7-12

Four series (mystery, romance, horror, and sports) in *Double Fastback Books.* Seven sets (spy, crime, science fiction, mystery, romance, horror, sports) in *Fastback Books.* Each series contains ten books.

The Every Reader Series (McGraw-Hill) **RL** 4 **IL** 5-12

15 paperbacks of adapted classics (*Kidnapped, Cases of Sherlock Holmes*).

First Reading Books (formerly Dolch Books) (DLM) **RL** 1-2 **IL** 1-8

Each book (e.g., *Stories from Canada, Fairy Stories*) has several short stories written using Dolch basic words.

Flashbacks (Opportunities for Learning) **RL** 4-5 **IL** 6-12

Three series of sports, war disasters. Three copies of ten titles in each series. Skillcheck cards.

Galaxy 5 (Children's Press) **RL** 2 **IL** 4-12

Six fantasy space adventures follow heroes on spaceship Voyager.

High Noon Books (Educational Performance Associates)   **RL** 1-4 **IL** 4-12

Series include *Tom and Rick Mysteries* (nine titles); *The Road Aces* (two titles) and *Meg Parker Mysteries* (two titles).

Incredible Series (Barnell Loft)   **RL** 4-9 **IL** 4-11

Thirteen short books, each with one suspenseful tale, contain many illustrations and few words per page.

Jamestown Classics (Jamestown)   **RL** 4-5 **IL** 5-adult

Each of 24 books is a simplified classic (O. Henry, Poe, Jack London, etc.). Skills development; audiocassettes.

Know Your World Extra (Weekly Reader)   **RL** 2-3 **IL** 7-12

Weekly newspaper of news, movie reviews, sports, etc. increases in difficulty throughout year. Skills exercises.

Laura Brewster Mysteries (Opportunities for Learning)   **RL** 2-3 **IL** 6-12

Six mystery novels; includes workbooks.

Let's Discover Library (Raintree)   **RL** 2 **IL** K-6

Sixteen volume general reference set covers animals, outer space, earth, etc. Illustrations and photographs in text.

Meg Parker Mysteries (Opportunities for Learning)   **RL** 2 **IL** 4-6

Ten books in set. Teacher's guides contain activity sheets.

Movers and Shapers (Raintree)   **RL** 4-5 **IL** 4-8

Six books focus on achievement of American women. Biographies sketch struggles of 30 women in various fields.

Myth, Magic and Superstition (Raintree)   **RL** 5 **IL** 4-8

Eighteen titles with short stories about ghosts, haunted houses, and magic.

Pacemaker Classics Previews (Fearon)   **RL** 2 **IL** 5-12

Sound filmstrips and books of 16 classics include *Treasure Island, 20,000 Leagues Under the Sea.*

Pacemaker True Adventures (Fearon)   **RL** 2 **IL** 5-12

Eleven books about adventurers such as Charles Lindbergh and Mata Hari. Each book contains three stories.

Phonics Practice Readers (Modern Curriculum Press)   **RL** 1-2 **IL** 1-4

Sets A and B each contain 40 eight-page books with a story using words of one phonics element (such as short *a*). *Vowels and Values* series has two sets of ten similar books.

Profiles: A Collection of Short Biographies (Globe)   **RL** 3-4 **IL** 7-12

Book contains 24 two–three page biographies, including Boris Karloff, Jim Thorpe, Enrico Caruso. Skill exercises.

Quest, Adventure, Survival (Raintree)   **RL** 5 **IL** 4-12

25 rewritten classics of adventure. Each book has 48 pages.

Reach: The Reading Extravaganza of American Cycling and Hydroplane Show (Economy)   **RL** 3–5 **IL** 4–9

21 cassettes of show business include audition, rehearsal, shows, and grand finale. Consumable *Show Magazine* with exercises and 12 supplementary readers.

Secret Stories of the Sensational Super Heroes (Children's Press)   **RL** 4 **IL** 3–adult

Comic-book format presents *Captain America, Fantastic Four, Spiderman,* and *Incredible Hulk* in separate books. Comprehension questions included.

Stories of Surprise and Wonder; Beyond Time and Space; Tales of Mystery and the Unknown (Globe)   **RL** 3–6 **IL** 4–12

Three books each contain several adapted stories. Study aids included.

Stories That are Not Boring (Opportunities for Learning)   **RL** 4–7 **IL** 6–adult

Book with stories, each containing a motivational vignette. Comprehension and study aids.

Stories of the Unusual (Opportunities for Learning)   **RL** 2–4 **IL** 4–7

Six units explore *The Bermuda Triangle, Close Encounters,* etc. Audio cassettes introduce story up to a "cliff hanger."

Sundown Books (New Readers Press)   **RL** 2–3 **IL** 9–adult

14 books and a study pack foster comprehension.

Tales with a Twist (New Readers Press)   **RL** 4 **IL** 9–adult

Book contains stories of adventure and intrigue. Study guide. Program available on audiocassette.

Thunder the Dinosaur (Cypress)   **RL** 1.5–2 **IL** 1–4

20 short paperbacks about a fantasy dinosaur. Based on children's language patterns. Sound filmstrips, coloring book, build-a-dinosaur set available.

Tom and Ricky Mysteries (Opportunities for Learning)   **RL** 1 **IL** 4–9

Thirty books have an adult look.

Turning Point: A Collection of Short Biographies (Globe)   **RL** 3 **IL** 7–adult

Book with short biographies of famous people at "turning points" in their careers. Skills exercises included.

Which Way Books (Pocket Books)   **RL** 3–5 **IL** 3–9

Several liberally illustrated paperbacks allow readers to choose how the story will develop.

Wildlife Series (Crestwood House)   **RL** 5–6 **IL** 3 and up

Over 50 48-page books, each devoted to one animal. Maps and illustrations.

The World of Sports Series; The Challenge of Sports (Globe)   **RL** 4–5 **IL** 4–12

Two books of *The World of Sports* contain short biographies of famous athletes. *Challenge of Sports* details different sports. Skills exercises provided.

III.B.   Predictable Books

City Kids (Cypress; Rigby)   RL 2-3   IL 3-6

Short comic paperbacks include titles such as *And the Teacher Got Mad*. No text versions, without words, encourage writing.

Predictable Books (Scholastic)   RL 1-2   IL 1-3

15 books in each of two sets. Set one: grades K-1. Set two: Grades 1-2.

Ready to Read (Richard C. Owens)   RL K-2   IL K-4

From New Zealand come 45 excellent paperback books each with a different format and appealing natural language. Depending on level, books can be used for shared reading, guided reading, or independent reading. Many big books available.

The Story Box (Wright Group)   RL K-3   IL K-4

Short, enchanting predictable books from New Zealand include 117 titles. Seven color-coded levels. Big books and cassettes available. Different levels suitable for reading to children, assisted reading, or independent reading.

Sunshine Books (Wright Group)   RL K-1   IL K-2

Short, small predictable books include very easy reading. Contains levels A–I with eight titles at each level.

Theme Packs (Rigby)   RL K-2   IL K-4

Each set includes one big book and several matching small ones. Packs include fiction and nonfiction. Samples of themes are space, technology, dinosaurs, family.

Willie MacGurkle and Friends; Finnigin and Friends
(Curriculum Associates)   RL 1-3; 4-6   IL 1-3; 4-6

Ten student books in each set develop language skills with rhymes, rhythm, and humorous characters.

IV.   LANGUAGE DEVELOPMENT AND ENRICHMENT

Building Real Life English Skills (Opportunities for Learning)   RL 5

Text for remedial and ESL students incorporates survival skills normally given in language arts curriculum.

Peabody Language Development Kits

(American Guidance Services)   Ages 3-5; 5-6; 6-7; 7-8

Stimulates cognitive skills and oral language. Multisensory approach. Cards, puppets, mascots used.

Wordless Books (Sundance)   RL K-2   IL K-2

Five titles, each with seven titles. Activity sheets. Titles include: *Moonlight, Pancakes for Breakfast*.

V. MATERIAL FOR FOCUSED INSTRUCTION

These provide instruction in six areas:

A. Multi-Area development   D. Vocabulary
B. Word recognition   E. Study strategies/Content areas
C. Comprehension   F. Rate

V.A. Multi-Area Development

Activity Concept English (ACE) (Scott Foresman)   RL 5 IL 7–12

Two books at each of four levels integrate reading, writing, listening, speaking for remedial students. Each contains 12 stories and one novel.

LARC: Language Arts Resource Center (Arista)   RL 2 IL 2–6

Modules on word skills and comprehension include stories, filmstrips, records, games, workbooks, puzzles.

Merrill Reading Skill Text Series (Merrill)   RL K–6

Ten consumable workbooks. Includes two-page stories with exercises. Includes audiovisual materials.

Skill by Skill Workbook (Modern Curriculum Press)   RL 2–6

Separate workbook series for comprehension, vocabulary, study skills. Each book covers four-six skills. Has puzzles, treasure maps.

Specific Skills Series (Barnell Loft)   RL 1–12

Separate skills booklets on each of 12 levels focus on one skill. Nine booklets at each level include *Getting the Main Idea, Drawing Conclusions.*

Supportive Reading Skills (Barnell Loft)   RL 2–9

Books on different levels each focus on one skill, including *Reading Schedules, Interpreting Idioms, Understanding Questions.*

V.B. Word Recognition

BEST: Building Essential Skills Together 8 (Bomar/Noble)   RL 1–3 IL 1–adult

Tutorial program includes 200 3″ by 5″ picture and letter cards, 80 instructional cards, cassette tape.

Brigance Prescriptive Word Analysis: Strategies and Practices
(Curriculum Associates)   RL 1–6

Two volumes of activities for teaching word analysis skills keyed to *Brigance Diagnostic Inventory*

Discovering Phonics We Use (Riverside)   RL 1–6

Eight workbooks with one-page lessons. No contextual reading.

Dolch Word Cards (DLM)   **RL** 1–3

Sets include *Dolch Picture Word Cards* (95 nouns, pictures on back), *Dolch Words* (220 basic words), *Popper Words* (*Dolch Words* divided into two sets), and *Dolch Sight Phrase Cards.*

MCP Phonics Program (Modern Curriculum Press)   **RL** 1–6

Series of workbooks presents phonics skills.

Merrill Phonics Skilltext Series (Merrill)   **RL** 1–4   **IL** K–4

Five leveled workbooks include phonics, structural analysis, vocabulary, and dictionary exercises.

Pacemaker Core Vocabularies 1 and 2 (Fearon)   **RL** 3–4   **IL** 7–9

Lists of words recognized by junior high students reading at third (Core 1) and fourth (Core 2) grade levels.

Vocabulary Fluency (Curriculum Associates)   **RL** 1–?   **IL** 4–6; 7–9

Two books provide practice matching oral to written language to foster fluency. Exercises move from words to sentences.

V.C.   Comprehension

Basic Reading Units Multi-Skills Kits (Continental Press)   **RL** 2–4.9   **IL** 6–12

Each of two kits contains 12 titles reinforcing one skill (e.g., main idea). High interest, short passages with questions.

Big Leagues Comprehension Kits (Educational Insights)   **RL** 2–4   **IL** 4–8

Four kits each with 40 true sports stories presented on cards. Vocabulary and comprehension questions.

Building Basic Reading Skills (Continental Press)   **RL** 1–6   **IL** 7–12

Three workbooks (main ideas, inferences, sequencing) provide high interest materials. Short passages with questions.

Building Language Power with Cloze (Modern Curriculum Press)   **RL** 2–6   **IL** 2–9

Five worktexts with one page stories designed as cloze exercises, with deleted words and phrases. Available as skill station.

Catching On (Open Court)   **RL** 1–6

Six leveled soft-cover books use humor and absurdity to motivate thoughtful reading and reasoning.

Clues for Better Reading (Curriculum Associates)   **RL** 1–6.2   **IL** 1–9

Skill book A and kits I, II, and III develop comprehension through clues in exciting stories.

Comprehension Skills (Jamestown)   **RL** 4–8; 6–12   **IL** 6–12; 9–

Advanced and middle levels each contain 10 books on one skill (judgments, understanding character). Cassettes available.

Corrective Reading (SRA)   **RL** PP–adult   **IL** 4–adult

Employs direct teaching to improve cognitive skills. Level A–*Thinking Basics;* Level B–*Comprehension Skills;* Level C–*Concept Applications.* One book at each level.

Guidebook to Better Reading Series (Bowmar/Noble)   **RL** 2–6   **IL** 5–adult

Attractively packaged stories of adventure, intrigue, etc. Supplementary readers and audio-cassette available.

Life Skills Reading (Price, Stern, Sloan)   **RL** 3–5   **IL** 5–8

14 paperback reproducible books emphasize menus, telephone use. 12 colored posters for each book.

New Reading-Thinking Skills (Continental Press)   **RL** 3–4   **IL** 6–12

Six leveled workbooks for comprehension and critical thinking.

Open-Ended Plays; Open-Ended Stories (Globe)   **RL** 3–5   **IL** 7–12

Two books of 20 short, open-ended plays and stories let students work out real-life problems. Topics include lifestyles, values, drugs, cheating, prejudice, and loneliness.

Reading Comprehension (Educational Insights)   **RL** 3–4   **IL** 4–8

Eight kits, each with 25 selections (three copies of each) on cards. Questions follow reading. Topics are cars, fads, etc.

Reading Comprehension Series (Steck-Vaughn)   **RL** 1–6   **IL** 1–9

Seven workbooks of stories containing controlled vocabulary followed by varied exercises. Review lessons.

Reading for Understanding (SRA)   **RL** 3–adult

Three kits with 300 activity cards. Cards have ten short passages with last word missing. Develops inference skills.

The Reading Power Tapes Program (Globe)   **RL** 4–5   **IL** 6–12

12 audio cassettes present mysteries, adventures, biographies. Skills developed in story breaks. Workbooks.

Reading, Thinking and Reasoning Skills Program, Revised (Steck-Vaughn)   **RL** 1–8

14 leveled worktexts with one page exercises for higher-order comprehension: abstract judging, developing conclusions, etc.

Signal/Tactics (Scott Foresman)   **RL** 5–10   **IL** 7–12

Signal contains literature units and is correlated with *Tactics*, covering nine skill units.

Single Skills (Jamestown)   **RL** 3–12   **IL** 6–12

One book for each of six comprehension skills on each of ten grade levels. Passages followed by questions.

Skills/Drills (Jamestown)   **RL** 4–6   **IL** 6–12

Three sets of worksheets provide comprehension practice.

Thinking About Reading (Modern Curriculum Press)   **RL** 2–6   **IL** 2–10

Two sets of innovative worktexts each contain ten stories divided into segments. Students read using DRTA (see Chapter 10). Story mapping and vocabulary self-selection included. Levels B, C, D, E, F available for reading levels 2–6.

Thinklab Series (SRA)   **Grades 2–adult**

Contains *Junior Thinklab* (Grades 2–4); *Thinklab* (Grades 3–adult) and *Thinklab II* (Grades 5–adult). Challenging set of activity cards teach reasoning, classifying, logic, etc.

TR Reading Comprehension Series (DLM)   **RL 1–4 IL 2–7**

Eight book series teaches comprehension. Each book has 42 lessons of high-interest, nonfiction content.

The World of Reading (Educational Insights)   **RL 3–6 IL 5–12**

Five kits each contain 48 colorful cards with 16 passages on biographies, mysteries, myths, etc. Comprehension follow-up.

V.D.   Meaning Vocabulary

Base: Basic Approaches to the Structure of English (Bowmar/Noble)   **RL 4–adult**

17 audiocassettes with music and sound effects highlight the teaching of base words and affixes.

Houghton Mifflin Vocabulary for Achievement (Houghton Mifflin)   **RL 6–12**

Worktexts present lessons centered around theme. Passage provided in each lesson. Teaches context, dictionary, word analysis, and test taking.

In Other Words (Scott Foresman)   **RL 3–4; 5–10**

Two levels of thesaurus, *Beginning Thesaurus* and *Junior Thesaurus*, present thousands of synonyms for word study.

Lessons in Vocabulary Development (Curriculum Associates)   **RL 4–6**

Word clusters used. 12 to 14 words of similar and opposite meaning introduced in each lesson.

Picto-Cabulary (Barnell Loft)   **RL 5–9**

Two exercise books use theme and pictures to present vocabulary words.

Reading Around Words (Instructional/Communications Technology)   **RL 4–12**

Workbook series introduces words in text and students infer meanings. Cassettes and Apple computer program available.

Reading Vocabulary Laboratories (Arista Publishing)   **RL 2–6**

Five kits with cards each teach the 1,000 most used words in basals using context clues in stories. Each lab contains three reading levels: one year below; on level; one year above.

Survival Vocabulary Set (Opportunities for Learning)   **RL 2**

Ten workbooks present survival words for consumer skills (banking, job application, etc.) Each book teaches 30 words.

V.E.   Study Strategies/Content Areas

Be a Better Reader (Prentice Hall)   **RL 4–12**

Eight leveled worktexts apply comprehension and studying to content areas of literature, social studies, science, etc.

Brigance Prescriptive Study Skills (Curriculum Associates)   **RL** 1–7 **IL** 3–adult

Single volume provides objectives, rationale, skill sequence, etc. for each skill area. Teaches reference and map skills.

Bright Ideas; First Ideas (Modern Curriculum Press)   **RL** K–2 **IL** K–4

Short, colorful paperbacks give background information on *Knights and Castles, Out of an Egg*, etc.

Content Reading Program (Opportunities for Learning)   **RL** 2 **IL** 4–12

Five workbooks, each concentrating on a content area: History, literature, science, geography, and government.

Learning to Study (Jamestown)   **RL** 3–8

Six graded workbooks teach organization, location, interpretation, retention, test taking, studying.

Newslab (Science Research Associates)   **RL** 4–8

Kit teaches how to read newspaper. In addition, teaches content area skill development and study skills.

Reading in the Content Areas (Modern Curriculum Press)   **RL** 3–6

Four graded worktexts teach using graphic aids, textbook aids, outlining, summarizing, etc.

Reading Skills for the Content Areas (Arista)   **RL** 4–5 **IL** 4–6

Kit with cards teaches reading strategies for science, math, social studies.

Reading the Content Fields (Jamestown)   **RL** 4–12

Each of five books covers science, math, practical arts, etc. Each book contains 25 passages. Audiocassettes available.

Usborne-Hayes Informational Books (Hayes)   **RL** 2–8 **IL** 2–12

Over 150 paperback titles deal with the world, history, science, etc. Motivating comic-book format in many books.

Young Explorers; World Explorers (National Geographic)   **RL** 3–8 **IL** 3–10

Two sets geared, respectively, to lower elementary and upper elementary/junior high, explore science topics with beautiful illustrations and text. Over 100 titles. Hardbound.

V.F.   Rate

Reading Accelerator (Alexander Simpson Associates)

Advanced instrument for increasing reading speed covers book page at a predetermined speed

VI.   MATERIALS FOR SEVERELY DISABLED READERS

These materials develop reading abilities in the most disabled students.

VI.A.   Development of Prerequisite Abilities

VI.A1   VISUAL PERCEPTUAL-VISUAL MOTOR MATERIALS

Fitzhugh Plus (Allied Educational Press)

Programmed workbooks in matching, completing, analyzing shapes.

Frostig Program for the Development of Visual Perception (Modern Curriculum Press)

Written activities develop visual and auditory perception.

Pictures and Patterns (Modern Curriculum Press)

Exercises for body awareness, visual-motor coordination, figure-ground discrimination, etc.

VI.A2   AUDITORY PERCEPTUAL MATERIALS

Auditory Discrimination in Depth (DLM)

Multisensory program by Lindamood and Lindamood develops auditory skills including phonological awareness. Filmstrips and cassettes included.

Auditory Perception Training (DLM)

Two graded sets teach memory, motor skills, imagery, etc.

High Hat Early Reading Program (American Guidance Service)

Originally *Goldman-Lynch Sounds and Symbols Development Kit.* Teaches (1) sounds to symbols, and (2) symbols to letters associations. Puppets, cassettes, etc.

Semel Auditory Processing Program (Modern Curriculum Press)

Assesses and remediates basic language disorders.

Sound-Order-Sense (Modern Curriculum Press)

Develops auditory perception for disabled older students.

VI.B. Special Remedial Approaches

The Basic Reading Series (Science Research Associates)   **RL** PP–2.2

Workbook and six books of basal series uses phonics approach in structured format. Uses stories, poems, plays.

Breaking the Code (Open Court)   **RL** 1–4   **IL** 4–8

Uses synthetic, highly structured phonics approach. Alphabet cards teach letter sounds rather than names.

Corrective Reading: Decoding ABC (Science Research Associates)   **RL** PP–6   **IL** 4–adult

Daily 35–45 lessons with teacher scripts. Three graded levels move from word attack basics (A), to decoding (B), to skill applications (C).

Glass Analysis for Decoding Only (Easier to Learn) **RL** 1–4 **IL** 2–6

Cards teaching decoding using word groups containing the same letter clusters. Supplementary small reading books.

Language Arts Phonics (Scholastic) **RL** 1–3

Three graded workbooks present chants and poems and break them into word and sound components. Cloze, sentence making, and reading included.

Merrill Linguistic Reading Program (Merrill) **RL** K–3

Highly structured basal program uses linguistic phonics approach to teach reading.

Multisensory Approach to Language Arts for Specific Language Disability Children (Educators Publishing Service) **RL** 1–3

Gillingham-Stillman program is structured phonics approach. Written exercises, manipulatives, "jewel box" of words.

Palo Alto Reading Program (Harcourt Brace) **RL** 1–3

Supplementary program of 21 soft-cover books teaches phonics using exercises and reading selections.

Phonics Remedial Reading Lessons (Academic Therapy)

Book of sequential phonics drills by Kirk, Kirk, Minskoff.

Programmed Reading (McGraw-Hill) **RL** 1–3 **IL** 1–6

Series of programmed workbooks lets students check answers. Uses phonics approach. Has 22 independent storybooks.

Reading Mastery: Distar Program I,II (Science Research Associates) **RL** 1–3 **IL** 1–4

Structured, synthetic basal phonics program with teacher script uses special alphabet with regular sound/symbol relationships. Two levels.

Recipe for Reading (Educators Publishing Service)

Core book presents many synthetic phonics exercises. Supplementary books provide practice in context.

Speech to Print Phonics (Harcourt Brace) **RL** 1–3 **IL** 1–6

Kit containing cards teaches phonics with teacher-led lessons.

VII. REAL-LIFE MATERIALS/FUNCTIONAL READING

These materials help students to prepare for life and work.

Basic Life Skills (Continental Press) **RL** 4–5 **IL** 9–adult

Boxed kits with file folders foster home and business life skills of recipes, appliances, warranties, leases, etc.

Follett Coping Skills Series (Cambridge) **RL** 3–6 **IL** 9–adult

Sixteen workbooks organized around Adult Performance Objectives. Titles include *Finding Work, Child Care*.

Follett Success Skills Series (Cambridge)   **RL** 3–5   **IL** 10–adult

Eighteen workbooks in three series: personal competence (money, friends), communications (television), career guidance.

Job Tips: The World of Work (Fearon)   **RL** 2–7   **IL** 7–12

A photo illustrated booklet for each of 112 entry-level jobs: food services, building trades, clerical work, etc.

Know-How Series (Cambridge)   **RL** 4–5   **IL** 9–adult

Eight competency-based workbooks. Develops basic skills using daily situations. Includes insurance, taxes, jobs.

The Lifeschool Program (Fearon)   **RL** 1–4   **IL** 9–12

Four binders contain 40 learning modules in six areas, including consumer economies, occupations, health.

News for You (New Reader's Press)   **RL** 4–6   **IL** adult

Four to six page newspaper with adult format is published every Wednesday.

Pacemaker Career Readers (Fearon)   **RL** 2   **IL** 7–12

Ten career exploration books including nurse's aide, machinist, retail sales, beauty salon work, security guard.

Pacemaker Vocational Readers (Fearon)   **RL** 2   **IL** 7–12

Ten career-oriented stories show entry-level jobs (gardener, waitress, cook) and information on the work world.

People Working Today (Opportunities for Learning)   **RL** 1.9   **IL** 9–12

Ten stories of entry level jobs (clerk, bellhop, gas station attendant) feature information on the work world.

Real Life Reading (Academic Therapy)   **RL** 4–6   **IL** 9–12

Six workbooks feature survival reading skills such as food, shopping, reading labels, prescriptions, traveling.

B

Appendix:
ADDRESSES
OF PUBLISHERS
AND RESOURCES

ABBOTT LABORATORIES, Abbott Park, North Chicago, IL 60064.

ACADEMIC THERAPY PUBLICATIONS (Div. of Educational Performance Associates), 20 Commercial Boulevard, Novato, CA 94947–6191.

ACORN PRODUCTS, 8717 Mockingbird Rd., Platteville, WI 54818.

ADVANCED IDEAS 1442A Walnut, Berkeley, CA 94701.

ALADDIN BOOKS (See Macmillan).

ALEXANDER SIMPSON ASSOCIATES, P.O. Box 377658, Chicago, IL 60637.

ALLIED EDUCATIONAL PRESS, P. O. Box 337, Niles, MI 49120.

ALLYN & BACON, INC. (See Prentice Hall).

AMERICAN ASSOCIATION ON MENTAL DEFICIENCY, 1719 Kalorama Road, Washington, DC 20009.

AMERICAN GUIDANCE SERVICE, Publishers' Bldg., P.O. Box 99, Circle Pines, MN 55014–1796

AMERICAN OPTICAL CO., Box 1, Southbridge, MA 01550.

AMERICAN ORTHOPSYCHIATRIC ASSOCIATION, 1775 Broadway, New York, NY 10019.

ARISTA PUBLISHING (Div. of Regents Publishing Co., Inc.), Two Park Avenue, New York, NY 10016.

ATHENEUM PUBLISHERS (Subs. of Scribner Book Cos, Inc.), 115 Fifth Avenue, New York, NY 10003.

BARNELL LOFT, LTD., 958 Church St., Baldwin, NY 11510.

BAUSCH AND LOMB OPTICAL CO., Rochester, NY 14602.

BOBBS-MERRILL CO., INC. (Div. of Macmillan Publishing Co.), 4300 W. 62 St., Indianapolis, IN 46206.

BOWMAR/NOBLE (Subs. The Economy Co.) 1200 N.W. 63rd St., P.O. Box 25308, Oklahoma City, OK 73125.

BRADBURY PRESS (See Macmillan).

WILLIAM C. BROWN CO., 2460 Kerper Blvd., Dubuque, IA 52001.

CALIFORNIA TESTING BUREAU (CTB) McGraw-Hill, Del Monte Research Park, Monterey, CA 93940.

CAMBRIDGE, The Adult Education Co., 888 Seventh Ave., New York, NY 10106.

CHECKERBOARD PRESS (See Macmillan).

CHILDREN'S PRESS (Div. of Regensteiner Publishing Enterprises, Inc.), 1224 W. Van Buren St., Chicago, IL 60607.

CLARIS CORPORATIION, 440 Clyde Ave., Mountain View, CA 94043.

COLLEGE BOARD, 45 Columbus Ave., New York, NY 10023.

COMMUNICATION RESEARCH ASSOCIATES, P.O. Box 11012, Salt Lake City, UT 84147.

COMP UNIQUE, 4615 Clausen Avenue, Western Springs, IL 60558.

CONTINENTAL PRESS, INC., 520 E. Bainbridge St., Elizabethtown, PA 17022.

COWARD-MCCANN, (Div. of The Putnam Young Readers Group), 51 Madison Ave., New York, NY 10010.

CRESTWOOD HOUSE, INC., Highway 66 So., Box 3427, Mankato, MN 56002-3427.

C.P.S., Box 83, Larchmont, NY 10538.

THOMAS Y. CROWELL (See Harper & Row).

CROWN PUBLISHERS, INC., 225 Park Ave. S., New York, NY 10003.

CURRICULUM ASSOCIATES, INC., 5 Esquire Rd., North Billerica, MA 01862-2589.

CUE SOFTSWAP, P.O. Box 271704, Concord, CA 94527-1704.

CYPRESS PUBLISHING GROUP, 1763 Gardena Ave., Glendale, CA 91204.

D.C. HEATH, 125 Spring St., Lexington, MA 02173.

DIAL BOOKS FOR YOUNG READERS (Div. of E.P. Dutton), 2 Park Ave., New York, NY 10016.

DLM/TEACHING RESOURCES, One DLM Park, Allen, TX 75002.

DRIER EDUCATIONAL SYSTEMS (see Jamestown).

E.M. COLEMAN ENTERPRISES, P.O. Box T, Crugers, NY 10521.

E. P. DUTTON & CO., INC. (Div. of New American Library), 2 Park Ave., New York, NY 10016.

EASIER TO LEARN MATERIALS, Box 329, Garden City, NY 11530.

THE ECONOMY COMPANY, 1200 NW 63rd St., P.O. Box 25308, Oklahoma City, OK 73125.

EDUCATIONAL CHALLENGES (see McGraw-Hill Book Company).

EDUCATIONAL DEVELOPMENTAL LABORATORIES, INC. (Div. of McGraw-Hill Book Company), 1221 Avenue of the Americas, New York, NY 10020.

EDUCATIONAL INSIGHTS, 19560 S. Rancho Way, Dominguez Hills, CA 90220.

EDUCATIONAL PERFORMANCE ASSOCIATES, INC., 600 Broad Ave., Ridgefield, NJ 07657.

EDUCATIONAL TEACHING AIDS, 199 Carpenter Ave., Wheeling, IL 60090.

EDUCATORS PUBLISHING SERVICE, 75 Moulton St., Cambridge, MA 02238-9101.

ENRICH EDUCATION (Div. of Price, Stern, Sloan Publishers), 410 N. Cienega Blvd., Los Angeles, CA 90048-1996.

ESSAY PRESS, P. O. Box 2323, La Jolla, CA 92037.

FEARON EDUCATION (Div. of David S. Lake Publishers), 19 Davis Drive, Belmont, CA 94002.

FIELDING PUBLICATIONS (See William Morrow).

FIRST BYTE, 2845 University Drive, Long Beach, CA 90806.

FOUR WINDS PRESS (See Macmillan).

FIELD PUBLICATIONS, 245 Long Hill Road, Middletown, CN 06457.

GESSLER EDUCATIONAL SOFTWARE, 900 Broadway, New York, NY 10003.

GINN, Secondary Materials (See Prentice Hall).

GLOBE BOOK CO., INC. (Subs. of Simon & Schuster, Inc.), 50 W. 23rd St. New York, NY 10010.

GOLDEN BOOKS (See Western Publishing Co., Inc.).

GOLDENCRAFT (See Childrens Press).

GORSUCH SCARISBRICK PUBLISHERS, 8233 Via Paseo del Norte, Suite E-400, Scottsdale, AZ. 85258.

GREENWILLOW BOOKS (See William Morrow).

GROSSET & DUNLAP (See Putnam Young Readers Group).

GRUNE & STRATTON, INC. (Subs. of Harcourt Brace Jovanovich, Inc.), 6277 Sea Harbor Drive, Orlando, FL 32887.

HARCOURT BRACE JOVANOVICH, INC., 1250 Sixth Ave., San Diego, CA 92101.

HARPER JUNIOR BOOKS (See Harper & Row).

HARPER & ROW, PUBLISHERS, INC., 10 E. 53rd St., New York, NY 10022.

HARTLEY COURSEWARE, INC., P.O. Box 431, Dimondale, MI 48821.

HARVARD UNIVERSITY PRESS, 79 Garden St., Cambridge, MA 02138.

HAYES BOOKS, 10302 E. 55th Place, Tulsa, OK 74146-6508.

HEARST BOOKS (See William Morrow).

HENRY HOLT AND COMPANY, 521 Fifth Ave., New York, NY 10175.

HISKEY-NEBRASKA CO., 5640 Baldwin, Lincoln, NE 68507.

HOLT, RINEHART AND WINSTON (Div. of CBS Inc. Educational and Professional Publishing Co.), 383 Madison Ave., New York, NY 10017.

HOUGHTON MIFFLIN COMPANY, One Beacon St., Boston, MA 02108.

IBM, 101 Paragon Dr., Montvale, NJ 07645.

INSTRUCTIONAL/COMMUNICATIONS TECHNOLOGY, INC., 10 Stepar Pl., Huntington Station, NY 11746.

INSTITUTE FOR PERSONALITY AND ABILITY TESTING, P.O. Box 188, Champaign, IL 61820-0188.

JAMESTOWN PUBLISHERS, Box 9168, Providence, RI 02904.

JASTAK ASSOCIATES, 1526 Gilpin Ave., Wilmington, DE 19806.

JULIAN MESSNER (See Simon & Schuster).

KENDALL/HUNT PUBLISHING CO. (Subs. of William C. Brown Co.), 2460 Kerper Blvd., Dubuque, IA 52001.

KEYSTONE VIEW CO., 2212 E. 12th St., Davenport, IA 52803.

KLAMATH PIONEER PUBLISHING CO., 132 S. Seventh St., Klamath Falls, OR 97601.

KNOPF, 201 E. 50th St., New York, NY 10022.

LAUBACH LITERACY INTERNATIONAL, 1320 Jamesville Ave., Box 131, Syracuse, NY 13210.

LEARNING COMPANY, 545 Middlefield Rd., Ste. 170, Menlo Park, CA 94025.

LEARNING CONCEPTS., INC., 8517 Production Ave., San Diego, CA 92121.

LERNER PUBLICATIONS, 241 First Ave. N., Minneapolis, MN 55401.

J. P. LIPPINCOTT COMPANY (See Harper & Row).

LITTLE SIMON (See Simon & Schuster).

LOTHROP, LEE AND SHEPARD CO. INC., 105 Madison Ave., New York, NY 10016.

MACMILLAN PUBLISHING CO. INC., 866 Third Ave., New York, NY 10022.

MAICO HEARING INSTRUCTIONS, 7375 Bush Lake Rd., Minneapolis, MN 55435.

MCGRAW-HILL BOOK CO., School Division, 1200 NW 63rd St., P.O. Box 25308, Oklahoma City, OK 73125.

MECC, 3490 Lexington Ave. N., St. Paul, MN 55126.

MERRILL PUBLISHING CO. (Div. of Bell & Howell Co.), P.O. Box 508, 1300 Alum Creek Dr., Columbus, OH 43216–0508.

MIAMI UNIVERSITY ALUMNI ASSOCIATION, Murstein Alumni Center, Miami University, Oxford, OH 45056.

MICRO POWER & LIGHT CO., 12820 Hillcrest Road, Suite 224, Dallas, TX 75230.

MINDSCAPE, INC., 3444 Dundee Rd., Northbrook, IL 60062.

MODERN CURRICULUM PRESS (Subs. of Simon & Schuster), 13900 Prospect Rd., Cleveland, OH 44136.

WILLIAM MORROW AND CO., 105 Madison Ave., New York, NY 10016.

NATIONAL GEOGRAPHIC SOCIETY, 17th and M Streets, Washington, D.C. 20036.

C.H. NEVINS PRINTING, 311 Bryn Mawr Island Bayshore Gardens, Brandenton, FL 33507.

NEW DIMENSIONS OF EDUCATION (Div. of Arista Corp.), 2 Park Ave., New York, NY 10016.

NEW READERS PRESS (Div. of Laubach Literacy International), 1320 Jamesville Ave., Box 131, Syracuse, NY 13210.

NORTHWESTERN UNIVERSITY PRESS, Box 1093X, 1735 Benson Ave., Evanston, IL 60201.

OPEN COURT PUBLISHING CO. (Div. of Carus Corp.), Box 599, Peru, IL 61354.

OPPORTUNITIES FOR LEARNING, INC., 20417 Nordhoff St., Dept. EAS, Chatsworth, CA 91311.

RICHARD C. OWENS PUBLISHERS, INC., 135 Katonah Ave., Katonah, NY 10535.

OXFORD PRESS, 200 Madison Ave., New York, NY 10016.

PACER BOOKS (See Putnam Young Readers Group).

PERSONAL PRESS, 1515 Riebl Rd., Santa Rosa, CA 95404.

PHILOMEL BOOKS (Div. of Putnam Young Readers Group), 51 Madison Ave., New York, NY 10010.

PLATT & MUNK, Cricket Books, Putnam Young Readers Group, 51 Madison Ave., New York, NY 10010.

PRENTICE HALL, Allyn & Bacon, Prentice-Hall Bldg., Englewood Cliffs, NJ 07632.

PRENTICE-HALL BOOKS FOR YOUNG READERS (See Simon & Schuster).

PRICE/STERN/SLOAN PUBLISHERS, INC., 410 North La Cienega Blvd., Los Angeles, CA 90048.

PRO-ED, 5341 Industrial Oaks Blvd., Austin, TX 78735.

PSYCHOLOGICAL CORP. (See Harcourt Brace Jovanovich).

PSYCHOTECHNICS, INC., 1900 Pickwick Ave., Glenview, IL 60025.

PTI-KOALA, 296 Mount Hermon Rd., Scotts Valley, CA 95066.

PUFFIN BOOKS, Viking Penguin Children's Books, 40 W. 23rd St., New York, NY 10010.

THE PUTNAM YOUNG READERS GROUP, 51 Madison Ave., New York, NY 10010.

G.P. PUTNAM'S SONS (See Putnam Young Readers Group).

RAINTREE PUBLISHERS, INC., 310 W. Wisconsin Ave., Milwaukee, WI 53203.

RAND MCNALLY & COMPANY (See Riverside Publishing Co.).

RANDOM HOUSE, INC., 201 E. 50th St., New York, NY 10022.

R.C. SYSTEMS, INC., 121 West Winesap Rd., Bothell, WA 98012.

READER'S DIGEST SERVICES, Educational Division (Div. of Random House), 400 Hahn Road, Westminster, MD 21157.

REYNAL & CO. (See William Morrow).

RIGBY EDUCATION, 454 S. Virginia St., Crystal Lake, IL 60014.

THE RIVERSIDE PUBLISHING CO. (Subs. of Houghton Mifflin Co.), 8420 W. Bryn Mawr Ave., Suite 1000, Chicago, IL 60631.

SCHOLASTIC INC., P.O. Box 7501, 2931 East McCarty St., Jefferson City, Mo 65102.

SCHOLASTIC SOFTWARE, P.O. Box 7502, 2931 E. McCarty St., Jefferson City, MO 65102.

SCHOLASTIC TESTING SERVICE, 480 Meyer Road, Bensenville, IL 60106.

SCIENCE RESEARCH ASSOCIATES, 155 North Wacker Drive, Chicago IL 60606–1780.

SCOTT, FORESMAN AND COMPANY (Subs. of SFM Cos Inc.), 1900 E. Lake Ave., Glenview, IL 60025.

SCRIBNER EDUCATIONAL PUBLISHERS, Front and Brown Streets, Riverside, NJ 08075.

SERENDIPITY BOOKS (See Price/Stern/Sloan).

SIERRA ON-LINE, Sierra On-Line Bldg., Coursegold, CA 93614.

SILVER BURDETT, Secondary Materials (See Prentice Hall).

SIMON & SCHUSTER JUVENILE PUBLISHING DIVISION, 1230 Avenue of the Americas, New York, NY 10020.

SLOSSON EDUCATIONAL PUBLICATIONS, 140 Pine St., P.O. Box 280, East Aurora, NY 14052.

SPINNAKER, 1 Kendall Square, Cambridge, MA 02139.

SPRINGBOARD SOFTWARE, INC., 7808 Creekridge Circle, Minneapolis, MN 55435.

SRA (See Science Research Associates).

STECK-VAUGHN CO. (Div. of National Education Corp.), P.O. Box 26015, Austin, TX 78768.

C. H. STOELTING CO., 1350 South Kostner Ave., Chicago, IL 60623.

STREET ELECTRONICS, 1140 Mark Ave., Carpenteria, CA 93013.

SUNBURST COMMUNICATIONS, 39 Washington St., Pleasantville, NY 10570.

SUNDANCE, P.O. Box 1326, Littleton, MA 01460.

TEACHERS COLLEGE PRESS, 1234 Amsterdam Ave., New York, NY 10027.

TEACHER SUPPORT SOFTWARE, P.O. Box 7130, Gainesville, FL 32605–7130.

TROPHY (See Harper & Row).

UNIVERSITY OF ILLINOIS PRESS, 54 E. Gregory Dr., P.O. Box 5081, Sta. A, Champaign, IL 61820.

GEORGE WAHR PUBLISHING CO., 304 1/2 S. State Street, Ann Arbor, MI 48104.

WANDERER BOOKS (Div. of Simon & Schuster, Inc.), 1230 Avenue of the Americas, New York, NY 10020.

WEEKLY READER Secondary Periodicals (Div. of Field Publications), 4343 Equity Drive, P.O. Box 16618, Columbus, OH 43216.

WESTERN PSYCHOLOGICAL SERVICES (Div. of Manson Western Corp.), 12031 Wilshire Blvd., Los Angeles, CA 90025.

WESTERN PUBLISHING CO., INC., 850 Third Ave., New York., NY 10022.

WESTWOOD PRESS, 251 Park Ave. S., 14th Floor, New York, NY 10010.

WINDMILL BOOKS, INC. (Div. of Intext), 1230 Avenue of the Americas, New York, NY 10020.

THE WRIGHT GROUP, 10949 Technology Place, San Diego, CA 92127.

XEROX EDUCATION PUBLICATIONS, 245 Long Hill Road, Middletown, CN 06457.

ZANER-BLOSER, P.O. BOX 16764, Columbus, OH 43216–6764.

SAMPLE DIAGNOSTIC READING REPORT

This report is intended to serve as a sample for diagnosticians preparing intensive diagnostic examinations. Space is given at several points in the report to fill in relevant information. In addition, continuous text should be filled in at many points. Diagnosticians should realize that no standardized report form will completely suit the very individual needs of a remedial student and that this form must be adapted to the needs of every case. In addition, certain portions may be deleted, since the report covers a wider range of abilities than would be presented by any individual student. Portions may, of course, also be added. While this report attempts to take a broad view of reading diagnosis, it will probably not be suitable for every theoretical framework of the reading process. The report is intended only as a model that may be adapted freely, in whole or in part.*

I. DIAGNOSTIC READING REPORT

Name of student   Date of report
Birthdate of student   Diagnostician

*Notes on interpretation: Parentheses enclosing slashes indicate alternatives; that is, (we/they) indicates "we" *or* "they."

Sex of student   Name of school/institution
Present age   Address of school/institution
School (or setting) and grade   Phone of school/institution
Parents' names   Dates of diagnosis
Home address
Home phone

This is a diagnostic reading report of (student), who is currently _____ years of age. (Student) was referred to the reading clinic by _____. The reason for referral was _____.

II. ASSESSMENT INSTRUMENTS USED

Name of Test   *Level*   *Form*   *Score/Range*   *Administered by*

III. CURRENT EXPECTED READING LEVEL*

III.A. Discrepancy Criteria

The level at which a student might be expected to read is important in determining whether or not that student has a reading disability. To determine (student's) current reading expectancy, the (test of intelligence) was administered. The score indicated that (student's) intellectual potential is currently in the (below-average/average/above-average) range.

It should be remembered that intellectual potential is influenced by many factors and is changeable under certain conditions. Previous estimates of potential level by (previous referrals) (agreed/did not agree) with the estimates of the current diagnosis.

Using a reading expectancy formula, it was estimated that (student) currently has the potential to read at the _____ grade level. Since (student's) reading achievement level† is at the _____ grade level, there is a discrepancy between current achievement and current potential of _____. At (student's) grade level, this indicates (student) (does/does not) have a reading disability.

III.B. Practical Criteria

The student's current instructional and life situation (pragmatic considerations) are important in determining if there is a reading disability. At present, (student) functions (considerably below/somewhat below/about as well as) the other students in

---

*Both discrepancy criteria and practical criteria are given in this section. Diagnosticians may choose one or use both. Discrepancy criteria are given first.

†This score is usually the *total* score on the standardized survey test that was given to the student.

(his/her) instructional situation. In addition, (student) (shows/does not show) a consistent pattern of reading failure.

In summary, (student's) reading disability can be classified as (mild/moderate/severe/not apparent).

IV. PRESENT READING ACHIEVEMENT LEVEL

To determine (student's) current reading level, the (survey test) was given. Currently (student's) achievement level is

at the _____ grade level. (This means that (student) reads about as well as the average student at the _____ grade level who took this test,

at the _____ percentile when compared with others of (his/her) grade. This means that about _____ % of the other students perform less well than (student).

In addition, the results of the (informal reading inventory/oral reading inventory) show that (student) is reading at the _____ grade level.

Classroom observations and reports of (student), (his/her) teachers, and parents show that (student) is working at the _____ grade level in (his/her) class.

Informally administered diagnostic teaching tasks showed that (student) is working at the _____ grade level and has difficulty with _____.
(DESCRIBE RANGE OF READING ABILITIES, IF APPROPRIATE.)

The results of these and other tests and observations reveal that the area(s) of (word recognition/comprehension/word meaning/study strategies/rate of reading) are currently most in need of remediation.

V. ANALYSIS OF READING STRENGTHS AND WEAKNESSES

Several diagnostic tests and procedures revealed patterns of reading strengths and weaknesses in (student's) performance.

V.A. Informally Observed Reading Abilities

As mentioned previously, an (informal reading inventory/oral reading inventory) was given. This test permits close observation of many facets of the student's reading.

Results are given as an independent level (where the student can read without assistance), an instructional level (where the student can read with assistance), and a frustration level (where the student can no longer read). These levels were determined from (oral reading/both oral and silent reading).

READING LEVEL   GRADE

Independent   _____
Instructional   _____
Frustration   _____

(Student) does relatively well in passages dealing with the subject matter of _____. He/she appears to have less background and interest for dealing with passages dealing with _____.

Some of the more difficult passages were read orally to (student). (His/her) oral comprehension indicated that the listening level (does not exceed the reading level/exceeds the reading level by _____ years).

(ADDITIONAL OBSERVATIONS OF (1) ORAL VERSUS SILENT READING, (2) PERFORMANCE ON WORD RECOGNITION PLACEMENT TEST, (3) ORAL READING PERFORMANCE VERSUS COMPREHENSION AND (4) THE INFLUENCE OF INTEREST AND BACKGROUND IN READING PERFORMANCE MAY BE ADDED HERE.)

(Student's) comprehension patterns on this test revealed that (summarize strengths, weaknesses).

The strategies a student uses during the oral reading of passages reveals many things about reading. (Student's) strategies revealed that _____.

(HERE, THE STUDENT'S PATTERNS OF MISCUES, SUCH AS USE OF PHONICS CLUES, CONTEXT, AND SO ON CAN BE NOTED.* ACTUAL EXAMPLES OF MISCUES ARE HELPFUL. PATTERNS OF REPETITIONS, AID, INSERTIONS, OMISSIONS, AND SUBSTITUTIONS MAY ALSO BE NOTED.)

(Student's) oral reading was (fluent/not fluent). (He/she) (recognized/did not recognize) words without hesitation and (did not depend/depended) upon teacher aid. In addition _____.

(SECTIONS V$_B$ V$_C$, V$_D$, V$_E$, and V$_F$ INCLUDED ONLY IF RELEVANT.)

V.B. Word Recognition

The ability to recognize words is basic to good reading. To investigate further competencies in word recognition, tests, observations, and informal teaching procedures were given in the areas of (sight word recognition/phonics/structural analysis/context clues).

(USE THE FOLLOWING INTRODUCTIONS, IF RELEVANT.)

Sight Words. The term sight words refers to the words a student can read instantly without hesitation. (KNOWLEDGE OF BASIC SIGHT WORDS MAY BE SEPARATED FROM MORE ADVANCED SIGHT WORDS.)

---

*If the reading miscue inventory framework is used, then terms may be described as graphophonic, syntactic, semantic, etc.

Phonics. This refers to the student's abilities to use the relationships between letters and sounds to "sound out" or decode words. (THIS SECTION CONTAINS STATEMENTS OF SKILLS AND STRATEGIES THAT THE STUDENT HAS OR HAS NOT MASTERED.)

Context Clues/Use of Language Clues in Reading. A student's knowledge of language structure and information about the world are powerful tools for recognizing words. (DESCRIBE STRATEGIES.)

Structural Analysis. Students may recognize words by their component parts, such as recognizing the word "walked" by the components "walk" and "ed." (DESCRIBE STRATEGIES.)

V.c. Comprehension

Comprehension is central to the ability to read; without comprehension, no reading actually takes place. (DESCRIBE COMPREHENSION STRATEGIES, STRENGTHS AND WEAKNESSES, ABILITY TO DEAL WITH LONGER MATERIAL, SILENT AND ORAL COMPREHENSION, INFORMAL OBSERVATIONS.)

V.d. Meaning Vocabulary

The number of words a student understands is an important factor in reading achievement. (DESCRIBE VOCABULARY TESTS, VOCABULARY LISTENING LEVEL ON READING TESTS, AND INFORMAL OBSERVATIONS.)

V.e. Study Strategies

It is important that students learn to apply their reading strategies to the school studying situation. (DESCRIBE TEACHER REPORTS, OBSERVATIONS, TESTS.)

V.f. Reading Rate

The ability to read at an appropriate speed is an important factor in upper-level reading skills. (DESCRIBE TEACHER REPORTS, OBSERVATIONS, TESTS.)

V.g. Class Performance

According to reports from (student's) school by the teacher/principal, at present he/she is functioning well/at an average level/with some difficulty/with great difficulty in class. (HERE, DETAIL STUDENT'S FUNCTIONING IN THE SCHOOL SITUATION.)

Special services being provided include (HERE, DETAIL SPECIAL PLACEMENTS, RESOURCE ROOM SERVICES, ETC.)

VI. ANALYSIS OF PREREQUISITE ABILITIES UNDERLYING READING

(SECTION *VI* USUALLY FOR VERY DISABLED, YOUNG, OR BEHAVIOR PROBLEMS ONLY.)

Students must possess certain underlying abilities before they can learn to read. These include (visual-motor and auditory skills/a knowledge of reading concepts/appropriate learning styles). These skills are often lacking in (severely disabled readers/younger students).

(INCLUDE *VI.A*, *VI.B*, AND *VI.C* ONLY IF RELEVANT.)

VI.A. Visual-Motor Skills and Auditory Skills

These skills form a basis for further learning. Tests, informal teaching tasks, and observations were done to assess these areas. (DESCRIBE. AN INFORMAL WORD LEARNING TASK MAY BE DESCRIBED HERE; SEE CHAPTER 13.)

VI.B. Knowledge of Reading Concepts

Students need knowledge of several fundamental concepts (letter, word) to be able to read effectively. Informal observations and tests revealed that (student) lacks some of these concepts. (DESCRIBE.)

VI.C. Appropriate Learning Style

Often, disabled readers are hampered by personal styles that distract them from learning. Informal observation of (student) revealed that there were difficulties with (impulsive behavior/behavior being too dependent on the surroundings or "field"/attending to the instructor and the instructional task). (DESCRIBE TESTS AND SPECIFIC INCIDENTS, IF POSSIBLE.)

VII. FACTORS ASSOCIATED WITH READING PERFORMANCE

Often, difficulty with the reading situation is associated with several factors such as the environment of the home and school, emotional factors, physical factors, intellectual factors, and language factors. Although these factors do not necessarily cause a reading disability, they may be important in treating the disability. The factors most important in (student's) case seem to be (home environment/school environment/emotional factors/intellectual factors/physical factors/language factors).

(INCLUDE *VII.A*, *VII.B*, *VII.C*, *VII.D*, *VII.E* AND *VIII.F* ONY IF RELEVANT.)

VII.A. **Home Environment**

(Student's) home environment (appears to be supportive/may be a factor in the reading disability). (DESCRIBE RELEVANT INFORMATION.)

VII.B. **School Environment**

Teacher reports, observations, and interviews indicate that (student) (functions well/has some difficulties) in the school environment. (DESCRIBE FACTORS INCLUDING COMFORT IN SCHOOL, ABILITY TO RELATE TO TEACHERS AND PEERS, ABILITY TO COMPLETE WORK.)

Some factors in (student's) school history may have affected reading performance. These include (frequent absences/frequent transfers/starting reading instruction at a young age/difficulties in previous classrooms). (DESCRIBE FURTHER.)

VII.C. **Emotional Factors, Interest, and Motivation**

Emotional and motivational factors (seem to be/do not seem to be) hampering reading performance.

(Student's) behavior during the testing situation was (appropriate and friendly/somewhat inappropriate). (DESCRIBE.) In addition, reported life adjustment with peers, parents, and other adults seems to be (normal/not entirely normal). (DESCRIBE.)

An informal instrument where (student) was asked to complete sentences such as "I like . . . " revealed _____.
(DESCRIBE FURTHER TESTS OF EMOTIONAL FACTORS, IF RELEVANT.)

Attitude toward reading and interest in reading are other ways in which emotions affect reading performance. (Student's) attitude toward reading is (positive/neutral/negative). (He/she) (shows/does not show) a desire to learn to read better. (OBSERVATIONS ABOUT VIEWING READING AS A MEANINGFUL PROCESS MAY BE INCLUDED HERE; SEE CHAPTER 5.)

(Student's) interests include _____.
These will help to plan an effective reading program.

VII.D. **Physical Factors**

(Student's) general health and health history is (good/fair/poor), indicating that health considerations (have not/may have) affected the present level of reading performance. Health problems that may have affected reading are _____. (GENERAL LEVEL OF MATURATION MAY ALSO BE DESCRIBED AS A PROBLEM.)

The (vision test) was administered as a screening test to determine whether visual factors could be interfering with reading. Results showed that (student's) vision (appears to be adequate for reading/may be interfering with reading). The areas

of _____ showed some problems. Additional signs of visual strain were _____).
(He/she) should be seen by an optometrist or opthamologist for further examination.

The (hearing test) was administered as a screening test to determine whether (student's) auditory acuity, or hearing, was adequate for reading. (Student's) hearing (appears to be adequate/may be interfering with reading). Additional signs of hearing problems were _____). (He/she) should be referred to an audiologist, otologist, or otolaryngologist.

VII.E. Intellectual Factors

The (test of intelligence) was administered to (student). As reported previously, (he/she) scored in the (above-average/average/below-average) range. Patterns of intellectual strengths and weaknesses revealed that _____. In addition, informal observations revealed that _____.

VII.F. Language Factors

Since reading is based on language, a student's oral language development is an important determinant of reading abilities. (Student's) history indicates (normal speech and language development/problems in speech and language development). (DESCRIBE SPEECH OR LANGUAGE PROBLEMS.) Informal observations of (student's) language revealed that language and verbal interactions are (well developed/adequate/a potential source of difficulty). (DESCRIBE TESTS OF LANGUAGE IF RELEVANT.)

(INCLUDE *VIII* IF RELEVANT.)

VIII.   RECOMMENDATIONS FOR REFERRAL

It is recommended that (student) be referred to a (type of specialist) for further investigation of vision/hearing/language, etc.

IX.   RECOMMENDATIONS FOR INSTRUCTION

(Student) (is recommended for/is not recommended for) remedial instruction at this time. This instruction should take place in (describe setting), approximately _____ times per week.

The most important goals for (student's) instruction are presently _____. (DESCRIBE METHODS AND MATERIALS FOR ACCOMPLISHING THESE GOALS.)

X. RECOMMENDATIONS FOR PARENTS
AND CLASSROOM TEACHER

Parents can be an important help in the reading situation. It is recommended that (student's) parents (maintain a positive attitude toward remediation, complimenting each success/provide enriching activities such as reading to (student) and take (him/her) on field trips/maintain an attitude of objectivity and some distance from the reading remediation). (EXPLAIN FURTHER.)

Classroom adjustments will help (student) overcome reading difficulties and feel more comfortable in the reading situation. It is recommended that (student's) classroom teacher make the following adjustments in the instructional situation: _____.

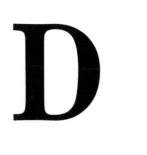

Appendix:
AN INFORMAL
READING
INVENTORY

This informal reading inventory was developed at the University of the Virgin Islands. It contains many selections taken from the Macmillan basal reading series, and it is used with the approval of Macmillan publishers. Other sections, also used with approval, are from the Houghton-Mifflin basal.

The IRI was extensively fieldtested at the University of the Virgin Islands and was recently refined and revalidated by Kushner and Stecker (1987) using a sample of remedial readers. In addition, the level of each reading sample has been checked using two readability formulas.*

Questions are keyed as follows:

I = Inference	WR = Word Recognition
F = Fact	COMP = Comprehension
S = Sequence	IND = Independent Reading Level
V = Vocabulary	INSTR = Instructional Reading Level
M = Main Idea	FRUST = Frustration Reading Level

*This Informal Reading Inventory was developed by graduate students at the University of the Virgin Islands under the direction of Dr. Lynne K. List.

	(1) Word Recognition Scores (Instant) Total	Used to Compute Reading Level Passage Scores				Used to Compute Reading Level (6) Listening Level
Level		(2) Oral Reading Word Accuracy	(3) Oral Comprehension Score	(4) Silent Comprehension Score	(5) Average Comprehension Score	
PP						
P						
1						
2						
3						
4						
5						
6						
7						
8						

Estimated reading levels:
Independent level   _____
Instructional level   _____
Frustration level   _____
Listening level   _____

Figure A-1   IRI Summary Page

Table A-1   Graded Word Lists (Teacher's Worksheets)

(PP)	(P)	(1)
1. little _____	1. tree _____	1. birthday _____
2. is _____	2. something _____	2. them _____
3. and _____	3. she _____	3. many _____
4. ball _____	4. brown _____	4. could _____
5. no _____	5. black _____	5. ate _____
6. play _____	6. then _____	6. over _____
7. big _____	7. would _____	7. pretty _____
8. it _____	8. now _____	8. hand _____
9. mother _____	9. like _____	9. another _____
10. cat _____	10. friends _____	10. duck _____
11. funny _____	11. men _____	11. teacher _____
12. come _____	12. said _____	12. miss _____
13. a _____	13. home _____	13. crayon _____
14. rabbit _____	14. away _____	14. hot _____
15. I _____	15. please _____	15. stop _____

16. look ___	16. store ___	16. grow ___
17. blue ___	17. food ___	17. had ___
18. up ___	18. give ___	18. lunch ___
19. red ___	19. very ___	19. water ___
20. go ___	20. farm ___	20. those ___

(2)

1. field ___
2. banana ___
3. mine ___
4. awoke ___
5. sidewalk ___
6. chocolate ___
7. twenty ___
8. week ___
9. skin ___
10. drop ___
11. page ___
12. bicycle ___
13. yesterday ___
14. splash ___
15. till ___
16. between ___
17. coal ___
18. what ___
19. police ___
20. frighten ___

(3)

1. cousin ___
2. highway ___
3. allow ___
4. circle ___
5. wonderful ___
6. peach ___
7. laughed ___
8. sentence ___
9. sunrise ___
10. rather ___
11. sailor ___
12. market ___
13. through ___
14. promise ___
15. everything ___
16. became ___
17. glove ___
18. happiest ___
19. breathe ___
20. cabbage ___

(4)

1. alphabet ___
2. uncertain ___
3. sample ___
4. meant ___
5. exchange ___
6. baseball ___
7. yank ___
8. ideal ___
9. fire ___
10. seashore ___
11. zipper ___
12. butcher ___
13. merely ___
14. phone ___
15. forward ___
16. caterpillar ___
17. linger ___
18. mosquito ___
19. gobble ___
20. kennel ___

(5)

1. heroic ___
2. chemist ___
3. convention ___
4. location ___
5. anxious ___
6. stadium ___
7. therefore ___
8. nephew ___
9. migration ___
10. testimony ___
11. ungrateful ___
12. talkative ___
13. wharf ___
14. caravan ___
15. pavement ___
16. twilight ___
17. composer ___
18. vertical ___
19. bother ___
20. fleece ___

(6)

1. gigantic ___
2. wardrobe ___
3. friction ___
4. lament ___
5. reverence ___
6. valor ___
7. horrify ___
8. expression ___
9. cherished ___
10. haunt ___
11. ponderous ___
12. boulevard ___
13. shrewd ___
14. violin ___
15. barbaric ___
16. abbreviation ___
17. existence ___
18. hospitality ___
19. canopy ___
20. obligation ___

ORAL FORM—Level PP (27 words)*

MOTIVATION: If you climbed up a tree, you might need help to get down. Jeff and mother are trying to get a boy named Mike down from a tree. Let's see what happens.

Jeff said, "Here comes Daddy.

Here he comes with a ladder.

You can come down the ladder."

Mother said, "Mike can.

He can come down the ladder."†

COMPREHENSION CHECK

(F) 1. _____ Who is coming? (Daddy)
(F) 2. _____ What is Daddy bringing? (a ladder)
(I) 3. _____ What does Mother want Mike to do? (get down; come down the ladder)
(M) 4. _____ How is Mike going to get down? (using a ladder, climb down) 1/2 credit for one.

SCORING GUIDE: PREPRIMER

WR Errors		*Comp Errors*	
IND	0–1	IND	0
INSTR	1½–2½	INSTR	½–1
FRUST	3+	FRUST	2+

* These and the following 19 samples can be used as models for teacher's worksheets.

† Adapted from "Can Mike Get Down?," in A MAGIC BOX, Level 4, Preprimer 2, *The Macmillan Reading Program*—Albert J. Harris and Mae Knight Clark, Senior Authors, p. 50. Copyright © 1970 Macmillan Publishing Co., Inc.

SILENT FORM—Level PP (29 words)

MOTIVATION: In this story you will read about Mike and Jeff. One of these boys wants something.

Mike said, "I want a big boy's bike.

Make it a big boy's bike, Jeff."

Jeff said, "Can you ride it, Mike?

Can you ride a big boy's bike?"*

COMPREHENSION CHECK

(F)   1. _____ What does Mike want? (a big boy's bike)
(F)   2. _____ How is Jeff going to help Mike? (Jeff will make, buy, get a bike.)
(I)   3. _____ Who is older, Jeff or Mike? (Jeff)
(M)   4. _____ What is the story about? (a boy's wish for a bike)

SCORING GUIDE

Comp Errors

IND   0
INSTR   1
FRUST   2+

* Excerpted from "The Little Wheels," in THINGS YOU SEE, Level 5, Preprimer 3, *The Macmillan Reading Program*—Albert J. Harris and Mae Knight Clark, Senior Authors, p. 35. Copyright © 1974, 1965 Macmillan Publishing Co., Inc.

ORAL FORM—Level P (54 words)

MOTIVATION: There is a very worried mother in this story. Let's find out why she is worried.

Billy is a little goat on a farm. He likes to eat and play.

He likes to run and jump. One day Billy didn't eat.

He didn't run or jump. He didn't play.

"Oh!" said his mother.

"My little goat won't eat." Mother Goat ran to Daddy Goat.

Mother Goat said, "Billy won't eat."*

COMPREHENSION CHECK

(M) 1. _____ Give two reasons why Billy's mother is worried about him (He isn't running, jumping, playing, or eating.) 1/2 credit for one.

(F) 2. _____ What kind of an animal is Billy? (Goat)

(F) 3. _____ Who did Mother Goat go to for help? (Daddy Goat)

(I) 4. _____ How do we know that Mother Goat went quickly to Daddy Goat? (It said that she "ran.")

SCORING GUIDE: PRIMER

WR Errors		Comp Errors	
IND	0–2½	IND	0
INSTR	3–5	INSTR	1
FRUST	5½+	FRUST	2+

*Adapted from "The Goat Story," in WORLDS OF WONDER, Level 6, Primer, *The Macmillan Reading Program*—Albert J. Harris and Mae Knight Clark, Senior Authors, pp. 109–110. Copyright © 1974 Macmillan Publishing Co., Inc.

SILENT FORM—Level P (53 words)

MOTIVATION: This story is about a boy and his dog, Bolo. Let's read about how the boy is able to take Bolo on the bus.

"Bolo has to go to the dog show," said Jeff.

"How can I take him?"

"You can put him in something," said the busman.

"Then we will let him ride on the bus."

"That's good," said Jeff.

"I will get something to put him in.

Then we can ride to the show."*

COMPREHENSION CHECK

(F) 1. _____ Why does Bolo have to ride the bus? (to get to the dog show)

(I) 2. _____ Is Jeff happy Bolo can ride on the bus? (yes) How do you know? (Jeff said "that's good") 1/2 credit for one answer.

(I) 3. _____ The busman told Jeff to put Bolo in "something." What might the "something" be? (a box, etc.)

(M) 4. _____ Why does Jeff have to put Bolo in something? (so that he can ride the bus—or—be able to go to the dog show—or—so he doesn't bother other riders, etc.)

Comp Errors

IND   0
INSTR 1
FRUST 2+

*Adapted from "No Ride for Bolo," in WORLDS OF WONDER, Level 6, Primer, *The Macmillan Reading Program*—Albert J. Harris and Mae Knight Clark, Senior Authors, p. 63. Copyright © 1974 Macmillan Publishing Co., Inc.

ORAL FORM—Level 1 (73 words)

MOTIVATION: Have you ever tried to paint something? Let's read a story to see how a little boy felt about what he made.

One time at school Larry had to paint a flower.
Larry painted a blue and yellow one.
He thought it looked good.
Then Larry saw the flower that one of the other boys had painted. It was big and red. It had a bird on it. "My flower is not bad," thought Larry. "But that one is great. Why couldn't I paint a great flower?" Larry thought he would never do anything great.*

COMPREHENSION CHECK

(F) 1. _____ What did Larry do at school? (He painted a flower.)
(F) 2. _____ What colors did Larry use to paint his flower? (blue and yellow) give 1/2 credit for one.
(F) 3. _____ What did Larry think of the flower he painted? (He thought it looked good or it didn't look bad.)
(S) 4. _____ After Larry looked at his own flower, what else did he see? (He saw a flower another boy painted.)
(F) 5. _____ Tell me two things about the other boy's flower. (It was big, red, had a bird on it, and looked great.) full credit 2 of 4, half credit 1 of 4.

*Excerpted from "Never Great," in Elizabeth Levy, BEING ME, Grade 1, Level 10, *Series r: The New Macmillan Reading Program*—Carl B. Smith and Ronald Wardhaugh, Senior Authors, p. 127. Copyright © 1980 Macmillan Publishing Co., Inc.

WR Errors		Comp Errors	
IND	0–3½	IND	0–1
INSTR	4–7	INSTR	1½–3
FRUST	7½+	FRUST	3½+

SILENT FORM—Level 1 (104 words)

MOTIVATION: This story takes place on a farm. Let's read about something that happens to Tom and Ben on the farm.

One day Tommy had something for the little calf to eat. She ran at it so hard that Tommy fell over. It hurt, but Tommy didn't cry. Ben laughed when Tommy fell over. "I told you so!" he said. "You can't take care of a calf. You are not old enough. You have to be big like me to take care of a calf." Tommy was mad. He yelled, "I can too take care of my twin!"*

COMPREHENSION CHECK

(F)   1. _____   What did Tommy have that made the calf run over to him? (something to eat)

(F)   2. _____   What made Tommy mad? (Ben told him that he was too little to take care of the calf—or—Ben laughed at him—½ credit for Ben said he wasn't as big as he was)

*Excerpt adapted from THE LITTLE TWIN by Grace Paull. Copyright © 1953 by Grace Paull. Reprinted by permission of Doubleday, a division of Bantam, Doubleday, Dell Publishing Group, Inc.

(F) 3. _____ What did Ben do when Tommy fell over? (He laughed.)

(I) 4. _____ What did Tommy do to show that he was mad? (He yelled.)

(M) 5. _____ What does Tommy want to show to Ben? (He is big enough to take care of the calf.)

(I) 6. _____ Why do you think the calf ran so fast? (She was hungry, or might have been glad to see Tommy.)

(I) 7. _____ Who was older, Ben or Tommy? (Ben) How do you know? (He said Tommy was little—or—he was big)

SCORING GUIDE: LEVEL 1

Comp Errors

IND   1
INSTR   1–2
FRUST   2½ +

ORAL FORM—Level 2 (109 words)

MOTIVATION: Let's read a story about a boy who wants to learn something.

Tommy and his mother and father went to the country each summer. This summer they took a house right beside a lake. "I'm so glad we're here," said Tommy. "I didn't learn how to swim last year, but *this* year I will. You wait and see." "Good," said his father. "I'm glad you want to learn now. Many of the boys and girls here don't know how to swim. We're getting a lifeguard to teach you. His name is Big Jim, and I'm sure you'll like him." Tommy did like Big Jim. Just the same he couldn't do the things Big Jim asked him to do. *

COMPREHENSION CHECK

(F) 1. _____ What was the name of the boy who couldn't swim? (Tommy)

(F) 2. _____ Where did Tommy's family go every summer? (the country—or—the lake)

(I) 3. _____ Where do you think Tommy and the other children go to swim? (the lake)

(F) 4. _____ What did Tommy want to do this summer? (learn how to swim)

(F) 5. _____ How did Tommy feel about Big Jim? (He liked him.)

(V) 6. _____ What does it mean when the story says, "they took a house right beside a lake"? (They rented, stayed in, or lived in a house by the lake)

(I) 7. _____ Was it easy for Tommy to learn to swim? (No) How do you know? (He couldn't do the things Big Jim asked him to do.) 1/2 credit for one correct answer.

SCORING GUIDE: LEVEL 2

WR Errors		Comp Errors	
IND	0–5	IND	0
INSTR	5½–10½	INSTR	1–2
FRUST	11+	FRUST	3+

* Adapted from "The Boy Who Couldn't Swim," in SHINING BRIDGES, Grade 2, Level 2, *The Macmillan Reading Program*—Albert J. Harris and Mae Knight Clark, Senior Authors, p. 94. Copyright © 1974 Macmillan Publishing Co., Inc.

SILENT FORM—Level 2 (112 words)

MOTIVATION: Let's read a story about a girl and a boy and how they spend their summer.

Jane Turner lived in a small hotel right on the beach. Her mother and father owned the hotel, and Jane was glad they did. People came there with children, and the children became Jane's friends. They went swimming almost every day. One of Jane's friends was a boy named Billy. One day Jane and Billy were playing with a beach ball, and Billy got hurt. The beach ball hit him on the mouth. For a second Billy was angry. He threw the ball so hard that it went way out over the water. Then a strange thing happened. As Jane and Billy watched, a big, dark animal jumped out of the water.*

* Adapted from "Jane and the Dolphin," in SHINING BRIDGES, Grade 2, Level 2, *The Macmillan Reading Program*—Albert J. Harris and Mae Knight Clark, Senior Authors, pp. 63–64. Copyright © 1974 Macmillan Publishing Co., Inc.

COMPREHENSION CHECK

(F) 1. _____ Where did Jane Turner live? (in a hotel—or—by the beach)

(F) 2. _____ Who owned the hotel that Jane lived in? (her mother and father)

(F) 3. _____ How often did the children go swimming? (almost every day)

(F) 4. _____ How did Billy get hurt? (The ball hit him in the mouth.)

(I) 5. _____ How can you tell that Billy wasn't the only friend Jane had? (It said that he was *one* of her friends and the children who came to the hotel became her *friends*.)

(S) 6. _____ What did Billy do after he got angry? (He threw the ball so hard that it went out over the water.)

(F) 7. _____ What did the big, dark animal do? (jumped out of the water)

SCORING GUIDE: LEVEL 2

Comp Errors

IND   0
INSTR 1–2
FRUST 2½+

ORAL FORM—Level 3 (159 words)

MOTIVATION: Grandmother was helping Alicia. Read to find out how grandmother was helping her.

"Hold very still now, Alicia," Grandmother said. "I don't want to stick you with these pins."

Alicia stood carefully on the stool. She imagined herself to be made out of stone as Grandmother pinned up the dress she would wear to her cousin's wedding. Alicia wondered if she would have to stand still like this during the wedding. She had never been a flower girl before and was really looking forward to it. "I'll never be able to wait until Saturday," she thought.

"There," Grandmother said as she put in the last pin. "Now, step down. Come and look in the mirror."

As they stood in front of the long bedroom mirror, Grandmother put her hands on Alicia's shoulders. "What do you think, Alicia?" she asked.

"Oh, Grandma! It's the most beautiful dress I've ever seen." She gave her grandmother a big hug. "Thank you! Thank you for making it for me."

"Tomorrow, I'll finish the dress so that it will be ready for the wedding on Saturday."*

COMPREHENSION CHECK

(F)   1. _____ What was grandmother doing to the dress? (pinning it up)

(I)   2. _____ Did Alicia like the dress? (yes) How do you know? (She hugged her grandmother—or—she told her grandmother it was a beautiful dress) 1/2 credit for one.

(M)   3. _____ What were Alicia and her grandmother preparing for? (a wedding) What was Alicia going to be? (a flower girl)

(I)   4. _____ Why did Alicia pretend she was made out of stone? (she had to stand still while she was being pinned—or—so she wouldn't get stuck)

(I)   5. _____ Why was grandmother putting pins in Alicia's dress? (She was hemming it—or—shortening it—or—fixing it)

(V)   6. _____ In this story, what is a long bedroom mirror? (a tall mirror—or—a mirror that shows you from head to toe—or—full-length mirror)

(S)   7. _____ What did Alicia do after grandmother was finished pinning up the dress? (stood in front of the mirror)

(F)   8. _____ When was the wedding going to take place? (Saturday)

(F)   9. _____ Who was getting married? (Alicia's cousin)

(I)   10. _____ Why did grandmother want Alicia to look in the mirror? (to see if she liked the dress)

SCORING GUIDE: LEVEL 3

WR Errors		*Comp Errors*	
IND	0–7½	IND	0–1
INSTR	8–15	INSTR	2–3
FRUST	15½+	FRUST	4+

*From "A Gift for Alicia" by Lorenca Consuelo Rosal with Patricia Oliverez from *Caravans*, Houghton Mifflin Reading, Copyright © 1986 Houghton Mifflin Co. Used with permission.

SILENT FORM—Level 3 (132 words)

MOTIVATION: John and Si were looking for another football player to play on the team. John is running over to Si's house to meet the hot prospect.

"Where is he?" he asked, as he came up onto the porch. "I want to see him catch." "Sit down John," Si said very seriously. I think I'd better tell you how it all started. Don't interrupt until I finish."

But when Si came to the part where Faith had come over to his yard, John burst out, "You mean to tell me that Faith Cummings is our new left end? You got me away from the Ohio State-Purdue game to tell me this? A girl! I lost five pounds just running over here."

"Hold your horses until I finish the story. It's unbelievable," Si said. He quickly told John the rest. "I threw seven passes and she didn't miss once. Imagine what we would do with her on the team!"*

COMPREHENSION CHECK

(F)   1. _____ What position on the team were John and Si trying to find a player for? (left end)

(M)   2. _____ What was so unusual about the situation Si and John were in? (Faith, a girl, wasn't supposed to be that good a football player.)

(I)   3. _____ Who was more excited about the new player, Si or John? Why? (Si, because he already knew how well she could catch.)

(F)   4. _____ What game was John watching on T.V.? (Ohio State-Purdue—or—football)

(M)   5. _____ Why were John and Si excited about having Faith on the Team? (Because she was a good player.)

(I)   6. _____ Do you think that Si and John could convince the rest of the team to accept Faith as the new left end? Why? (Yes; because they were so enthusiastic—or—she was so good.); 1/2 credit for yes. Full credit for yes plus one reason.

(F)   7. _____ How many passes did Faith catch? (7)

(F)   8. _____ How many pounds did John say he lost running over to Si's house? (5)

(F)   9. _____ Si asked John not to interrupt his story. Did John interrupt? If so, what did he say first? (Yes; He said, "You mean Faith Cummings is our new left end?") 1/2 credit for one.

(V)   10. _____ What did Si mean when he said, "Hold your horses until I finish the story."? (Don't interrupt me.)

* From "The Secret Deal" from *Mystery Guest at Left End* by Beman Lord. Used by permission of Henry Z. Walck, Inc.

SCORING GUIDE: LEVEL 3

Comp Errors

IND	0–1
INSTR	1½–3
FRUST	3½+

ORAL FORM—Level 4 (198 words)

MOTIVATION: In this story Ernie gets a visitor. You will find out who this visitor is.

One October afternoon Ernie was home from school waiting for the scabs from his chicken pox spots to fall off. Even though nobody could catch the chicken pox from him anymore, he looked pretty awful. Now that he didn't itch and feel terrible, he was bored. Ernie was so bored he couldn't wait to get back to school. He wondered what exciting things his friends in the fourth grade and Mrs. Crownfeld, his teacher, were doing while he spent his time waiting for scabs to fall off. When the doorbell suddenly rang, Ernie was glad. Even answering the door was something to do.

When Ernie looked through the peephole in the door to find out who was there before opening it, he saw it was his Uncle Simon, his mother's brother, who was a sailor. Ernie and his mother hadn't seen Uncle Simon in two years because he had been away at sea. Ernie had thought of Uncle Simon often during those two years and had imagined Uncle Simon climbing the rigging, doing things with the mizzenmast, swabbing the deck, and standing watch with a spy glass—all the things that sailors did in the stories Ernie read.*

COMPREHENSION CHECK

(F)   1. _____ What illness did Ernie have? (chicken pox)

(I)   2. _____ Why do you suppose that Ernie was thinking about going back to school? (He was bored.)

(F)   3. _____ Why was Ernie glad when he heard the doorbell ring? (It gave him something to do.)

(I)   4. _____ Who was Ernie's visitor? (Uncle Simon)

*From "Ernie and the Mile-Long Muffler," by Marjorie Lewis, in *Flights*. Copyright 1982, Coward, McCann & Geoghegan. Reprinted by permission of the author.

(S) 5. _____ What did Ernie do before he opened the door? (looked through the peep-hole)

(F) 6. _____ What did Uncle Simon do for a living? (He was a sailor.)

(F) 7. _____ Where did Ernie get his information about what sailors did? (in stories)

(I) 8. _____ Why can we say that Uncle Simon had probably done many things since Ernie had seen him? (he had been gone two years—or—the story says he had done many things)

(V) 9. _____ What does "peephole" mean? (a hole in the door to look through)

(S) 10. _____ How did Ernie's feelings change in this story? (First he was bored—then he was glad.)

SCORING GUIDE: LEVEL 4

WR Errors		Comp Errors	
IND	0–8½	IND	0–1
INSTR	9–17	INSTR	1½–3
FRUST	17½+	FRUST	3½+

SILENT FORM—Level 4 (244 words)

MOTIVATION: Paul Revere, a hero of the American Revolution, rode on horseback to warn the other colonists that the enemy was coming. Let's read to find out how his ride was interrupted.

For a while all went well. And then suddenly from out of the shadows appeared six English officers. They rode with their pistols in their hands and ordered Paul to stop. But Paul didn't stop immediately.

One of the officers shouted, "If you go an inch farther, you are a dead man."

Paul and his companions tried to ride through the group, but they were surrounded and ordered into a pasture at one side of the road.

In the pasture six other officers appeared with pistols in their hands.

One of them spoke like a gentleman. He took Paul's horse by the reins and asked Paul where he came from.

Paul told him, "Boston."

The officer asked what time he had left Boston.

Paul told him.

The officer said, "Sir, may I crave your name?"

Paul answered that his name was Revere.

"What! *Paul Revere?*"

Paul said, "Yes."

Now, the English officers certainly did not want to let Paul Revere loose, so they put him, along with other prisoners, at the center of their group, and they rode off toward Lexington. As they approached town, they heard gunfire.

"What was that?" The officer asked.

Paul said it was a signal to alarm the countryside.

With this piece of news, the English decided they'd like to get back to their own troops in a hurry. Indeed, they were in such a hurry that they no longer wanted to be bothered with prisoners. So after relieving the prisoners of their horses, they set them free.*

COMPREHENSION CHECK

(F) 1. _____ Who appeared from out of the shadows? (English officers, the enemy)

(F) 2. _____ Did Paul stop immediately when he was ordered to? (No, not immediately)

(F) 3. _____ Where was Paul Revere coming from? (Boston)

(V) 4. _____ What do you think the officer meant when he said "Sir, may I crave your name?" (What is your name?)

(F) 5. _____ What did Paul say when the officer asked his name. (He said, "Paul Revere.")

(F) 6. _____ What did the officer do when he found out the rider was the famous Paul Revere? (He put him with the other prisoners)

7. _____ What did they hear as they approached town? (gunfire)

8. _____ What was the name of the town? (Lexington)

(F) 9. _____ What happened to the soldiers at the end of the story? (They hurried back to their own troops—or—they fled—or—they left the prisoners)

(M) 10. _____ Do you think Paul Revere was a hero in this story? Why? (Yes; He was risking his life by going out when enemy soldiers were near.)

SCORING GUIDE: LEVEL 4

Comp Errors

IND   0–1
INSTR   2–3
FRUST   4+

*Excerpt from *And Then What Happened, Paul Revere?* by Jean Fritz, text © 1973 by Jean Fritz. Reprinted by permission of Coward, McCann & Geoghegan.

ORAL FORM—Level 5 (195 words)

MOTIVATION: This is a story about a boy and his father.

Father pulled on his pants and boots and heavy jacket and lit his lantern. By the time he'd done that, I had my things on, too. My mother was up then and objecting, but my father shushed her. So I went with him. The late moon was up and we could see our way easy. I stayed in the shack with the operator and my father went off to set his signal and tend his switch. Sure enough, in about twenty minutes the train came along, swung into the second line of track and stopped. The telegraph operator stepped out and started talking to a brakeman. I was scared stiff. I stood in the shack doorway and looked at the train and I was shaking inside like I had some kind of fever. It wasn't much of a train. Just an engine and little fuel car and four old coaches. I mean the railroad wasn't wasting any good equipment or any extra men on this train, and it was being shoved along slow between other trains. Except for the wheezing engine, the train was a tired and sleeping or dead thing on the track.*

COMPREHENSION CHECK

(F)   1. _____ Name the items of clothing that father put on. (pants—boots—and heavy jacket) Full credit for two items.

(I)   2. _____ Why do you think the child's mother objected to his going out with his father? (the child had already been undressed for the night—or—it was dark outside—or—it was dangerous)

(V)   3. _____ What does "father shushed her" mean? (father told her to be quiet—shut up, etc.) ½ credit for told her not to worry.

(F)   4. _____ Where was the father taking his son? (to the track—or—to the railroad track)

(F)   5. _____ How many coaches did the train have? (four)

(F)   6. _____ Where did the child wait when father went to set his signal? (in the shack—with the operator)

(I)   7. _____ Was it night or day when the father and the child went out from home? (night) How do you know? (father lit his lantern—or—on the way to the track the late moon was up) 1/2 credit for either part.

(I)   8. _____ Why do you think the child was shaking inside? (he was scared—nervous—afraid—or excited)

(M)   9. _____ What is this story mainly about? Choose one of the following ideas: A. A Trip with Father B. A Trip to the Track during the Night C. Visiting New Train Engines (B).

(I)   10. _____ Why did the train seem "a tired and sleeping or dead thing on the track?" (the coaches were old—or—it make quiet sounds—or—it moved slowly, etc.)

* Adapted from "Jacob," in Jack Schaefer, *The Plainsmen* (Boston: Houghton-Mifflin, 1954), pp. 243–44. Copyright © 1954 by Jack Schaefer, copyright © renewed 1982. Reprinted by permission of Don Congdon Associates, Inc.

SCORING GUIDE: LEVEL 5

WR Errors		*Comp Errors*	
IND	0–9½	IND	0–1
INSTR	10–19½	INSTR	1½–3
FRUST	20+	FRUST	3½+

SILENT FORM—Level 5 (118 words)

MOTIVATION: The story we are about to read tells about what the early settlers in America did to trees and forests.

The forests made America the richest and most fertile country on earth. There was abundant wood for buildings. The rich earth could be farmed when the trees had been felled. There were more than one billion acres of untouched forest—enough wood, everyone thought, to last forever.

Trees were slashed and land was cleared for farming without a thought for the future. Great stretches of forest were fired and burned to clear the land for farms. Logs were used to build homes and schools, barns, churches, bridges, and forts. After the early settlers came the loggers.

It was during the days of the Gold Rush, in the middle 1800's, that cutting timber for profit became a really big business.*

COMPREHENSION CHECK

(F)   1. _____ What made America the richest and most fertile country on Earth? (the forests)

(V)   2. _____ What does "abundant wood" mean? (plenty of wood—or—more than enough wood)

(V)   3. _____ What does "trees were slashed" mean? (Trees were cut down.)

(F)   4. _____ Why were the forests cut down and fired? (to clear land for farms—½ credit for making homes)

(F)   5. _____ Name three things the story says that the early settlers built from wood. (homes, schools, barns, churches, forts, bridges) 1/2 credit for two, full credit for three.

(F)   6. _____ Who came after the early settlers? (loggers)

(I)   7. _____ Why do you think a particular period of time was referred to as the days of the "Gold Rush"? (People were rushing for gold in that period.)

(F)   8. _____ About when was the Gold Rush? (100–150 years ago—or—middle 1800's)

*Adapted from *The Friendly Forests* by Alma Chesnut Moore. Copyright © 1954, renewed 1982 by Alma Chesnut Moore. All rights reserved. Reprinted by permission of Viking Penguin Inc.

(I)   9. _____   What could the settlers have done during the time they were cutting down the trees to make sure that the forests remain? (young trees could have been planted—or—seeds could have been sown in their place)

(M)   10. _____   Give the story a title.   A. Early Settlers Waste the Forest   B. The Forests are Being Cut Down   C. Forests are a Big Business.   (B)

SCORING GUIDE: LEVEL 2

Comp Errors

IND	0–1
INSTR	1½–3
FRUST	3½+

ORAL FORM—Level 6 (239 words)

MOTIVATION: Let's see how thinking like a successful scientist can be applied to a fishing trip.

What is the "scientific method" of thinking? An example will answer a number of questions about it.

Suppose you have been out trout fishing, using worms for bait, and after several hours you have not even had a nibble. You saw another fisherman bring home a day's limit of trout the day before from the same place you have been fishing. You wonder why he caught so many and you none at all.

Puzzled, you stop fishing and just watch the stream for a while. Presently you see fish breaking the surface of the water. Why? What makes them jump up to the surface this way? perhaps they are coming up for air, or just feeling playful. Or possibly the light attracts them.

Another idea seems more likely. Maybe these trout like insects to eat, and leap up to strike when they see one near the surface of the water.

This seems like a good lead, so you decide to test your idea. You just slapped a mosquito that lit on your arm; now you toss it onto the surface of the water. You see a swirl, and the mosquito is gone. In fact, you find that every time you toss a mosquito onto the surface of the water, a fish strikes at it. After a few tests in this fashion you come to a conclusion; these trout do not like worms, but they seem to find mosquitos irresistible.*

*Adapted and abridged from *So You Want To Be a Scientist* by Alan E. Nourse, M.D., p. 61. Copyright © 1960 by Alan Edward Nourse. By permission of Harper & Row Publishers, Inc.

COMPREHENSION CHECK

(F) 1. _____ What kind of fish were you trying to catch? (trout)

(I) 2. _____ What kind of bait was the successful fisherman using in an attempt to catch fish? (insects—or—mosquitos)

(F) 3. _____ What fact in the story caused you to stop fishing and just observe the surroundings? (the fact that he wasn't catching any fish—or—that another fisherman was having luck where he was not)

(F) 4. _____ What reasons did you first think of for the fishes' behavior? (coming up for air, feeling playful, attracted to light, like insects) Any two of these count for full credit.

(F) 5. _____ What did you throw into the water that the trout seemed to like? (mosquitos)

(F) 6. _____ What conclusion was formed at the end of this story about the eating habits of the trout? (The trout did not like worms, but they found mosquitos irresistible.) Must include both halves for full credit.

(V) 7. _____ In the phrase, "slapped a mosquito that lit on your arm," what does the word "lit" mean? (landed—or—came to rest)

(F) 8. _____ What do you see just before the mosquito disappears? (a swirl)

(M) 9. _____ Explain how the scientific method of thinking was used in this story. (accept answers that state: you find a problem—think of solutions—test them—arrive at conclusions) full credit for any three ½ credit for two

(M) 10. _____ Give this story a title. Choose from the following: A. Scientists like to Fish   B. Fishing Is Fun to Do   C. A Scientific Method to Catch Trout.   (C)

SCORING GUIDE: LEVEL 6

WR Errors		*Comp Errors*	
IND	0–11½	IND	0–1
INSTR	12–23½	INSTR	1½–3
FRUST	24+	FRUST	3½+

SILENT FORM—Level 6 (231 words)

MOTIVATION: A man observed a pond for a long time to gain knowledge about one particular creature. Let's read the following passage to see what creature held this man's interest.

This was the day: I knew it. For a month I had been watching, brooding over this pond, and now I knew. I felt a stirring of the pulse of things that the cold-hearted turtles could no more escape than could the clouds and I.

Leaving my horse unhitched, as if he too understood, I slipped eagerly into my hidden nook for a look at the pond. As I did so, a large fish ploughed a furrow through the still pond water. And in this wake rose the head of an enormous turtle. Swinging slowly around, the creature headed straight for the shore, and without a pause scrambled out on the sand.

She was about the size of a big scoop shovel. But that was not what excited me so much as her manner and the gait at which she moved. For I could see there was method in it, and fixed purpose. On she came, shuffling over the sand toward the higher open fields. She had a hurried, determined seesaw motion that was taking her somewhere in particular, and that was bound to get her there on time.

I held my breath.

Over the strip of sand, without a stop, she paddled. Up a narrow cowpath into the high grass along a fence she went. Then up the narrow cowpath, on all fours, just like another turtle, I paddled, and into the high wet grass along the fence.*

COMPREHENSION CHECK

(F) 1. _____ What creature in the story was the man so interested in? (turtle)

(I) 2. _____ How long had the man been watching and brooding over the pond? (for a month; 30–31 days)

(F) 3. _____ What creature in the story ploughed a furrow through the water? (a fish)

(F) 4. _____ To what object was the size of the turtle compared? (scoop shovel)

(F) 5. _____ What about the turtle excited the man most? (her manner and the gait at which she moved.)

(V) 6. _____ If the turtle is "enormous," what do we know about it? (very big, large)

(V) 7. _____ What is meant by the word "nook" in the following phrase: "I slipped eagerly into my hidden nook for a look at the pond"? (hiding place—or—secluded place)

(I) 8. _____ What method of transportation did the man use to get to the pond? (a horse)

(I) 9. _____ Why did the man find it necessary to follow the turtle on all fours? (so the turtle wouldn't notice that he was there)

(M) 10. _____ Give this story a title. Choose from the following: A. Studying Nature for a Living B. Riding My Horse in the Woods C. Learning about a Turtle D. Studying Fish in a Pond   (C)

SCORING GUIDE: LEVEL 2

Comp Errors

IND	0–1
INSTR	2–3
FRUST	4+

* Excerpted from Dallas Lore Sharp, "Turtle Eggs for Agassiz," in *The Atlantic Monthly* (November 1932).

ORAL FORM—Level 7 (218 words)

> MOTIVATION: Have you ever had a relative stay with you while your parents were away? Let's read a story about some children who didn't enjoy their aunt's visit.

After we moved to Montclair, Aunt Anne came to stay with us for several days while Mother and Dad were away on a lecture tour. She made it plain from the start that she was not a guest, but the temporary commander-in-chief. She even used the front stairs, leading from the front hall to the second floor, instead of the back stairs, which led from the kitchen to a hallway near the girls' bathroom. None of us was allowed to use the front stairs, because Dad wanted to keep the varnish on them looking nice.

"Daddy will be furious if he comes home and finds you've been using his front stairs," we told Aunt Anne.

"Nonsense," she cut us off. "The back stairs are narrow and steep, and I for one don't propose to use them. As long as I'm here, I'll use any stairs I have a mind to. Now rest your features and mind your business."

She sat at Dad's place at the foot of the table, and we resented this, too. Ordinarily, Frank, as the oldest boy, sat in Dad's place, and Anne, as the oldest girl, sat at Mother's. We also disapproved of Aunt Anne's blunt criticism of how we kept our bedrooms, and some of the changes she made in the family routine.*

COMPREHENSION CHECK

(F) 1. _____ Where were the children's parents going when Aunt Anne came to stay? (They were going away on a lecture tour.)

(F) 2. _____ What stairway did Aunt Anne use? (the front stairs)

(F) 3. _____ Why weren't the children allowed to use the front stairs? (because Dad wanted to keep the varnish on them looking nice)

(I) 4. _____ What did Aunt Anne mean when she said, "Now rest your features?" (relax, don't worry, any comparable answer)

(V) 5. _____ What does the word "propose" mean in the phrase "I for one don't propose to use them?" (intend, plan, etc.)

(I) 6. _____ Were Frank and Anne the only children in the family? (No) How do you know? (The passage said that Frank was the oldest of the *boys* and Anne was the oldest of the *girls*.) 1/2 credit for one.

(F) 7. _____ Where did Aunt Anne sit at the table? (in Dad's place—or—at the foot of the table)

*From *Cheaper By the Dozen* by Frank B. Gilbreth, Jr., and Ernestine Gilbreth Carey (New York: Thomas Y. Crowell Co., 1948), pp. 175–76. Copyright © 1948, 1963 by Frank B. Gilbreth, Jr., and Ernestine Gilbreth Carey. By permission of Harper & Row, Publishers, Inc., and Heinemann Ltd.

(I) 8. _____ Why did Frank and Anne resent Aunt Anne choosing to sit where she did at the table? (because being the oldest generally meant that they could sit in Mother and Dad's places when they were away)

(I) 9. _____ How did Aunt Anne feel about the way the children kept their bedrooms? (she didn't like it—or—she criticized it.)

(M) 10. _____ Why did the children resent Aunt Anne? (because she changed things that seemed important to them, etc.)

SCORING GUIDE: LEVEL 7

WR Errors		Comp Errors	
IND	0–10½	IND	0–1
INSTR	11–21½	INSTR	2–3
FRUST	22+	FRUST	4+

SILENT FORM—Level 7 (201 words)

MOTIVATION: In some cases it is necessary to observe animals in their natural settings in order to understand them. Let's read a story about observing animals this way.

Now the larger and commoner creatures from most parts of the world are well represented in nearly all zoological collections, and quite a lot is known about them. So it was the smaller and rarer beasts, about which we know so little, that I wanted to collect. It is about them that I am going to write.

From many points of view it is sometimes the small animals in a country that influence man more than the large ones. At home, for instance, the brown rat does more damage every year than any of the larger creatures. It was for this reason that I concentrated during my collecting trips on the smaller forms of life. For my first expedition I chose the Cameroons, since it is a small, almost forgotten corner of Africa, which is more or less as it was before the advent of the white man. Here, in the gigantic rain forests, the animals live their lives as they have done for thousands of years.

It is of great value to get to know and study these wild creatures before they are influenced by civilization, for wild animals can be affected just as much by change as people.*

---

*Excerpted from "Collecting in the Cameroons," in Gerald Durrell, *The New Noah* (New York: Viking Penguin Inc., 1967). Used by permission of Curtis Brown Ltd.

COMPREHENSION CHECK

(F)   1. _____ What kinds of creatures are well represented in most zoos? (larger and commoner ones) Need both·answers for full credit.

(F)   2. _____ What animal does more damage every year than any of the larger animals, back at home? (the brown rat)

(I)   3. _____ Why do you suppose he concentrated on the smaller forms of life during his collecting trips? (little research has been done on them—or—any logical answer)

(F)   4. _____ Where did he choose to go on his first expedition? (the Cameroons—or—Africa)

(F)   5. _____ Where are the Cameroons? (in a small, almost forgotten corner of Africa)

(V)   6. _____ What does the word "expedition" mean in the phrase "For my first expedition I chose the Cameroons"? (trip, adventure)

(F)   7. _____ What kind of place within the Cameroons did the author work in? (rain forest)

(F)   8. _____ Why were the animals of the Cameroons chosen to be observed? (They have lived the same way for thousands of years.)

(I)   9. _____ Why is it important to study wild animals as they are in nature? (so we can see how they act and live when they are not disturbed)

(M) 10. _____ Give this story a title. Choose from the following: A. The Rainy Cameroons   B. Large Animals Found in Zoos   C. Small Animals Can Cause Lots of Damage   D. Learning about Small Creatures   (D)

SCORING GUIDE: LEVEL 7

Comp Errors

IND   0–1
INSTR   1½–3
FRUST   3½+

ORAL FORM—Level 8 (245 words)

MOTIVATION: Most of us take the ability to walk for granted. Let's read a story about a boy who lost that ability as a result of having polio, a crippling disease.

The massages were continued. I lay in bed most of the time. Each day I tried to walk a bit. The weakness in my legs gradually disappeared. My feet would flop a bit; the muscles of my knees would twitch; curious numb sensations would come and go. But before many months I relearned to walk, and the frailty which the disease had caused seemed to pass. Someone said that the salt water and massages had effected wonders. Mother was silent awhile and then said, "So did my prayers."

But the ordeal had left its scars. Mother believed the doctor implicitly, and was convinced that the sand would fast run out of my glass. So she set about to guard my health, to protect me against physical strain, to do all sorts of favors designed to save my energy. I was waited on, hand and foot. Worse than that, I began to hear what Mother was saying to others: "he's not as strong as other boys; he has to be careful what he does—you know, his legs were almost paralyzed."

This solicitousness set up a severe reaction. It seemed to me I was being publicly recognized as a puny person—a weakling. Thus there began to grow in me a great rebellion. I protested against Mother's descriptions of me. But I believe my rebellion was not so much against her as it was against the kind of person I thought I was coming to be.*

COMPREHENSION CHECK

(F)   1. _____ What did the boy do most of the time? (lay in bed)

(F)   2. _____ What things did he feel as the strength gradually went out of his legs? (knee muscles twitching; numb sensations coming and going) Full credit for one.

(I)   3. _____ What did Mother think helped him improve? (her prayers—or—God)

(I)   4. _____ Why did Mother work so hard to save his energy? (Because she believed he wouldn't survive long and wanted to protect him for as long as she could)

(I)   5. _____ What treatments aided the boy's recovery? (salt water, massages, rest) 1/2 credit for one; full credit for two.

(F)   6. _____ What was Mother saying to other people? (He's not as strong as other boys; he has to be careful what he does)

(I)   7. _____ Why did Mother's actions and statements upset the boy? (Because he believed them—or—because he felt publicly humiliated or embarrassed)

(V)   8. _____ What does "implicitly" mean in the sentence "mother believed the doctor implicitly?" (without further questioning)

(F)   9. _____ What was the boy rebelling against more than his mother? (the kind of person he was afraid he was becoming)

(M)   10. _____ What lesson can be learned from this story? (certain kinds of help can do more harm than good—or—lack of confidence can cause rebellion—or—any reasonable answer)

SCORING GUIDE: LEVEL 8

WR Errors		Comp Errors	
IND	0–12	IND	0–1
INSTR	12½–24½	INSTR	1½–3
FRUST	25+	FRUST	3½+

*Text excerpt from *Of Men and Mountains* by William O. Douglas, pp. 31–32. Copyright 1950, by William O. Douglas. By permission of Harper & Row, Publishers, Inc. and The Lantz Office Incorporated.

SILENT FORM—Level 8 (247 words)

MOTIVATION: You've probably seen many Cowboy and Indian movies on TV. Eventually the Indians lost. Read this story to find out how Chief Jacob was actually defeated.

They chased Jacob farthest and almost penned him a few times and killed a lot of braves and got wind of where his women and their kids were hidden, and forced him to move them farther into the mountains with them getting out just in time, not being able to carry much with them. But that wasn't catching Jacob and stopping him and his braves from carrying on their hop-skip-and-jump war against all whites in general and these troops in particular. Then a second general went in and about a thousand more soldiers with them and they had hard fighting off and on over a couple hundred miles and more, and the days drove on into deep winter and Jacob was licked. Not by the government and its soldiers and their guns. By the winter. He and his braves, what was left of them, had kept two generals and up to two thousand troops busy for four months fighting through parts of three states and then the winter licked him. He came to the second general under truce in what remained of his chief's rig and took off his headdress and laid it on the ground and spoke. His children were scattered in the mountains, he said, and the cold bit sharp and they had few blankets and no food. Several of the small ones had been found frozen to death. From the moment the sun passed overhead that day he would fight no more.*

COMPREHENSION CHECK

(I)   1. _____ Who was Jacob? (the chief of the Indian tribe—or—head of the group)

(V)   2. _____ What are "braves" in the phrase "they killed a lot of braves"? (North American Indian warriors) must mention warriors or fighters to receive credit.

(I)   3. _____ Why do you suppose they were called "braves?"(The word brave means showing courage or not afraid and warriors should possess these qualities) ½ credit for they were fighters.

(F)   4. _____ Who or what was Jacob and his braves' hop-skip-and-jump war aimed against? (whites—or—white soldiers)

(F)   5. _____ How did the soldier's discovery of the women and children's hiding place hurt the Indians?(They were forced to move—or—had to leave behind supplies)

(F)   6. _____ How long did Jacob keep fighting before giving up? (four months)

(I)   7. _____ The second general gained an unexpected advantage. What was it? (The Indians were not prepared for the hardships of winter.)

---

* Adapted from "Jacob," in Jack Schaefer, *The Plainsmen* (Boston: Houghton-Mifflin, 1954), pp. 243–44. Copyright © 1954 by Jack Schaefer, copyright © renewed 1982. Reprinted by permission of Don Congdon Associates, Inc.

(F)   8. _____ What happened to several of Jacob's small children? (They were found frozen to death.)

(I)   9. _____ Why do you suppose Jacob took off his headdress and laid it on the ground before he spoke to the second general? (to show that he surrendered)

(M) 10. _____ Give this story a title. Choose from the following: A. How Jacob was Finally Defeated   B. Surviving in the Bitter Cold Mountains   C. Braves Are Great Indian Fighters   D. Defeating Jacob was an Easy Job   (A.)

SCORING GUIDE: LEVEL 8

Comp Errors

IND	0–1
INSTR	1½–3
FRUST	3½+

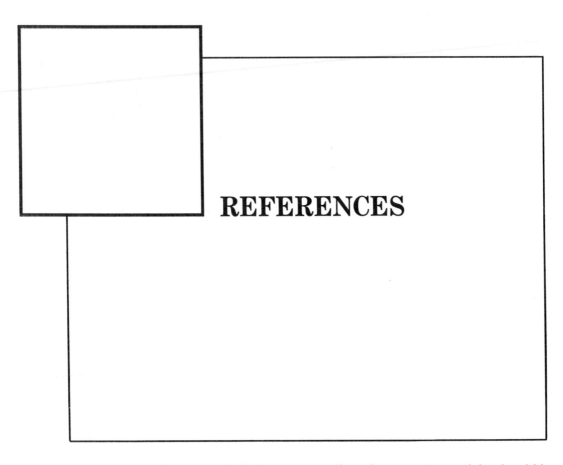

REFERENCES

AARON, P. G. Dyslexia, an imbalance in cerebral information processing strategies. *Perceptual and Motor Skills*, 1978, *47*, 699–706.

ABRAMS, J. C. and KASLOW, F. Family systems and the learning disabled child: Intervention and treatment. *Journal of Learning Disabilities*, 1977, *10*, 86–90.

ACKERMAN, P. T., ANHALT, J. M., and DYKMAN, R. A. Inferential word-decoding weakness in reading disabled children. *Learning Disabilities Quarterly*, 1986, *9*, 315–324.

ADAMS, A. The incidence of reversal errors in normal and LD readers. Paper presented at the American Educational Research Association, New Orleans, LA, April 8, 1988.

AFFLERBACH, P. How are main idea statements constructed? Watch the experts! *Journal of Reading*, 1987, *30*, 512–518.

ALLEY, G., and DESHLER, P. *Teaching the learning disabled adolescent.* Denver: Love Publishing, 1979.

ALLINGTON, R. L. If they don't get to read much in reading groups, how they ever gonna get good? *Journal of Reading*, 1977, *21*, 57–61.

———. Teacher interruption behaviors during primary grade oral reading. *Journal of Educational Psychology*, 1980, *72*, 371–377.

———. The reading instruction provided readers of differing abilities. *The Elementary School Journal*, 1983, *83*, 548–559.

———. Content coverage and contextual reading in reading groups. *Journal of Reading Behavior*, 1984, *16*, 85–97.

———. Policy constraints and effective compensatory reading instruction: A review. In J. B. Hoffman (Ed.), *Effective teaching of reading: Research and practice*, Newark, DE: International Reading Association, 1986.

ALLINGTON, R. L. and BROIKOU, K. A. Development of shared knowledge: A new role for classroom and specialist teachers. *The Reading Teacher*, 1988, *41* (8), 806–812.

ALLINGTON, R. L. and SHAKE, M. C. Remedial reading: Achieving curricular congruence in classroom and clinic. *The Reading Teacher*, 1986, *39*, 648–655.

ANASTASI, A. *Psychological testing.* New York: Macmillan, 1976.

ANDERSON, B. The missing ingredient: Fluent oral reading. *Elementary School Journal*, 1981, *81*, 173–177.

ANDERSON, R., and FREEBODY, P. Vocabulary knowledge in J. Guthrie (Ed.), *Comprehension and teach-*

ing: *Research Views.* Newark, DE: International Reading Association, 1981, 77–117.

ANDERSON, R. D., HIEBERT, E. H., SCOTT, J. A., and WILKINSON, I. A. *Becoming a nation of readers: The report of the commission on reading.* Washington, D.C.: National Institute of Education, 1985.

ANDERSON, S. *A whole-language approach to reading.* Lanham, MD.: University Press of America, 1984.

ANDERSON-INMAN, L. The reading-writing connection: Classroom applications for the computer. Part I *The Computing Teacher,* 1986, *14,* 23–26.

APPLEBY, A. N. *The child's concept of story: Ages 2–17.* Chicago: University of Chicago Press, 1978.

ARIAS, M. B. The context of education for Hispanic students: An overview. *Journal of Educational Research,* 1986, *95,* 26–57.

ARMBRUSTER, B. B. The problem of "inconsiderate" text in G. G. Duffy, L. R. Roehler, and J. Mason, (Eds.). *Comprehension Instruction: Perspectives and Suggestions,* New York. Longman, 1984.

ARMSTRONG, R. J. and JENSEN, J. A. *Slosson Intelligence Test: 1981 norms tables, application and development.* East Aurora, NY: Slosson Educational Publications.

ASHTON WARNER, S. *Teacher.* New York: Simon and Schuster, 1963.

AULLS, M. W. *Developing readers in today's elementary school.* Boston: Allyn & Bacon, 1982.

AULLS, M. W., and GELBART, F. Effects of a method of instruction and ability on literal comprehension of short stories. *Research in the teaching of English,* 1980, *14,* 51–59.

BALOW, B. The long-term effect of remedial reading instruction. *The Reading Teacher,* 1965, *18,* 581–586.

BANNATYNE, A. D. Diagnosis: A note on recategorization of the WISC scaled scores. *Journal of Learning Disabilities,* 1974, *7,* 272–273.

BARNES, D. *From communication to curriculum.* Middlesex, England: Penguin, 1975.

BARR, R. Development of a word learning task to predict success and identify methods by which kindergarten children learn to read. Final Report to the U.S. Department of Health, Education, and Welfare, Office of Education, Contract 9E125, 1971.

———. The influence of instructional conditions on word recognition errors. *Reading Research Quarterly,* 1972, *7,* 509–529.

———. National College of Education, Evanston, IL. Personal communication, 1988.

BARR, R., and DREEBEN, R. *How schools work.* Chicago: University of Chicago Press, 1983.

BARR, R. and SADOW, M. *Reading diagnosis for teachers.* New York: Longman, 1985.

BARRETT, T. C. *The evaluation of children's reading achievement.* Perspectives in Reading No. 8. Newark, DE: International Reading Association, 1967.

BAUMANN, J. F. The effectiveness of a direct instruction paradigm for teaching main idea comprehension, *Reading Research Quarterly,* 1984, *20,* 93–115.

BECK, I. L., PERFETTI, C. A., and MCKEOWN, M. G. The effects of long-term vocabulary instruction on lexical access and reading comprehension. *Journal of Educational Psychology,* 1982, *74,* 506–521.

BEEBE, J., FEENEY, B., and HILL, R. Tying a chapter 1 language-based reading program to the classroom basal. Presentation at the Fifteenth Great Plains Regional Reading Conference, International Reading Association, Des Moines, IA, October 23, 1987.

BERLINER, D. C. Tempus Educare. In P. L. Peterson and H. J. Walberg (Eds.), *Research on teaching: Concepts, findings, and implications.* Berkeley, Calif.: McCutchan Publications, 1979.

———. Academic learning time and reading achievement. In J. T. Guthrie (Ed.), *Comprehension and teaching: Research views.* Newark, DE: International Reading Association, 1981.

BETTS, E. *Foundations of reading instruction.* New York: American Book, 1946.

BLACHOWICZ, C. L. Z. Cloze activities for primary readers. *The Reading Teacher,* 1977, *31,* 300–302.

———. Making connections: Alternatives to the vocabulary notebook. *Journal of Reading* 1986, *29,* 643–649.

BLOOM, B. S. *Human characteristics and school learning.* New York: McGraw-Hill, 1976.

BOND, B., TINKER, M., WASSON, B., and WASSON, J. *Reading difficulties: Their diagnosis and correction* (5th ed.). Englewood Cliffs, NJ: Prentice-Hall, 1984.

BORMUTH, J. R. The cloze readability procedure. *Elementary English,* 1968, *45,* 236–249.

———. Development of readability analyses. Final Report 7–0052, U.S. Department of Health, Education, and Welfare, Office of Education, Bureau of Research, 1969.

BOSS, C. Process-oriented writing: Instructional implications for handicapped students. *Exceptional Children,* 1988, *54,* 521–527.

BOWLBY, J. *Attachment.* New York: Basic Books, 1969.

BRADLEY, J. M. Evaluating reading achievement for placement in special education. *The Journal of Special Education,* 1976, *10,* 291–296.

BRADLEY, L., and BRYANT, P. *Rhyme and Reason in Reading and Spelling.* Monograph Series of the International Academy for Research in Learning Disabilities, Number 1, Ann Arbor: University of Michigan Press, 1985.

BREEN, M. J. Cognitive patterns of learning disability subtypes as measured by the *Woodcock-Johnson Psycho-Educational Battery. Journal of Learning Disabilities,* 1986, *19,* 86–90.

BRIDGE, C. A., and TIERNEY, R. J. The inferential operations of children across text with narrative and expository tendencies. *Journal of Reading Behavior,* 1981, *31,* 201–214.

BRIGANCE, A. H. *Brigance diagnostic inventory of basic skills.* North Billerica, ME: Curriculum Associates, 1977.

BROWN, A. L., and DAY, J. D. Macrorules for summarizing text: The development of expertise. Technical

Report No. 270, Champaign, IL: Center for the Study of Reading: University of Illinois, 1983.

BROWN, A. L., and PALINSCAR, A. S. Inducing strategic learning from texts by means of informed, self-control training. Technical Report No. 262, Champaign , IL: Center for the Study of Reading, University of Illinois, 1982.

BRUININKS, V. L. Actual and perceived peer status of learning disabled students in mainstream programs. *Journal of Special Education*, 1978, *12*, 51–58.

BRYAN, T. H. Personality and situational factors in learning disabilities. In G. Pavlidis and D. Fisher (eds.). *Dyslexia: Its neuropsychology and treatment.* NY: Wiley and Sons, 1986 (a).

———. Self concept and attribution of the learning disabled. *Learning disabilities Focus*, 1986, *1*, 82–89 (b).

BUSWELL, G. T. Relationship between rate of thinking and rate of reading. *School Review*, 1951, *49*, 339–346.

CALDWELL, J. A. A new look at the old informal reading inventory. *The Reading Teacher*, 1985, *39*, 168–173.

CARR, E., and OGLE, D. K-W-L plus: A strategy for comprehension and summarization. *Journal of Reading*, 1987, *30*, 626–631.

CARR, E., and WIXON, K. K. Guidelines for evaluating vocabulary instruction. *Journal of Reading*, 1986, *29*, 588–596.

CARTER, T. P., and CHATFIELD, M. Effective bilingual schools: Implications for policy and practice. *American Journal of Education*, 1986, *95*, 220–231.

CARVER, R. P. Measuring readability using DRP units. *Journal of Reading Behavior*, 1985, *17*, 303–316.

CASHDAN, A., PUMFREY, P. D., and LUNZER, E. A. Children receiving remedial teaching in reading. *Educational Research*, 1971, *13*, 98–105.

CHALL, J. S. *Learning to read: The great debate* (Updated edition). New York: McGraw-Hill, 1983.

CHOMSKY, C. Write first, read later. *Childhood Education*, 1971, *47*, 296–299.

———. When you still can't read in third grade. After decoding, what? In S. J.: Samuels (Ed.), *What research has to say about reading instruction.* Newark, DE: International Reading Association, 1978.

———. Approaching reading through invented spelling. In L. B. Resnick and P. A. Weaver (Eds.), *Theory and practice of early reading* (Vol. 2). Hillsdale, NJ: Lawrence Erlbaum, 1979.

CLAY, M. M. Emergent Reading Behavior. Unpublished doctoral dissertation, University of Auckland Library, 1966. Cited in Clay, M. M. *The early detection of reading difficulties: A diagnostic survey with recovery procedures* (3rd ed.). Portsmouth, NH.: Heinemann, 1985.

———. *Reading: The patterning of complex behavior* (2nd. ed.). Portsmouth, NH: Heinemann, 1979.

———. Reading recovery: A follow-up study in M. M. Clay, *Observing young readers: Selected papers.* Portsmouth, NH: Heinemann, 1982.

———. *The early detection of reading difficulties: A diagnostic survey with recovery procedures* (3rd ed.). Portsmouth, NH: Heinemann, 1985.

COHEN, J. Learning disabilities and psychological development in childhood and adolescence. *Annals of Dyslexia* 1986, *36*, 287–300.

COLLINS, J. P. A linguistic perspective on minority education: Discourse analysis and early literacy. Unpublished doctoral dissertation, University of California, Berkeley, 1983.

COOLEY, W. W. Effectiveness in compensatory education. *Educational Leadership*, 1981, *38*, 298–301.

COSDEN, M., GERBER, M., SEMMEL, D., GOLDMAN, S., and SEMMEL, M. Microcomputer uses within microeducation environments. *Exceptional Children*, 1987, *53*, 399–409.

CRAFTON, L. K. Learning from reading: What happens when students generate their own background information? *Journal of Reading*, 1983, *26*, 586–592.

CRITCHLEY, M. *The dyslexic child.* Springfield, IL: Charles C. Thomas, 1970.

CROOK, W. *Can your child read? Is he hyperactive?* Jacobson, TN: Professional Books, 1977.

CRUIKSHANK, W. Foreward. In G. Pavlidis and D. Fisher (Eds.), *Dyslexia: Its neurology and treatment.* New York: Wiley, 1986.

CULLINAN, D., and EPSTEIN, M. *Special education for adolescents: Issues and perspectives.* Columbus, OH: Charles E. Merrill, 1979.

CUNNINGHAM, P. M. Teaching were, with, what, and other "four letter" words. *The Reading Teacher*, 1980, *34*, 160–163.

DALE, E., and CHALL, J. S. A formula for predicting readability. *Educational Research Bulletin*, Ohio State University, 1948, 27, 11–20, 28, 37–54.

DAVEY, B. Think aloud—Modeling the cognitive processes of reading comprehension. *Journal of Reading*, 1983, *27*, 44–47.

DEFRIES, J. C., and DECKER, S. N. Genetic aspects of reading disability: A family study. In R. N. Malatesha and P. G. Aaron (Eds.), *Reading disorders: Varieties and treatments.* New York: Academic Press, 1982.

DENCKLA, M., and RUDEL, R. Rapid automized naming (R.A.N.) Dyslexia differentiated from other learning disabilities. *Neuropsychologia*, 1976, *14*, 471–478.

DENO, S., MIRKIN, P. K., and CHIANG, B. Identifying valid measures of reading. *Exceptional Children*, 1982, *49*, 36–45.

DESHLER, D., SCHUMAKER, J., and LENZ, B. Academic and cognitive intervention for learning disabled adolescents. Part I. *Journal of Learning Disabilities*, 1984, *17*, 170–187.

Diagnostic and statistical manual of mental disorders III-R (DSM III-R). Washington, D.C.: American Psychiatric Association, 1987, 52–53.

DORE-BOYCE, K., MISNER, M. S., and McGUIRE, L. D. Comparing reading expectancy formulas. *The Reading Teacher*, 1975, *29*, 8–14.

DREYER, S. S. *The book finder: A guide to children's literature about the needs and problems of youth* (3rd ed.). Circle Pines, MN.: American Guidance Service, 1985.

DUANE, D. D. Neurodiagnostic tools in dyslexic syndromes in children: Pitfalls and proposed comparative study of computer tomography, nuclear magnetic resonance, and brain electrical activity mapping. In Pavlidis and D. Fisher (Eds.), *Dyslexia: Its neurology and treatment.* New York: Wiley, 1986.

DUDLEY-MARLING, C. Microcomputers, reading and writing: Alternatives to drill and practice. *The Reading Teacher*, 1985, 38, 380–389.

DURKIN, D. What classroom observations reveal about reading comprehension instruction. *Reading Research Quarterly*, 1978–1979, 14, 481–533.

DURRELL, D. *Improving reading instruction.* New York: Harcourt, Brace, and World, 1956.

DYKSTRA, R. *The relationship between measures of auditory discrimination and reading achievement at the end of first grade.* Unpublished doctoral dissertation. University of Minnesota, 1962.

DYSON, A. H. "N spell my Grandmama": Fostering early thinking about print. *The Reading Teacher*, 1984, 38, 262–271.

EHRI, L. C., and WILCE, L. S. Movement into reading: Is the first stage of printed word learning visual or phonetic? *Reading Research Quarterly*, 1985, 20, 163–179.

Elementary writing guide, Fairfax, VA: County School Board of Fairfax County, 1983.

ENGLEMANN, S., BECKER, J., BECKER, W., CORINE, L., JOHNSON, G., and MEYERS, L. *Corrective reading program.* Chicago: Science Research Associates, 1978.

ESTES, T., and VAUGHAN, J. L. Reading interest and comprehension: Implications. *The Reading Teacher*, 1973, 27, 149–153.

FARR, R. and CAREY, R. F. *Reading: What can be measured?* 2nd edition. Newark, DE: International Reading Association, 1986.

FEINGOLD, B. *Why your child is hyperactive.* New York: Random House, 1975.

FERNALD, G. M. *Remedial techniques in basic school subjects.* New York: McGraw-Hill, 1943.

——. *Remedial techniques in basic school subjects.* L. Idol (Ed.), Austin, TX: Pro-Ed, 1988.

FEUERSTEIN, R. *Instrumental enrichment.* Baltimore: University Park Press, 1979.

FISHER, C. W., FILBY, N. W., MARLIAVE, R., CAHEN, L. S., DISHAW, M. M., and MOORE, J. E., *Teaching and learning in the elementary school: A summary of the beginning teacher evaluation study* (BTES Rep. VII-I). San Francisco: Far West Laboratory for Educational Research and Development, 1978. (a)

FISHER, C. W., FILBY, N. W., MARLIAVE, R., CAHEN, L. S., DISHAW, M. M., MOORE, J. E., and BERLINER, D. C., *Teaching behaviors, academic learning time and student achievement.* (Final report of Phase III–B Beginning Teacher Evaluation Study.) San Francisco: Far West Laboratory for Educational Research and Development, 1978. (b)

FITZGERALD, J., and SPIEGEL, D. Enhancing children's reading comprehension through instruction in narrative structure. *Journal of Reading Behavior*, 1983, 15, 1–17.

FREY, L., and REIGELUTH, C. Instructional models for tutoring: A review. *Journal of Instructional Development*, 1986, 9, 2–7.

FRY, E. A. The new instant word list. *The Reading Teacher*, 1980, 34, 284–289.

——. A readability formula that saves time. *Journal of Reading*, 1968, 11, 513–516.

GALABURDA, A. M. Animal studies of the neurology of developmental dyslexia. In Pavlidis and D. Fisher (Eds.), *Dyslexia: Its neurology and treatment.* New York: Wiley, 1986.

GAMBRELL, L. B. Functions of children's oral language during reading instruction. Paper presented at the 36th Annual Meeting of the National Reading Conference, Austin, TX, Dec. 3, 1986.

GAMBRELL, L. B., and BALES, R. J. Mental imagery and the comprehension-monitoring performance of fourth- and fifth-grade poor readers. *Reading Research Quarterly*, 1986, 21, 454–464.

GAMEZ, G. I. Reading in a second language: "Native language approach" vs. "direct method." *The Reading Teacher*, 1979, 32, 665–670.

GASKINS, R. W. The missing ingredients: Time on task, direct instruction, and writing. *The Reading Teacher*, 1988, 41, (8), 750–756.

GENESEE, F. Second language learning through immersion: A review of U.S. programs. *Review of Educational Research*, 1985, 55, 541–561.

GENTILE, L., LAMB, P., and RIVERS, C. A neurologist's views of reading difficulty: Implications for remedial instruction. *The Reading Teacher*, 1985, 39, 174–183.

GENTRY, J. R. Early spelling strategies. *The Elementary School Journal*, 1987, 79, 88–92.

GERBER, M. M. Generalizations of spelling strategies of LD students as a result of contingent imitation/modeling and mastery criteria. *Journal of Learning Disabilities*, 1986, 19, 530–537.

——. Teaching with microcomputers. *Academic Therapy* 1986, 22, 117–124.

GESCHWIND, N. Dyslexia, cerebral dominance, autoimmunity and sex hormones. In Pavlidis and D. Fisher (Eds.), *Dyslexia: Its neurology and treatment.* New York: Wiley, 1986.

GILFORD, H. *Plays for reading.* New York: Walker and Co., 1967.

GILLINGHAM, A., and STILLMAN, B. W. *Remedial training for children with specific difficulty in reading, spelling, and penmanship* (7th ed.). Cambridge, MA: Educators Publishing Service, 1970.

GIPE, J. P. Investigating techniques for teaching word meaning. *Reading Research Quarterly*, 1978–1979, 14, 624–644.

——. Use of relevant context helps kids learn new

word meanings. *The Reading Teacher*, 1980, *33*, 398–402.

GLASS, G. G. *Teaching decoding as separate from reading.* Garden City, NY: Adelphi University Press, 1973.

GLASS, G. V., and SMITH, M. L. Pull out in compensatory education. Boulder, CO.: University of Colorado, Boulder, Laboratory of Educational Research, ED 160723, 1977.

GOLDMAN, S. R., and PELLEGRINO, J. W. Information processing and educational microcomputer technology: Where do we go from here? *Journal of Learning Disabilities*, 1987, *20*, 144–154.

GOOD, T. Research on classroom teaching. In L. S. Schulman and G. Sykes (Eds.), *Handbook on Teaching and Policy*, New York: Longman, 1983.

GOODMAN, K. S. A linguistic study of cues and miscues in reading. *Elementary English*, 1965, *42*, 639–643.

———. Reading: A psycholinguistic guessing game. *Journal of the Reading Specialist*, 1967, *6*, 126–135.

———. Analysis of oral reading miscues. *Reading Research Quarterly*, 1969, *5*, 9–30.

GOODMAN, K. S., and GOLLASCH, F. V. Word omissions: Deliberate and non-deliberate. *Reading Research Quarterly*, 1980–1981, *14*, 6–31.

GOODMAN, K., and GOODMAN, Y. Reading and writing relationships: Pragmatic functions. *Language Arts*, 1983, *60*, 590–599.

GOODMAN, Y. M. Miscues, errors and reading comprehension in J. Meritt (Ed.), *New Horizons in Reading*. Newark, DE: International Reading Association, 1976.

———. Kid watching: An alternative to testing, *National Elementary Principal*, 1978, *57*, 41–45.

GOODMAN, Y. M., and BURKE, C. *Reading strategies: Focus on comprehension.* New York: Holt, Rinehart and Winston, 1980.

GOODMAN, Y. M., WATSON, D. J., and BURKE, C. L. *Reading Miscue Inventory: Alternative Procedures.* Katonah, NY: R. C. Owens, 1987.

GOULDNER, H. *Teachers' pets, troublemakers, and nobodies.* Westport, CT: Greenwood Press, 1978.

GRABE, M., and GRABE, C. The microcomputer and the language experience approach. *The Reading Teacher*, 1985, *38*, 508–511.

GRAVES, D. H. *Writing: Teachers and children at work*, Portsmouth, NH: Heinemann, 1983.

GROSS, A. The relationship between sex differences and reading ability in an Israeli kibbutz system. In D. Feitleson (Ed.), *Crosscultural perspectives on reading and reading research*. Newark, DE: International Reading Association, 1978.

GUINET, L. *Evaluation of DISTAR materials in three junior learning assistance programs* (Report RR 71–16). Vancouver, British Columbia: University of Vancouver, Board of Trustees, 1971

GUTHRIE, J. T., SIEFERT, M., and KLINE, M. Clues from research on programs for poor readers. In S. J. Samuels (Ed.), *What research has to say about reading instruction*. Newark, DE: International Reading Association, 1978.

HANSEN, J. Authors respond to authors. *Language Arts*, 1983, *60*, 176–183.

HAGGARD, M. R. Developing critical thinking with the DR-TA. *The Reading Teacher*, 1988, *41*, 526–535.

HARING, N., and BATEMAN, B. *Teaching the learning disabled child.* Englewood Cliffs, NJ: Prentice-Hall, 1977.

HARRIS, A. What is new in remedial reading? *The Reading Teacher*, 1981, *34*, 405–410.

HARRIS, A. J., and SIPAY, E. R. *How to increase reading ability*, 8th edition. New York: Longman, 1985, p. 533.

HARSTE, J. C., and CAREY, R. F. Comprehension as setting. In J. C. Harste and R. F. Carey *New Perspectives in Comprehension*. Monographs in language and reading studies, *Monographs in teaching and learning*. Bloomington, IN: Indiana University, School of Education. Nov. 3, 1979.

HAYNES, M. C., and JENKINS, J. R. Reading instruction in special education resource rooms. *American Education Research Journal*, 1986, *23*, 161–190.

HECKELMAN, R. G. The neurological impress method of remedial reading instruction. *Academic Therapy*, 1969, *4*, 277–282.

HENDERSON, E. *Teaching Spelling.* Boston: Houghton Mifflin, 1985.

HERBER, H. L. *Teaching Reading in content areas*, 2nd ed., Englewood Cliffs, NJ: Prentice Hall, 1978.

HIRSCH, E. D. Jr. *Cultural Literacy.* Boston: Houghton Mifflin, 1987.

HINSHELWOOD, J. *Congenital word-blindness.* London: H. K. Lewis, 1917.

HITTLEMAN, D. R. *Developmental reading: A psycholinguistic perspective.* Boston: Houghton Mifflin (formerly Rand McNally), 1978.

HOFFMAN, J. V. *The oral recitation lesson: A teacher's guide.* Austin, TX: Academic Resource Consultants, 1985.

———. Rethinking the role of oral reading in basal instruction. *The Elementary School Journal*, 1987, *87*, 367–373.

HOFFMAN, J. V., O'NEAL, S. V., KASTLER, L. A., CLEMENTS, R. D., SEGEL, K. W., and NASH, M. F. Guided oral reading and miscue focused verbal feedback in second grade classrooms. *Reading Research Quarterly*, 1984, *14*, 367–384.

HOLCOMB, W. R., HARDESTY, R. A., ADAMS, N. A., and PONDER, H. M. WISC-R types of learning disabilities: A profile analysis with cross-validation. *Journal of Learning Disabilities*, 1987, *20*, 369–374.

HOLDAWAY, D. *The foundations of literacy.* Portsmouth, NH: Heinemann, 1979.

HORNBY, P. A. Achieving second language fluency through immersion education. *Foreign Language Annals*, 1980, *13*, 107–113.

HOSKISSON, K. The many facets of assisted reading. *Elementary English*, 1975, *52*, 653–659.

HOUGH, R. A., NURSS, J. R., and ENRIGHT, D. S. Story reading with limited English speaking children in the regular classroom. *The Reading Teacher*, 1986, *39*, 500–514.

HUMES, A. Research on the composing process. *Review of Educational Research*, 1983, *53*, 201–216.

HUNTER, M. *The science of the art of teaching from controversy in education*. Philadelphia: W.S. Saunders, 1978.

IDOL, L. Group story mapping: A comprehension strategy for both skilled and unskilled readers. *Journal of Learning Disabilities*, 1987, *20*, 196–205.

International Reading Association. Misuse of grade equivalents. (Printed in *Reading Research Quarterly*, 1981, *16*, follows p. 611.)

IPSEN, S. M., MCMILLAN, J. H., and FALLEN, N. H. An investigation of the reported discrepancy between the *Woodcock-Johnson Tests of Cognitive Ability and the Weschler Intelligence Scale for Children-Revised*. *Diagnostique*, 1983, *9*, 32–44.

IVES, J., BURSUK, Z., and IVES, S. *Word recognition*. Boston: Houghton Mifflin (formerly Rand McNally), 1979.

JENKINS, J. R., HELIOTIS, J., HAYNES, M., BECK, K. Does passive learning account for readers' comprehension deficits in ordinary reading situations? *Learning Disabilities Quarterly*, 1986, *9*, 69, 76.

JENKINS, J. R., STEIN, M. L., and WYSOCKI, K. Learning vocabulary through reading. *American Educational Research Journal*, 1984, *21*, 767–787.

JOHNSON, D., and MYKLEBUST, H. R. *Learning disabilities: Educational principles and practices*. New York: Grune & Stratton, 1967.

JOHNSON, D. D. The Dolch list reexamined. *The Reading Teacher*, 1971, *24*, 455–456.

JOHNSON, M. J., KRESS, R. A., and PIKULSKI, J. J. *Informal reading inventories*, (2nd ed.). Newark, DE: International Reading Association, 1987.

JOHNSTON, P. H. Instruction and student independence. *Elementary School Journal*, 1984, *84*, 338–344.

———. Understanding reading disability: A case study approach. *Harvard Educational Review*, 1985, *55*, 153–177.

JOHNSTON, P. H., ALLINGTON, R. L., and AFFLERBACH, P. The congruence of classroom and remedial instruction. *The Elementary School Journal*, 1985, *85*, 465–478.

JONES, M. B., and PIKULSKI, E. C. Cloze for the classroom. *The Reading Teacher*, 1974, *17*, 432–438.

JOSEL, C. A. A silent DRTA for remedial eighth graders. *Journal of Reading*, 1986, *29*, 434–439.

———. In a different context. *Journal of Reading*, 1988, *31*, 374–377.

KAUFMAN, A. S. The WISC and learning disabilities assessment: State of the art. *Journal of Learning Disabilities*, 1981, *14*, 520–526.

KAUFMAN, A. and MCLEAN, J. K-ABC/WISC-R factor analysis for a learning disabled population. *Journal of Learning Disabilities*, 1986, *19*, 145–153.

KAVALE, K. Functions of the *Illinois Test of Psycholinguistic Abilities* (ITPA): Are they trainable? *Exceptional Children*, 1981, *47*, 20, 496–513.

KAVALE, K. A., and FORNESS, S. R. The far side of heterogeneity: A critical analysis of empirical subtyping research in learning disabilities. *Journal of Learning Disabilities*, 1987, *6*, 374–382.

KEOGH, B. K. Future of the LD field: Research and practice. *Journal of Learning Disabilities*, 1986, *19*, 455–460.

KEOGH, B. K., MAJOR-KINGSLEY, S., OMORI-GORDEN, H., and READ, H. P. *A system of marker variables for the field of learning disabilities*. Syracuse, NY: Syracuse University Press, 1982.

KEOGH, B., and MARGOLIS, J. Learning to labor and to wait: Attentional problems of children with learning disorders. *Journal of Learning Disabilities*, 1976, *9*, 276–286.

KEOGH, B. K., TCHIR, C., and WINDEGUTH-BEHN, A. Teachers' perceptions of educationally high risk children. *Journal of Learning Disabilities*, 1974, *7*, 367–374.

KIBBY, M. Passage readability affects the oral reading strategies of disabled readers. *The Reading Teacher*, 1979, *32*, 390–396.

KIESLING, H. Productivity of instructional time by mode of instruction for students at varying levels of reading skill. *Reading Research Quarterly*, 1977–1978, *13*, 554–582.

KIRK, S. A. Redesigning delivery systems for learning disabled students. *Learning Disabilities Focus*, 1986, *2*, 4–6.

KIRK, S., and ELKINS, J. Characteristics of children enrolled in child service demonstration centers. *Journal of Learning Disabilities*, 1975, *8*, 630–637.

KIRK, S., KIRK, W., and MINSKOFF, E. Phonic remedial reading lessons. Novato, CA: Academic Therapy Publications, 1985.

KIRK, S., KLIEBHAN, J., and LERNER, J. *Teaching reading to slow and disabled learners*. Boston: Houghton Mifflin, 1978.

KLESIUS, J. P., and HOMAN, S. P. A validity and reliability update on the informal reading inventory with suggestions for improvement. *Journal of Learning Disabilities*, 1985, *18*, 71–76.

KLINE, C., and KLINE, C. Follow-up study of 216 dyslexic children. *Bulletin of the Orton Society*, 1975, *25*, 127–144.

KNAFLE, J. D., and GEISSAL, M. A. Auditory discrimination tests: A linguistic approach. *The Reading Teacher*, 1977, *31*, 134–141.

KRASHEN, STEPHEN D. *The natural approach: Language acquisition in the classroom*. Haward, CA.: Alemany Press, 1983.

KRISE, B. M. Reversals in reading: A problem in space perception. *Elementary School Journal*, 1949, *49*, 278–284.

KUDER, G. F., and RICHARDSON, M. W. The theory of

the estimate of test reliability. *Psychometrica*, 1937, 2, 151–160.

KUSHNER, S., and STECKER, J. Field testing of informal reading inventory, Chicago, IL, 1987.

LABERGE, D., and SAMUELS, S. M. Toward a theory of automatic information processing in reading. *Cognitive Psychology*, 1974, 6, 293–323.

LABOV, W. Some sources of reading problems for Negro speakers of nonstandard English. In A. Frasier (Ed.), *New directions in elementary English*. Champaign IL: National Council of Teachers of English, 1967.

LABOV, W., COHEN, P., ROBINS, C., and LEWIS, J. A note on the relationship of reading failures to peer-group status in urban ghettoes. *The Florida F. L. Report*, 1969, 7, 54–57, 167.

———. *A study of the nonstandard English of Negro and Puerto Rican speakers in New York City*. Final report, Cooperative Research Project 3288, Office of Education, Washington, D.C., 1968.

LEINHARDT, G., ZIGMOND, N., and COOLEY, W. Reading instruction and its effects. *American Educational Research Journal*, 1981, 18, 343–361.

LERNER, J. W. The regular education initiative: Some unanswered questions. *Learning Disabilities Focus*, 1987, 3, 3–7.

———. *Learning disabilities: Theories, diagnosis, and teaching strategies* (5th ed.). Boston: Houghton Mifflin, 1989.

LERNER, J. W., DAWSON, D., and HORVATH, L. *Cases in learning and behavior problems: A guide to individual education programs*. Boston: Houghton Mifflin, 1980.

LERNER, J. W., MARDELL-CZUDNOWSKI, C., and GOLDENBERG, D. *Special education in the early childhood years* (2nd ed.). Englewood Cliffs, NJ: Prentice-Hall, 1987.

LEVINSON, H. N. *Smart But Feeling Dumb*. New York: Warner Books, 1984.

LEWITTER, F. I., DeFRIES, J. C., and ELSON, R. C. Genetic models of reading disability. *Behavior Genetics*, 1980, 10, 9–30.

LIBERMAN, I. Y. A language-oriented view of reading and its disabilities. *Thalamus*, 1984, 4, 1–41.

LIBERMAN, I. Y., and SHANKWEILER, D. Phonology and the problems of learning to read and write. *Remedial and Special Education*, 1985, 6, 8–17.

LIBERMAN, I., SHANKWEILER, D., CAMP, L., BLACHMAN, B., and WERFELMAN, M. In H. Myklebust (Ed.), *Progress in Learning Disabilities* (Vol. V.) New York: Grune and Stratton, 1983.

LIBERMAN, I., SWANKWEILER, D., FOWLER, C., and FISCHER, F. Phonetic segmentation and recoding in the beginning reader. In A. S. Reber and D. Scarborough (Eds.), *Toward a psychological theory of reading*. Hillsdale, NJ: Erlbaum, 1977.

LICHT, B., and KISTNER, J. Motivational problems of learning disabled children: Individual differences and their implications for treatment. In J. Torgesen and B. Wong (Eds.), *Psychological and educational perspectives on learning disabilities*. New York: Academic Press, 1986.

LIPSON, M. Y., COX, C. H., IWANKOWSKI, S., and SIMON, M. Exploration of the interactive nature of reading: Using commercial IRI's to gain insights. *Reading Psychology: An International Quarterly*, 1984, 5, 209–218.

LIST, L. K. *Music, art and drama experiences for the elementary curriculum*. New York: Teachers College Press, 1982.

LONG, R. Washington Update. *Reading Today*, 1987, 5 (number 1), p. 3.

LYON, G. R. Educational validation studies of learning disabled readers: Essentials of Subtype Analysis. In B. P. Rourke (Ed.), *Neuropsychology of learning disabilities*. New York: Guilford Publications, 1985.

———. Learning-disabled readers: Identification of Subgroups. In H. Myklebust (Ed.). *Progress in Learning Disabilities* (Vol V.) New York: Grune and Stratton, 1983.

LYONS, C., PINNELL, G. S., SHORT, K. G., and YOUNG, P. *The Ohio reading recovery project*, vol. IV, State of Ohio, Pilot year, 1985–1986, Columbus, OH: Ohio State University, 1986.

MACARTHUR, C. The impact of computers on the writing process. *Exceptional Children*, 1988, 54, 536–542.

MANZO, A. V. The ReQuest procedure. *Journal of Reading*, 1969, 13, 123–126, 163.

———. Psychologically induced dyslexia and learning disabilities. *The Reading Teacher*, 1987, 40, 408–413.

MARTIN, H. Nutrition, injury, illness and minimal brain dysfunction. In H. Rie and E. Rie (Eds.), *Handbook of minimal brain dysfunction: A critical view*. New York: John Wiley, 1980.

MATUTE-BIANCHI, M. E. Ethnic identities and patterns of school success and failure among Mexican-descent and Japanese-American students in a California high school: An ethnographic analysis. *American Journal of Education*, 1986, 95, 233–253.

McDAVID, R. I. Language and prestige: "Standard English." Revision of H. L. Mencken, *The American Language*. In N. A. Johnson (Ed.), *Current topics in language*. Cambridge, MA: Winthrop, 1976.

McDERMOTT, R. P. Pirandello in the classroom: On the possibility of equal educational opportunity in American culture. In M. C. Reynolds (Ed.), *Futures of exceptional children: Emerging structures*. Reston, VA: Council for Exceptional Children, 1978.

———. The ethnography of speaking and reading. In R. Shuy, (Ed.), *Linguistic theory: What can it say about reading?* Newark, DE: International Reading Association, 1977.

McKENNA, M. C. Informal reading inventories: A review of the issues. *The Reading Teacher*, 1983, 38, 870–879.

McKINNEY, J. D. Research on conceptually and empirically defined subtypes of learning disabilities. In M. Wang, H. Walberg, and M. Reynolds (Eds.), *The*

Handbook of special education: Research and practice. Oxford, England: Pergamon Press, 1986.

MCNEILL, D. *The acquisition of language: The study of developmental psycholinguistics.* New York: Harper and Row, 1970.

Miami Herald, October 11, 1980.

MILLER, G. A. The magical number seven plus or minus two: Some limits on our capacity for processing information. *Psychological Review,* 1956, *63,* 89–97.

MOFFETT, J., and WAGNER, B. J. *Student-centered language arts and reading, K-12* (2nd ed.). Boston: Houghton Mifflin, 1976.

MONAHAN, J., Orange County Public Schools, Orlando, FL, personal communication, 1987.

MOORE, D. W., and ARTHUR, S. V. Possible sentences. In E. D. Dishner, T. W. Bean and J. E. Readence (Eds.), *Reading in the Content Areas: Improving classroom instruction.* Dubuque IA.: Kendall/Hunt, 1981.

MOORE D., and WIELAN, O. WISC-R scatter indexes of children referred for reading diagnosis. *Journal of Learning Disabilities,* 1981, *14,* 511–514.

MORRIS, D., National College of Education, Evanston, IL, personal communication, 1986.

MOZZI, L. Northeastern Illinois University, Chicago, IL, personal communication, 1980.

NAGY, W., HERMAN, P., and ANDERSON, R. Learning words from context. *Reading Research Quarterly,* 1985, *20,* 233–253.

NATIONAL COMMISSION ON EXCELLENCE IN EDUCATION. *A nation at risk: The imperative for educational reform.* Washington, DC: National Commission on Excellence in Education, 1983.

NELSON, L., and MORRIS, D. Supported oral reading: A year-long intervention study in two inner-city primary grade classrooms. Paper presented at the 36th National Reading Conference, Austin, TX, December 3, 1986.

NEW DIRECTIONS IN READING INSTRUCTION (flip chart), Tallahasee, FL: Department of Education, in connection with Florida Reading Association; now available from Newark, DE, International Reading Association, 1987.

NEWCOMER, P. L. A comparison of two published reading inventories. *Remedial and Special Education,* 1985, *6,* 31–36.

NEWKIRK, T. Young writers as critical readers. *Language Arts,* 1982, *59,* 451–457.

News for Counselors, Is there a "real world" reading standard for high school graduates? Fall, 1985.

NORMAN C., and ZIGMOND, N. Characteristics of children labled and served as learning disabled in school systems affiliated with the child service demonstration centers. *Journal of Learning Disabilities,* 1980, *13,* 542–547.

NORTON, A. J., and GLICK, P. C. One parent families: A social and economic profile. *Family Relations,* 1986, *35,* 9–17.

OGLE, D. K-W-L: A teaching model that develops active reading of expository text. *The Reading Teacher,* 1986, *39,* 564–570.

OLLILA, L., JOHNSON, T., and DOWNING, J. Adopting a Russian method for auditory discrimination training. *Elementary English,* 1974, *51,* 1138–1145.

ORFIELD, G. Hispanic education: Challenges, research, and policies. *American Journal of Education,* 1986, *95,* 1–25.

ORTIZ, B. Reading activities and reading proficiency among Hispanic, black, and white students. *American Journal of Education,* 1986, *95,* 58–76.

ORTON, S. T. *Reading, writing and speech problems in children.* New York: W. W. Norton, 1937.

ORTON DYSLEXIA SOCIETY. Some facts about illiteracy in America, *Perspectives on dyslexia,* 1986, *13,* 1.

———. Perspectives on dyslexia: Medical research update. Baltimore: Orton Dyslexia Society, 1987.

PAGE, W. D., and CARLSON, K. L. The process of observing oral reading scores. *Reading Horizons,* 1975, *15,* 147–150.

PAPERT, S. *Mindstorms: Children, computers, and powerful ideas.* New York: Basic Books, 1980.

PARATORE, J. R., and INDRISANO, R. Intervention assessment of reading comprehension. *The Reading Teacher,* 1987, *40,* 778–783.

PARIS, S. G. Teaching children to guide their reading and learning. In T. E. Raphael (Ed.), *The contexts of school-based literacy,* New York: Random House, 1986.

PARIS, S. G., CROSS, D. R., and LIPSON, M. Y. Informed strategies for learning: A program to improve children's reading awareness and comprehension. *Journal of Educational Psychology,* 1984, 76, 1239–1252.

PATTISON, L. Software writing made easy. *Electronic Learning,* March, 1985, 30–35.

PAUK, W. *How to study in college* (3rd ed.). Boston: Houghton Mifflin, 1984.

PEARL R., DONAHUE M., and BRYAN. T. H. Social relationships of learning-disabled children. In J. J. Torgesen, and B. Y. L. Wong (Eds.), *Psychological and Educational perspectives on learning disabilities.* New York: Academic Press, 1986.

PEARSON, P. D., and JOHNSON, D. D. *Teaching reading comprehension.* New York: Holt, Rinehart and Winston, 1978.

PETERSEN, B. *The characteristics of texts that support beginning readers.* Unpublished Doctoral Dissertation, Columbus OH: The Ohio State University, 1988.

PEREZ, E. Oral language competence improves reading skills of Mexican American third graders. *The Reading Teacher,* 1981, *35,* 24–27.

PFLAUM, S. W., WALBERG, H. J., KAREGIANES, M. L., and RASHER, S. W. Reading instruction: A quantitative analysis. *Educational Researcher,* 1980, (July), 12–18.

PIAGET, J. *The language and thought of the child.* New York: Harcourt Brace, 1926.

PIKULSKI, J. J., and SHANAHAN, T. Informal reading

inventories: A critical analysis. In J. J. Pikulski and T. Shanahan (Eds.), *Approaches to the informal evaluation of reading.* Newark, DE: International Reading Association, 1982, 94–116.

POWELL, W. R. Reappraising the criteria for interpreting informal inventories. In D. L. DeBoer (Ed.), *Reading diagnosis and evaluation.* Newark, DE: International Reading Association, 1970.

PRESSLEY, M. Imagery and children's learning: Putting the picture in developmental perspective. *Review of Educational Research,* 1977, *47,* 585–622.

PRESSLEY, M., HORTON, M., RETSON, J., and NIELSON, W. *Mind's Eye: Creating mental pictures from printed words.* Escondido, CA: Escondido Union School District, 1979.

PRESTON, R. C. Reading achievement of German boys and girls related to sex of teacher. *The Reading Teacher,* 1979, *32,* 521–526.

QUIRK, T. J., TRISTMAN, D. A., NAILN, K., and WEINBERG, S. Classroom behavior of teachers during compensatory reading instruction. *Journal of Educational Research,* 1975, *68,* 185–192.

RABINOVITCH, R. Dyslexia: Psychiatric considerations. In J. Money (Ed.), *Reading disability: Progress and research needs in dyslexia.* Baltimore: Johns Hopkins University Press, 1969.

RAMIREZ, J. D. Comparing structured English immersion and bilingual education: First-year results of a national study. *American Journal of Education,* 1986, *95,* 122–148.

RAPHAEL, T. E. Question-answering strategies for children. *The Reading Teacher,* 1982, *36,* 186–190.

———. Teaching question-answer relationships, revisited. *The Reading Teacher,* 1986, *39,* 516–522.

RAPP, D. Food allergy treatment for hyperkinesis. *Journal of Learning Disabilities,* 1979, *12,* 608–616.

RAUSCHER-DAVOUST, L. The LEARN program, unpublished manuscript, 1986.

———. LEARN: An after-school language arts program. *AARSIC (Administrators in Reading Special Reading Council) Abstracts,* 1987, *2,* 506.

Reading Recovery in Ohio, 1984–1986. Vol. 1 (number 1), Columbus Ohio: The Ohio State University, College of Education, 1984–1988.

Reading resource specialist handbook, Orlando FL: Orange County Public Schools, 1985.

RENNIE, B. J., BRAUN, C., and GORDON, C. J. Longterm effects of clinical intervention: An in-depth study. *Reading Horizons,* 1986, *27,* 12–18.

REYNOLDS, M., WANG, M., and WALBERG, H. The necessary restructuring of special and regular education. *Exceptional Children,* 1987, *53,* 391–398.

RICHEK, M. A. A study of the affix structure of English: Affix frequency, and teaching methods. Unpublished paper. Chicago: University of Chicago, 1969.

———. Readiness skills that predict initial word learning using two different methods of instruction. *Reading Research Quarterly,* 1977–1978, *13,* 200–222.

———. *Increasing the achievement of your remedial reading students.* Paso Robles, CA: Bureau of Education and Research, 1983–1989.

———. DRTA: 5 variations that facilitate independence in reading narratives. *Journal of Reading* 1987, *30,* 636.

———. Meaning vocabulary: An interesting and profitable study. *Greater Washington Reading Council Journal,* 1987, *12,* 9–11.

———. *The World of Words* (2nd ed.). Boston: Houghton Mifflin, 1989.

RICHEK, M. A., and MCTAGUE, B. The "Curious George" strategy for students with reading problems. *The Reading Teacher,* 1988 (in press).

RICHGELS, J. J. Experimental reading with invented spelling (ERIS): A preschool and kindergarten method. *The Reading Teacher,* 1987, *40,* 522–529.

ROBBINS, P., and WOLFE, P. Reflections on a Hunterbased staff development project. *Educational Leadership,* 1987, *44,* 56–61.

ROBINSON, H. *Why pupils fail in reading.* Chicago: University of Chicago Press, 1946.

———. Visual and auditory modalities related to methods for beginning readng. *Reading Research Quarterly,* 1972, *8,* 7–41.

ROSSMAN, L. The disabled adolescent reader. In D. Sawyer (Ed.), *Disabled readers: Insight, assessment, instruction.* Newark, DE: International Reading Association, 1980.

ROSSWELL, F., and NATCHEZ, G. *Reading disability: A human approach to learning* (3rd ed.). New York: Basic Books, 1977.

RUNION, H. J. Hypoglycemia—fact or fiction? In W. Cruickshank (Ed.), *Approaches to learning disabilities. Vol. 1. The best of ACLD.* Syracuse, NY: Syracuse University Press, 1980.

RUST, K. Wordprocessing: The missing key for writing. *The Reading Teacher,* 1986, *39,* 611–612.

SALVIA, J., and YSSELDYKE, J. E. *Assessment in special and remedial education* (4th ed.). Boston: Houghton Mifflin, 1988.

SAMUELS, S. J. Effects of pictures on learning to read. *Review of Educational Research,* 1970, *40,* 397–407.

———. Effects of letter name knowledge on learning to read. *American Educational Research Journal,* 1972, *9,* 65–74.

———. The method of repeated readings. *The Reading Teacher,* 1979, *32,* 403–408.

———. Information processing abilities and reading. *Journal of Learning Disabilities,* 1987, *10,* 88–122.

———. Decoding and automaticity: Helping poor readers become automatic at word recognition. *The Reading Teacher,* 1988, *41,* (8), 756–761.

SCHALLERT, D. L., KLEINMAN, G. M., and RUBIN, A. Analyses of differences between written and oral language. Technical Report 29. Urbana, IL: University of Illinois, Center for the Study of Reading, April, 1977.

SCHELL, L. M., and HANNA, G. S.   Can informal reading inventories reveal strengths and weaknesses in comprehension subskills? *The Reading Teacher*, 1981, *35*, 263–268.

SCHUDER, T., CLEWELL, S. F., and JACKSON, N.   Getting the gist of expository text: Teaching reading as a decision making process. In D. M. Glynn (Ed.), *Children's comprehension of Narrative and Expository Text: Research into Practice*. Newark, DE, International Reading Association, 1988.

SCHUMAKER, J. B., DESHLER, D. D., and ELLIS, E. S.   Intervention issues related to the education of learning disabled adolescents. In J. J. Torgeson and B. Y. L. Wong (Eds.) *Psychological and educational perspectives on learning disability*, Orlando, FL: Academic Press, 1986.

SHEENAN, L. D., FELDMAN, R. S., and ALLEN, V. L.   Research on children tutoring children: A critical review. *Review of Educational Research*, 1976, *16*, 355–385.

SHEPARD, D.   Special students and regular software. *The Computing Teacher*, 1986, *14*, 18–19.

SILVER, L. B.   Controversal approaches to treating learning disabilities and attention deficit disorder. *American Journal of Diseases of Children*, 1986, *140*, 1045–1052.

——.   The "magic cure": A review of the current controversial approaches to treatment of learning disabilities. *Journal of Learning Disabilities*, 1987, *20*, 498–504.

SIMPSON, J.   A shallow labor pool spurs business to act to bolster education. *Wall Street Journal*, October 28, 1987, p. 1.

SIPAY, E. R.   A comparison of standard reading scores and functional reading levels. *Reading Teacher*, 1964, *17*, 265–268.

SLINGERLAND, B.   A multisensory approach to language arts for specific learning disability children. Cambridge, MA: Educators Publishing Service, 1974.

SMITH, N.   The wordprocessing approach to language experience. *The Reading Teacher*, 1985, *36*, 556–559.

SMITH, N. B.   *American reading instruction* (rev. ed.). Newark, DE: International Reading Association, 1965.

SMITH, S. L.   Retellings as measures of comprehension. In J. C. Harste and R. F. Carey (Eds.), *New perspectives in comprehension*, Monographs in reading and language studies, Monographs in Teaching and Learning. Bloomington, IN: Indiana University, School of Education, 1979.

SNIDER, V. E., and TARVER, S. G.   The effect of early reading failure on acquisition of knowledge among students with learning disabilities. *Journal of Learning Disabilities*, 1987, *20*, 351–356, 373.

SPACHE, G. D.   A new readability for primary-grade materials. *Elementary School Journal*, 1953, *53*, 410–413.

——.   *Diagnosing and correcting reading disabilities*. Boston: Allyn & Bacon, 1981.

SPACHE, G. D., and SPACHE, E. B.   *Reading in the elementary school* (4th ed.). Boston: Allyn & Bacon, 1977.

STAHL, S. A., and FAIRBANKS, M. M.   The effects of vocabulary instruction: A model-based meta-analysis. *Review of Educational Research*, 1986, *56*, 72–110.

STANOVICH, K. E.   Individual differences in the cognitive processes of reading I: Word decoding. *Journal of Learning Disabilities*, 1982, *15*, 485–493.

——.   Explaining the variance in reading ability in terms of psychological processes: What have we learned? *Annals of Dyslexia*, 1985, *35*, 69–96.

——.   Cognitive processes and the reading problems of learning-disabled children: Evaluating the assumptions of specificity. In J. Torgesen and B. Wong (Eds.), *Psychological and educational perspectives on learning disabilities*. New York: Academic Press, 1986. (a)

——.   Matthew effects in reading: Some consequences of individual differences in the acquisition of literacy. *Reading Research Quarterly*, 1986, *21*, 360–406. (b)

STANOVICH, K. E., CUNNINGHAM, A. E., and FEEMAN, D. J.   Intelligence, cognitive skills, and early reading progress. *Reading Research Quarterly*, 1984, *19*, 278–303.

STAUFFER, R. G.   *Directing the reading-thinking process*. New York: Harper and Row, 1975.

——.   *The language experience approach to the teaching of reading*. 2nd ed. New York: Harper and Row, 1980.

STEIRNAGLE, E.   A five-year summary of a remedial reading program. *The Reading Teacher*, 1971, *24*, 537–43.

STEPHENS, R.   Write/Read/Write some more. Presentation at the 4th Annual Conference on Adult Reading Problems, Chicago State University, Chicago, September 27, 1986.

STERNBERG, R. G.   *Beyond IQ: A triarchic theory of human intelligence*. New York: Cambridge University Press, 1985.

STOIBER, K. C., BRACKEN, B. A., and GISSAL, T. J.   Cognitive processing styles in reading-disabled and a matched group of normal children. *Journal of Psychoeducational Assessment*, 1983, *1*, 219–234.

STOTSKY, S.   Research on reading/writing relationships: A synthesis and suggested directions. *Language Arts*, 1983, *60*, 627–642.

STRANG, R.   *Reading diagnosis and remediation*. Newark, DE: International Reading Association. ERIC-CRIER, 1968.

STRAUSS, A., and LEHTINEN, L.   *Psychopathology and education of the brain-injured child*. New York: Grune & Stratton, 1947.

SWANSON, H. L.   Information processing theory and learning disabilities: An overview. *Journal of Learning Disabilities*, 1987, *20*, 3–7.

TAYLOR, R. L., PARTENIO, I., and ZIEGLER, E. Diagnostic use of WISC-R subtest scatter: A note of caution. *Diagnostique*, 1983, 9, 26–31.

THANE, A. *Plays from famous stories and fairy tales.* Boston: Plays Inc., 1967.

TIERNEY, R. J., and PEARSON, P. D. Toward a composing model of reading. *Language Arts*, 1983, 60, 568–580.

TINDAL, G., and MARSTON D. Approaches to assessment. In J. K. Torgensen and B. Wong. *Psychological and Educational Perspectives in Learning Disabilities.* New York: Academic Press, 1986.

TORGESON, J. K. Computers and cognition in reading: A focus on decoding fluency. *Exceptional Children*, 1986, 53, 157–162.

———. Using computers to help learning disabled children practice reading: A research-based perspective. *Learning Disabilities Focus*, 1986, 1, 72–81.

TRAUB, N., and BLOOM, F. *Recipe for Reading.* Cambridge, MA: Educator's Publishing Service, 1978.

TUNMER, W. E., HERRIMAN, M. L., and NESDALE, A. R. Metalinguistic abilities and beginning reading. *Reading Research Quarterly*, 1988, 23, (2), 134–158.

U.S. DEPARTMENT OF EDUCATION. *To assure the free appropriate public education of all children.* Second Annual Report to Congress on the Implementation of Public Law 94-142, The Education of All Handicapped Children Act. State Program Implementation Studies. Office of Special Education, 1980.

———. National Assessment of Educational Progress. *The reading report card: Progress toward excellence in our schools.* Washington, DC: Government Printing Office, 1986.

———. *To assure the free appropriate public education of all handicapped children.* Ninth and tenth Annual Report of Congress on the Implementation of the Education of the Handicapped Act. Washington, DC: Government Printing Office, 1987, 1988.

VANCOUVER, BRITISH COLUMBIA: University of Vancouver, Board of Trustees, 1971.

VAUGHN, S. Why teach social skills to learning disabled students? *Journal of Learning Disabilities*, 1985, 18, 588–591.

VELLUTINO, F. R. Dyslexia. *Scientific American*, 1987, 256, 34–41.

VENEZKY, R. L. The curious role of letter names in reading instruction. *Visible Language*, 1975, 9, 7–23.

VENEZKY, R. L., KAESTLE, C. F., and SUM, A. M. *The subtle danger: Reflections on the literacy abilities of America's young adults.* Princeton, NJ: Educational Testing Service, 1987.

VERNOT, D. Writing to Read works because it motivates. *Electronic Learning*, 1987, 6, 38–39.

VOGEL, S. A. Syntactic abilities in normal and dyslexic children. *Journal of Learning Disabilities*, 1974, 7, 103–109.

WAGGONER, D. *Minority language population from the 1980 census.* National Clearinghouse for Bilingual Education Forum, 1984, 7, 6–7.

WAGNER, R. K. Phonological processing abilities and reading: Implications for disabled readers. *Journal of Learning Disabilities*, 1986, 19, 623–630.

WALLACE, G., and LARSEN, S. C. *Educational assessment of learning problems: testing for teaching.* Boston: Allyn & Bacon, 1978.

WALLACH, L., and WALLACH, M. A. Phonemic analysis training in the teaching of reading. In W. M. Cruickshank and J. W. Lerner (Eds.), *Coming of age.* (Vol. 3) *The Best of ACLD*, Syracuse, NY: Syracuse University Press, 1982.

WALSH, D. J., PRICE, G. G., GILLINGHAM, M. G. The critical but transitory importance of letter naming. *Reading Research Quarterly*, 1988, 23, 108–122.

WECHSLER, D. *Wechsler intelligence scale for children—revised.* New York: Psychological Corp., 1974.

———. *The measurement and appraisal of adult intelligence* (4th ed.). Baltimore, Md.: Williams and Wilkins, 1975.

WEINBERG, W. A., and REHMET, A. Childhood affective disorders and school problems. In D. Cantwell and G. Carlson (Eds.), *Affective disorders in childhood and adolescence—an update.* Jamaica, NY: Spectrum Publication, 1983.

WHITE, B. *The first years of life.* Englewood Cliffs, NJ: Prentice-Hall, 1975.

WIIG, E. and SEMEL, E.H. *Language assessment and intervention for the learning disabled.* Columbus, OH: Charles E. Merrill, 1984.

WILL, M. Educating children with learning problems: A shared responsibility. *Exceptional Children*, 1986, 52, 411–416.

WILLIAMS, J. P. Teaching decoding with an emphasis on phoneme analysis and phoneme blending. *Journal of Educational Psychology*, 1980, 12, 1–15.

———. Phonemic analysis and how it relates to reading. *Journal of Learning Disabilities*, 1984, 17, 240–245.

———. The role of phonemic analysis in reading. In J. J. Torgeson and B. Wong (Eds.) *Psychological and educational perspectives on learning disabilty*, Orlando, FL: Academic Press, 1986.

WIXON, K. Questions about a text: What you ask about is what children learn. *The Reading Teacher*, 1983, 37, 287–293.

———. An interactive view of reading disability. Presentation given at Florida Reading Association Conference, Bal Harbour, FL, October 15, 1987.

WIXON, K., and LIPSON, M. Y. Reading (Dis)Ability: An interactionist perspective. In T. E. Raphael (Ed.) *The contexts of school-based literacy.* New York: Random House, 1986.

WIXON, K., PETERS, C., WEBER, E., and ROEBER, E. New directions in statewide reading assessment. *The Reading Teacher*, 1987, 40, 749–755.

WOLFRAM, W. *A sociolinguistic description of Detroit Negro speech.* Washington, D.C.: Center for Applied Linguistics, 1969.

WONG, B. Y. A cognitive approach to teaching spelling. *Exceptional Children*, 1986, 53, 169–172.

WONG, B., and WONG, W. Role-taking skills in normal achieving and learning disabled children. *Learning Disability Quarterly*, 1980, 3, 11–18.

YSSELDYKE, J., THURLOW, M., MECHLENBURG, C., and GRADEN, J. Opportunity to learn for regular and special education students during reading instruction. *Remedial and Special Education*, 1984, 5, 29–37.

INDEX

SUBJECT INDEX

TEST INDEX